THE JOURNALS OF ALEXANDER MACKENZIE

VOYAGES FROM MONTREAL, ON THE RIVER ST. LAURENCE, THROUGH THE CONTINENT OF NORTH AMERICA, TO THE FROZEN AND PACIFIC OCEANS; IN THE YEARS, 1789 AND 1793. WITH A PRELIMINARY ACCOUNT OF THE RISE, PROGRESS, AND PRESENT STATE OF THE FUR TRADE OF THAT COUNTRY.

By Sir Alexander Mackenzie

THE NARRATIVE PRESS
TRUE FIRST PERSON ACCOUNTS OF HIGH ADVENTURE

To
His Most Sacred Majesty
George the Third
This Volume is Inscribed
By His Majesty's
Most Faithful Subject,
And
Devoted Servant,
Alexander Mackenzie.

The Narrative Press
P.O. Box 2487, Santa Barbara, California 93120 U.S.A.
Telephone: (805) 884-0160 Web: www.narrativepress.com

ISBN 1-58976-036-0 (Paperback)
ISBN 1-58976-037-9 (eBook)

Produced in the United States of America

TABLE OF CONTENTS

US
Lewis &
Clarke
1804

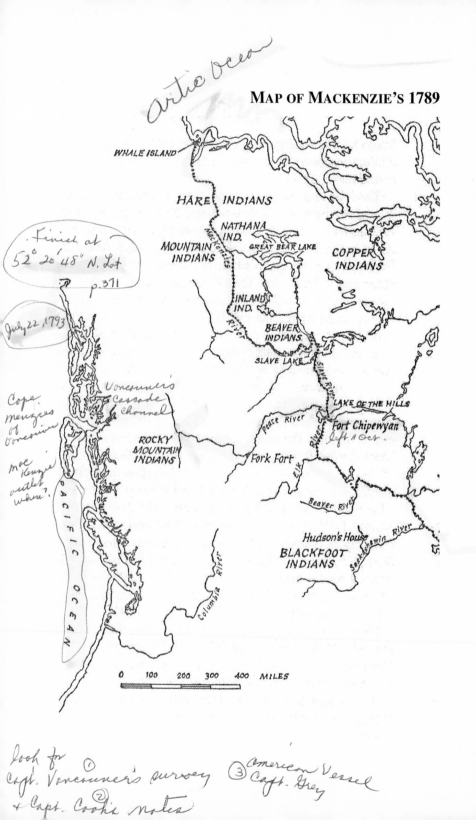

MAP OF MACKENZIE'S 1789

artic Ocean

WHALE ISLAND

HARE INDIANS

NATHANA IND.

MOUNTAIN INDIANS

GREAT BEAR LAKE

COPPER INDIANS

Mackenzie River

INLAND IND.

BEAVER INDIANS.

SLAVE LAKE

Slave River

LAKE OF THE HILLS

Peace River

Fort Chipewyan
left 11 Oct.

ROCKY MOUNTAIN INDIANS

Vancouver's Cascade Channel

Fork Fort

Elk River

Beaver River

PACIFIC OCEAN

Hudson's House

BLACKFOOT INDIANS

Saskatchewin River

Columbia River

· Finish at 52° 20' 48" N. Lat
p.371

July 22 1793

Cape. menzies of Vancouver

mac Kenzie outlet where?

0   100   200   300   400   MILES

look for ① Capt. Vancouver's survey   ③ American Vessel Capt. Grey
+ Capt. Cooke ② notes

TRANS-CANADA ROUTES

DAVIS STRAIT

LABRADOR

HUDSON'S BAY

Churchill Fort

NEW

York Fort   Severn House

SOUTH   WALES

EAST MAIN

JAMES'S BAY

East-Main Factory

LAKE WINNIPIC

Moose Fort

Brunswick House

LAKE OF THE WOODS

Montreal

LAKE SUPERIOR

Ottawa River

LAKE HURON

LAKE ONTARIO

LAKE MICHIGAN

PREFACE

On presenting this Volume to my Country, it is not necessary to enter into a particular account of those voyages whose journals form the principal part of it, as they will be found, I trust, to explain themselves. It appears, however, to be a duty, which the Public have a right to expect from me, to state the reasons which have influenced me in delaying the publication of them.

It has been asserted, that a misunderstanding between a person high in office and myself, was the cause of this procrastination. It has also been propagated, that it was occasioned by that precaution which the policy of commerce will sometimes suggest; but they are both equally devoid of foundation. The one is an idle tale; and there could be no solid reason for concealing the circumstances of discoveries, whose arrangements and prosecution were so honourable to my associates and myself, at whose expence they were undertaken. The delay actually arose from the very active and busy mode of life in which I was engaged since the voyages have been completed; and when, at length, the opportunity arrived, the apprehension of presenting myself to the Public in the character of an Author, for which the course and occupations of my life have by no means qualified me, made me hesitate in committing my papers to the Press; being much better calculated to perform the voyages, arduous as they might be, than to write an account of them. However, they are now offered to the Public with the submission that becomes me.

I was led, at an early period of life, by commercial views, to the country North-West of Lake Superior, in North America, and being endowed by Nature with an inquisitive mind and enterprising spirit; possessing also a constitution and frame of body equal to the most arduous undertakings, and being familiar with toilsome exertions in the prosecution of mercantile pursuits, I not only contemplated the practicability of penetrating across the continent of America, but was confident in the qualifications, as I was animated by the desire, to undertake the perilous enterprise.

The general utility of such a discovery, has been universally acknowledged; while the wishes of my particular friends and commercial associates, that I should proceed in the pursuit of it, contributed to quicken the execution of this favourite project of my own ambition: and as the completion of it extends the boundaries of geographic science, and adds new countries to the realms of British commerce, the danger I have encountered, and the toils I have suffered, have found their recompence; nor will the many tedious and weary days, or the gloomy and inclement nights which I have passed, have been passed in vain.

The first voyage has settled the dubious point of a practicable North-West passage; and I trust, that it has set that long agitated question at rest, and extinguished the disputes respecting it for ever. An enlarged discussion of that subject will be found to occupy the concluding pages of this volume.

In this voyage, I was not only without the necessary books and instruments, but also felt myself deficient in the sciences of astronomy and navigation: I did not hesitate, therefore, to undertake a winter's voyage to this country, in order to procure the one and acquire the other. These objects being accomplished, I returned, to determine the practicability of a commercial communication through the continent of North America, between the Atlantic and Pacific Oceans, which is proved by my second journal. Nor do I hesitate to declare my decided opinion, that very great and essential advantages may be derived by extending our trade from one sea to the other.

Some account of the fur trade of Canada from that country, of the native inhabitants, and of the extensive districts connected with it, forms a preliminary discourse, which will, I trust, prove interesting to a nation whose general policy is blended with, and whose prosperity is supported by, the pursuits of commerce. It will also qualify the reader to pursue the succeeding voyages with superior intelligence and satisfaction.

These voyages will not, I fear, afford the variety that may be expected from them; and that which they offered to the eye, is not of a nature to be effectually transferred to the page. Mountains and vallies, the dreary waste, and wide-spreading forests, the lakes and rivers succeed each other in general description; and, except on the coasts of the Pacific Ocean, where the villages were permanent, and the inhabitants in a great measure stationary, small bands of wandering Indians are the only people whom I shall introduce to the acquaintance of my readers.

The beaver and the buffalo, the moose-deer and the elk, which are the principal animals to be found in these countries, are already so familiar to the naturalists of Europe, and have been so often as well as correctly described in their works, that the bare mention of them, as they enlivened the landscape, or were hunted for food; with a cursory account of the soil, the course and navigation of lakes and rivers, and their various produce, is all that can be reasonably expected from me.

I do not possess the science of the naturalist; and even if the qualifications of that character had been attained by me, its curious spirit would not have been gratified. I could not stop to dig into the earth, over whose surface I was compelled to pass with rapid steps; nor could I turn aside to collect the plants which nature might have scattered on the way, when my thoughts were anxiously employed in making provision for the day that was passing over me. I had to encounter perils by land and perils by water; to watch the savage who was our guide, or to guard against those of his tribe who might meditate our destruction. I had, also, the passions and fears of others to control and subdue. To day I had to assuage the rising discontents, and on the morrow to cheer the fainting spirits, of the people who accompanied me. The toil of our navigation was incessant, and oftentimes extreme; and in our progress over land we had no protection from the severity of the elements, and possessed no accommodations or conveniences but such as could be contained in the burden on our shoulders, which aggravated the toils of our march, and added to the wearisomeness of our way.

Though the events which compose my journals may have little in themselves to strike the imagination of those who love to be astonished, or to gratify the curiosity of such as are enamoured of romantic adventures; nevertheless, when it is considered that I explored those waters which had never before borne any other vessel than the canoe of the savage; and traversed those deserts where an European had never before presented himself to the eye of its swarthy natives; when to these considerations are added the important objects which were pursued, with the dangers that were encountered, and the difficulties that were surmounted to attain them, this work will, I flatter myself, be found to excite an interest, and conciliate regard, in the minds of those who peruse it.

The general map which illustrates this volume, is reduced by Mr. Arrowsmith from his three-sheet map of North America, with the latest discoveries, which he is about to republish. His professional abilities are well known, and no encomium of mine will advance the general and merited opinion of them.

Before I conclude, I must beg leave to inform my readers, that they are not to expect the charms of embellished narrative, or animated description; the approbation due to simplicity and to truth is all I presume to claim; and I am not without the hope that this claim will be allowed me. I have described whatever I saw with the impressions of the moment which presented it to me. The successive circumstances of my progress are related without exaggeration or display. I have seldom allowed myself to wander into conjecture; and whenever conjecture has been indulged, it will be found, I trust, to be accompanied with the temper of a man who is not disposed to think too highly of himself: and if at any time I have delivered myself with confidence, it will appear, I hope, to be on those subjects which, from the habits and experience of my life, will justify an unreserved communication of my opinions. I am not a candidate for literary fame: at the same time, I cannot but indulge the hope that this volume, with all its imperfections, will not be thought unworthy the attention of the scientific geographer; and that, by unfolding countries hitherto unexplored, and which, I presume, may now be considered as part of the British dominions, it will be received as a faithful tribute to the prosperity of my country.

Alexander Mackenzie.

London,

November 30, 1801.

PART 1

A GENERAL HISTORY
OF THE
FUR TRADE
FROM
CANADA
TO THE
NORTH-WEST

A GENERAL HISTORY OF THE FUR TRADE FROM CANADA TO THE NORTH-WEST

The fur trade, from the earliest settlement of Canada, was considered of the first importance to that colony. The country was then so populous, that, in the vicinity of the establishments, the animals whose skins were precious, in a commercial view, soon became very scarce, if not altogether extinct. They were, it is true, hunted at former periods, but merely for food and clothing. The Indians, therefore, to procure the necessary supply, were encouraged to penetrate into the country, and were generally accompanied by some of the Canadians, who found means to induce the remotest tribes of natives to bring the skins which were most in demand, to their settlements, in the way of trade,

It is not necessary for me to examine the cause, but experience proves that it requires much less time for a civilised people to deviate into the manners and customs of savage life, than for savages to rise into a state of civilisation. Such was the event with those who thus accompanied the natives on their hunting and trading excursions; for they became so attached to the Indian mode of life, that they lost all relish for their former habits and native homes. Hence they derived the title of *Coureurs des Bois,* became a kind of pedlars, and were extremely useful to the merchants engaged in the fur trade; who gave them the necessary credit to proceed on their commercial undertakings. Three or four of these people would join their stock, put their property into a birch-bark canoe, which they worked themselves, and either accompanied the natives in their excursions, or went at once to the country where they knew they were to hunt.

At length, these voyages extended to twelve or fifteen months, when they returned with rich cargoes of furs, and followed by great numbers of the natives. During the short time requisite to settle their accounts with the merchants, and procure fresh credit, they generally contrived to squander away all their gains, when they returned to renew their favourite mode of life: their views being answered, and their labour sufficiently rewarded, by indulging themselves in extravagance and dissipation during the short space of one month in twelve or fifteen.

This indifference about amassing property, and the pleasure of living free from all restraint, soon brought on a licentiousness of manners which could not long escape the vigilant observation of the missionaries, who had much reason to complain of their being a disgrace to the Christian religion; by not only swerving from its duties themselves, but by thus bringing it into disrepute with those of the natives who had become converts to it; and, consequently, obstructing the great object to which those pious men had devoted their lives. They, therefore, exerted their influence to procure the suppression of these people, and accordingly, no one was allowed to go up the country to traffic with the Indians, without a licence from the government.

At first these permissions were, of course, granted only to those whose character was such as could give no alarm to the zeal of the missionaries: but they were afterwards bestowed as rewards for services, on officers, and their widows; and they, who were not willing or able to make use of them, (which may be supposed to be always the case with those of the latter description) were allowed to sell them to the merchants, who necessarily employed the Coureurs des bois, in quality of their agents; and these people, as may be imagined, gave sufficient cause for the renewal of former complaints; so that the remedy proved, in fact, worse than the disease.

At length, military posts were established at the confluence of the different large lakes of Canada, which, in a great measure, checked the evil consequences that followed from the improper conduct of these foresters, and, at the same time, protected the trade. Besides, a number of able and respectable men retired from the army, prosecuted the trade in person, under their respective licences, with great order and regularity, and extended it to such a distance, as, in those days, was considered to be an astonishing effort of commercial enterprize. These persons and the missionaries having combined their views at the same time, secured the respect of the natives, and the obedience of the people necessarily employed in the laborious parts of this undertaking. These gentlemen denominated themselves commanders, and not traders, though they were intitled to both those characters: and, as for the missionaries, if sufferings and hardships in the prosecution of the great work which they had undertaken, deserved applause and admiration, they had an undoubted claim to be admired and applauded: they spared no labour and avoided no danger in the execution of their important office; and it is to be seriously lamented, that their pious endeavours did not meet with the success which they deserved: for there is hardly a trace to be found beyond the cultivated parts, of their meritorious functions.

The cause of this failure must be attributed to a want of due consideration in the mode employed by the missionaries to propagate the religion of which they were the zealous ministers. They habituated themselves to the savage life, and naturalised themselves to the savage manners, and, by thus becoming dependant, as it were, on the natives, they acquired their contempt rather than their veneration. If they had been as well acquainted with human nature, as they were with the articles of their faith, they would have known, that the uncultivated mind of an Indian must be disposed by much preparatory method and instruction to receive the revealed truths of Christianity, to act under its sanctions, and be impelled to good by the hope of its reward, or turned from evil by the fear of its punishments. They should have began their work by teaching some of those useful arts which are the inlets of knowledge, and lead the mind by degrees to objects of higher comprehension. Agriculture so formed to fix and combine society, and so preparatory to objects of superior consideration, should have been the first thing introduced among a savage people: it attaches the wandering tribe to that spot where it adds so much to their comforts; while it gives them a sense of property, and of lasting possession, instead of the uncertain hopes of the chase, and the fugitive produce of uncultivated wilds. Such were the means by which the forests of Paraguay were converted into a scene of abundant cultivation, and its savage inhabitants introduced to all the advantages of a civilized life.

The Canadian missionaries should have been contented to improve the morals of their own countrymen, so that by meliorating their character and conduct, they would have given a striking example of the effect of religion in promoting the comforts of life to the surrounding savages; and might by degrees have extended its benign influence to the remotest regions of that country, which was the object, and intended to be the scene, of their evangelic labours. But by bearing the light of the Gospel at once to the distance of two thousand five hundred miles from the civilized part of the colonies, it was soon obscured by the cloud of ignorance that darkened the human mind in those distant regions.

The whole of their long route I have often travelled, and the recollection of such a people as the missionaries having been there, was confined to a few superannuated Canadians, who had not left that country since the cession to the English, in 1763, and who particularly mentioned the death of some, and the distressing situation of them all. But if these religious men did not attain the objects of their persevering piety, they were, during their mission, of great service to the commanders who engaged in those distant expeditions, and spread the fur trade as far West as the banks of the Saskatchiwine river, in 53° North latitude, and longitude 102 West.

At an early period of their intercourse with the savages, a custom was introduced of a very excellent tendency, but is now unfortunately discontinued, of not selling any spirituous liquor to the natives. This admirable regulation was for some time observed, with all the respect due to the religion by which it was sanctioned, and whose severest censures followed the violation of it. A painful penance could alone restore the offender to the suspended rites of the sacrament. The casuistry of trade, however, discovered a way to gratify the Indians with their favourite cordial, without incurring the ecclesiastical penalties, by giving, instead of selling it to them.

But notwithstanding all the restrictions with which commerce was oppressed under the French Government, the fur trade was extended to the immense distance which has been already stated; and surmounted many most discouraging difficulties, which will be hereafter noticed; while, at the same time, no exertions were made from Hudson's Bay to obtain even a share of the trade of a country which, according to the charter of that company, belonged to it, and, from its proximity, is so much more accessible to the mercantile adventurer.

Of these trading commanders, I understood, that two attempted to penetrate to the Pacific Ocean, but the utmost extent of their journey I could never learn; which may be attributed, indeed, to a failure of the undertaking.

For some time after the conquest of Canada, this trade was suspended, which must have been very advantageous to the Hudson's Bay Company, as all the inhabitants to the Westward of Lake Superior, were obliged to go to them for such articles as their habitual use had rendered necessary. Some of the Canadians who had lived long with them, and were become attached to a savage life, accompanied them thither annually, till mercantile adventurers again appeared from their own country, after an interval of several years, owing, as I suppose, to an ignorance of the country in the conquerors, and their want of commercial confidence in the conquered. There were, indeed, other discouragements, such as the immense length of the journey necessary to reach the limits beyond which this commerce must begin; the risk of property; the expences attending such a long transport; and an ignorance of the language of those who, from their experience, must be necessarily employed as the intermediate agents between them and the natives. But, notwithstanding these difficulties, the trade, by degrees, began to spread over the different parts to which it had been carried by the French, though at a great risk of the lives, as well as the property, of their new pos-

How did The English
Then affect The ?
natives!

sessors, for the natives had been taught by their former allies to entertain hostile dispositions towards the English, from their having been in alliance with their natural enemies the Iroquois; and there were not wanting a sufficient number of discontented, disappointed people to keep alive such a notion; so that for a long time they were considered and treated as objects of hostil- ity. To prove this disposition of the Indians, we have only to refer to the conduct of Pontiac, at Detroit, and the surprise and taking of Michilimakinac, about this period.

Hence it arose, that it was so late as the year 1766, before which, the trade I mean to consider, commenced from Michilimakinac. The first who attempted it were satisfied to go the length of the River Camenistiquia, about thirty miles to the Eastward of the Grande Portage, where the French had a principal establishment, and was the line of their communication with the interior country. It was once destroyed by fire. Here they went and returned successful in the following spring to Michilimakinac. Their success induced them to renew their journey, and incited others to follow their example. Some of them remained at Camenistiquia, while others proceeded to and beyond the Grande Portage, which, since that time has become the principal entrepôt of that trade, and is situated in a bay, in latitude 48 North, and longitude 90 West. After passing the usual season there, they went back to Michilimakinac as before, and encouraged by the trade, returned in increased numbers. One of these, Thomas Curry, with a spirit of enterprize superior to that of his contemporaries, determined to penetrate to the furthest limits of the French discoveries in that country; or at least till the frost should stop him. For this purpose he procured guides and interpreters, who were acquainted with the country, and with four canoes arrived at Fort Bourbon, which was one of their posts, at the West end of the Cedar Lake, on the waters of the Saskatchiwine. His risk and toil were well recompensed, for he came back the following spring with his canoes filled with fine furs, with which he proceeded to Canada, and was satisfied never again to return to the Indian country.

From this period people began to spread over every part of the country, particularly where the French had established settlements.

Mr. James Finlay was the first who followed Mr. Curry's example, and with the same number of canoes, arrived, in the course of the next season, at Nipawee, the last of the French settlements on the bank of the Saskatchiwine River, in latitude nearly 43½ North, and longitude 103 West: he found the good fortune, as he followed, in every respect, the example, of his predecessor.

As may be supposed, there were now people enough ready to replace them, and the trade was pursued with such avidity, and irregularity, that in a few years it became the reverse of what it ought to have been. An animated competition prevailed, and the contending parties carried the trade beyond the French limits, though with no benefits to themselves or neighbours, the Hudson's-Bay Company; who in the year 1774, and not till then, thought proper to move from home to the East bank of Sturgeon Lake, in latitude 53.56 North, and longitude 102.15 West, and became more jealous of their fellow subjects; and, perhaps, with more cause, than they had been of those of France. From this period to the present time, they have been following the Canadians to their different establishments, while, on the contrary, there is not a solitary instance that the Canadians have followed them; and there are many trading posts which they have not yet attained. This, however, will no longer be a mystery when the nature and policy of the Hudson's Bay Company is compared with that which has been pursued by their rivals in this trade. – But to return to my subject.

This competition, which has been already mentioned, gave a fatal blow to the trade from Canada, and, with other incidental causes, in my opinion, contributed to its ruin. This trade was carried on in a very distant country, out of the reach of legal restraint, and where there was a free scope given to any ways or means in attaining advantage. The consequence was not only the loss of commercial benefit to the persons engaged in it, but of the good opinion of the natives, and the respect of their men, who were inclined to follow their example; so that with drinking, carousing, and quarrelling with the Indians along their route, and among themselves, they seldom reached their winter quarters; and if they did, it was generally by dragging their property upon sledges, as the navigation was closed up by the frost. When at length they were arrived, the object of each was to injure his rival traders in the opinion of the natives as much as was in their power, by misrepresentation and presents, for which the agents employed were peculiarly calculated. They considered the command of their employer as binding on them, and however wrong or irregular the transaction, the responsibility rested with the principal who directed them. This is Indian law. Thus did they waste their credit and their property with the natives, till the first was past redemption, and the last was nearly exhausted; so that towards the spring in each year, the rival parties found it absolutely necessary to join, and make one common stock of what remained, for the purpose of trading with the natives, who could entertain no respect for persons who had conducted themselves with so much irregularity and deceit. The winter, therefore was one continued scene of disagreements and quarrels. If any one had the precaution or good sense to keep clear of these proceedings, he derived a proportionable advantage from his good conduct, and frequently proved a peacemaker between the parties. To such an height had they carried this licentious conduct, that they were in a continual state of alarm, and were even frequently stopped to pay tribute on their route into the country; though they had adopted the plan of travelling together in parties of thirty or forty canoes, and keeping their men armed; which sometimes, indeed, proved necessary for their defence.

Thus was the trade carried on for several years, and consequently becoming worse and worse, so that the partners, who met them at the Grande Portage, naturally complained of their ill success. But specious reasons were always ready to prove that it arose from circumstances which they could not at that time control; and encouragements were held forth to hope that a change would soon take place, which would make ample amends for past disappointments.

It was about this time, that Mr. Joseph Frobisher, one of the gentlemen engaged in the trade, determined to penetrate into the country yet unexplored, to the North and Westward, and, in the spring of the year 1775, met the Indians from that quarter on their way to Fort Churchill, at Portage de Traite, so named from that circumstance on the banks of the Missinipi, or Churchill River, latitude 55.25 North, longitude, 103¼ West. It was, indeed, with some difficulty that he could induce them to trade with him, but he at length procured as many furs as his canoes would carry. In this perilous expedition he sustained every kind of hardship incident to a journey through a wild and savage country, where his subsistence depended on what the woods and the waters produced. These difficulties, nevertheless, did not discourage him from returning in the following year, when he was equally successful. He then sent his brother to explore the country still further West, who penetrated as far as the lake of Isle a la Crosse, in latitude 55.26 North, and longitude 108 West.

He, however, never after wintered among the Indians, though he retained a large interest in the trade, and a principal share in the direction of it till the year 1798, when he retired to enjoy the fruits of his labours; and, by his hospitality, became known to every respectable stranger who visited Canada.

The success of this gentleman induced others to follow his example, and in the spring of the year 1778, some of the traders on the Saskatchiwine River, finding they had a quantity of goods to spare, agreed to put them into a joint stock, and gave the charge and management of them to Mr. Peter Pond, who, in four canoes, was directed to enter the English River, so called by Mr. Frobisher, to follow his track, and proceed still further; if possible, to Athabasca, a country hitherto unknown but from Indian report. In this enterprise he at length succeeded, and pitched his tent on the banks of the Elk River, by him erroneously called the Athabasca River, about forty miles from the Lake of the Hills, into which it empties itself.

Here he passed the winter of 1778-9; saw a vast concourse of the Knisteneaux and Chepewyan tribes, who used to carry their furs annually to Churchill; the latter by the barren grounds, where they suffered innumerable hardships, and were sometimes even starved to death. The former followed the course of the lakes and rivers, through a country that abounded in animals, and where there was plenty of fish: but though they did not suffer from want of food, the intolerable fatigue of such a journey could not be easily repaid to an Indian: they were, therefore, highly gratified by seeing people come to their country to relieve them from such long, toilsome, and dangerous journies; and were immediately reconciled to give an advanced price for the articles necessary to their comfort and convenience. Mr. Pond's reception and success was accordingly beyond his expectation; and he procured twice as many furs as his canoes would carry. They also supplied him with as much provision as he required during his residence among them, and sufficient for his homeward voyage. Such of the furs as he could not embark, he secured in one of his winter huts, and they were found the following season, in the same state in which he left them.

These, however, were but partial advantages, and could not prevent the people of Canada from seeing the improper conduct of some of their associates, which rendered it dangerous to remain any longer among the natives. Most of them who passed the winter at the Saskatchiwine, got to the Eagle hills, where, in the spring of the year 1780, a few days previous to their intended departure, a large band of Indians being engaged in drinking about their houses, one of the traders, to ease himself of the troublesome importunities of a native, gave him a dose of laudanum in a glass of grog, which effectually prevented him from giving further trouble to any one, by setting him asleep for ever. This accident produced a fray, in which one of the traders, and several of the men, were killed, while the rest had no other means to save themselves but by a precipitate flight, abandoning a considerable quantity of goods, and near half the furs which they had collected during the winter and the spring.

About the same time, two of the establishments on the Assiniboin river, were attacked with less justice, when several white men, and a great number of Indians were killed. In short, it appeared, that the natives had formed a resolution to extirpate the traders; and, without entering into any further reasonings on the subject, it appears to be incontrovertible, that the irregularity pursued in carrying on the trade has brought it into its present forlorn situation; and nothing but the greatest calamity that could have befallen the natives, saved the traders from destruction: this was the small pox, which spread its destructive and desolating power, as the fire consumes the dry grass of the fields The fatal infection spread around with a baneful rapidity which no flight could escape, and with a fatal effect that nothing could resist. It destroyed with its pestilential breath whole families and tribes; and the horrid scene presented to those who had the melancholy and afflicting opportunity of beholding it, a combination of the dead, the dying, and such as to avoid the horrid fate of their friends around them, prepared to disappoint the plague of its prey, by terminating their own existence.

The habits and lives of these devoted people, which provided not to-day for the wants of to-morrow, must have heightened the pains of such an affliction, by leaving them not only without remedy, but even without alleviation. Nought was left them but to submit in agony and despair.

To aggravate the picture, if aggravation were possible, may be added, the putrid carcasses which the wolves, with a furious voracity, dragged forth from the huts, or which were mangled within them by the dogs, whose hunger was satisfied with the disfigured remains of their masters. Nor was it uncommon for the father of a family, whom the infection had not reached, to call them around him, to represent the cruel sufferings and horrid fate of their relations, from the influence of some evil spirit who was preparing to extirpate their race; and to incite them to baffle death, with all its horrors, by their own poniards. At the same time, if their hearts failed them in this necessary act, he was himself ready to perform the deed of mercy with his own hand, as the last act of his affection, and instantly to follow them to the common place of rest and refuge from human evil.

It was never satisfactorily ascertained by what means this malignant disorder was introduced, but it was generally supposed to be from Missisouri, by a war party.

The consequence of this melancholy event to the traders must be self-evident; the means of disposing of their goods were cut off; and no furs were obtained, but such as had been gathered from the habitations of the deceased Indians, which could not be very considerable: nor did they look from the losses of the present year, with any encouraging expectations to those which were to come. The only fortunate people consisted of a party who had again penetrated to the Northward and Westward in 1780, at some distance up the Missinipi, or English River, to Lake la Rouge. Two unfortunate circumstances, however, happened to them; which are as follow.

Mr. Wadin, a Swiss gentleman, of strict probity and known sobriety, had gone there in the year 1779, and remained during the summer 1780. His partners and others, engaged in an opposite interest, when at the Grande Portage, agreed to send a quantity of goods on their joint account, which was accepted, and Mr. Pond was proposed by them to be their representative to act in conjunction with Mr. Wadin. Two men, of more opposite characters, could not, perhaps, have been found. In short from various causes, their situations became very uncomfortable to each other, and mutual ill-will was the natural consequence: without entering, therefore, into a minute history of these transactions, it will be sufficient to observe, that, about the end of the year 1780, or the beginning of the year 1781, Mr. Wadin had received Mr. Pond and one of his own clerks to dinner; and, in the course of the night, the former was shot through the lower part of the thigh, when it was said that he expired from the loss of blood, and was buried next morning at eight o'clock. Mr. Pond, and the clerk, were tried for this murder at Montreal, and acquitted: nevertheless, their innocence was not so apparent as to extinguish the original suspicion.

The other circumstance was this. In the spring of the year, Mr. Pond sent the abovementioned clerk to meet the Indians from the Northward, who used to go annually to Hudson's Bay; when he easily persuaded them to trade with him, and return back, that they might not take the contagion which had depopulated the country to the Eastward of them: but most unfortunately they caught it here, and carried it with them, to the destruction of themselves and the neighbouring tribes.

The country being thus depopulated, the traders and their friends from Canada, who, from various causes already mentioned, were very much reduced in number, became confined to two parties, who began seriously to think of making permanent establishments on the Missinipi river, and at Athabasca; for which purpose, in 1781-2, they selected their best canoe-men, being ignorant that the small pox penetrated that way. The most expeditious party got only in time to the Portage la Loche, or Mithy-Ouinigam, which divides the waters of the Missinipi from those that fall into the Elk river, to dispatch one canoe strong handed, and light-loaded, to that country; but, on their arrival there, they found, in every direction, the ravages of the small pox; so that, from the great diminution of the natives, they returned in the spring with no more than seven packages of beaver. The strong woods and mountainous countries afforded a refuge to those who fled from the contagion of the plains; but they were so alarmed at the surrounding destruction, that they avoided the traders, and were dispirited from hunting except for their subsistence. The traders, however, who returned into the country in the year 1782-3, found the inhabitants in some sort of tranquillity, and more numerous than they had reason to expect, so that their success was proportionably better.

During the winter of 1783-4, the merchants of Canada, engaged in this trade, formed a junction of interests, under the name of the North-West Company, and divided it into sixteen shares, without depositing any capital; each party furnishing a proportion or quota of such articles as were necessary to carry on the trade: the respective parties agreeing to satisfy the friends they had in the country, who were not provided for, according to this agreement, out of the proportions which they held. The management of the whole was accordingly entrusted to Messrs. Benjamin and Joseph Frobisher, and Mr. Simon M'Tavish, two distinct houses, who had the greatest interest and influence in the country, and for which they were to receive a stipulated commission in all transactions.

In the spring, two of those gentlemen went to the Grande Portage with their credentials, which were confirmed and ratified by all the parties having an option, except Mr. Peter Pond, who was not satisfied with the share allotted him. Accordingly he, and another gentlemen, Mr. Peter Pangman, who had a right to be a partner, but for whom no provision had been made, came to Canada, with a determination to return to the country, if they could find any persons to join them, and give their scheme a proper support.

The traders in the country, and merchants at Montreal, thus entered into a co-partnership, which, by these means, was consolidated and directed by able men, who, from the powers with which they were entrusted, could carry on the trade to the utmost extent it would bear. The traders in the country, therefore, having every reason to expect that their past and future labours would be recompensed, forgot all their former animosities, and engaged with the utmost spirit and activity, to forward the general interest; so that, in the following year, they met their agents at the Grande Portage, with their canoes laden with rich furs from the different parts of that immense tract of country. But this satisfaction was not to be enjoyed without some interruption; and they were mortified to find that Mr. Pangman had prevailed on Messrs. Gregory and Macleod to join him, and give him their support in the business, though deserted by Mr. Pond, who accepted the terms offered by his former associates.

In the counting house of Mr. Gregory I had been five years; and at this period had left him, with a small adventure of goods, with which he had entrusted me, to seek my fortune at Detroit. He, without any solicitation on my part, had procured an insertion in the agreement, that I should be admitted a partner in this business, on condition that I would proceed to the Indian country in the following spring, 1785. His partner came to Detroit to make such a proposition. I readily assented to it, and immediately proceeded to the Grande Portage, where I joined my associates.

We now found that independent of the natural difficulties of the undertaking, we should have to encounter every other which they, who were already in possession of the trade of the country, could throw in our way, and which their circumstances enabled them to do. Nor did they doubt, from their own superior experience, as well as that of their clerks and men, with their local knowledge of the country and its inhabitants, that they should soon compel us to leave the country to them. The event, however, did not justify their expectations; for, after the severest struggle ever known in that part of the world, and suffering every oppression which a jealous and rival spirit could instigate; after the murder of one of our partners, the laming of another, and the narrow escape of one of our clerks, who received a bullet through his powder horn, in the execution of his duty, they were compelled to allow us a share of the trade. As we had already incurred a loss, this union was, in every respect, a desirable event to us, and was concluded in the month of July 1787.

This commercial establishment was now founded on a more solid basis than any hitherto known in the country; and it not only continued in full force, vigour, and prosperity, in spite of all interference from Canada, but maintained at least an equal share of advantage with the Hudson's-Bay Company, notwithstanding the superiority of their local situation. The following account of this self-erected concern will manifest the cause of its success.

It assumed the title of the North-West Company, and was no more than an association of commercial men, agreeing among themselves to carry on the fur trade, unconnected with any other business, though many of the parties engaged had extensive concerns altogether foreign to it. It may be said to have been supported entirely upon credit; for, whether the capital belonged to the proprietor, or was borrowed, it equally bore interest, for which the association was annually accountable. It consisted of twenty shares, unequally divided among the persons concerned. Of these, a certain proportion was held by the people who managed the business in Canada, and were styled agents for the Company. Their duty was to import the necessary goods from England, store them at their own expence at Montreal, get them made up into the articles suited to the trade, pack and forward them, and supply the cash that might be wanting for the outfits; for which they received, independent of the profit on their shares, a commission on the amount of the accounts, which they were obliged to make out annually, and keep the adventure of each year distinct. Two of them went annually to the Grande Portage, to manage and transact the business there, and on the communication at Detroit, Michilimakinac, St. Mary's, and at Montreal, where they received, stored, packed up, and shipped the company's furs for England, on which they had also a small commission. The remaining shares were held by the proprietors, who were obliged to winter and manage the business of the concern with the Indians and their respective clerks, &c. They were not supposed to be under any obligation to furnish capital, or even credit. If they obtained any capital by the trade, it was to remain in the hands of the agents; for which they were allowed interest. Some of them, from their long services and influence, held double shares, and were allowed to retire from the business at any period of the existing concern, with one of those shares, naming any young man in the company's service to succeed him in the other. Seniority and merit were, however, considered as affording a claim to the succession, which, nevertheless, could not be disposed of without the concurrence of the majority of the concern; who, at the same time relieved the seceding person from any responsibility respecting the share that he transferred, and accounted for it according to the annual value or rate of the property; so that the seller could have no advantage but that of getting the share of stock which he retained realised, and receiving for the transferred share what was fairly determined to be the worth of it. The former was also discharged from all duty, and became a dormant partner. Thus, all the young men who were not provided for at the beginning of the contract, succeeded in succession to the character and advantages of partners. They entered into the Company's service for five or seven years, under such expectations, and their reasonable prospects were seldom disappointed: there were, indeed, instances when they succeeded to shares, before their apprenticeship was expired, and it frequently happened that they were provided for while they were in a state of articled clerkship. Shares were transferable only to the concern at large, as no person could be admitted as a partner who had not served his time to the trade. The dormant partner indeed might dispose of his interest to any one he chose, but if the transaction were not acknowledged by his associates, the purchaser could only be considered as his agent or attorney. Every share had a vote, and two thirds formed a majority. This regular and equitable mode of providing for the clerks of the company, excited a spirit of emulation in the discharge of their various duties, and in fact, made every agent a principal, who perceived his own prosperity to be immediately connected with that of his employers. Indeed, without such a spirit, such a trade could not have become so extended and advantageous, as it has been and now is.

In 1788, the gross amount of the adventure for the year did not exceed forty thousand pounds,[1] but by the exertion, enterprise, and industry of the proprietors, it was brought in eleven years to triple that amount and upwards; yielding proportionate profits, and surpassing, in short, any thing known in America.

Such, therefore, being the prosperous state of the company, it, very naturally, tempted others to interfere with the concern in a manner by no means beneficial to the company, and commonly ruinous to the undertakers.

In 1798 the concern underwent a new form, the shares were increased to forty-six, new partners being admitted, and others retiring. This period was the termination of the company, which was not renewed by all the parties concerned in it, the majority

---

1.   This might be properly called the stock of the company, as it included, with the expenditure of the year, the amount of the property unexpended, which had been appropriated for the adventure of that year, and was carried on to the account of the following adventure.

continuing to act upon the old stock, and under the old firm; the others beginning a new one; and it now remains to be decided, whether two parties, under the same regulations and by the same exertions, though unequal in number, can continue to carry on the business to a successful issue. The contrary opinion has been held, which, if verified, will make it the interest of the parties again to coalesce; for neither is deficient in capital to support their obstinacy in a losing trade, as it is not to be supposed that either will yield on any other terms than perpetual participation.

It will not be superfluous in this place, to explain the general mode of carrying on the fur trade.

The agents are obliged to order the necessary goods from England in the month of October, eighteen months before they can leave Montreal; that is, they are not shipped from London until the spring following, when they arrive in Canada in the summer. In the course of the following winter they are made up into such articles as are required by the savages; they are then packed into parcels of ninety pounds weight each, but cannot be sent from Montreal until the May following; so that they do not get to market until the ensuing winter, when they are exchanged for furs, which come to Montreal the next fall, and from thence are shipped, chiefly to London, where they are not sold or paid for before the succeeding spring, or even as late as June; which is forty-two months after the goods were ordered in Canada; thirty-six after they had been shipped from England, and twenty-four after they had been forwarded from Montreal; so that the merchant, allowing that he has twelve months credit, does not receive a return to pay for those goods, and the necessary expences attending them, which is about equal to the value of the goods themselves, till two years after they are considered as cash, which makes this a very heavy business. There is even a small proportion of it that requires twelve months longer to bring round the payment, owing to the immense distance it is carried, and from the shortness of the seasons, which prevents the furs, even after they are collected, from coming out of the country for that period.[2]

The articles necessary for this trade, are coarse woollen cloths of different kinds; milled blankets of different sizes; arms and ammunition; twist and carrot tobacco; Manchester goods; linens, and coarse sheetings; thread, lines and twine; common hardware; cutlery and ironmongery of several descriptions; kettles of brass and copper, and sheet-iron; silk and cotton handkerchiefs; hats, shoes and hose; calicoes and printed cottons, &c. &c. &c. Spirituous liquors and provisions are purchased in Canada. These, and the expence of transport to and from the Indian country, including wages to clerks, interpreters, guides, and canoe-men, with the expence of making up the goods for the market, form about half the annual amount against the adventure.

This expenditure in Canada ultimately tends to the encouragement of British manufactory, for those who are employed in the different branches of this business, are enabled by their gains to purchase such British articles as they must otherwise forego.

The produce of the year for which I am now speaking, consisted of the following furs and peltries:

106,000 Beaver skins; 6,000 Lynx skins; 2,100 Bear skins; 600 Wolverine skins; 1,500 Fox skins; 1,650 Fisher skins; 4,000 Kitt Fox skins; 100 Rackoon skins; 4,600 Otter skins; 3,800 Wolf skins; 17,000 Musquash skins; 700 Elk skins; 32,000 Marten skins; 750 Deer skins; 1,800 Mink skins; 1,200 Deer skins, dressed; 500 Buffalo robes, and a quantity of castorum.

Of these were diverted from the British market, being sent through the United States to China, 13,364 skins, fine beaver,

---

2.   This will be better illustrated by the following statement:

We will suppose the goods for 1798;

The orders for the goods are sent to this country 25th Oct. 1796

They are shipped from London March 1797.

They arrive in Montreal June 1797.

They are made in the course of that summer and winter

They are sent from Montreal May 1798.

They arrive in the Indian country, and are exchanged for furs the following winter 1798-9.

Which furs come to Montreal Sept. 1799.

And are shipped to London, where they are sold in March and April, and paid for in May or June 1800.

weighing 19,283 pounds; 1,250 fine otters, and 1,724 kitt foxes. They would have found their way to the China market at any rate, but this deviation from the British channel arose from the following circumstance:

An adventure of this kind was undertaken by a respectable house in London, half concerned with the North-West Company in the year 1792. The furs were of the best kind, and suitable to the market; and the adventurers continued this connexion for five successive years, to the annual amount of forty thousand pounds. At the winding up of the concern of 1792, 1793, 1794, 1795, in the year 1797, (the adventure of 1796 not being included, as the furs were not sent to China, but disposed of in London), the North-West Company experienced a loss of upwards of £40,000 (their half,) which was principally owing to the difficulty of getting home the produce procured in return for the furs from China, in the East India Company's ships, together with the duty payable, and the various restrictions of that company. Whereas, from America there are no impediments; they get immediately to market, and the produce of them is brought back, and perhaps sold in the course of twelve months. From such advantages the furs of Canada will no doubt find their way to China by America, which would not be the case if British subjects had the same privileges that are allowed to foreigners, as London would then be found the best and safest market.

But to return to our principal subject. – We shall now proceed to consider the number of men employed in the concern: viz. fifty clerks, seventy-one interpreters and clerks, one thousand one hundred and twenty canoe men, and thirty-five guides. Of these, five clerks, eighteen guides, and three hundred and fifty canoe men, were employed for the summer season in going from Montreal to Grande Portage, in canoes, part of whom proceeded from thence to Rainy Lake, as will be hereafter explained, and are called Pork-eaters, or Goers and Comers. These were hired in Canada or Montreal, and were absent from the 1st of May till the latter end of September. For this trip the guides had from eight hundred to a thousand livres, and a suitable equipment; the foreman and steersman from four to six hundred livres; the middlemen from two hundred and fifty to three hundred and fifty livres, with an equipment of one blanket, one shirt, and one pair of trowsers; and were maintained during that period at the expence of their employers. Independent of their wages, they were allowed to traffic, and many of them earned to the amount of their wages. About one third of these went to winter: and had more than double the above wages and equipment. All the winterers were hired by the year, and some times for three years; and of the clerks many were apprentices, who were generally engaged for five or seven years, for which they had only one hundred pounds, provision and clothing. Such of them who could not be provided for as partners, at the expiration of this time, were allowed from one hundred pounds to three hundred pounds per annum, with all necessaries, till provision was made for them. Those who acted in the twofold capacity of clerk and interpreter, or were so denominated, had no other expectation than the payment of wages to the amount of from one thousand to four thousand livres per annum, with clothing and provisions. The guides, who are a very useful set of men, acted also in the additional capacity of interpreters, and had a stated quantity of goods, considered as sufficient for their wants, their wages being from one to three thousand livres. The canoe men are of two descriptions, foremen and steersmen, and middlemen. The two first were allowed annually one thousand two hundred, and the latter eight hundred, livres each. The first class had what is called an equipment, consisting of two blankets, two shirts, two pair of trowsers, two handkerchiefs, fourteen pounds of carrot tobacco, and some trifling articles. The latter had ten pounds of tobacco, and all the other articles: those are called North Men, or Winterers; and to the last class of people were attached upwards of seven hundred Indian women and children, victualled at the expence of the company.

The first class of people are hired in Montreal five months before they set out, and receive their equipments, and one third of their wages in advance; and an adequate idea of the labour they undergo may be formed from the following account of the country through which they pass, and their manner of proceeding.

The necessary number of canoes being purchased, at about three hundred livres each, the goods formed into packages, and the lakes and rivers free of ice, which they usually are in the beginning of May, they are then dispatched from La Chine, eight miles above Montreal, with eight or ten men in each canoe, and their baggage; and sixty-five packages of goods, six hundred weight of biscuit, two hundred weight of pork, three bushels of pease, for the men's provision; two oil cloths to cover the goods, a sail, &c. an axe, a towing-line, a kettle, and a sponge to bail out the water, with a quantity of gum, bark, and watape, to repair the vessel. An European on seeing one of these slender vessels thus laden, heaped up, and sunk with her gunwale within six inches of the water, would think his fate inevitable in such a boat, when he reflected on the nature of her voyage; but the Canadians are so expert that few accidents happen.

Leaving La Chine, they proceed to St. Ann's, within two miles of the Western extremity of the island of Montreal, the lake of the two mountains being in sight, which may be termed the commencement of the Utawas River. At the rapid of St. Ann they are obliged to take out part, if not the whole of their lading. It is from this spot that the Canadians consider they take their departure, as it possesses the last church on the island, which is dedicated to the tutelar saint of the voyagers.

The lake of the two mountains is about twenty miles long, but not more than three wide, and surrounded by cultivated fields, except the Seignory belonging to the clergy, though nominally in possession of the two tribes of Iroquois and Algonquins, whose village is situated on a delightful point of land under the hills, which, by the title of mountains, give a name to the lake. Near the extremity of the point their church is built, which divides the village in two parts, forming a regular angle along the water side. On the East is the station of the Algonquins, and on the West, one of the Iroquois, consisting in all of about five hundred warriors. Each party has its missionary, and divine worship is performed according to the rites of the Roman

Catholic religion, in their respective languages in the same church: and so assiduous have their pastors been, that these people have been instructed in reading and writing in their own language, and are better instructed than the Canadian inhabitants of the country of the lower ranks: but notwithstanding these advantages, and though the establishment is nearly coeval with the colonization of the country, they do not advance towards a state of civilization, but retain their ancient habits, language, and customs, and are becoming every day more depraved, indigent, and insignificant. The country around them, though very capable of cultivation, presents only a few miserable patches of ground, sown by the women with maize and vegetables. During the winter season, they leave their habitations, and pious pastors, to follow the chase, according to the custom of their forefathers. Such is, indeed, the state of all the villages near the cultivated parts of Canada. But we shall now leave them to proceed on our voyage.

At the end of the lake the water contracts into the Utawas River, which, after a course of fifteen miles, is interrupted by a succession of rapids and cascades for upwards of ten miles, at the foot of which the Canadian Seignories terminate; and all above them were waste land, till the conclusion of the American war, when they were surveyed by order of government, and granted to the officers and men of the eighty-fourth regiment, when reduced; but principally to the former, and consequently little inhabited, though very capable of cultivation.

The voyagers are frequently obliged to unload their canoes, and carry the goods upon their backs, or rather suspended in slings from their heads. Each man's ordinary load is two packages, though some carry three. Here the canoe is towed by a strong line. There are some places where the ground will not admit of their carrying the whole; they then make two trips, that is, leave half their lading, and go and land it at the distance required; and then return for that which was left. In this distance are three carrying-places, the length of which depends in a great measure upon the state of the water, whether higher or lower; from the last of these the river is about a mile and a half wide, and has a regular current for about sixty miles, when it ends at the first Portage de Chaudiere, where the body of water falls twenty-five feet, over cragged, excavated rocks, in a most wild, romantic manner. At a small distance below, is the river Rideau on the left, falling over a perpendicular rock, near forty feet high, in one sheet, assuming the appearance of a curtain; and from which circumstance it derives its name. To this extent the lands have been surveyed, as before observed, and are very fit for culture. Many loyalists are settled upon the river Rideau, and have, I am told, thriving plantations. Some American families preferring the British territory, have also established themselves along a river on the opposite side, where the soil is excellent. Nor do I think the period is far distant, when the lands will become settled from this vicinity to Montreal.

Over this portage, which is six hundred and forty-three paces long, the canoe and all the lading is carried. The rock is so steep and difficult of access, that it requires twelve men to take the canoe out of the water: it is then carried by six men, two at each end on the same side, and two under the opposite gunwale in the middle. From hence to the next is but a short distance, in which they make two trips to the second Portage de Chaudiere, which is seven hundred paces, to carry the loading alone. From hence to the next and last Chaudiere, or Portage des Chenes, is about six miles, with a very strong current, where the goods are carried seven hundred and forty paces; the canoe being towed up by the line, when the water is not very high. We now enter Lac des Chaudieres, which is computed to be thirty miles in length. Though it is called a lake, there is a strong draught downwards, and its breadth is from one to four miles. At the end of this is the Portage des Chats, over which the canoe and lading are carried two hundred and seventy-four paces; and very difficult it is for the former. The river is here barred by a ridge of black rocks, rising in pinnacles and covered with wood, which, from the small quantity of soil that nourishes it, is low and stinted. The river finds its way over and through these rocks, in numerous channels, falling fifteen feet and upwards. From hence two trips are made through a serpentine channel, formed by the rocks, for several miles, when the current slackens, and is accordingly called the Lake des Chats. To the channels of the grand Calumet, which are computed to be at the distance of eighteen miles, the current recovers its strength, and proceeds to the Portage Dufort, which is two hundred and forty-five paces long; over which the canoe and baggage are transported. From hence the current becomes more rapid, and requires two trips to the Décharge des Sables,[3] where the goods are carried one hundred and thirty-five paces, and the canoe towed. Then follows the Mountain Portage, where the canoe and lading are also carried three hundred and eighty-five paces; then to the Décharge of the Derige where the goods are carried two hundred and fifty paces; and thence to the grand Calumet. This is the longest carrying-place in this river, and is about two thousand and thirty-five paces. It is a high hill or mountain. From the upper part of this Portage the current is steady, and is only a branch of the Utawas River, which joins the main channel, that keeps a more Southern course, at the distance of twelve computed leagues. Six leagues further it forms Lake Coulonge, which is about four leagues in length: from thence it proceeds through the channels of the Allumettes to the Décharge, where part of the lading is taken out, and carried three hundred and forty-two paces. Then succeeds the Portage des Allumettes, which is but twenty-five paces, over a rock difficult of access, and at a very short distance from the Décharge. From Portage de Chenes to this spot, is a fine deer-hunting country, and the land in many parts very fit for cultivation. From hence the river spreads wide, and is full of islands, with some current for seven leagues, to the beginning of *Riviere Creuse,* or Deep River, which runs in the form of a canal, about a mile and a half wide, for about thirty-six miles; bounded upon the North by very high rocks, with low land on the South, and sandy; it is intercepted again by falls and cataracts so that the Portages of the two Joachins almost join. The first is nine hundred and twenty-six paces, the next seven hundred and twenty, and both very bad roads. From hence is a steady current of nine miles to the River

---

3.   The place where the goods alone are carried is called a *Decharge,* and that where goods and canoes are both transported, overland, is denominated a *Portage.*

du Moine, where there has generally been a trading house; the stream then becomes strong for four leagues, when a rapid succeeds, which requires two trips. A little way onward is the Décharge, and close to it, the Portage of the Roche Capitaine, seven hundred and ninety-seven paces in length. From hence two trips are made through a narrow channel of the Roche Capitaine, made by an island four miles in length. A strong current now succeeds, for about six leagues to the Portage of the two rivers, which is about eight hundred and twenty paces; from thence it is three leagues to the Décharge of the Trou, which is three hundred paces. Near adjoining is the rapid of Levellier; from whence, including the rapids of Matawoen, where there is no carrying-place, it is about thirty-six miles to the forks of the same name; in latitude 46¾ North, and longitude 78¾ West, and is at the computed distance of four hundred miles from Montreal. At this place the Petite Riviere falls into the Utawas. The latter river comes from a North-Westerly direction, forming several lakes in its course. The principal of them is Lake Temescamang, where there has always been a trading post, which may be said to continue, by a succession of rivers and lakes, upwards of fifty leagues from the Forks, passing near the waters of the Lake Abbitiby, in latitude 48½, which is received by the Moose River, that empties itself into James Bay.

The Petite Riviere [the Mattawa] takes a South-West direction, is full of rapids and cataracts to its source, and is not more than fifteen leagues in length, in the course of which are the following interruptions – The Portage of Plein Champ, three hundred and nineteen paces; the Décharge of the Rose, one hundred and forty-five paces; the Décharge of Campion, one hundred and eighty-four paces; the Portage of the Grosse Roche, one hundred and fifty paces; the Portage of Paresseux, four hundred and two paces; the Portage of Prairie, two hundred and eighty-seven paces; the Portage of La Cave, one hundred paces; Portage of Talon, two hundred and seventy-five paces; which, for its length, is the worst on the communication; Portage Pin de Musique, four hundred and fifty-six paces, next to this is Mauvais de Musique, where many men have been crushed to death by the canoes, and others have received irrecoverable injuries. The last in this river is the Turtle Portage, eighty-three paces, on entering the lake of that name, whence the great river is said to take its source. At the first vase the country has the appearance of having been over-run by fire, and consists in general of huge rocky hills. The distance of this portage which is the height of land, between the waters of the St. Laurence and the Utawas, is one thousand five hundred and thirteen paces to a small canal in a plain, that is just sufficient to carry the loaded canoe about one mile to the next vase, which is seven hundred and twenty-five paces. It would be twice this distance, but the narrow creek is dammed in the beaver fashion, to float the canoes to this barrier, through which they pass, when the river is just sufficient to bear them through a swamp of two miles to the last vase, of one thousand and twenty-four paces in length. Though the river is increased in this part, some care is necessary to avoid rocks and stumps of trees. In about six miles is the lake Nepisingui, which is computed to be twelve leagues long, though the route of the canoes is something more: it is about fifteen miles wide in the widest part, and bounded with rocks. Its inhabitants consist of the remainder of a numerous converted tribe, called Nepisinguis of the Algonquin nation. Out of it flows the Riviere des François, over rocks of a considerable height. In a bay to the East of this, the road leads over the Portage of the Chaudiere des François, five hundred and forty-four paces, to still water. It must have acquired the name of Kettle, from a great number of holes in the solid rock of a cylindrical form, and not unlike that culinary utensil. They are observable in many parts along strong bodies of water, and where, at certain seasons, and distinct periods, it is well known the water inundates; at the bottom of them are generally found a number of small stones and pebbles. This circumstance justifies the conclusion, that at some former period these rocks formed the bed of a branch of the discharge of this lake, although some of them are upwards of ten feet above the present level of the water at its greatest height. They are, indeed, to be seen along every great river throughout this wide extended country. The French river is very irregular, both as to its breadth and form, and is so interspersed with islands, that in the whole course of it the banks are seldom visible. Of its various channels, that which is generally followed by the canoes is obstructed by the following Portages, viz. des Pins, fifty-two paces; Feausille, thirty-six paces; Parisienne, one hundred paces; Recolet, forty-five paces; and the Petite Feausille, twenty-five paces. In several parts there are guts or channels, where the water flows with great velocity, which are not more than twice the breadth of a canoe. The distance to Lake Huron is estimated at twenty-five leagues, which this river enters in the latitude 45-53 North, that is, at the point of land three or four miles within the lake. There is hardly a foot of soil to be seen from one end of the French river to the other, its banks consisting of hills of entire rock. The coast of the lake is the same, but lower, backed at some distance by high lands. The course runs through numerous islands to the North of West to the river Tessalon, computed to be about fifty leagues from the French river, and which I found to be in latitude 46.12.21 North; and from thence crossing, from island to island, the arm of the lake that receives the water of Lake Superior (which continues the same course), the route changes to the South of West ten leagues to the Detour, passing the end of the island of St. Joseph, within six miles of the former place. On that island there has been a military establishment since the upper posts were given up to the Americans in the year 1794; and is the Westernmost military position which we have in this country. It is a place of no trade, and the greater part, if not the whole of the Indians, come here for no other purpose but to receive the presents which our government annually allows them. They are from the American territory (except about thirty families, who are the inhabitants of the lake from the French river, and of the Algonquin nation) and trade in their peltries, as they used formerly to do at Michilimakinac, but principally with British subjects. The Americans pay them very little attention, and tell them that they keep possession of their country by right of conquest: that, as their brothers, they will be friends with them while they deserve it; and that their traders will bring them every kind of goods they require, which they may procure by their industry.

Our commanders treat them in a very different manner, and, under the character of the representatives of their father; (which parental title the natives give to his present Majesty, the common father of all his people) present them with such things as the actual state of their stores will allow.

How far this conduct, if continued, may, at a future exigency, keep these people in our interest, if they are even worthy of it, is not an object of my present consideration: at the same time, I cannot avoid expressing my perfect conviction, that it would not be of the least advantage to our present or future commerce in that country, or to the people themselves; as it only tends to keep many of them in a state of idleness about our military establishments. The ammunition which they receive is employed to kill game, in order to procure rum in return, though their families may be in a starving condition: hence it is, that, in consequence of slothful and dissolute lives, their numbers are in a very perceptible state of diminution.

From the Detour to the island of Michilimakinac, at the confluence of the Lakes Huron and Michigan, in latitude 45-54 North is about forty-miles. To keep the direct course to Lake Superior, the north shore from the river Tessalon should be followed; crossing to the North-West end of St. Joseph, and passing between it and the adjacent islands, which makes a distance of fifty miles to the fall of St. Mary, at the foot of which, upon the South shore, there is a village, formerly a place of great resort for the inhabitants of Lake Superior, and consequently of considerable trade: it is now, however, dwindled to nothing, and reduced to about thirty families, of the Algonquin nation, who are one half of the year starving, and the other half intoxicated, and ten or twelve Canadians, who have been in the Indian country from an early period of life, and intermarried with the natives who have brought them families. Their inducement to settle there, was the great quantity of white fish that are to be taken in and about the falls, with very little trouble, particularly in the autumn, when that fish leaves the lakes, and comes to the running and shallow waters to spawn. These, when salt can be procured, are pickled just as the frost sets in, and prove very good food with potatoes, which they have of late cultivated with success. The natives live chiefly on this fish, which they hang up by the tails, and preserve throughout the winter, or at least as long as they last; for whatever quantity they may have taken, it is never known that their economy is such as to make them last through the winter, which renders their situation very distressing; for if they had activity sufficient to pursue the labours of the chase, the woods are become so barren of game as to afford them no great prospect of relief. In the spring of the year they, and the other inhabitants, make a quantity of sugar from the maple tree, which they exchange with the traders for necessary articles, or carry it to Michilimakinac, where they expect a better price. One of these traders was agent for the North-West Company, receiving, storing, and forwarding such articles as come by the way of the lakes upon their vessels; for it is to be observed, that a quantity of their goods are sent by that route from Montreal in boats to Kingston, at the entrance of Lake Ontario, and from thence in vessels to Niagara, then over land ten miles to a water communication, by boats, to Lake Erie, where they are again received into vessels and carried over that lake up the river Detroit, through the lake and river Sinclair to Lake Huron, and from thence to the Falls of St. Mary's, when they are again landed and carried for a mile above the falls, and shipped over Lake Superior to the Grande Portage. This is found to be a less expensive method than by canoes, but attended with more risk, and requiring more time, than one short season of this country will admit; for the goods are always sent from Montreal the preceding fall; and besides, the company get their provisions from Detroit, as flour and Indian corn; as also considerable supplies from Michilimakinac of maple sugar, tallow, gum, &c. &c.

For the purpose of conveying all these things, they have two vessels upon the Lakes Erie and Huron, and one on Lake Superior, of from fifty to seventy tons burthen. This being, therefore, the depot for transports, the Montreal canoes, on their arrival, were forwarded over Lake Superior, with only five men in each; the others were sent to Michilimakinac for additional canoes, which were required to prosecute the trade, and then taking a lading there, or at St. Mary's, and follow the others. At length they all arrive at the Grande Portage, which is one hundred and sixty leagues from St. Mary's coastways, and situated on a pleasant bay on the North side of the lake, in latitude 48 North and longitude 90 West from Greenwich, where the compass has not above five degrees East variation.

At the entrance of the bay is an island which screens the harbour from every wind except the South. The shallowness of the water, however, renders it necessary for the vessel to anchor near a mile from the shore, where there is not more than fourteen feet water. This lake justifies the name that has been given to it: the Falls of St. Mary, which is its Northern extremity, being latitude 46.31 North, and in longitude 84 West, where there is no variation of the compass whatever, while its Southern extremity, at the River St. Louis, is in latitude 46.45 North, and longitude 92.10 West: its greatest breadth is one hundred and twenty miles, and its circumference, including its various bays, is not less than one thousand two hundred miles. Along its North shore is the safest navigation, as it is a continued mountainous embankment of rock, from three hundred to one thousand five hundred feet in height. There are numerous coves and sandy bays to land, which are frequently sheltered by islands from the swell of the lake. This is particularly the case at the distance of one hundred miles to the Eastward of the Grande Portage, and is called the Pays Plat.

This seems to have been caused by some convulsion of nature, for many of the islands display a composition of lava, intermixed with round stones of the size of a pigeon's egg. The surrounding rock is generally hard, and of a dark blue-grey, though it frequently has the appearance of iron and copper. The South side of the lake, from Point Shagoimigo East, is almost a continual straight line of sandy beach, interspersed with rocky precipices of limestones, sometimes rising to an hundred feet in height, without a bay. The embankments from that point Westward are, in general, of strong clay, mixed with stones, which renders the navigation irksome and dangerous. On the same side, at the River Tonnagan, is found a quantity of virgin copper.

The Americans, soon after they got possession of that country, sent an engineer thither; and I should not be surprised to hear of their employing people to work the mine. Indeed, it might be well worthy the attention of the British subjects to work the mines on the North coast, though they are not supposed to be so rich as those on the South.

Lake Superior is the largest and most magnificent body of fresh water in the world: it is clear and pellucid, of great depth, and abounding in a great variety of fish, which are the most excellent of their kind. There are trouts of three kinds, weighing from five to fifty pounds, sturgeon, pickerel, pike, red and white carp, black bass, herrings, &c. &c. and the last and best of all, the Ticamang, or white fish, which weighs from four to sixteen pounds, and is of a superior quality in these waters.

This lake may be denominated the grand reservoir of the River St. Laurence, as no considerable rivers discharge themselves into it. The principal ones are, the St. Louis, the Nipigon, the Pic, and the Michipicoten. Indeed, the extent of country from which any of them flow, or take their course, in any direction, cannot admit of it, in consequence of the ridge of land that separates them from the rivers that empty themselves into Hudson's-Bay, the gulph of Mexico, and the waters that fall in Lake Michegan, which afterwards becomes part of the St. Laurence.

This vast collection of water is often covered with fog, particularly when the wind is from the East, which, driving against the high barren rocks on the North and West shore, dissolves in torrents of rain. It is very generally said, that the storms on this lake are denoted by a swell on the preceding day; but this circumstance did not appear from my observation to be a regular phenomenon, as the swells more frequently subsided without any subsequent wind.

Along the surrounding rocks of this immense lake, evident marks appear of the decrease of its water, by the lines observable along them. The space, however, between the highest and the lowest, is not so great as in the smaller lakes, as it does not amount to more than six feet, the former being very faint.

The inhabitants that are found along the coast of this water, are all of the Algonquin nation, the whole of which do not exceed 150 families.[4]

These people live chiefly on fish; indeed, from what has been said of the country, it cannot be expected to abound in animals, as it is totally destitute of that shelter, which is so necessary to them. The rocks appear to have been over-run by fire, and the stinted timber, which once grew there, is frequently seen lying along the surface of them: but it is not easy to be reconciled, that any thing should grow where there is so little appearance of soil. Between the fallen trees there are briars, with hurtleberry and gooseberry bushes, raspberries, &c. which invite the bears in greater or lesser numbers, as they are a favourite food of that animal: beyond these rocky banks are found a few moose and fallow deer. The waters alone are abundantly inhabited.

A very curious phenomenon was observed some years ago at the Grande Portage, for which no obvious cause could be assigned. The water withdrew with great precipitation, leaving the ground dry that had never before been visible, the fall being equal to four perpendicular feet, and rushing back with great velocity above the common mark. It continued thus falling and rising for several hours, gradually decreasing till it stopped at its usual height. There is frequently an irregular influx and deflux, which does not exceed ten inches, and is attributed to the wind.

The bottom of the bay, which forms an amphitheatre, is cleared of wood and inclosed; and on the left corner of it, beneath a hill, three or four hundred feet in height, and crowned by others of a still greater altitude, is the fort, picketed in with cedar pallisadoes, and inclosing houses built with wood and covered with shingles. They are calculated for every convenience of trade, as well as to accommodate the proprietors and

---

4. In the year 1668, when the first missionaries visited the South of this lake, they found the country full of inhabitants. They relate, that, about this time a band of the Nepisingues [Nipis-sings], who were converted, emigrated to the Nipigon country, which is to the North of Lake Superior. Few of their descendants are now remaining, and not a trace of the religion communicated to them is to be discovered.

clerks during their short residence there. The North men live under tents: but the more frugal pork-eater lodges beneath his canoe. The soil immediately bordering on the lake has not proved very propitious, as nothing but potatoes have been found to answer the trouble of cultivation. This circumstance is probably owing to the cold damp fogs of the lake, and the moisture of the ground from the springs that issue from beneath the hills. There are meadows in the vicinity that yield abundance of hay for the cattle; but, as to agriculture, it has not hitherto been an object of serious consideration.

I shall now leave these geographical notices, to give some further account of the people from Montreal. – When they are arrived at the Grande Portage which is near nine miles over, each of them has to carry eight packages of such goods and provisions as are necessary for the interior country. This is a labour which cattle cannot conveniently perform in summer, as both horses and oxen were tried by the company without success. They are only useful for light, bulky articles; or for transporting upon sledges, during the winter, whatever goods may remain there, especially provision, of which it is usual to have a year's stock on hand.

Having finished this toilsome part of their duty, if more goods are necessary to be transported, they are allowed a Spanish dollar for each package: and so inured are they to this kind of labour, that I have known some of them set off with two packages of ninety pounds each, and return with two others of the same weight, in the course of six hours, being a distance of eighteen miles over hills and mountains. This necessary part of the business being over, if the season be early they have some respite, but this depends upon the time the North men begin to arrive from their winter quarters, which they commonly do early in July. At this period, it is necessary to select from the pork-eaters, a number of men, among whom are the recruits, or winterers, sufficient to man the North canoes necessary to carry, to the river of the rainy lake, the goods and provisions requisite for the Athabasca country; as the people of that country, (owing to the shortness of the season and length of the road, can come no furer), are equipped there, and exchange ladings with the people of whom we are speaking, and both return from whence they came. This voyage is performed in the course of a month, and they are allowed proportionable wages for their service.

The north men being arrived at the Grande Portage, are regaled with bread, pork, butter, liquor, and tobacco, and such as have not entered into agreements during the winter, which is customary, are contracted with, to return and perform the voyage for one, two, or three years: their accounts are also settled, and such as choose to send any of their earnings to Canada, receive drafts to transmit to their relations or friends: and as soon as they can be got ready, which requires no more than a fortnight, they are again dispatched to their respective departments. It is, indeed, very creditable to them as servants, that though they are sometimes assembled to the number of twelve hundred men, indulging themselves in the free use of liquor, and quarrelling with each other, they always shew the greatest respect to their employers, who are comparatively but few in number, and beyond the aid of any legal power to enforce due obedience. In short, a degree of subordination can only be maintained by the good opinion these men entertain of their employers, which has been uniformly the case, since the trade has been formed and conducted on a regular system.

The people being dispatched to their respective winter quarters, the agents from Montreal, assisted by their clerks, prepare to return there, by getting the furs across the portage, and remaking them into packages of one hundred pounds weight each, to send them to Montreal; where they commonly arrive in the month of September.

The mode of living at the Grande Portage, is as follows: The proprietors, clerks, guides, and interpreters, mess together, to the number of sometimes an hundred, at several tables, in one large hall, the provision consisting of bread, salt pork, beef, hams, fish, and venison, butter, peas, Indian corn, potatoes, tea, spirits, wine, &c. and plenty of milk, for which purpose several milch cows are constantly kept. The mechanics have rations of such provision, but the canoe-men, both from the North and Montreal, have no other allowance here, or in the voyage, than Indian corn and melted fat. The corn for this purpose is prepared before it leaves Detroit, by boiling it in a strong alkali, which takes off the outer husk; it is then well washed, and carefully dried upon stages, when it is fit for use. One quart of this is boiled for two hours, over a moderate fire, in a gallon of water; to which, when it has boiled a small time, are added two ounces of melted suet; this causes the corn to split, and in the time mentioned makes a pretty thick pudding. If to this is added a little salt, (but not before it is boiled, as it would interrupt the operation), it makes an wholesome, palatable food, and easy of digestion. This quantity is fully sufficient for a man's subsistence during twenty-four hours; though it is not sufficiently heartening to sustain the strength necessary for a state of active labour. The Americans call this dish hominee[5].

The trade from Grande Portage, is, in some particulars, carried on in a different manner with that from Montreal. The canoes used in the latter transport are now too large for the former, and some of about half the size are procured from the natives, and are navigated by four, five, or six men, according to the distance which they have to go. They carry a lading of about thirty-five packages, on an average; of these twenty-three are for the purpose of trade, and the rest are employed for provisions, stores and baggage. In each of these canoes are a foreman and steersman; the one to be always on the look out, and direct the passage of the vessel, and the other to attend the helm. They also carry her, whenever that office is necessary. The foreman has the command, and the middle-men obey both; the latter earn only two-thirds of the wages which are paid to the two former. Independent of these a conductor or pilot is appointed to every four or six of these canoes, whom they are all obliged to obey; and is, or at least intended to be, a person of superior experience, for which he is proportionably paid.

---

5. Corn is the cheapest provision that can be procured, though from the expence of transport, the bushel costs about twenty shillings sterling, at the Grande Portage. A man's daily allowance does not exceed ten-pence.

In these canoes, thus loaded, they embark at the North side of the portage, on the river Au Tourt, which is very inconsiderable; and after about two miles of a Westerly course, is obstructed by the Partridge Portage, six hundred paces tong. In the spring this makes a considerable fall, when the water is high, over a perpendicular rock of one hundred and twenty feet. From thence the river continues to be shallow, and requires great care to prevent the bottom of the canoe from being injured by sharp rocks, for a distance of three miles and an half to the Prairie, or Meadow, when half the lading is taken out, and carried by part of the crew, while two of them are conducting the canoe among the rocks, with the remainder, to the Carreboeuf Portage, three miles and an half more, when they unload and come back two miles, and embark what was left for the other hands to carry, which they also land with the former; all of which is carried six hundred and eighty paces, and the canoe led up against the rapid. From hence the water is better calculated to carry canoes, and leads by a winding course to the North of West three miles to the Outard Portage, over which the canoe, and every thing in her, is carried for two thousand four hundred paces. At the further end is a very high hill to descend, over which hangs a rock upwards of seven hundred feet high. Then succeeds the Outard Lake, about six miles long, lying in a North-West course, and about two miles wide in the broadest part. After passing a very small rivulet, they come to the Elk Portage, over which the canoe and lading are again carried one thousand one hundred and twenty paces; when they enter the lake of the same name, which is an handsome piece of water, running North-West about four miles, and not more than one mile and an half wide.[6] They then land at the Portage de Cerise, over which, and in the face of a considerable hill, the canoe and cargo are again transported for one thousand and fifty paces. This is only separated from the second Portage de Cerise, by a mud-pond (where there is plenty of water lilies), of a quarter of a mile in length; and this is again separated by a similar pond, from the last Portage de Cerise,

---

6.   Here is a most excellent fishery for white fish, which are exquisite.

which is four hundred and ten paces. Here the same operation is to be performed for three hundred and eighty paces. They next enter on the Mountain Lake, running North-West by West six miles long, and about two miles in its greatest breadth. In the centre of this lake, and to the right is the Old Road, by which I never passed; but an adequate notion may be formed of it from the road I am going to describe, and which is universally preferred. This is first, the small new portage over which every thing is carried for six hundred and twenty-six paces, over hills and gullies; the whole is then embarked on a narrow line of water, that meanders South-West about two miles and an half. It is necessary to unload here, for the length of the canoe, and then proceed West half a mile, to the new Grande Portage, which is three thousand one hundred paces in length, and over very rough ground, which requires the utmost exertions of the men, and frequently lames them: from hence they approach the Rose Lake, the portage of that name being opposite to the junction of the road from the Mountain Lake. They then embark on the Rose Lake, about one mile from the East end of it, and steer West by South, in an oblique course, across it two miles; then West-North-West passing the Petite Peche to the Marten Portage three miles. In this part of the lake the bottom is mud and slime, with about three or four feet of water over it; and here I frequently struck a canoe pole of twelve feet long, without meeting any other obstruction than if the whole were water: it has, however, a peculiar suction or attractive power, so that it is difficult to paddle a canoe over it. There is a small space along the South shore, where the water is deep, and this effect is not felt. In proportion to the distance from this part, the suction becomes more powerful: I have, indeed been told that loaded canoes have been in danger of being swallowed up, and have only owed their preservation to other canoes, which were lighter. I have, myself, found it very difficult to get away from this attractive power, with six men, and great exertion, though we did not appear to be in any danger of sinking.

Over against this is a very high, rocky ridge, on the South side, called Marten Portage, which is but twenty paces long, and

separated from the Peche Portage, which is four hundred and
eighty paces, by a mud-pond, covered with white lilies. From
thence the course is on the lake of the same name, West-South-
West three miles to the height of land, where the waters of the
Dove or Pigeon River terminate, and which is one of the sources
of the great St. Laurence in this direction. Having carried the
canoe and lading over it, six hundred and seventy-nine paces,
they embark on the lake of Hauteur de Terre,[7] which is in the
shape of an horse-shoe. It is entered near the curve, and left at
the extremity of the Western limb, through a very shallow channel, where the canoe passes half loaded for thirty paces with the
current, which conducts these waters through the succeeding
lakes and rivers, till they discharge themselves, by the river Nelson, into Hudson's-Bay. The first of these is Lac de pierres à
fusil, running West-South-West seven miles long, and two wide,
and, making an angle at North-West one mile more, becomes a
river for half a mile, tumbling over a rock, and forming a fall and
portage, called the Escalier, of fifty-five paces; but from hence it
is neither lake or river, but possesses the character of both, and
runs between large rocks, which cause a current or rapid, for
about two miles and an half, West-North-West, to the portage of
the Cheval du Bois. Here the canoe and contents are carried
three hundred and eighty paces, between rocks; and within a
quarter of a mile is the Portage des Gros Pins, which is six hundred and forty paces over an high ridge. The opposite side of it is
washed by a small lake three miles round; and the course is
through the East end or side of it, three quarters of a mile North-
East, where there is a rapid. An irregular, meandering channel,
between rocky banks, then succeeds, for seven miles and a half,
to the Maraboeuf Lake, which extends North four miles, and is
three quarters of a mile wide, terminating by a rapid and
décharge, of one hundred and eighty paces, the rock of Saginaga

---

7.   The route which we have been travelling hitherto, leads along the high rocky
land or bank of Lake Superior on the left. The face of the country offers a wide scene of huge
hills and rocks, separated by stony vallies, lakes, and ponds. Wherever there is the least soil,
it is well covered with trees.

being in sight, which causes a fall of about seven feet, and a portage of fifty-five paces.

Lake Saginaga takes its name from its numerous Islands. Its greatest length from East to West is about fourteen miles, with very irregular inlets, is no where more than three miles wide, and terminates at the small portage of Le Roche, of forty-three paces. From thence is a rocky, stony passage of one mile, to Prairie Portage, which is very improperly named, as there is no ground about it that answers to that description, except a small spot at the embarking place at the West end: to the East is an entire bog; and it is with great difficulty that the lading can be landed upon stages, formed by driving piles into the mud, and spreading branches of trees over them. The portage rises on a stony ridge, over which the canoe and cargo must be carried for six hundred and eleven paces. This is succeeded by an embarkation on a small bay, where the bottom is the same as has been described in the West end of Rose Lake, and it is with great difficulty that a laden canoe is worked over it, but it does not comprehend more than a distance of two hundred yards.

From hence the progress continues through irregular channels, bounded by rocks, in a Westerly course for about five miles, to the little Portage des Couteaux, of one hundred and sixty-five paces, and the Lac des Couteaux, running about South-West by West twelve miles, and from a quarter to two miles wide. A deep bay runs East three miles from the West end, where it is discharged by a rapid river, and after running two miles West, it again becomes still water. In this river are two carrying-places, the one fifteen, and the other one hundred and ninety paces. From this to the Portage des Carpes is one mile North-West, leaving a narrow lake on the East that runs parallel with the Lake des Couteaux, half its length, where there is a carrying-place, which is used when the water in the river last mentioned is too low. The Portage des Carpes is three hundred and ninety paces, from whence the water spreads irregularly between rocks, five miles North-West and South-East to the portage of Lac Bois Blanc, which is one hundred and eighty paces. Then follows the lake of that name, but I think improperly so called as the natives name it the Lake Passeau Minac Sagaigan, or lake of Dry Berries.

Before the small pox ravaged this country, and completed, what the Nodowasis, in their warfare, had gone far to accomplish, the destruction of its inhabitants, the population was very numerous: this was also a favourite part, where they made their canoes, &c. the lake abounding in fish, the country round it being plentifully supplied with various kinds of game, and the rocky ridges, that form the boundaries of the water, covered with a variety of berries.

When the French were in possession of this country, they had several trading establishments on the islands and banks of this lake. Since that period, the few people remaining, who were of the Algonquin nation, could hardly find subsistence; game having become so scarce, that they depended principally for food upon fish, and wild rice which grows spontaneously in these parts.

This lake is irregular in its form, and its utmost extent from East to West is fifteen miles; a point of land, called Point au Pin, jutting into it, divides it in two parts: it then makes a second angle at the West end, to the lesser Portage de Bois Blanc, two hundred paces in length. This channel is not wide, and is intercepted by several rapids in the course of a mile: it runs West-North-West to the Portage des Pins, over which the canoe and lading is again carried four hundred paces. From hence the channel is also intercepted by very dangerous rapids for two miles Westerly, to the point of Pointe du Bois, which is two hundred and eighty paces. Then succeeds the portage of Lake Croche one mile more, where the carrying-place is eighty paces, and is followed by an embarkation on that lake, which takes its name from its figure. It extends eighteen miles, in a meandering form, and in a westerly direction; it is in general very narrow, and at about two-thirds of its length becomes very contracted, with a strong current.

Within three miles of the last Portage is a remarkable rock, with a smooth face, but split and cracked in different parts, which hang over the water. Into one of its horizontal chasms a great number of arrows have been shot, which is said to have been done by a war party of the Nadowasis or Sieux, who had done much mischief in this country, and left these weapons as a warning to the Chebois or natives, that, notwithstanding its lakes, rivers, and rocks, it was not inaccessible to their enemies.

Lake Croche is terminated by the Portage de Rideau, four hundred paces long, and derives its name from the appearance of the water, falling over a rock of upwards of thirty feet. Several rapids succeed, with intervals of still water, for about three miles to the Flacon portage, which is very difficult, is four hundred paces long, and leads to the Lake of La Croix, so named from its shape. It runs about North-West eighteen miles to the Beaver Dam, and then sinks into a deep bay nearly East. The course to the Portage is West by North for sixteen miles more from the Beaver Dam, and into the East bay is a road which was frequented by the French, and followed through lakes and rivers until they came to Lake Superior by the river Caministiquia, thirty miles East of the Grand Portage.

Portage la Croix is six hundred paces long: to the next portage is a quarter of a mile, and its length is forty paces; the river winding four miles to Vermillion Lake, which runs six or seven miles North-North-West, and by a narrow strait communicates with Lake Namaycan, which takes its name from a particular place at the foot of a fall, where the natives spear sturgeon. Its course is about North-North-West and South-South-East, with a bay running East, that gives it the form of a triangle: its length is about sixteen miles to the Nouvelle Portage. The discharge of the lake is from a bay on the left, and the portage one hundred and eighty paces, to which succeeds a very small river, from whence there is but a short distance to the next Nouvelle Portage, three hundred and twenty paces long. It is then necessary to embark on a swamp, or overflowed country, where wild rice grows in great abundance. There is a channel or small river in the centre of this swamp, which is kept with difficulty, and runs South and North one mile and a half. With deepening water, the course continues North-North-West one mile to the Chaudiere Portage, which is caused by the discharge of the waters running on the left of the road from Lake Naymaycan, which used to be the common route, but that which I have described is the fastest as well as the shortest. From hence there is some current though the water is wide spread, and its course about North by West three miles and an half to the Lac de la Pluie, which lies nearly East and West; from thence about fifteen miles is a narrow strait that divides the lake into two unequal parts, from whence to its discharge is a distance of twenty-four miles. There is a deep bay running North-West on the right, that is not included, and is remarkable for furnishing the natives with a kind of soft, red stone, of which they make their pipes; it also affords an excellent fishery both in the summer and winter; and from it is an easy, safe, and short road to the Lake du Bois, (which I shall mention presently) for the Indians to pass in their small canoes, through a small lake and on a small river, whose banks furnish abundance of wild rice. The discharge of this lake is called Lake de la Pluie River, at whose entrance there is a rapid, below which is a fine bay, where there had been an extensive picketted fort and building when possessed by the French; the site of it is at present a beautiful meadow, surrounded with groves of oaks. From hence there is a strong current for two miles, where the water falls over a rock twenty feet, and, from the consequent turbulence of the water, the carrying-place, which is three hundred and twenty paces long, derives the name of Chaudiere. Two miles onward is the present trading establishment, situated on an high bank on the North side of the river, in 48.37 North latitude.

Here the people from Montreal come to meet those who arrive from the Athabasca country, as has been already described, and exchange lading with them. This is also the residence of the first chief, or Sachem, of all the Algonquin tribes, inhabiting the different parts of this country. He is by distinction called Nectam, which implies personal pre-eminence. Here also the elders meet in council to treat of peace or war.

This is one of the finest rivers in the North-West, and runs a course West and East one hundred and twenty computed miles; but in taking its course and distance minutely I make it only eighty. Its banks are covered with a rich soil, particularly to the

North, which, in many parts, are clothed with fine open groves of oak, with the maple, the pine, and the cedar. The Southern bank is not so elevated, and displays the maple, the white birch, and the cedar, with the spruce, the alder, and various under-wood. Its waters abound in fish, particularly the sturgeon, which the natives both spear and take with drag-nets. But notwith-standing the promise of this soil, the Indians do not attend to its cultivation, though they are not ignorant of the common process, and are fond of the Indian corn, when they can get it from us.

Though the soil at the fort is a stiff clay, there is a garden, which, unassisted as it is by manure, or any particular attention, is tolerably productive.

We now proceed to mention the Lake du Bois, into which this river discharges itself in latitude 49 North, and was formerly famous for the richness of its banks and waters, which abounded with whatever was necessary to a savage life. The French had several settlements in and about it; but it might be almost con-cluded, that some fatal circumstance had destroyed the game, as war and small pox had diminished the inhabitants, it having been very unproductive in animals since the British subjects have been engaged in travelling through it; though it now appears to be recovering its pristine state. The few Indians who inhabit it might live very comfortably, if they were not so immoderately fond of spirituous liquors.

This lake is also rendered remarkable, in consequence of the Americans having named it as the spot, from which a line of boundary, between them and British America, was to run West, until it struck the Mississippi; which, however, can never hap-pen, as the North-West part of the Lake du Bois is in latitude 49.37 North, and longitude 94.31 West, and the Northernmost branch of the source of the Mississippi is in latitude 47.38 North, and longitude 95.6 West, ascertained by Mr. Thomson, astrono-mer to the North-West Company, who was sent expressly for that purpose in the spring of 1798. He, in the same year, deter-mined the Northern bend of the Missisoury to be in latitude 47.32 North, and longitude 101.25 West; and, according to the Indian accounts, it runs to the south of West, so that if the Missisoury were even to be considered as the Mississippi, no Western line could strike it.

It does not appear to me to be clearly determined what course the Line is to take, or from what part of Lake Superior it strikes through the country to the Lake du Bois: were it to follow the principal waters to their source, it ought to keep through Lake Superior to the River St. Louis, and follow that river to its source; close to which is the source of the waters falling into the river of Lake la Pluie, which is a common route of the Indians to the Lake du Bois: the St. Louis passes within a short distance of a branch of the Mississippi, where it becomes navigable for canoes. This will appear more evident from consulting the map; and if the navigation of the Mississippi is considered as of any consequence, by this country, from that part of the globe, such is the nearest way to get at it.

But to return to our narrative. The Lake du Bois, is, as far as I could learn, nearly round, and the canoe course through the centre of it among a cluster of islands, some of which are so extensive that they may be taken for the main land. The reduced course would be nearly South and North. But following the navigating course, I make the distance seventy-five miles, though in a direct line it would fall very short of that length. At about two-thirds of it there is a small carrying-place, when the water is low. The carrying-place out of the lake is on an island, and named Portage du Rat, in latitude 49-37 North and longitude 94¼ West, it is about fifty paces long. The lake discharges itself at both ends of this island, and forms the River Winipic, which is a large body of water, interspersed with numerous islands, causing various channels and interruptions of portages and rapids. In some parts it has the appearance of lakes, with steady currents; I estimate its winding course to the Dalles eight miles; to the Grand Décharge twenty-five miles and an half, which is a long carrying-place for the goods; from thence to the little Décharge one mile and an half; to the Terre Jaune Portage two miles and an half; then to its galet seventy yards; two miles and three quarters to the Terre Blanche, near which is a fall of from four to five feet; three miles and an half to Portage de L'Isle, where there is a trading-post, and, about eleven miles, on the North shore, a trading establishment, which is the road, in boats to Albany River, and from thence to Hudson's Bay. There is also a communication with Lake Superior, through what is called the Nipigan country, which enters that Lake about thirty-five leagues East of the Grande Portage. In short, the country is so broken by lakes and rivers, that people may find their way in canoes in any direction they please. It is now four miles to Portage de L'isle, which is but short, though several canoes have been lost in attempting to run the rapid. From thence it is twenty-six miles to Jacob's Falls, which are about fifteen feet high; and six miles and an half to the woody point; forty yards from which is another Portage. They both form an high fall, but not perpendicular. From thence to another galet, or rocky Portage, is about two miles, which is one continual rapid and cascade; and about two miles further is the Chute a l'Esclave, which is upwards of thirty feet. The Portage is long, through a point covered with wood: it is six miles and an half more to the barrier, and ten miles to the Grand Rapid. From thence, on the North side, is a safe road, when the waters are high, through small rivers and lakes, to the Lake du Bonnet, called the Pinnawas, from the man who discovered it: to the White River, so called from its being, for a considerable length, a succession of falls and cataracts, is twelve miles. Here are seven portages, in so short a space, that the whole of them are discernible at the same moment. From this to Lake du Bonnet is fifteen miles more, and four miles across it to the rapid. Here the Pinnawas road joins, and from thence it is two miles to the Galet du Lac du Bonnet; from this to the Galet du Bonnet one mile and an half; thence to the Portage of the same name is three miles. This Portage is near half a league in length, and derives its name from a custom the Indians have of crowning stones, laid in a circle, on the highest rock in the portage, with wreaths of herbage and branches. There have been examples of men taking seven packages of ninety pounds each, at one end of the portage, and putting them down at the other without stopping.

To this, another small portage immediately succeeds, over a rock producing a fall. From thence to the fall of Terre Blanche is two miles and an half; to the first portage Des Eaux qui Remuent is three miles; to the next, of the same name, is but a few yards distant; to the third and last, which is a Décharge, is three miles and an half; and from this to the last portage of the river one mile and an half; and to the establishment, or provision house, is two miles and an half. Here also the French had their principal inland depot, and got their canoes made.

It is here, that the present traders, going to great distances, and where provision is difficult to procure, receive a supply to carry them to the Rainy Lake, or Lake Superior. From the establishment to the entrance of Lake Winipic is four miles and an half, latitude 50.37 North.

The country, soil, produce, and climate, from Lake Superior to this place bear a general resemblance, with a predominance of rock and water: the former is of the granite kind. Where there is any soil it is well covered with wood, such as oak, elm, ash of different kinds, maple of two kinds, pines of various descriptions, among which are what I call the cypress, with the hickory, iron-wood, liard, poplar, cedar, black and white birch, &c. &c. Vast quantities of wild rice are seen throughout the country, which the natives collect in the month of August for their winter stores.[8] To the North of fifty degrees, it is hardly known, or at least does not come to maturity.

Lake Winipic [Winnipeg] is the great reservoir of several large rivers, and discharges itself by the River Nelson into Hudson's Bay. The first in rotation, next to that I have just described, is the Assiniboin, or Red River, which, at the distance of forty miles coastwise, disembogues on the South-West side of the lake Winipic. It alternately receives those two denominations from its dividing, at the distance of about thirty miles from the lake, into two large branches. The Eastern branch, called the Red River, runs in a Southern direction to near the head waters

---

8.   The fruits are, strawberries, hurthberries, plumbs, and cherries, hazlenuts, gooseberries, currants, raspberries, poires, &c.

of the Mississippi. On this are two trading establishments. The country on either side is but partially supplied with wood, and consists of plains covered with herds of the buffalo and the elk, especially on the Western side. On the Eastern side are lakes and rivers, and the whole country is well wooded, level, abounding in beavers, bears, moose-deer, fallow-deer, &c. &c. The natives, who are of the Algonquin tribe, are not very numerous, and are considered as the natives of Lake Superior. This country being near the Mississippi, is also inhabited by the Nadowasis, who are the natural enemies of the former; the head of the water being the war-line, they are in a continual state of hostility; and though the Algonquins are equally brave, the others generally outnumber them; it is very probable, therefore, that if the latter continue to venture out of the woods, which form their only protection, they will soon be extirpated. There is not, perhaps, a finer country in the world for the residence of uncivilised man, than that which occupies the space between this river and Lake Superior. It abounds in every thing necessary to the wants and comforts of such a people. Fish, venison, and fowl, with wild rice, are in great plenty; while, at the same time, their subsistence requires that bodily exercise so necessary to health and vigour.

This great extent of country was formerly very populous, but from the information I received, the aggregate of its inhabitants does not exceed three hundred warriors; and, among the few whom I saw, it appeared to me that the widows were more numerous than the men. The rackoon is a native of this country, but is seldom found to the Northward of it.

The other branch is called after the tribe of the Nadawasis, who here go by the name of Assiniboins, and are the principal inhabitants of it. It runs from the North-North-West, and, in the latitude of 51¼ West, and longitude 103 1/3, rising in the same mountains as the river Dauphin, of which I shall speak in clue order. They must have separated from their nation at a time beyond our knowledge, and live in peace with the Algonquins and Knisteneaux.

The country between this and the Red River, is almost a continual plain to the Missisoury. The soil is sand and gravel, with a slight intermixture of earth, and produces a short grass. Trees are very rare; nor are there on the banks of the river sufficient, except in particular spots, to build houses and supply fire-wood for the trading establishments, of which there are four principal ones. Both these rivers are navigable for canoes to their source, without a fall; though in some parts there are rapids, caused by occasional beds of lime-stone, and gravel; but in general they [have] a sandy bottom.

The Assiniboins, and some of the Fall, or Big-bellied Indians, are the principal inhabitants of this country, and border on the river, occupying the centre part of it; that next Lake Winipic, and about its source, being the station of the Algonquins and Knisteneaux, who have chosen it in preference to their own country. They do not exceed five hundred families. They are not beaver hunters, which accounts for their allowing the division just mentioned, as the lower and upper parts of this river have those animals, which are not found in the intermediate district. They confine themselves to hunting the buffalo, and trapping wolves, which cover the country. What they do not want of the former for raiment and food, they sometimes make into pemmican, or pounded meat, while they melt the fat, and prepare the skins in their hair, for winter. The wolves they never eat, but produce a tallow from their fat, and prepare their skins; all which they bring to exchange for arms and ammunition, rum, tobacco, knives, and various baubles, with those who go to traffic in their country.

The Algonquins, and the Knisteneaux, on the contrary, attend to the fur-hunting, so that they acquire the additional articles of cloth, blankets, &c. but their passion for rum often puts it out of their power to supply themselves with real necessaries.

The next river of magnitude is the river Dauphin, which empties itself at the head of St. Martin's Bay, on the West side of the Lake Winipic, latitude nearly 52.15 North, taking its source in the same mountains as the last-mentioned river, as well as the Swan and Red-Deer River, the latter passing through the lake of the same name, as well as the former, and both continuing their course through the Manitoba Lake, which, from thence, runs parallel with Lake Winipic, to within nine miles of the Red River, and by what is called the river Dauphin, disembogues its waters, as already described, into that lake. These rivers are very rapid, and interrupted by falls, &c. the bed being generally rocky. All this country, to the South branch of the Saskatchiwine, abounds in beaver, moose-deer, fallow-deer, elks, bears, buffalos, &c. The soil is good, and wherever any attempts have been made to raise the esculent plants, &c. it has been found productive.

On these waters are three principal forts for trade. Fort Dauphin, which was established by the French before the conquest. Red-Deer-River, and Swan-River Forts, with occasional detached posts from these. The inhabitants are the Knisteneaux, from the North of Lake Winipic; and Algonquins from the country between the Red River and Lake Superior; and some from the Rainy Lake: but as they are not fixed inhabitants, their number cannot be determined: they do not, however, at any time exceed two hundred warriors. In general they are good hunters. There is no other considerable river except the Saskatchiwine, which I shall mention presently, that empties itself into the Lake Winipic.

Those on the North side are inconsiderable, owing to the comparative vicinity of the high land that separates the waters coming this way, from those discharging into Hudson's bay. The course of the lake is about West-North-West, and South-South-East, and the East end of it is in 50.37 North. It contracts at about a quarter of its length to a strait, in latitude 51.45 and is no more than two miles broad, where the South shore is gained through islands, and crossing various bays to the discharge of the Saskatchiwine, in latitude 53.15. This lake, in common with those of this country, is bounded on the North with banks of black and grey rock, and on the South by a low, level country, occasionally interrupted with a ridge or bank of lime-stones, lying in stratas, and rising to the perpendicular height of from twenty to forty feet; these are covered with a small quantity of earth, forming a level surface, which bears timber, but of a moderate growth, and declines to a swamp. Where the banks are low, it is evident in many places that the waters are withdrawn, and never rise to those heights which were formerly washed by them.

The inhabitants who are found along this lake, are of the Knisteneaux and Algonquin tribes, and but few in number, though game is not scarce, and there is fish in great abundance. The black bass is found there, and no further West; and beyond it no maple trees are seen, either hard or soft.

On entering the Saskatchiwine, in the course of a few miles, the great rapid interrupts the passage. It is about three miles long. Through the greatest part of it the canoe is towed, half or full laden, according to the state of the waters: the canoe and its contents are then carried one thousand one hundred paces. The channel here is near a mile wide, the waters tumbling over ridges of rocks that traverse the river. The south bank is very high, rising upwards of fifty feet, of the same rock as seen on the South side of the Lake Winipic, and the North is not more than a third of that height. There is an excellent sturgeon-fishery at the foot of this cascade, and vast numbers of pelicans, cormorants, &c. frequent it, where they watch to seize the fish that may be killed or disabled by the force of the waters.

About two miles from this Portage the navigation is again interrupted by the Portage of the Roche Rouge, which is an hundred yards long; and a mile and an half from thence the river is barred by a range of islands, forming rapids between them; and through these it is the same distance to the rapid of Lake Travers, which is four miles right across, and eight miles in length. Then succeeds the Grande Décharge, and several rapids, for four miles to the Cedar Lake, which is entered through a small channel on the left, formed by an island, as going round it would occasion loss of time. In this distance banks of rocks (such as have already been described), appear at intervals on either side; the rest of the country is low. This is the case along the South bank of the lake and the islands, while the North side, which is very uncommon, is level throughout. This lake runs first West four miles, then as much more West-South-West, across a deep bay on the right, then six miles to the Point de Lievre, and across another bay again on the right; then North-West eight miles, across a still deeper bay on the right; and seven miles parallel with the North coast, North-North-West through islands, five miles more to Fort Bourbon[9], situated on a small island, dividing this from Mud-Lake.

The Cedar Lake is from four to twelve miles wide, exclusive of the bays. Its banks are covered with wood, and abound in game, and its waters produce plenty of fish, particularly the sturgeon. The Mud-Lake, and the neighbour-hood of the Fort Bourbon, abound with geese, ducks, swans, &c. and was formerly remarkable for a vast number of martens, of which it cannot now boast but a very small proportion.

The Mud-Lake must have formerly been a part of the Cedar Lake, but the immense quantity of earth and sand, brought down by the Saskatchiwine, has filled up this part of it for a circumference whose diameter is at least fifteen or twenty miles: part of which space is still covered with a few feet of water, but the greatest proportion is shaded with large trees, such as the liard, the swamp-ash, and the willow. This land consists of many islands, which consequently form various channels, several of which are occasionally dry, and bearing young wood. It is, indeed, more than probable that this river will, in the course of time, convert the whole of the Cedar Lake into a forest. To the North-West the cedar is not to be found.

From this lake the Saskatchiwine may be considered as navigable to near its sources in the rocky mountains, for canoes, and without a carry-place, making a great bend to Cumberland House, on Sturgeon Lake. From the confluence of its North and South branches its course is Westerly; spreading itself, it receives several tributary streams, and encompasses a large track of country, which is level, particularly along the South branch, but is little known. Beaver, and other animals, whose furs are valuable, are amongst the inhabitants of the North-West

---

9.   This was also a principal post of the French, who gave it its name.

branch, and the plains are covered with buffalos, wolves, and small foxes; particularly about the South branch, which, however, has of late claimed some attention, as it is now understood, that where the plains terminate towards the rocky mountain, there is a space of hilly country clothed with wood, and inhabited also by animals of the fur kind. This has been actually determined to be the case towards the head of the North branch, where the trade has been carried to about the latitude 54 North, and longitude 114½ West. The bed and banks of the latter, in some few places, discover a stratum of free-stone; but, in general, they are composed of earth and sand. The plains are sand and gravel, covered with fine grass, and mixed with a small quantity of vegetable earth. This is particularly observable along the North branch, the West side of which is covered with wood.

There are on this river five principal factories for the convenience of trade with the natives. Nepawi House, South-branch House, Fort-George House, Fort-Augustus House, and Upper Establishment. There have been many others, which, from various causes, have been changed for these, while there are occasionally others depending on each of them.

The inhabitants, from the information I could obtain, are as follow:

At Nepawi, and South-branch House, about thirty tents of Knisteneaux, or ninety warriors; and sixty tents of Stone-Indians, or Assiniboins, who are their neighbours, and are equal to two hundred men: their hunting ground extends upwards to about the Eagle Hills. Next to them are those who trade at Forts George and Augustus, and are about eighty tents or upwards of Knisteneaux: on either side of the river, their number may be two hundred. In the same country are one hundred and forty tents of Stone-Indians; not quite half of them inhabit the West woody country; the others never leave the plains, and their numbers cannot be less than four hundred and fifty men. At the Southern Headwaters of the North branch dwells a tribe called Sarsees, consisting of about thirty-five tents, or one hundred and twenty men. Opposite to those Eastward, on the head-waters of the South Branch, are the Picaneaux, to the number of from twelve to fifteen hundred men. Next to them, on the same water, are the Blood-Indians, of the same nation as the last, to the number of about fifty tents, or two hundred and fifty men. From them downwards extend the Black-Feet Indians, of the same nation as the two last tribes: their number may be eight hundred men. Next to them, and who extend to the confluence of the South and North branch, are the Fall, or Big-bellied Indians, who may amount to about six hundred warriors.

Of all these different tribes, those who inhabit the broken country on the North-West side, and the source of the North branch, are beaver-hunters; the others deal in provisions, wolf, buffalo, and fox skins; and many people on the South branch do not trouble themselves to come near the trading establishments. Those who do, choose such establishments as are next to their country. The Stone-Indians here, are the same people as the Stone-Indians, or Assiniboins, who inhabit the river of that name already described, and both are detached tribes from the Nada-wasis, who inhabit the Western side of the Mississippi, and the lower part of the Missisoury. The Fall, or Big-bellied Indians, are from the South-Eastward also, and of a people who inhabit the plains from the North bend of the last mentioned river, latitude 47.32 North, longitude 101.25 West, to the South bend of the Assiniboin River, to the number of seven hundred men. Some of them occasionally come to the latter river to exchange dressed buffalo robes, and bad wolf-skins for articles of no great value.

The Picaneaux, Black-Feet, and Blood-Indians, are a distinct people, speak a language of their own, and, I have reason to think, are travelling North-Westward, as well as the others just mentioned: nor have I heard of any Indians with whose language, that which they speak has any affinity. They are the people who deal in horses and take them upon the war-parties towards Mexico; from which, it is evident, that the country to the South-East of them, consists of plains, as those animals could not well be conducted through an hilly and woody country, intersected by waters.

The Sarsees, who are but few in number, appear from their language, to come on the contrary from the North-Westward, and are of the same people as the Rocky-Mountain Indians described in my second journal, who are a tribe of the Chepewyans; and, as for the Knisteneaux, there is no question of their having been, and continuing to be, invaders of this country, from the Eastward. Formerly, they struck terror into all the other tribes whom they met; but now they have lost the respect that was paid them; as those whom they formerly considered as barbarians, are now their allies, and consequently become better acquainted with them, and have acquired the use of fire-arms. The former are still proud without power, and affect to consider the others as their inferiors; those consequently are extremely jealous of them, and, depending upon their own superiority in numbers, will not submit tamely to their insults; so that the consequences often prove fatal, and the Knisteneaux are thereby decreasing both in power and number: spirituous liquors also tend to their diminution, as they are instigated thereby to engage in quarrels which frequently have the most disastrous termination among themselves.

The Stone-Indians must not be considered in the same point of view respecting the Knisteneaux, for they have been generally obliged, from various causes, to court their alliance. They, however, are not without their disagreements, and it is sometimes very difficult to compose their differences. These quarrels occasionally take place with the traders, and sometimes have a tragical conclusion. They generally originate in consequence of stealing women and horses: they have great numbers of the latter throughout their plains, which are brought, as has been observed, from the Spanish settlements in Mexico; and many of them have been seen even in the back parts of this country, branded with the initials of their original owners names. Those horses are distinctly employed as beasts of burden, and to chase the buffalo. The former are not considered as being of much value, as they may be purchased for a gun, which costs no more than twenty-one shillings in Great Britain. Many of the hunters cannot be purchased with ten, the comparative value of which exceeds the property of any native.

Of these useful animals no care whatever is taken, as when they are no longer employed, they are turned loose winter and summer to provide for themselves. Here, it is to be observed, that the country, in general, on the West and North side of this great river, is broken by the lakes and rivers with small intervening plains, where the soil is good, and the grass grows to some length. To these the male buffalos resort for the winter, and if it be very severe, the females also are obliged to leave the plains.

But to return to the route by which the progress West and North is made through this continent.

We leave the Saskatchiwine[10] by entering the river which forms the discharge of the Sturgeon Lake, on whose East bank is situated Cumberland house, in latitude 53.56 North, longitude 102.15. The distance between the entrance and Cumberland house is estimated at twenty miles. It is very evident that the mud which is carried down by the Saskatchiwine River, has formed the land that lies between it and the lake, for the distance of upwards of twenty miles in the line of the river, which is inundated during one half of the summer, though covered with wood. This lake forms an irregular horseshoe, one side of which runs to the North-West, and bears the name of Pine-Island Lake, and the other known by the name already mentioned, runs to the East of North, and is the largest: its length is about twenty-seven miles, and its greatest breadth about six miles. The North side of the latter is the same kind of rock as that described in Lake Winipic, on the West shore. In latitude 54.16 North, the Sturgeon-Weir River discharges itself into this lake, and its bed appears to be of the same kind of rock, and is almost a continual rapid. Its direct course is about West by North, and with its windings, is about thirty miles. It takes its waters into the Beaver Lake, the South-West side of which consists of the same rock lying in thin

10. It may be proper to observe, that the French had two settlements upon the Saskatchiwine, long before, and at the conquest of Canada; the first at the Pasquia, near Carrot River, and the other at Nipawi, where they had agricultural instruments and wheel carriages, marks of both being found about those establishments, where the soil is excellent.

stratas: the route then proceeds from island to island for about twelve miles, and along the North shore, for about four miles more, the whole being a North-West course to the entrance of a river, in latitude 54.32 North. The lake, for this distance, is about four or five miles wide, and abounds with fish common to the country. The part of it upon the right of that which has been described, appears more considerable. The islands are rocky, and the lake itself surrounded by rocks. The communication from hence to the Bouleau Lake, alternately narrows into rivers and spreads into small lakes. The interruptions are, the Pente Portage, which is succeeded by the Grand Rapid, where there is a Décharge, the Carp Portage, the Bouleau Portage in latitude 54.50 North, including a distance, together with the windings, of thirty-four miles, in a Westerly direction. The Lake de Bouleau then follows. This lake might with greater propriety, be denominated a canal, as it is not more than a mile in breadth. Its course is rather to the East of North for twelve miles to Portage de L'Isle. From thence there is still water to Portage d'Epinettes, except an adjoining rapid. The distance is not more than four miles Westerly. After crossing this Portage, it is not more than two miles to Lake Miron, which is in latitude 55.7 North. Its length is about twelve miles, and its breadth irregular, from two to ten miles. It is only separated from Lake du Chitique, or Pelican Lake, by a short, narrow, and small strait. That lake is not more than seven miles long, and its course about North-West. The Lake des Bois then succeeds, the passage to which is through small lakes, separated by falls and rapids. The first is a Décharge: then follow the three galets, in immediate succession. From hence Lake des Bois runs about twenty-one miles. Its course is South-South-East, and North-North-West, and is full of islands. The passage continues through an intricate, narrow, winding, and shallow channel for eight miles. The interruptions in this distance are frequent, but depend much on the state of the waters. Having passed them, it is necessary to cross the Portage de Traite, or, as it is called by the Indians, Athiquisipichigan Ouinigam, or the Portage of the Stretched Frog-Skin, to the Missinipi. The waters already described discharge themselves into Lake Winipic, and augment those of the river Nelson. These which we are now entering are called the Missinipi, or great Churchill River.

All the country to the South and East of this, within the line of the progress that has been described, is interspersed by lakes, hills, and rivers, and is full of animals, of the fur-kind, as well as the moose-deer. Its inhabitants are the Knisteneaux Indians, who are called by the servants of the Hudson's-Bay Company, at York, their home-guards.

The traders from Canada succeeded for several years in getting the largest proportion of their furs, till the year 1793, when the servants of that company thought proper to send people amongst them, (and why they did not do it before is best known to themselves), for the purpose of the trade, and securing their credits, which the Indians were apt to forget. From the short distance they had to come, and the quantity of goods they supplied, the trade has, in a great measure, reverted to them, as the merchants from Canada could not meet them upon equal terms. What added to the loss of the latter, was the murder of one of their traders, by the Indians, about this period. Of these people not above eighty men have been known to the traders from Canada, but they consist of a much greater number.

The Portage de Traite, as has already been hinted, received its name from Mr. Joseph Frobisher, who penetrated into this part of the country from Canada, as early as the years 1774 and 1775, where he met with the Indians in the spring, on their way to Churchill, according to annual custom, with their canoes full of valuable furs. They traded with him for as many of them as his canoes could carry, and in consequence of this transaction, the Portage received and has since retained its present appellation. He also denominated these waters the English River. The Missinipi, is the name which it received from the Knisteneaux, when they first came to this country, and either destroyed or drove back the natives, whom they held in great contempt, on many accounts, but particularly for their ignorance in hunting the beaver, as well as in preparing, stretching, and drying the skins of those animals. And as a sign of their derision, they stretched the skin of a frog, and hung it up at the Portage. This was, at that time, the utmost extent of their conquest or warfaring-progress West, and is in latitude 55.25 North, and longitude 103¾ West. The river here, which bears the appearance of a lake, takes its name from the Portage, and is full of islands. It runs from East to West about sixteen miles, and is from four to five miles broad. Then succeed falls and cascades which form what is called the grand rapid. From thence there is a succession of small lakes and rivers, interrupted by rapids and falls, viz. the Portage de Bared, the Portage de L'Isle, and that of the Rapid River. The course is twenty miles from East-South-East to North-North-West. The Rapid-River Lake then runs West five miles, and is of an oval form. The rapid river is the discharge of Lake la Ronge, where there has been an establishment for trade from the year 1782. Since the small pox ravaged these parts, there have been but few inhabitants; these are of the Knisteneaux tribe, and do not exceed thirty men. The direct navigation continue to be through rivers and canals, interrupted by rapids; and the distance to the first Décharge is four miles, in a Westerly direction. Then follows Lake de la Montagne, which runs South-South-West three miles and an half, then North six miles, through narrow channels, formed by islands, and continues North-North-West five miles, to the portage of the same name, which is no sooner crossed, than another appears in sight, leading to the Otter Lake, from whence it is nine miles Westerly to the Otter Portage, in latitude 57.39. Between this and the Portage du Diable, are several rapids, and the distance three miles and an half. Then succeeds the lake of the same name, running from South-East to North-West, five miles, and West four miles and an half. There is then a succession of small lakes, rapids, and falls, producing the Portage des Ecors, Portage du Galet, and Portage des Morts, the whole comprehending a distance of six miles, to the lake of the latter name. On the left side is a point covered with human bones, the relics of the small pox; which circumstance gave the Portage and the lake this melancholy denomination. Its course is South-West fifteen miles, while its breadth does not exceed three miles. From thence a rapid river leads to Portage de Hallier, which is followed by Lake de L'Isle d'Ours; it is, however, improperly called a lake, as it contains frequent impediments amongst its islands, from rapids. There is a very dangerous one about the centre of it, which is named the Rapid qui ne parle point, or that never speaks, from its silent whirlpool-motion. In some of the whirlpools the suction is so powerful, that they are carefully avoided. At some distance from the silent rapid, is a narrow strait, where the Indians have painted red figures on the face of a rock, and where it was their custom formerly to make an offering of some of the articles which they had with them, in their way to and from Churchill. The course in this lake, which is very meandering, may be estimated at thirty-eight miles, and is terminated by the Portage du Canot Tourner, from the danger to which those are subject who venture to run this rapid. From thence a river of one mile and a half North-West course leads to the Portage de Bouleau, and in about half a mile to the Portage des Epingles, so called from the sharpness of its stones. Then follows the Lake des Souris, the direction across which is amongst islands, North-West by West six miles. In this traverse is an island, which is remarkable for a very large stone, in the form of a bear, on which the natives have painted the head and snout of that animal; and here they also were formerly accustomed to offer sacrifices. This lake is separated only by a narrow strait from the Lake du Serpent, which runs North-North West seven miles, to a narrow channel, that connects it with another lake, bearing the same name, and running the same course for eleven miles, when the rapid of the same denomination is entered on the West side of the lake. It is to be remarked here, that for about three or four miles on the North-West side of this lake, there is an high bank of clay and sand, clothed with cypress trees, a circumstance which is not observable on any lakes hitherto mentioned, as they are bounded, particularly on the North, by black and grey rocks. It may also be considered as a most extraordinary circumstance, that the Chepewyans, go North-West from hence to the barren grounds, which are their own country, without the assistance of canoes; as it is well known that in every other part which has been described, from Cumberland House, the country is broken on either side of the direction to a great extent: so that a traveller could not go at right angles with any of the waters already mentioned, without meeting with others in every eight or ten miles. This will also be found to be very much the case in proceeding to Portage la Loche.

The last mentioned rapid is upwards of three miles long, North-West by West; there is, however, no carrying, as the line and poles are sufficient to drag and set the canoe against the current. Lake Croche is then crossed in a Westerly direction of six miles, though its whole length may be twice that distance; after which it contracts to a river that runs Westerly for ten miles, when it forms a bend, which is left to the South, and entering a portion of its waters called the Grass River, whose meandering course is about six miles, but in a direct line not more than half that length, where it receives its waters from the great river, which then runs Westerly eleven miles before it forms the Knee Lake, whose direction is to the North of West. It is full of islands for eighteen miles, and its greatest apparent breadth is not more than five miles. The portage of the same name is several hundred yards long, and over large stones. Its latitude is 55.50 and longitude 106.30. Two miles further North is the commencement of the Croche Rapid, which is a succession of cascades for about three miles, making a bend due South to the Lake du Primeau, whose course is various, and through islands, to the distance of about fifteen miles. The banks of this lake are low, stony, and marshy, whose grass and rushes, afford shelter and food to great numbers of wild fowl. At its Western extremity is Portage la Puise, from whence the river takes a meandering course, widening and contracting at intervals, and is much interrupted by rapids. After a Westerly course of twenty miles, it reaches Portage Pellet. From hence, in the course of seven miles, are three rapids, to which succeeds the Shagoina Lake, which may be eighteen miles in circumference. Then Shagoina strait and rapid lead into the Lake of Isle a la Crosse, in which the course is South twenty miles, and South-South-West fourteen miles, to the Point au Sable; opposite to which is the discharge of the Beaver-River, bearing South six miles: the lake in the distance run, does not exceed twelve miles in its greatest breadth. It now turns West-South-West, the isle a la Crosse being on the South, and the main land on the North; and it clears the one and the other in the distance of three miles, the water presenting an open horizon to right and left: that on the left formed by a deep narrow bay, about ten leagues in depth; and that to the right by what is called la Riviere Creuse, or Deep River, being a canal of still water, which is here four miles wide. On following the last course, Isle a la Crosse Fort appears on a low isthmus, at the distance of five miles, and is in latitude 55.25 North, and longitude 107.48 West.

This lake and fort take their names from the island just mentioned, which, as has been already observed, received its denomination from the game of the cross, which forms a principal amusement among the natives. The situation of this lake, the abundance of the finest fish in the world to be found in its waters, the richness of its surrounding banks and forests, in moose and fallow deer, with the vast numbers of the smaller tribes of animals, whose skins are precious, and the numerous flocks of wild fowl that frequent it in the spring and fall, make it a most desirable spot for the constant residence of some, and the occasional rendezvous of others of the inhabitants of the country, particularly of the Knisteneaux.

Who the original people were that were driven from it, when conquered by the Knisteneaux is not now known, as not a single vestige remains of them. The latter, and the Chepewyans, are the only people that have been known here; and it is evident that the last-mentioned consider themselves as strangers, and seldom remain longer than three or four years, without visiting their relations and friends in the barren grounds, which they term their native country. They were for sometime treated by the Knisteneaux as enemies; who now allow them to hunt to the North of the track which has been described, from Fort du Traite upwards, but when they occasionally meet them, they insist on contributions, and frequently punish resistance with their arms. This is sometimes done at the forts, or places of trade, but then it appears to be a voluntary gift. A treat of rum is expected on the occasion, which the Chepewyans on no other account ever purchase; and those only who have had frequent intercourse with the Knisteneaux have any inclination to drink it.

When the Europeans first penetrated into this country, in 1777, the people of both tribes were numerous, but the small pox was fatal to them all, so that there does not exist of the one, at present, more than forty resident families; and the other has been from about thirty to two hundred families. These numbers are applicable to the constant and less ambitious inhabitants, who are satisfied with the quiet possession of a country affording, without risk or much trouble, every thing necessary to their comfort; for since traders have spread themselves over it, it is no more the rendezvous of the errant Knisteneaux, part of whom used annually to return thither from the country of the Beaver River, which they had explored to its source in their war and hunting excursions and as far as the Saskatchiwine, where they sometimes met people of their own nation, who had prosecuted similar conquests up that river. In that country they found abundance of fish and animals, such as have been already described, with the addition of the buffalos, who range in the partial patches of meadow scattered along the rivers and lakes. From thence they returned in the spring to the friends whom they had left; and, at the same time met with others who had penetrated, with the same designs, into the Athabasca country, which will be described hereafter.

The spring was the period of this joyful meeting, when their time was occupied in feasting, dancing, and other pastimes, which were occasionally suspended for sacrifice, and religious solemnity: while the narratives of their travels, and the history of their wars, amused and animated the festival. The time of rejoicing was but short, and was soon interrupted by the necessary preparations for their annual journey to Churchill, to exchange their furs for such European articles as were now become necessary to them. The shortness of the seasons, and the great length of their way requiring the utmost dispatch, the most active men of the tribe, with their youngest women, and a few of their children undertook the voyage, under the direction of some of their chiefs, following the waters already described, to their discharge at Churchill Factory, which are called, as has already been observed, the Missinipi, or Great Waters. There they remained no longer than was sufficient to barter their commodities, with a supernumerary day or two to gratify themselves with the indulgence of spirituous liquors. At the same time the inconsiderable quantity they could purchase to carry away with them, for a regale with their friends, was held sacred, and reserved to heighten the enjoyment of their return home, when the amusements, festivity, and religious solemnities of the spring were repeated. The usual time appropriated to these convivialities being completed, they separated, to pursue their different objects; and if they were determined to go to war, they made the necessary arrangements for their future operations.

But we must now renew the progress of the route. It is not more than two miles from Isle a la Crosse Fort, to a point of land which forms a cheek of that part of the lake called the Riviere Creuse, which preserves the breadth already mentioned for upwards of twenty miles; then contracts to about two, for the distance of ten miles or more, when it opens to Lake Clear, which is very wide, and commands an open horizon, keeping the West shore for six miles. The whole of the distance mentioned is about North-West, when, by a narrow, crooked channel, turning to the South of West, the entry is made into Lake du Boeuf, which is contracted near the middle, by a projecting sandy point; independent of which it may be described as from six to twelve miles in breadth, thirty-six miles long, and in a North-West direction. At the North-West end, in latitude 76.8 it receives the waters of the river la Loche, which, in the fall of the year, is very shallow, and navigated with difficulty even by half-laden canoes. Its water is not sufficient to form strong rapids, though from its rocky bottom the canoes are frequently in considerable danger. Including its meanders, the course of this river may be computed at twenty-four miles, and receives its first waters from the lake of the same name, which is about twenty miles long, and six wide; into which a small river flows, sufficient to bear

loaded canoes, for about a mile and an half, where the navigation ceases; and the canoes, with their lading, are carried over
the Portage la Loche for thirteen miles.

This portage is the ridge that divides the waters which discharge themselves into Hudson's Bay, from those that flow into
the Northern ocean, and is in the latitude 56.20 and longitude
109.15 West. It runs South West until it loses its local height
between the Saskatchiwine and Elk Rivers; close on the bank of
the former, in latitude 53.36 North, and longitude 113.45 West,
it may be traced in an Easterly direction toward latitude 58.12
North, and longitude 103½ West, when it appears to take its
course due North, and may probably reach the Frozen Seas.

From Lake le Souris, the banks of the rivers and lakes display a smaller portion of solid rock. The land is low and stony,
intermixed with a light, sandy soil, and clothed with wood. That
of the Beaver River is of a more productive quality: but no part
of it has ever been cultivated by the natives or Europeans, except
a small garden at the Isle a la Crosse, which well repaid the
labour bestowed upon it.

The Portage la Loche is of a level surface, in some parts
abounding with stones, but in general it is an entire sand, and
covered with the cypress, the pine, the spruce fir, and other trees
natural to its soil. Within three miles of the North-West termination, there is a small round lake, whose diameter does not exceed
a mile, and which affords a trifling respite to the labour of carrying. Within a mile of the termination of the Portage is a very
steep precipice, whose ascent and descent appears to be equally
impracticable in any way, as it consists of a succession of eight
hills, some of which are almost perpendicular; nevertheless, the
Canadians contrive to surmount all these difficulties, even with
their canoes and lading.

This precipice, which rises upwards of a thousand feet above
the plain beneath it, commands a most extensive, romantic, and
ravishing prospect. From thence the eye looks down on the
course of the little river, by some called the Swan river, and by
others, the Clear-Water and Pelican river, beautifully meandering for upwards of thirty miles. The valley, which is at once

refreshed and adorned by it, is about three miles in breadth, and is confined by two lofty ridges of equal height, displaying a most delightful intermixture of wood and lawn, and stretching on till the blue mist obscures the prospect. Some parts of the inclining heights are covered with stately forests, relieved by promontories of the finest verdure, where the elk and buffalo find pasture. These are contrasted by spots where fire has destroyed the woods, and left a dreary void behind it. Nor, when I beheld this wonderful display of uncultivated nature, was the moving scenery of human occupation wanting to complete the picture. From this elevated situation, I beheld my people, diminished, as it were, to half their size, employed in pitching their tents in a charming meadow, and among the canoes, which, being turned upon their sides, presented their reddened bottoms in contrast with the surrounding verdure. At the same time, the process of gumming them produced numerous small spires of smoke, which, as they rose, enlivened the scene, and at length blended with the larger columns that ascended from the fires where the suppers were preparing. It was in the month of September when I enjoyed a scene, of which I do not presume to give an adequate description; and as it was the rutting season of the elk, the whistling of that animal was heard in all the variety which the echoes could afford it.

This river, which waters and reflects such enchanting scenery, runs, including its windings, upwards of eighty miles, when it discharges itself in the Elk River, according to the denomination of the natives, but commonly called by the white people, the Athabasca River, in latitude 56.42 North.

At a small distance from Portage la Loche, several carrying-places interrupt the navigation of the river; about the middle of which are some mineral springs, whose margins are covered with sulphureous incrustations. At the junction or fork, the Elk River is about three quarters of a mile in breadth, and runs in a steady current, sometimes contracting, but never increasing its channel, till, after receiving several small streams, it discharges itself into the Lake of the Hills, in latitude 58.36 North. At about twenty-four miles from the Fork, are some bitumenous fountains, into which a pole of twenty feet long may be inserted without the least resistance. The bitumen is in a fluid state, and when mixed with gum, or the resinous substance collected from the spruce fir, serves to gum the canoes. In its heated state it emits a smell like that that of sea-coal. The banks of the river, which are there very elevated, discover veins of the same bitumenous quality. At a small distance from the Fork, houses have been erected for the convenience of trading with a party of the Knisteneaux, who visit the adjacent country for the purpose of hunting.

At the distance of about forty miles from the lake, is the Old Establishment, which has been already mentioned, as formed by Mr. Pond in the year 1778-9, and which was the only one in this part of the world, till the year 1785. In the year 1788, it was transferred to the Lake of the Hills, and formed on a point on its Southern side, at about eight miles from the discharge of the river. It was named Fort Chepewyan, and is in latitude 58.38 North, longitude 110.26 West, and much better situated for trade and fishing, as the people here have recourse to water for their support.

This being the place which I made my head-quarters for eight years, and from whence I took my departure, on both my expeditions, I shall give some account of it, with the manner of carrying on the trade there, and other circumstances connected with it.

The laden canoes which leave Lake la Pluie about the first of August, do not arrive here till the latter end of September, or the beginning of October, when a necessary proportion of them is dispatched up the Peace River to trade with the Beaver and Rocky-Mountain Indians. Others are sent to the Slave River and Lake, or beyond them, and traffic with the inhabitants of that country. A small part of them, if not left at the Fork of the Elk River, return thither for the Knisteneaux, while the rest of the people and merchandise remain here to carry on trade with the Chepewyans.

Here have I arrived with ninety or an hundred men without any provision for their sustenance; for whatever quantity might have been obtained from the natives during the summer, it could not be more than sufficient for the people dispatched to their different posts; and even if there were a casual superfluity, it was absolutely necessary to preserve it untouched, for the demands of the spring. The whole dependance, therefore, of those who remained, was on the lake, and fishing implements for the means of our support. The nets are sixty fathom in length, when set, and contain fifteen meshes of five inches in depth. The manner of using them is as follows: A small stone and wooden buoy are fastened to the side-line opposite to each other, at about the distance of two fathoms: when the net is carefully thrown into the water, the stone sinks it to the bottom, while the buoy keeps it at its full extent, and it is secured in its situation by a stone at either end. The nets are visited every day, and taken out every other day to be cleaned and dried. This is a very ready operation when the waters are not frozen, but when the frost has set in, and the ice has acquired its greatest thickness, which is sometimes as much as five feet, holes are cut in it at the distance of thirty feet from each other, to the full length of the net; one of them is larger than the rest, being generally about four feet square, and is called the bason: by means of them, and poles of a proportionable length, the nets are placed in and drawn out of the water. The setting of hooks and lines is so simple an employment as to render a description unnecessary. The white fish are the principal object of pursuit: they spawn in the fall of the year, and, at about the setting in of the hard frost, crowd in shoals to the shallow water, when as many as possible are taken, in order that a portion of them may be laid by in the frost to provide against the scarcity of winter; as, during that season, the fish of every description decrease in the lakes, if they do not altogether disappear. Some have supposed that during this period they are stationary, or assume an inactive state. If there should be any intervals of warm weather during the fall, it is necessary to suspend the fish by the tail, though they are not so good as those which are altogether preserved by the frost. In this state they remain to the beginning of April, when they have been found as sweet as when they were caught.[11]

Thus do these voyagers live, year after year, entirely upon fish, without even the quickening flavour of salt, or the variety of any farinaceous root or vegetable. Salt, however, if their habits had not rendered it unnecessary, might be obtained in this country to the Westward of the Peace River, where it loses its name in that of the Slave River, from the numerous salt-ponds and springs to be found there, which will supply in any quantity, in a state of concretion, and perfectly white and clean. When the Indians pass that way they bring a small quantity to the fort, with other articles of traffic.

During a short period of the spring and fall, great numbers of wild fowl frequent this country, which prove a very gratifying food after such a long privation of flesh-meat. It is remarkable, however, that the Canadians who frequent the Peace, Saskatchi-wine, and Assiniboin rivers, and live altogether on venison, have a less healthy appearance than those whose sustenance is obtained from the waters. At the same time the scurvy is wholly unknown among them.

In the fall of the year the natives meet the traders at the forts, where they barter the furs or provisions which they may have procured: they then obtain credit, and proceed to hunt the beavers, and do not return till the beginning of the year; when they are again fitted out in the same manner and come back the latter end of March, or the beginning of April. They are now unwilling to repair to the beaver hunt until the waters are clear of ice, that they may kill them with fire-arms, which the Chepewyans are averse to employ. The major part of the latter return to the barren grounds, and live during the summer with their relations and friends in the enjoyment of that plenty which is derived from numerous herds of deer. But those of that tribe who are most partial to these desarts, cannot remain there in winter, and they are obliged, with the deer, to take shelter in the woods during that rigorous season, when they contrive to kill a few beavers,

11. This fishery requires the most unremitting attention, as the voyaging Canadians are equally indolent, extravagant, and improvident, when left to themselves, and rival the savages in a neglect of the morrow.

and send them by young men, to exchange for iron utensils and ammunition.

Till the year 1782, the people of Athabasca sent or carried their furs regularly to Fort Churchill, Hudson's Bay; and some of them have, since that time, repaired thither, notwithstanding they could have provided themselves with all the necessaries which they required. The difference of the price set on goods here and at that factory, made it an object with the Chepewyans, to undertake a journey of five or six months, in the course of which they were reduced to the most painful extremities, and often lost their lives from hunger and fatigue. At present, however, this traffic is in a great measure discontinued, as they were obliged to expend in the course of their journey, that very ammunition which was its most alluring object.

SOME ACCOUNT OF THE KNISTENEAUX INDIANS.

These people are spread over a vast extent of country. Their language is the same as that of the people who inhabit the coast of British America on the Atlantic, with the exception of the Esquimaux,[12] and continues along the Coast of Labrador, and the gulph and banks of St. Laurence to Montreal. The line then follows the Utawas [Ottawa] river to its source; and continues from thence nearly West along the high lands which divide the waters that fall into Lake Superior and Hudson's Bay. It then proceeds till it strikes the middle part of the river Winipic, following that water through the Lake Winipic, to the discharge of the Saskatchiwine into it; from thence it accompanies the latter to Fort George, when the line, striking by the head of the Beaver River to the Elk River, runs along its banks to its discharge in the Lake of the Hills; from which it may be carried back East, to the Isle a la Crosse, and so on to Churchill by the Missinipi. The whole of the tract between this line and Hudson's Bay and Straits, (except that of the Esquimaux in the latter), may be said to be exclusively the country of the Knisteneaux. Some of them, indeed, have penetrated further West and South to the Red River, to the South of Lake Winipic, and the South branch of the Saskatchiwine.

They are of moderate stature, well proportioned, and of great activity. Examples of deformity are seldom to be seen among them. Their complexion is of a copper colour, and their hair

---

12. The similarity between their language, and that of the Algonquins, is an unequivocal proof that they are the same people. Specimens of their respective tongues will be hereafter given.

black, which is common to all the natives of North America. It is cut in various forms, according to the fancy of the several tribes, and by some is left in the long, lank, flow of nature. They very generally extract their beards, and both sexes manifest a disposition to pluck the hair from every part of the body and limbs. Their eyes are black, keen, and penetrating; their countenance open and agreeable, and it is a principal object of their vanity to give every possible decoration to their persons. A material article in their toilettes is vermilion, which they contrast with their native blue, white, and brown earths, to which charcoal is frequently added.

Their dress is at once simple and commodious. It consists of tight leggins, reaching near the hip: a strip of cloth or leather, called assian, about a foot wide, and five feet long, whose ends are drawn inwards and hang behind and before, over a belt tied round the waist for that purpose: a close vest or shirt reaching down to the former garment, and cinctured with a broad strip of parchment fastened with thongs behind; and a cap for the head, consisting of a piece of fur, or small skin, with the brush of the animal as a suspended ornament: a kind of robe is thrown occasionally over the whole of the dress, and serves both night and day. These articles, with the addition of shoes and mittens, constitute the variety of their apparel. The materials vary according to the season, and consist of dressed moose-skin, beaver prepared with the fur, or European woollens. The leather is neatly painted, and fancifully worked in some parts with porcupine quills, and moose-deer hair: the shirts and leggins are also adorned with fringes and tassels; nor are the shoes and mittens without somewhat of appropriate decoration, and worked with a considerable degree of skill and taste. These habiliments are put on, however, as fancy or convenience suggests; and they will sometimes proceed to the chase in the severest frost, covered only with the slightest of them. Their head-dresses are composed of the feathers of the swan, the eagle, and other birds. The teeth, horns, and claws of different animals, are also the occasional ornaments of the head and neck. Their hair, however arranged, is always besmeared with grease. The making of every article of dress is a female occupation; and the women, though by no means inattentive to the decoration of their own persons, appear to have a still greater degree of pride in attending to the appearance of the men, whose faces are painted with more care than those of the women.

The female dress is formed of the same materials as those of the other sex, but of a different make and arrangement. Their shoes are commonly plain, and their leggins gartered beneath the knee. The coat, or body covering, falls down to the middle of the leg, and is fastened over the shoulders with cords, a flap or cape turning down about eight inches, both before and behind, and agreeably ornamented with quill-work and fringe; the bottom is also fringed, and fancifully painted as high as the knee. As it is very loose, it is enclosed round the waist with a stiff belt, decorated with tassels, and fastened behind. The arms are covered to the wrist, with detached sleeves, which are sewed as far as the bend of the arm; from thence they are drawn up to the neck, and the corners of them fall down behind, as low as the waist. The cap, when they wear one, consists of a certain quantity of leather or cloth, sewed at one end, by which means it is kept on the head, and, hanging down the back, is fastened to the belt, as well as under the chin. The upper garment is a robe like that worn by the men. Their hair is divided on the crown, and tied behind, or sometimes fastened in large knots over the ears. They are fond of European articles, and prefer them to their own native commodities. Their ornaments consist in common with all savages, in bracelets, rings, and similar baubles. Some of the women tatoo three perpendicular lines, which are sometimes double: one from the centre of the chin to that of the under lip, and one parallel on either side to the corner of the mouth.

Of all the nations which I have seen on this continent, the Knisteneaux women are the most comely. Their figure is generally well proportioned, and the regularity of their features would be acknowledged by the more civilized people of Europe. Their complexion has less of that dark tinge which is common to those savages who have less cleanly habits.

These people are, in general, subject to few disorders. The lues venerea, however, is a common complaint, but cured by the application of simples, with whose virtues they appear to well acquainted. They are also subject to fluxes, and pains in the breast, which some have attributed to the very cold and keen air which they inhale; but I should imagine that these complaints must frequently proceed from their immoderate indulgence in fat meat at their feasts, particularly when they have been preceded by long fasting.

They are naturally mild and affable, as well as just in their dealings, not only among themselves, but with strangers.[13] They are also generous and hospitable, and good-natured in the extreme, except when their nature is perverted by the inflammatory influence of spirituous liquors. To their children they are indulgent to a fault. The father, though he assumes no command over them, is ever anxious to instruct them in all the preparatory qualifications for war and hunting; while the mother is equally attentive to her daughters in teaching them every thing that is considered as necessary to their character and situation. It does not appear that the husband makes any distinction between the children of his wife, though they may be the offspring of different fathers. Illegitimacy is only attached to those who are born before their mothers have cohabited with any man by the title of husband.

It does not appear, that chastity is considered by them as a virtue; or that fidelity is believed to be essential to the happiness of wedded life. Though it sometimes happens that the infidelity of a wife is punished by the husband with the loss of her hair, nose, and perhaps life; such severity proceeds from its having been practised without his permission: for a temporary interchange of wives is not uncommon; and the offer of their persons is considered as a necessary part of the hospitality due to strangers.

---

13. They have been called thieves, but when that vice can with justice be attributed to them, it may be traced to their connection with the civilized people who come into their country to traffic.

When a man loses his wife, it is considered as a duty to marry her sister, if she has one; or he may, if he pleases, have them both at the same time.

It will appear from the fatal consequences I have repeatedly imputed to the use of spirituous liquors, that I more particularly consider these people as having been, morally speaking, great sufferers from their communication with the subjects of civilized nations. At the same time they were not, in a state of nature, without their vices, and some of them of a kind which is the most abhorrent to cultivated and reflecting man. I shall only observe that incest and bestiality are common among them.

When a young man marries, he immediately goes to live with the father and mother of his wife, who treat him, nevertheless, as a perfect stranger, till after the birth of his first child: he then attaches himself more to them than his own parents; and his wife no longer gives him any other denomination than that of the father of her child.

The profession of the men is war and hunting, and the more active scene of their duty is the field of battle, and the chase in the woods. They also spear fish, but the management of the nets is left to the women. The females of this nation are in the same subordinate state with those of all other savage tribes; but the severity of their labour is much diminished by their situation on the banks of lakes and rivers, where they employ canoes. In the winter, when the waters are frozen, they make their journies, which are never of any great length, with sledges drawn by dogs They are, at the same time, subject to every kind of domestic drudgery: they dress the leather, make the clothes and shoes, weave the nets, collect wood, erect the tents, fetch water, perform every culinary service; so that when the duties of maternal care are added, it will appear that the life of these women is an uninterrupted succession of toil and pain. This, indeed, is the sense they entertain of their own situation; and, under the influence of that sentiment, they are sometimes known to destroy their female children, to save them from the miseries which they themselves have suffered. They also have a ready way, by the use of certain simples, of procuring abortions, which they sometimes practise, from their hatred of the father, or to save themselves the trouble which children occasion: and, as I have been credibly informed, this unnatural act is repeated without any injury to the health of the women who perpetrate it.

The funeral rites begin, like all other solemn ceremonials, with smoking, and are concluded by a feast. The body is dressed in the best habiliments possessed by the deceased, or his relations, and is then deposited in a grave, lined with branches: some domestic utensils are placed on it, and a kind of canopy erected over it. During this ceremony, great lamentations are made, and if the departed person is very much regretted the near relations cut off their hair, pierce the fleshy part of their thighs and arms with arrows, knives, &c. and blacken their faces with charcoal. If they have distinguished themselves in war, they are sometimes laid on a kind of scaffolding; and I have been informed that women, as in the East, have been known to sacrifice themselves to the manes of their husbands. The whole of the property belonging to the departed person is destroyed, and the relations take in exchange for the wearing apparel, any rags that will cover their nakedness. The feast bestowed on the occasion, which is, or at least used to be, repeated annually, is accompanied with eulogiums of the deceased, and without any acts of ferocity. On the tomb are carved or painted the symbols of his tribe, which are taken from the different animals of the country.

Many and various are the motives which induce a savage to engage in war. To prove his courage, or to revenge the death of his relations, or some of his tribe, by the massacre of an enemy. If the tribe feel themselves called upon to go to war, the elders convene the people, in order to know the general opinion. If it be for war, the chief publishes his intention to smoke in the sacred stem at a certain period, to which solemnity, meditation and fasting are required as preparatory ceremonials. When the people are thus assembled, and the meeting sanctified by the custom of smoking, the chief enlarges on the causes which have called them together, and the necessity of the measures proposed on the occasion. He then invites those who are willing to follow him, to smoke out of the sacred stem, which is considered as the token of enrolment; and if it should be the general opinion, that assistance is necessary, others are invited, with great formality, to join them. Every individual who attends these meetings brings something with him as a token of his warlike intention, or as an object of sacrifice, which, when the assembly dissolves, is suspended from poles near the place of council.

They have frequent feasts, and particular circumstances never fail to produce them; such as a tedious illness, long fasting, &c. On these occasions it is usual for the person who means to give the entertainment, to announce his design, on a certain day, of opening the medicine bag and smoking out of his sacred stem. This declaration is considered as a sacred vow that cannot be broken. There are also stated periods, such as the spring and autumn, when they engage in very long and solemn ceremonies. On these occasions dogs are offered as sacrifices, and those which are very fat, and milk-white, are preferred. They also make large offerings of their property, whatever it may be. The scene of these ceremonies is in an open inclosure on the bank of a river or lake, and in the most conspicuous situation, in order that such as are passing along or travelling, may be induced to make their offerings. There is also a particular custom among them, that, on these occasions, if any of the tribe, or even a stranger, should be passing by, and be in real want of any thing that is displayed as an offering, he has a right to take it, so that he replaces it with some article he can spare, though it be of far inferior value: but to take or touch any thing wantonly is considered as a sacrilegious act, and highly insulting to the great Master of Life, to use their own expression, who is the sacred object of their devotion.

The scene of private sacrifice is the lodge of the person who performs it, which is prepared for that purpose by removing every thing out of it, and spreading green branches in every part. The fire and ashes are also taken away. A new hearth is made of fresh earth, and another fire is lighted. The owner of the dwelling remains alone in it; and he begins the ceremony by spreading a piece of new cloth, or a well-dressed moose-skin neatly painted, on which he opens his medicine-bag and exposes its contents, consisting of various articles. The principal of them is a kind of household god, which is a small carved image about eight inches long. Its first covering is of down, over which a piece of birch bark is closely tied, and the whole is enveloped in several folds of red and blue cloth. This little figure is an object of the most pious regard. The next article is his war-cap, which is decorated with the feathers and plumes of scarce birds, beavers, and eagle's claws, &c. There is also suspended from it a quill or feather for every enemy whom the owner of it has slain in battle. The remaining contents of the bag are, a piece of Brazil tobacco, several roots and simples, which are in great estimation for their medicinal qualities, and a pipe. These articles being all exposed, and the item resting upon two forks, as it must not touch the ground, the master of the lodge sends for the person he most esteems, who sits down opposite to him; the pipe is then filled and fixed to the stem. A pair of wooden pincers is provided to put the fire in the pipe, and a double-pointed pin, to empty it of the remnant of tobacco which is not consumed. This arrangement being made, the men assemble, and sometimes the women are allowed to be humble spectators, while the most religious awe and solemnity pervades the whole. The Michiniwais, or Assistant, takes up the pipe, lights it, and presents it to the officiating person, who receives it standing and holds it between both his hands. He then turns himself to the East, and draws a few whiffs, which he blows to that point. The same ceremony he observes to the other three quarters, with his eyes directed upwards during the whole of it. He holds the stem about the middle between the three first fingers of both hands, and raising them upon a line with his forehead, he swings it three times round from the East, with the sun, when, after pointing and balancing it in various directions, he reposes it on the forks: he then makes a speech to explain the design of their being called together, which concludes with an acknowledgment of past mercies, and a prayer for the continuance of them, from the Master of Life. He then sits down, and the whole company declare their approbation and thanks by uttering the word *ho!* with an emphatic prolongation of the last letter. The Michiniwais then takes up the pipe and holds it to the mouth of the officiating person, who, after smoking three whiffs out of it, utters a short prayer, and then goes round with it, taking his course from East to West, to every person present, who individually says something to him on the occasion: and thus the pipe is generally smoked out; when, after turning it three or four times round his head, he drops it downwards, and replaces it in its original situation. He then returns the company thanks for their attendance, and wishes them, as well as the whole tribe, health and long life.

These smoking rites precede every matter of great importance, with more or less ceremony, but always with equal solemnity. The utility of them will appear from the following relation.

If a chief is anxious to know the disposition of his people towards him, or if he wishes to settle any difference between them, he announces his intention of opening his medicine-bag and smoking in his sacred stem; and no man who entertains a grudge against any of the party thus assembled can smoke with the sacred stem; as that ceremony dissipates all differences, and is never violated.

No one can avoid attending on these occasions; but a person may attend and be excused from assisting at the ceremonies, by acknowledging that he has not undergone the necessary purification. The having cohabited with his wife, or any other woman, within twenty-four hours preceding the ceremony, renders him unclean, and, consequently, disqualifies him from performing any part of it. If a contract is entered into and solemnised by the ceremony of smoking, it never fails of being faithfully fulfilled. If a person, previous to his going on a journey, leaves the sacred stem as a pledge of his return, no consideration whatever will prevent him from executing his engagement.[14]

The chief, when he proposes to make a feast, sends quills, or small pieces of wood, as tokens of invitation to such as he wishes to partake of it. At the appointed time the guests arrive, each bringing a dish or platter, and a knife, and take their seats

---

14. It is however to be lamented, that of late there is a relaxation of the duties originally attached to these festivals.

on each side of the chief, who receives them sitting, according to their respective ages. The pipe is then lighted, and he makes an equal division of every thing that is provided. While the company are enjoying their meal, the chief sings, and accompanies his song with the tambourin, or shishiquoi, or rattle. The guest who has first eaten his portion is considered as the most distinguished person. If there should be any who cannot finish the whole of their mess, they endeavour to prevail on some of their friends to eat it for them, who are rewarded for their assistance with ammunition and tobacco. It is proper also to remark, that at these feasts a small quantity of meat or drink is sacrificed, before they begin to eat, by throwing it into the fire, or on the earth.

These feasts differ according to circumstances; sometimes each man's allowance is no more than he can dispatch in a couple of hours. At other times the quantity is sufficient to supply each of them with food for a week, though it must be devoured in a day. On these occasions it is very difficult to procure substitutes, and the whole must be eaten whatever time it may require. At some of these entertainments there is a more rational arrangement, when the guests are allowed to carry home with them the superfluous part of their portions. Great care is always taken that the bones may be burned, as it would be considered a profanation were the dogs permitted to touch them.

The public feasts are conducted in the same manner, but with some additional ceremony. Several chiefs officiate at them, and procure the necessary provisions, as well as prepare a proper place of reception for the numerous company. Here the guests discourse upon public topics, repeat the heroic deeds of their forefathers, and excite the rising generation to follow their example. The entertainments on these occasions consist of dried meats, as it would not be practicable to dress a sufficient quantity of fresh meat for such a large assembly; though the women and children are excluded.

Similar feasts used to be made at funerals, and annually, in honour of the dead; but they have been, for some time, growing into disuse, and I never had an opportunity of being present at any of them.

The women, who are forbidden to enter the places sacred to these festivals, dance and sing around them, and sometimes beat time to the music within them; which forms an agreeable contrast.

With respect to their divisions of time, they compute the length of their journeys by the number of nights passed in performing them; and they divide the year by the succession of moons. In this calculation, however, they are not altogether correct, as they cannot account for the odd days.

The names which they give to the moons are descriptive of the several seasons.

May: Atheiky o Pishim, Frog-Moon.

June: Oppinu o Pishim, The Moon in which birds begin to lay their eggs.

July: Aupascen o Pishim, The Moon when birds cast their feathers.

August: Aupahou o Pishim, The Moon when the young birds begin to fly.

September: Waskiscon o Pishim, The Moon when the moose-deer cast their horns.

October: Wisac o Pishim, The Rutting-Moon.

November: Thithigon Pewai o Pishim, Hoar-Frost-Moon. Kuskatinayoui o Pishim, Ice-Moon.

December: Pawatchicananasis o Pishim, Whirlwind-Moon.

January: Kushapawasticanum o Pishim, Extreme cold Moon.

February: Kichi Pishim, Big Moon; some say, Old Moon.

March: Mickysue Pishim, Eagle Moon.

April: Niscaw o Pishim, Goose-Moon.

These people know the medicinal virtues of many herbs and simples, and apply the roots of plants and the bark of trees with success. But the conjurers, who monopolize the medical science, find it necessary to blend mystery with their art, and do not communicate their knowledge. Their materia medica they administer in the form of purges and clysters; but the remedies and surgical operations are supposed to derive much of their effect from magic and incantation. When a blister rises in the foot from the frost, the chaffing of the shoe, &c. they immediately open it, and apply the heated blade of a knife to the part, which, painful as it may be, is found to be efficacious. A sharp flint serves them as a lancet for letting blood, as well as for scarification in bruises and swellings. For sprains, the dung of an animal just killed is considered as the best remedy. They are very fond of European medicines, though they are ignorant of their application: and those articles form an inconsiderable part of the European traffic with them.

Among their various superstitions, they believe that the vapour which is seen to hover over moist and swampy places, is the spirit of some person lately dead. They also fancy another spirit which appears, in the shape of a man, upon the trees near the lodge of a person deceased, whose property has not been interred with them. He is represented as bearing a gun in his hand, and it is believed that he does not return to his rest, till the property that has been withheld from the grave has been sacrificed to it.

Examples of the Knisteneaux and Algonquin Tongues

	Knisteneaux	Algonquin
Good Spirit	Ki jai Manitou	Ki jai Manitou.
Evil Spirit	Matchi manitou	Matchi manitou.
Man	Ethini	Inini.
Woman	Esquois	Ich-quois.
Male	Nap hew	Aquoisi.
Female	Non-gense	Non-gense.
Infant	A'wash ish	Abi nont-chen.

Head	Us ti quoin	O'chiti-goine.
Forehead	Es caa tick	O catick.
Hair	Wes ty-ky	Winessis.
Eyes	Es kis och	Oskingick.
Nose	Oskiwin	O'chengewane.
Nostrils	Oo tith ee go mow	Ni-de-ni-guom.
Mouth	O toune	O tonne.
My teeth	Wip pit tab	Nibit.
Tongue	Otaithani	O-tai-na-ni.
Beard	Michitoune	Omichitonn.
Brain	With i tip	Aba-e winikan.
Ears	O tow ee gie	O-ta wagane.
Neck	O qui ow	O'quoi gan.
Throat	O koot tas gy	Nigon dagane.
Arms	O nisk	O nic.
Fingers	Che chee	Ni nid gines.
Nails	Wos kos sia	Os-kenge.
Side	O's spig gy	Opikegan
My back	No pis quan	Ni-pi quoini.
My belly	Nattay	Ni my sat.
Thighs	O povam	Obouame.
My knees	No che quoin nah	Ni gui tick.
Legs	Nosk	Ni gatte.
Heart	O thea	Othai.
My father	Noo ta wie	Nossai.

My mother	Nigah wei	Nigah.
My boy (son)	Negousis	Nigouisses.
My girl (daughter)	Nidaniss.	Netanis
My brother, elder	Ni stess	Nis-a-yen.
My sister, elder	Ne miss	Nimisain.
My grandfather	Ne moo shum	Ni-mi-chomiss.
My grandmother	N'o kum	No-co-miss.
My uncle	N' o'ka miss	Ni ni michomen.
My nephew	Ne too sim	Ne do jim.
My niece	Ne too sim esquois	Ni-do-jim equois.
My mother-in-law	Nisigouse	Ni sigousiss.
My brother-in-law	Nistah	Nitah.
My companion	Ne wechi wagan	Ni-wit-chi-wagan.
My husband	Ni nap pem	Ni na bem.
Blood	Mith coo	Misquoi.
Old Man	Shi nap	Ajki win se.
I am angry	Ne kis si wash en	Nis Katissiwine.
I fear	Ne goos tow	Nisest guse.
Joy	Ne hea tha tom	Mamoud gikisi.
Hearing	Pethom	Oda wagan.
Track	Mis conna	Pemi ka wois
Chief, great ruler	Haukimah	Kitchi onodis.
Thief	Kismouthesk	Ke moutiske.
Excrement	Meyee	Moui.

Buffalo	Moustouche	Pichike.
Ferret	Sigous	Shingouss.
Polecat	Shicak	Shi-kak.
Elk	Moustouche	Michai woi.
Rein deer	Attick	Atick.
Fallow deer	Attick	Wa wasquesh.
Beaver	Amisk	Amic.
Woolverine	Qui qua katch	Quin quoagki.
Squirrel	Ennequachas	Otchi ta mou.
Minx	Sa quasue	Shaugouch.
Otter	Nekick	Ni guick.
Wolf	Mayegan	Maygan.
Hare	Wapouce	Wapouce.
Marten	Wappistan	Wabichinse.
Moose	Mouswah	Monse.
Bear	Masqua	Macqua.
Fisher	Wijask	Od-jisck.
Lynx	Picheu	Pechou.
Porcupine	Cau quah	Kack.
Fox	Ma kisew	Wagouche.
Musk Rat	Wajask	Wa-jack.
Mouse	Abicushiss	Wai wa be gou noge.
Cow Buffalo	Noshi Moustou-che	Nochena pichik.
Meat-flesh	Wias	Wi-ass.

Dog	Atim	Ani-mouse.
Eagle	Makusue	Me-guissis.
Duck	Sy Sip	Shi-sip.
Crow, Corbeau	Ca Cawkeu	Ka Kak.
Swan	Wapiseu	Wa-pe-sy.
Turkey	Mes sei thew	Mississay.
Pheasants	Okes kew	Ajack.
Bird	Pethesew	Pi-na-sy.
Outard	Niscag	Nic kack.
White Goose	Wey Wois	Woi wois.
Grey Goose	Pestasish	Pos ta kisk.
Partridge	Pithew	Pen ainse.
Water Hen	Chiquibish	Che qui bis.
Dove	Orni Mee	O mi-mis.
Eggs	Wa Wah	Wa Weni.
Pike or Jack	Kenonge	Kenonge.
Carp	Na may bin	Na me bine.
Sturgeon	Na May	Na Maiu.
White fish	Aticaming	Aticaming.
Pikrel	Oc-chaw	Oh-ga.
Fish (in general)	Kenonge	Ki-cons.
Spawn	Waquon	Wa quock.
Fins	Chichi kan	O nidj-igan.
Trout	Nay gouse	Na Men Gouse.

Craw Fish	A shag gee	A cha kens chacque.
Frog	Athick	O ma ka ki.
Wasp	Ah moo	A Mon.
Turtle	Mikinack	Mi-ki-nack.
Snake	Kinibick	Ki nai bick.
Awl	Oscajick	Ma-gose.
Needle	Saboinigan	Sha-bo nigan.
Fire Steel	Appet	Scoutecgan.
Fire wood	Mich-tah	Missane.
Cradle	Teckinigan	Tickina-gan.
Dagger	Ta comagau	Na-ba-ke-gou-man.
Arrow	Augusk or Atouche	Mettic ka nouins.
Fish Hook	Quosquipichican	Maneton Miquis cane
Ax	Shegaygan	Wagagvette.
Ear-bob	Chi-kisebisoun	Na be chi be soun.
Comb	Sicahoun	Pin ack wan.
Net	Athabe	Assap.
Tree	Mistick	Miti-coum.
Wood	Mistick	Mitic.
Paddle	Aboi	Aboui.
Canoe	Chiman	S-chiman.
Birch Rind	Wasquoi Kigigah	Wig nass.

Bark	Wasquoi	On-na-guege.
Touch Wood	Pousagan	Sa-ga-tagan.
Leaf	Nepeshah	Ni-biche.
. Grass	Masquosi	Masquosi.
Raspberries	Misqui-meinac	Misqui meinac.
Strawberries	O'-tai-e minac	O'-tai-e minac.
Ashes	Pecouch	Pengoui.
Fire	Scou tay	Scou tay.
Grapes	Shomenac	Shomenac.
Fog	Pakishihow	A Winni.
Mud	Asus ki	A Shiski.
Currant	Kisijiwin	Ki si chi woin.
Road	Mescanah	Mickanan.
Winter	Pipoun	Pipone.
Island	Ministick	Miniss.
Lake	Sagayigan	Sagayigan.
Sun	Pisim	Kijis.
Moon	Tibisca pesim (the night Sun)	Dibic kijiss.
Day	Kigi gatte	Kigi gatte.
Night	Tibisca	Dibic kawte.
Snow	Counah	So qui po.
Rain	Kimiwoin	Ki mi woini.
Drift	Pewan	Pi-woine.
Hail	Shes eagan	Me qua mensan.

Ice	Mesquaming	Me quam.
Frost	Aquatin	Gas-ga-tin.
Mist	Picasyow	An-quo-et.
Water	Nepec	Ni-pei.
World	Messe asky (all the earth)	Missi achki.
Mountain	Wachee	Watchive.
Sea	Kitchi kitchi ga ming	Kitchi-kitchi ga ming
Morning	Kequishepe	Ki-ki-jep.
Mid-day	Abetah quisheik	Na ock quoi.
Portage	Unygam	Ouni-gam.
Spring	Menouscaming	Mino ka ming.
River	Sipee	Sipi.
Rapid	Bawastick	Ba wetick.
Rivulet	Sepeesis	Sipi wes chin.
Sand	Thoeaw	Ne gawe.
Earth	Askee	Ach ki.
Star	Attack	Anang.
Thunder	Pithuseu	Ni mi ki.
Wind	Thoutin	No tine.
Calm	Athawostin	A-no-a-tine.
Heat	Quishipoi	Aboycd.
Evening	Ta kashike	O'n-a guche.
North	Kywoitin	Ke woitninak.
South	Sawena woon	Sha-wa-na-wang.

East	Coshawcastak	Wa-ba-no-notine.
West	Paquisimow	Panguis-chi-mo.
To-morrow	Wabank	Wa-bang.
Bone	Oskann	Oc-kann.
Broth	Michim waboi	Thaboub.
Feast	Ma qua see	Wi con qui wine.
Grease or oil	Pimis	Pimi-tais.
Marrow fat	Oscan pimis	Oska-pimitais.
Sinew	Asstis	Attiss.
Lodge	Wig-waum	Wi-gui-wam.
Bed	Ne pa win	Ne pai wine.
Within	Pendog ke	Pendig
Door	Squandam	Scouandam.
Dish	Othagan	O' na gann.
Fort	Wasgaigan	Wa-kuigan.
Sledge	Tabanask	Otabanac.
Cincture	Poquoatehoun	Ketche pisou.
Cap	Astotin	Pe matinang.
Socks	Ashican	A chi-gan.
Shirt	Papackeweyan	Pa pa ki weyan.
Coat	Papise-co-wegan	Papise-co-wagan.
Blanket	Wape weyang	Wape weyan.
Cloth	Maneto weguin	Maneto weguin.
Thread	Assabab	Assabab.

Garters	Chi ki-bisoon	Ni gaske-tase besoun.
Mittens	Astissack	Medjicawine.
Shoes	Maskisin	Makisin.
Smoking bag	Kusquepetagan	Kasquepetagan.
Portage sling	Apisan	Apican.
Strait on	Goi ask	Goi-ack.
Medicine	Mas ki kee	Macki-ki.
Red	Mes cob	Mes-cowa.
Blue	Kasqutch (same as black)	O-jawes-cowa.
White	Wabisca	Wabisca.
Yellow	Saw waw	O-jawa.
Green	Chibatiquare	O'jawes-cowa.
Brown		O'jawes-cowa.
Grey, &c.		O'jawes-cowa.
Ugly	Mache na gouseu	Mous-counu-gouse.
Handsome	Catawassiseu	Nam bissa.
Beautiful	Kissi Sawenogan	Quoi Natch.
Deaf	Nima petom	Ka ki be chai.
Good-natured	Mithiwashin	Onichishin.
Pregnant	Paawie	And-jioko.
Fat	Outhineu	Oui-ni-noe.
Big	Mushikitee	Messha.
Small or little	Abisasheu	Agu-chin.

Short	Chemasish	Tackosi.
Skin	Wian	Wian.
Long	Kinwain	Kiniwa.
Strong	Mascawa	Mache-cawa, Mas-cawise.
Coward	Sagatahaw	Cha-goutai-ye.
Weak	Nitha missew	Cha-gousi.
Lean	Mahta waw	Ka wa ca-tosa.
Brave	Nima Gustaw	Son qui taige.
Young man	Osquineguish	Oskinigui.
Cold	Kissin	Kissinan.
Hot	Kichatai	Kicha tai.
Spring	Minouscaming	Minokaming.
Summer	Nibin	Nibiqui.
Fall	Tagowagonk	Tagowag.
One	Peyac	Pecheik.
Two	Nisheu	Nige.
Three	Nishtou	Nis-wois.
Four	Neway	Ne-au.
Five	Ni-annan	Na-nan.
Six	Negoutawoesic	Ni gouta waswois.
Seven	Nish woisic	Nigi-was-wois.
Eight	Jannanew	She was wois.
Nine	Shack	Shang was wois.
Ten	Mitatat	Mit-asswois.

Eleven	Peyac osap	Mitasswois, hachi, pecheik.
Twelve	Nisheu osap	Mitasswois, hachi, nige.
Thirteen	Nichtou osap	Mitasswois hachi, niswois.
Fourteen	Neway osap	Mitasswois hachi, ne-au.
Fifteen	Niannan osap	Mitasswois hachi, nanan.
Sixteen	Nigoutawoesic osap	Mitasswois hachi, negoutawaswois.
Seventeen	Nish woesic osap	Mitasswois hachi, nigi waswois.
Eighteen	Jannanew osap	Mitasswois, hachi, shiwaswois.
Nineteen	Shack osap	Mitasswois hachi, shang as wois.
Twenty	Nisheu mitenah	Nigeta-nan.
Twenty-one	Nisheu mitenah peyac osap	Nigeta nan, hachi, pechic.
Twenty-two, &c.	Nisheu mitenah nishew osap	
Thirty	Nishtou mitenah	Niswois mitanan.
Forty	Neway mitenah	Neau mitanan.
Fifty	Niannan mitenah	Nanan mitanan.
Sixty	Negoutawoisic mitenah	Nigouta was wois mitanan.

Seventy	Nishwoisic mitenah	Nigi was wois mitanan.
Eighty	Jannaeu mitenah	She was wois mitanan.
Ninety	Shack mitenah	Shang was wois mitanan.
Hundred	Mitana mitenah	Ningoutwack.
Two hundred	Neshew mitena a mitenah	Nige wack.
One thousand	Mitenah mitena mitenah	Kitchi-wack.
First	Nican	Nitam.
Last	Squayatch	Shaquoiyanque.
More	Minah	Awa chi min.
Better	Athiwack mitha-washin	Awachimin o nichi shen.
Best	Athiwack mitha-washin	Kitchi o nichi shin.
I, or me	Nitha	Nin.
You, or thou	Kitha	Kin.
They, or them	Withawaw	Win na wa.
We	Nithawaw	Nina wa.
My, or mine	Nitayan	Nida yam.
Your's	Kitayan	Kitayam.
Who		Auoni.
Whom	Awoine	Kegoi nin.
What		Wa.

His, or her's	Otayan	Otayim mis.
All	Kakithau	Kakenan.
Some, or some few	Pey peyac	Pe-pichic.
The same	Tabescoutch	Mi ta yoche.
All the world	Missi acki wanque	Mishiwai asky.
All the men	Kakithaw Ethi nyock	Missi Inini wock.
More	Mina	Mina wa.
Now and then	Nannigoutengue.	
Sometimes	I as-cow-puco	
Seldom		Wica-ac-ko.
Arrive	Ta couchin	Ta-gouchin.
Beat	Otamaha	Packit-ais.
To burn	Mistascasoo	Icha-quiso.
To sing	Nagamoun	Nagam.
To cut	Kisquishan	Qui qui jan.
To hide	Catann	Caso tawe.
To cover	Acquahoun	A co na oune.
To believe	Taboitam	Tai hoitam.
To sleep	Nepan	Ni pann.
To dispute	Ke ko mi towock	Ki quaidiwine.
To dance	Nemaytow	Nimic.
To give	Mith	Mih.
To do	Ogitann	O-gitoune.

To eat	Wissinee	Wissiniwin.
To die	Nepew	Ni po wen.
To forget	Winnekiskisew	Woi ni mi kaw.
To speak	Athimetakcouse	Aninntagousse
To cry (tears)	Mantow	Ma wi.
To laugh	Papew	Pa-pe.
To set down	Nematappe	Na matape win.
To walk	Pimoutais	Pemoussai.
To fall	Packisin	Panguishin.
To work	Ah tus kew	Anokeh.
To kill	Nipahaw	Nishi-woes.
To sell	Attawoin	Ata wois.
To live	Pimatise	Pematis.
To see	Wabam	Wab.
To come	Astamoteh	Pitta-si-mouss.
Enough	Egothigog	Mi mi nic.
Cry (tears)	Manteau	Ambai ma wita.
It hails	Shisiagan	Sai saigaun.
There is, There is some	Aya wa	Aya wan.
It rains	Quimiwoin	Qui mi woin.
After to-morrow	Awls wabank	Awes wabang.
To-day	Anoutch	Non gum.
Thereaway	Netoi	Awoite.
Much	Michett	Ni bi wa.

Presently	Pichisqua	Pitchinac.
Make, heart	Quithipeh	Wai we be.
This morning	Shebas	Shai has.
This night	Tibiscag	De bi cong.
Above	Esplming	O kitchiai.
Below	Tabassish	Ana mai.
Truly	Taboiy	Ne de wache.
Already	Sashay	Sha shaye.
Yet, more	Minah	Mina wa.
Yesterday	Tacoushick	Pitchinago.
Far	Wathow	VC'assa.
Near	Quishiwoac	Paishou.
Never	Nima wecatch	Ka wi ka.
No	Nima	Ka wine.
Yes	Ah	In.
By-and-bye	Pa-nima	Pa-nima.
Always	Ka-ki-kee	Ka qui nick.
Make haste	Quethepeh	Niguim.
It's long since	Mewaisha	Mon wisha.

They are a numerous people, who consider the country between the parallels of latitude 60 and 65 North, and longitude 100 to 110 West, as their lands or home. They speak a copious language, which is very difficult to be attained, and furnishes dialects to the various emigrant tribes which inhabit the following immense track of country, whose boundary I shall describe.[15] It begins at Churchill, and runs along the line of separation between them and the Knisteneaux, up the Missinipi to the Isle a la Crosse, passing on through the Buffalo Lake, River Lake, and Portage la Loche: from thence it proceeds by the Elk River to the Lake of the Hills, and goes directly West to the Peace River; and up that river to its source and tributary waters; from whence it proceeds to the waters of the river Columbia; and follows that river to latitude 52.24 North, and longitude 122.54 West, where the Chepewyans have the Atnah or Chin Nation for their neighbours. It then takes a line due West to the sea-coast, within which, the country is possessed by a people who speak their language,[16] and are consequently descended from them: there can be no doubt, therefore, of their progress being to the Eastward. A tribe of them is even known at the upper establishments on the Saskatchiwine; and I do not pretend to ascertain how far they may follow the Rocky Mountains to the East.

It is not possible to form any just estimate of their numbers, but it is apparent, nevertheless, that they are by no means pro-portionate to the vast extent of their territories, which may, in some degree, be attributed to the ravages of the small pox, which are, more or less, evident throughout this part of the continent.

The notion which these people entertain of the creation, is of a very singular nature. They believe that, at the first, the globe was one vast and entire ocean, inhabited by no living creature, except a mighty bird, whose eyes were fire, whose glances were lightning, and the clapping of whose wings were thunder. On his descent to the ocean, and touching it, the earth instantly arose, and remained on the surface of the waters. This omnipotent bird then called forth all the variety of animals from the earth, except the Chepewyans, who were produced from a dog; and this cir-cumstance occasions their aversion to the flesh of that animal, as well as the people who eat it. This extraordinary tradition pro-ceeds to relate, that the great bird, having finished his work, made an arrow, which was to be preserved with great care, and

15. Those of them who come to trade with us, do not exceed eight hundred men, and have a smattering of the Knisteneaux tongue, in which they carry on their dealings with us.

16. The coast is inhabited on the North-West by the Eskimaux, and on the Pacific Ocean by a people different from both.

to remain untouched; but that the Chepewyans were so devoid of understanding, as to carry it away; and the sacrilege so enraged the great bird, that he has never since appeared.

They have also a tradition amongst them, that they originally came from another country, inhabited by very wicked people, and had traversed a great lake, which was narrow, shallow, and full of islands, where they had suffered great misery, it being always winter, with ice and deep snow. At the Copper-Mine River, where they made the first land, the ground was covered with copper, over which a body of earth had since been collected, to the depth of a man's height. They believe, also, that in ancient times their ancestors lived till their feet were worn out with walking, and their throats with eating. They describe a deluge, when the waters spread over the whole earth, except the highest mountains, on the tops of which they preserved themselves.

They believe, that immediately after their death, they pass into another world, where they arrive at a large river, on which they embark in a stone canoe, and that a gentle current bears them on to an extensive lake, in the centre of which is a most beautiful island; and that, in the view of this delightful abode, they receive that judgment for their conduct during life, which terminates their final state and unalterable allotment. If their good actions are declared to predominate, they are landed upon the island, where there is to be no end to their happiness; which, however, according to their notions, consists in an eternal enjoyment of sensual pleasure, and carnal gratification. But if their bad actions weigh down the balance, the stone canoe sinks at once, and leaves them up to their chins in the water, to behold and regret the rewards enjoyed by the good, and eternally struggling, but with unavailing endeavours, to reach the blissful island from which they are excluded for ever.

They have some faint notions of the transmigration of the soul; so that if a child be born with teeth, they instantly imagine, from its premature appearance, that it bears a resemblance to some person who had lived to an advanced period, and that he has assumed a renovated life, with these extraordinary tokens of maturity.

The Chepewyans are sober, timorous, and vagrant, with a selfish disposition which has sometimes created suspicions of their integrity. Their stature has nothing remarkable in it; but though they are seldom corpulent, they are sometimes robust. Their complexion is swarthy; their features coarse, and their hair lank, but not always of a dingy black; nor have they universally the piercing eye, which generally animates the Indian countenance. The women have a more agreeable aspect than the men, but their gait is awkward, which proceeds from their being accustomed, nine months in the year, to travel on snow-shoes and drag sledges of a weight from two to four hundred pounds. They are very submissive to their husbands, who have, however, their fits of jealousy; and, for very trifling causes, treat them with such cruelty as sometimes to occasion their death. They are frequently objects of traffic; and the father possesses the right of disposing of his daughter.[17] The men in general extract their beards, though some of them are seen to prefer a bushy, black beard, to a smooth chin. They cut their hair in various forms, or leave it in a long, natural flow, according as their caprice or fancy suggests. The women always wear it in great length, and some of them are very attentive to its arrangement. If they at any time appear despoiled of their tresses, it is to be esteemed a proof of the husband's jealousy, and is considered as a severer punishment than manual correction. Both sexes have blue or black bars, or from one to four straight lines on their cheeks or forehead, to distinguish the tribe to which they belong. These marks are either tatooed, or made by drawing a thread, dipped in the necessary colour, beneath the skin.

There are no people more attentive to the comforts of their dress, or less anxious respecting its exterior appearance. In the winter it is composed of the skins of deer, and their fawns, and dressed as fine as any chamois leather, in the hair. In the summer

---

17. They do not, however, sell them as slaves, but as companions to those who are supposed to live more comfortably than themselves.

their apparel is the same, except that it is prepared without the hair. Their shoes and leggins are sewn together, the latter reaching upwards to the middle, and being supported by a belt, under which a small piece of leather is drawn to cover the private parts, the ends of which fall down both before and behind. In the shoes they put the hair of the moose or rein-deer with additional pieces of leather as socks. The shirt or coat, when girted round the waist, reaches to the middle of the thigh, and the mittens are sewed to the sleeves, or are suspended by strings from the shoulders. A ruff or tippet surrounds the neck, and the skin of the head of the deer forms a curious kind of cap. A robe, made of several deer or fawn skins sewed together, covers the whole. This dress is worn single or double, but always in the winter, with the hair within and without. Thus arrayed, a Chepewyan will lay himself down on the ice in the middle of a lake, and repose in comfort, though he will sometimes find a difficulty in the morning to disencumber himself from the snow drifted on him during the night. If in his passage he should be in want of provision, he cuts an hole in the ice, when he seldom fails of taking some trout or pike, whose eyes he instantly scoops out, and eats as a great delicacy; but if they should not be sufficient to satisfy his appetite, he will, in this necessity make his meal on the fish in its raw state; but, those whom I saw, preferred to dress their victuals when circumstances admitted the necessary preparation. When they are in that part of their country which does not produce a sufficient quantity of wood for fuel, they are reduced to the same exigency, though they generally dry their meat in the sun.[18]

The dress of the women differs from that of the men. Their leggins are tied below the knee; and their coat or shift is wide, hanging down to the ancle, and is tucked up at pleasure by means of a belt, which is fastened round the waist. Those who have children have these garments made very full about the shoulders, as when they are travelling they carry their infants upon their backs, next their skin, in which situation they are perfectly comfortable and in a position convenient to be suckled. Nor do they discontinue to give their milk to them till they have another child. Child-birth is not the object of that tender care and serious attention among the savages as it is among civilised people. At this period no part of their usual occupation is omitted, and this continual and regular exercise must contribute to the welfare of the mother, both in the progress of parturition and in the moment of delivery. The women have a singular custom of cutting off a small piece of the navel-string of the new-born children, and hang it about their necks: they are also curious in the covering they make for it, which they decorate with porcupine's quills and beads.

Though the women are as much in the power of the men, as any other articles of their property, they are always consulted, and possess a very considerable influence in the traffic with Europeans, and other important concerns.

Plurality of wives is common among them, and the ceremony of marriage is of a very simple nature. The girls are betrothed at a very early period to those whom the parents think the best able to support them: nor is the inclination of the woman considered. Whenever a separation takes place, which sometimes happens, it depends entirely on the will and pleasure of the husband. In common with the other Indians of this country, they have a custom respecting the periodical state of a woman, which is rigorously observed: at that time she must seclude herself from society. They are not even allowed in that situation to keep the same path as the men, when travelling: and it is considered a great breach of decency for a women so circumstanced to touch any utensils of manly occupation. Such a circumstance is supposed to defile them, so that their subsequent use would be fol-

---

18. The provision called Pemican, on which the Chepewyans, as well as the other savages of this country, chiefly subsist in their journies, is prepared in the following manner. The lean parts of the flesh of the larger animals are cut in thin slices, and are placed on a wooden grate over a slow fire, or exposed to the sun, and sometimes to the frost. These operations dry it, and in that state it is pounded between two stones; it will then keep with care for several years. If, however, it is kept in large quantities, it is disposed to ferment in the spring of the year, when it must be exposed to the air, or it will soon decay. The inside fat, and that of the rump, which is much thicker in these wild than our domestic animals, is melted down and mixed, in a boiling state, with the pounded meat, in equal proportions; it is then put in baskets or bags for the convenience of carrying it. Thus it becomes a nutritious food, and is eaten, without any further preparation, or the addition of spice, salt, or any vegetable or farinaceous substance. A little time reconciles it to the palate. There is another sort made with the addition of marrow and dried berries, which is of a superior quality.

lowed by certain mischief or misfortune. There are particular skins which the women never touch, as of the bear and wolf; and those animals the men are seldom known to kill.

They are not remarkable for their activity as hunters, which is owing to the ease with which they snare deer and spear fish: and these occupations are not beyond the strength of their old men, women, and boys: so that they participate in those laborious occupations, which among their neighbours, are confined to the women. They make war on the Esquimaux, who cannot resist their superior numbers, and put them to death, as it is a principle with them never to make prisoners. At the same time they tamely submit to the Knisteneaux, who are not so numerous as themselves, when they treat them as enemies.

They do not affect that cold reserve at meeting, either among themselves or strangers, which is common with the Knisteneaux, but communicate mutually, and at once, all the information of which they are possessed. Nor are they roused like them from an apparent torpor to a state of great activity. They are consequently more uniform in this respect, though they are of a very persevering disposition when their interest is concerned.

As these people are not addicted to spirituous liquors, they have a regular and uninterrupted use of their understanding, which is always directed to the advancement of their own interest; and this disposition, as may be readily imagined, sometimes occasions them to be charged with fraudulent habits. They will submit with patience to the severest treatment, when they are conscious that they deserve it, but will never forget or forgive any wanton or unnecessary rigour. A moderate conduct I never found to fail, nor do I hesitate to represent them, altogether, as the most peaceable tribe of Indians known in North America.

There are conjurers and high-priests, but I was not present at any of their ceremonies; though they certainly operate in an extraordinary manner on the imaginations of the people in the cure of disorders. Their principal maladies are, rheumatic pains, the flux and consumption. The venereal complaint is very common; but though its progress is slow, it gradually undermines the constitution, and brings on premature decay. They have recourse to superstition for their cure, and charms are their only remedies, except the bark of the willow, which being burned and reduced to powder, is strewed upon green wounds and ulcers, and places contrived for promoting perspiration. Of the use of simples and plants they have no knowledge; nor can it be expected, as their country does not produce them.

Though they have enjoyed so long an intercourse with Europeans, their country is so barren, as not to be capable of producing the ordinary necessaries naturally introduced by such a communication; and they continue, in a great measure, their own inconvenient and awkward modes of taking their game and preparing it when taken. Sometimes they drive the deer into small lakes, where they spear them, or force them into inclosures, where the bow and arrow are employed against them. These animals are also taken in snares made of skin. In the former instance the game is divided among those who have been engaged in the pursuit of it. In the latter it is considered as private property; nevertheless, any unsuccessful hunter passing by, may take a deer so caught, leaving the head, skin, and saddle for the owner. Thus, though they have no regular government, as every man is lord in his own family, they are influenced, more or less, by certain principles which conduce to their general benefit.

In their quarrels with each other, they very rarely proceed to a greater degree of violence than is occasioned by blows, wrestling, and pulling of the hair, while their abusive language consists in applying the name of the most offensive animal to the object of their displeasure, and adding the term ugly, and chiay, or still-born.[19]

Their arms and domestic apparatus, in addition to the articles procured from Europeans, are spears, bows, and arrows, fishing-nets, and lines made of green deer-skin thongs. They have also nets for taking the beaver as he endeavours to escape from his lodge when it is broken open. It is set in a particular

---

19. This name is also applicable to the foetus of an animal, when killed, which is considered as one of the greatest delicacies.

manner for the purpose, and a man is employed to watch the moment when he enters the snare, or he would soon cut his way through it. He is then thrown upon the ice, where he remains as if he had no life in him.

The snow-shoes are of very superior workmanship. The inner part of their frame is straight, the outer one is curved, and it is pointed at both ends, with that in front turned up. They are also laced with great neatness with thongs made of deer-skin. The sledges are formed of thin slips of board turned up also in front, and are highly polished with crooked knives, in order to slide along with facility. Close-grained wood is, on that account, the best; but theirs are made of the red or swamp spruce-fir tree.

The country, which these people claim as their land, has a very small quantity of earth, and produces little or no wood or herbage. Its chief vegetable substance is the moss, on which the deer feed; and a kind of rock moss, which, in times of scarcity, preserves the lives of the natives. When boiled in water, it dissolves into a clammy, glutinous, substance, that affords a very sufficient nourishment. But, notwithstanding the barren state of their country, with proper care and economy, these people might live in great comfort, for the lakes abound with fish, and the hills are covered with deer. Though, of all the Indian people of this continent they are considered as the most provident, they suffer severely at certain seasons, and particularly in the dead of winter, when they are under the necessity of retiring to their scanty, stinted woods. To the Westward of them the musk-ox may be found, but they have no dependence on it as an article of sustenance. There are also large hares, a few white wolves, peculiar to their country, and several kinds of foxes, with white and grey partridges, &c. The beaver and moose-deer they do not find till they come within 60 degrees North latitude; and the buffalo is still further South. That animal is known to frequent an higher latitude to the Westward of their country. These people bring pieces of beautiful variegated marble, which are found on the surface of the earth. It is easily worked, bears a fine polish, and hardens with time; it endures heat, and is manufactured into pipes or calumets, as they are very fond of smoking tobacco; a luxury which the Europeans communicated to them.

Their amusements or recreations are but few. Their music is so inharmonious, and their dancing so awkward, that they might be supposed to be ashamed of both, as they very seldom practise either. They also shoot at marks, and play at the games common among them; but in fact they prefer sleeping to either; and the greater part of their time is passed in procuring food, and resting from the toil necessary to obtain it.

They are also of a querulous disposition, and are continually making complaints; which they express by a constant repetition of the word eduiy, "it is hard," in a whining and plaintive tone of voice.

They are superstitious in the extreme, and almost every action of their lives, however trivial, is more or less influenced by some whimsical notion. I never observed that they had any particular form of religious worship; but as they believe in a good and evil spirit, and a state of future rewards and punishments, they cannot be devoid of religious impressions. At the same time they manifest a decided unwillingness to make any communications on the subject.

The Chepewyans have been accused of abandoning their aged and infirm people to perish, and of not burying their dead; but these are melancholy necessities, which proceed from their wandering way of life. They are by no means universal, for it is within my knowledge, that a man, rendered helpless by the palsy, was carried about for many years, with the greatest tenderness and attention, till he died a natural death. That they should not bury their dead in their own country cannot be imputed to them as a custom arising from a savage insensibility, as they inhabit such high latitudes that the ground never thaws; but it is well known, that when they are in the woods, they cover their dead with trees. Besides, they manifest no common respect to the memory of their departed friends, by a long period of mourning, cutting off their hair, and never making use of the property of the deceased. Nay, they frequently destroy or sacrifice their own, as a token of regret and sorrow.

If there be any people who, from the barren state of their country, might be supposed to be cannibals by nature, these people, from the difficulty they, at times, experience in procuring food, might be liable to that imputation. But, in all my knowledge of them, I never was acquainted with one instance of that disposition; nor among all the natives which I met with in a route of five thousand miles, did I see or hear of an example of cannibalism, but such as arose from that irresistible necessity, which has been known to impel even the most civilised people to eat each other.

Examples of the Chepeweyan Tongue

Man	Dinnie
Woman	Chequois
Young man	Quelaquis
Young woman	Quelaquis chequoi
My son	Zi azay.
My daughter	Zi lengai.
My husband	Zi dinnie.
My wife	Zi zayunai.
My brother	Zi raing.
My father	Zi tah.
My mother	Zi nah.
My grandfather	Zi unai.
Me, or my	See.
I	Ne.
You	Nun.
They	Be.

Head	Edthie.
Hand	Law.
Leg	Edthen.
Foot	Cub.
Eyes	Nackhay.
Teeth	Goo.
Side	Kac-hey.
Belly	Bitt.
Tongue	Edthu.
Hair	Thiegah.
Back	Losseh.
Blood	Dell.
The Knee	Cha-gutt.
Clothes or Blanket	Etlunay.
Coat	Eeh.
Leggin	Thell.
Shoes	Kinchee.
Robe or Blanket	Thuth.
Sleeves	Bah.
Mittens	Geese.
Cap	Sah.
Swan	Kagouce.
Duck	Keth.
Goose	Gah.
White partridge	Cass bah.

Grey partridge	Deyee.
Buffalo	Giddy.
Moose-deer	Dinyai.
Rein-deer	Edthen.
Beaver	Zah.
Bear	Zass.
Otter	Naby-ai.
Martin	Thah.
Wolvereen	Naguiyai.
Wolf	Yess (Nouneay).
Fox	Naguethey.
Hare	Cah.
Dog	Sliengh.
Beaver-skin	Zah thith.
Otter-skin	Naby-ai thith.
Moose-skin	Deny-ai thith
Fat	Icah.
Grease	Thless.
Meat	Bid.
Pike	Uldiah.
White-fish	Slouey.
Trout	Slouyzinal.
Pickerel	O'Gah.
Fishhook	Ge-eth.
Fishline	Clulez.

One	Slachy.
Two	Naghur.
Three	Tagh-y.
Four	Dengk-y.
Five	Sasoulachee.
Six	Alki tar-hy-y.
Seven	
Eight	Alki deing-hy.
Nine	Cakina hanoth-na.
Ten	Ca noth na.
Twenty	Na ghur cha noth ha.
Fire	Counn.
Water	Toue.
Wood	Dethkin.
Ice	Thun.
Snow	Yath.
Rain	Thinnelsee.
Lake	Touey.
River	Tesse.
Mountain	Zeth.
Stone	Thaih.
Berries	Gui-eh.
Hot	Edowh.
Cold	Edzah.
Island	Nouey.

Gun	Telkithy.
Powder	Telkithy counna.
Knife	Bess.
Axe	Thynle.
Sun, Moon	Sah.
Red	Deli couse.
Black	Dell zin.
Trade, or barter	Na-houn-ny.
Good	Leyzong.
Not good	Leyzong houlley.
Stinking	Geddey.
Bad, ugly	Slieney.
Long since	Galladinna.
Now, to-day	Ganneh.
To-morrow	Gambeh.
By-and-bye, or presently	Carahoulleh.
House, or lodge	Cooen.
Canoe	Shaluzee.
Door	The o ball.
Leather-lodge	N'abalay.
Chief	Buchahudry.
Mine	Zidzy.
His	Bedzy.
Yours	Nuntzy.

Large	Unshaw.
Small, or little	Chautah.
I love you	Ba ehoinichdinh.
I hate you	Bucnoinichadinh hillay.
I am to be pitied	Est-chounest-hinay.
My relation	Sy lod, innay.
Give me water	Too hanniltu.
Give me meat	Beds-hanniltu.
Give me fish	Sloeeh anneltu.
Give me meat to eat	Bid Barheether.
Give me water to drink	To Barhithen.
Is it far off	Netha uzany.
Is it near	Nilduay uzany
It is not far	Nitha-hillai.
It is near	Nilduay.
How many	Etlaneldey.
What call you him, or that	Etla houllia.
Come here	Yeu dessay.
Pain, or suffering	I-yah.
It's hard	Eduyah.
You lie	Untzee.
What then	Eldaw-gueh.

PART 2

JOURNAL OF A VOYAGE
FROM
FORT CHIPEWYAN
TO THE ARCTIC OCEAN
IN 1789

Journey from Fort Chipewan to the Arctic Ocean in 1789

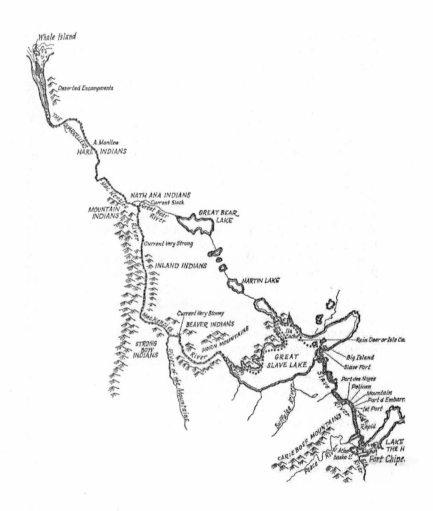

Journal of a Voyage performed by Order of the N.W. Company, in a Bark Canoe in search of a Passage by Water through the N.W. Continent of America from Athabasca to the Pacific Ocean in Summer 1789.

Wednesday, June 3. At 9 oClock embarked at Fort Chepwean (on the South side of the Lake of the Hills, in latitude 78.40 North, and longitude 110.30 West from Greenwich),[20] Mr. Leroux with Canoe for Slave Lake in Company. (The crew consisted of four Canadians, two of whom were attended by their wives, and a German; we were accompanied also by an Indian, who had acquired the title of English Chief, and his two wives, in a small canoe, with two young Indians; his followers in another small canoe. These men were engaged to serve us in the twofold capacity of interpreters and hunters. This Indian was one of the followers of the chief who conducted Mr. Hearne to the copper-mine river, and has since been a principal leader of his countrymen who were in the habit of carrying furs to Churchill Factory, Hudson's Bay, and till of late very much attached to the interest of that company. These circumstances procured for him the appellation of the English Chief.

(We were also accompanied by a canoe that I had equipped for the purpose of trade, and given the charge of it to M. Le Roux, one of the Company clerks. In this I was obliged to ship part of our provision; which, with the clothing necessary for us on the voyage, a proper assortment of the articles of merchandise as presents, to ensure us a friendly reception among the Indians, and the ammunition and arms requisite for defence, as well as a supply for our hunters, were more than our own canoe could carry, but by the time we should part company, there was every reason to suppose that our expenditure would make sufficient room for the whole.)

---

20. The material in parentheses appeared in the printed version of 1801, but did not appear in the manuscript. – ed.

Steered W. 21 Miles, then N.N.West 9 Miles when we entered the River, or one of the Branches or Outlets of this Lake, of which there are several. We steer North 6 Miles. Then N.N.E. 2 Miles. Here we camp'd at 7 oClock P.M. Our Hunters kill'd a Goose and *pair* Ducks. One of the Men [shot] a Duck which he swam for, our Canoe being taken out of the Water and the other Men Gumming her.

Thursday, June, 4. Embarked at 4 this Morning and steered N.N.E. ½ Mile, N. 1½ [Miles], N. 2 Miles, then W.N. 1½ Mile, N.N.W. ½ Mile, W.N.W. 2 Miles. Here this Branch joins the Peace River being the lowest. Its very remarkable that in all those Branches the Current when the Peace River is high in May and August run into the Lake (which in the other months of the year returns its waters to them): from the Lake to this (place, the branch is not more than) 200 yds wide nor their than 120. The Banks are low, here and there a Hugh (huge) Rock (rises above them). The Lowland is well covered with Wood, such as white Birch, Spruce or Pine of different Kind, Poplar, Willows of three Kinds and Aspen Tree. In this River we find the Current stronger (than that of the channel that communicates with the lake. It here, indeed, assumes the name of the *Slave* River), its about a Mile wide here, and its Course N.W. 2 Miles, N.N.W. through Islands 6 Miles, North 4½ Miles, N.b.E. 2 Miles, W.b.N., 6 Miles, N. 1 Mile, N.E.b.E. 2 Miles, N.N.W. 1 Mile, went down a rapid, N.W. 7½ Miles N.W. 9 Miles, N.b.W. 6 Miles, N.W.b.W. 1½ Miles, North W.b.N. ½ Mile, N.N.W. 6 Miles, N. 1 Mile, N.W.b.W. 4 Miles, N.N.E. 1 Mile. Land, unload our Canoes at the Dog River (at half past Seven) on the East Side close by the Rapids. The Hunters killed 2 Geese, and the Men killed a Goose and 2 Ducks. The River is near 2 leagues wide here.

Friday, June 5. We embarked at 3 oClock this Morning and unloaded our Canoe at this first Rapid. Here we enter a small River, or Channel which is occasioned by Islands. In half an hours time we came to the Carriers place. Its 380 paces long, and good except at the further End. We had some Difficulty in loading there being a quantity of Ice not yet thawed. From this to the next are 6 Miles [to the] Portage d'Embarras occasioned by Drift wood filling the small Channel, its 1020 Paces long. From here to the next 1½ Mile, 350 Paces long, to the next not above 150 yds. Its about the same length. From here to (the carrying place called) the Mountain about 4 Miles and we enter the Grand River. This small River is by much the best Road there being no Danger, tho' I believe a shorter road might be found upon the Outside of the Islands and not so many Carry Places. The Mountain [portage] is 335 Paces long, and from here to the Pelican Portage (820 Paces) about a Mile, all dangerous Rapids. The landing is very steep and quite close to the fall. All Hands were for some time handing the loading and Canoe up the Hill. One of the Indian Canoes went down the Fall, but (the woman who had the management of it) was lucky enough to jump out of her. She was broke to Pieces lost all her Menage. From where we started this Morning the Course is about N.W. and distance 15 Miles. From this to the next Carrying Place is about 9 Miles (in which distance there are) 3 Rapids. Course N.W.b.W. The Portage is very bad and 535 Paces long. Our Canoes light passed on the Outside of an Island opposite, made a portage of not more than the length of a Canoe. In rapids upon the other side of the River there were 5 Men drowned and 2 Canoes and some pieces lost going to the Slave Lake fall 1786 under charge of Mr. C. Grant (which occasioned this place to be called the *Portage des Noyes).* From this we steered S.W. 6 Miles and camped upon Point Du Roch half past 5P.M. Men and Indians much fatigued. They killed a Beaver 7 Geese and 4 Ducks.

Saturday, June 6. We embarked at ½ past 2 A.M. and steered N.W.b.N. 21 Miles, N.W.b.W. 5 Miles, W.N.W. 4 Miles, W. 6 Miles, Turned a point, N.N.E. 1 Mile, E. 5 Miles, N.E.b.E. 2 Miles: N.W.b.N. 1½ Miles, W.N.W. 3 Miles, N.E.b.E. 2 Miles, turn a point, W. 1½ Mile, W.b.N. 9 Miles, N.W.b.W. 6 Miles, N.N.W. 5 Miles. Here we landed, unloaded and camped for the Night at 6 oClock. Set a net in a small River close by. Had a Head wind the most part of the Day, so cold that the Indians made use of their Mittens. Killed 7 Geese and 6 Ducks.

Sunday, June 7. We set off at ½ past 3 A.M. steered W.N.W. I Mile round an Island, E. 1 Mile, N.b.W. 2½ Miles, S.b.W. 3 Miles, W.S.W. 1 Mile, S.W.b.S. ½ Miles, N.W. 3 Miles, W.N.W. 3½ Miles, N. 7½ Miles. Being raining for some time it came on so hard that we were obliged to land and unload to prevent our Goods getting wet. In an hours time it cleared up, and we reloaded and got underway. Steered N. 10 Miles, W. 1½ Mile, N. 1½ Mile. The rain came on again and obliged us to put on shore for the Night, about ½ past 3 P.M. We had a strong N.N.E. wind all Day which hindered us much. Mr. Leroux's People passed not finding this Place agreeable. The Men and Indians killed 2 Geese and 2 Ducks. Rained the rest of the Day.

Monday, June 8. It blew exceeding hard with rain all last Night and this Day till 2 in the afternoon when the Rain subsided, but the Wind continued which prevented our moving this Day.

Tuesday, June 9. We embarked at ½ past 2 A.M. Calm and Foggy. Soon after 2 young Men joined us that we had not seen for 2 days. They killed (during their absence) 4 Beavers and 10 Geese which they gave me. Our course N.W.b.N. 1 Mile. Opposite here is an opening in the right which we took for a Fork of the River but proved to be a Lake. We came back and steered S.W.b.S. 1½ Miles, W.S.W. 1½ Miles, W. 1 Mile. Here we entered a small River on the East side. They tell me that there used to be a Carrying Place at the Entry owing to Drift Wood filling up the Passages, but the Water has carried it away. The course of it is winding but suppose it will be about North distance 10 Miles to where it falls into the Slave Lake, and where we arrived at 9 A.M. We found a great change in the Weather, it being excessive Cold. The Lake is covered all over with Ice and does not seem to have yet moved, excepting along the shore. All along the River we were much troubled with Muskettows and Gnatts, but now I believe they must take their leave of us till the Weather gets warmer. From below the Rapids (as well as above) upon either side the River, the Banks are well covered with all kinds of Wood peculiar to this Country, particularly the West side, the land being lower and a richer soil (black Earth). (This artificial ground is carried down by the stream, and rests upon drift wood, so as to be eight or ten feet deep.) On the East side, the Banks are high, the soil is yellow Clay and Sand, so that the Wood is not so big nor so numerous. The ground is not yet thawed above 18 inches deep, notwithstanding the Leaf is at its full Growth, tho' there is hardly the appearance of any yet along the Lake. The Indians tell me that at a very little distance on both sides the River are very extensive Plains, where there are vast Herds of Buffaloes, and that the Moose Deer and the largest kind of Rain Deer keep in the Wood close by the River.

The Beaver (which are numerous) build their Houses in small Lakes, and Rivers, which they cannot do in the larger River as the Ice carries every thing along with it in the Spring. All the Banks of the River are covered with wild Fowl. We killed 2 swans 10 Geese 1 Beaver this morning without losing an hour's time, so that if we were for the purpose of hunting we might soon fill our Canoe.

From the small River we steered East on the Inside of a long Sand Bank (covered with Drift Wood and a few Willows) which reaches till opposite the Houses which Messrs. Grant and Leroux built here fall 1786. We ran aground often not finding 3 feet water when deepest for 6 Miles, and here we found Mr. Leroux who had arrived only in the Morning, had not seen him since the 7th. We unloaded our Canoe, and pitched our Tents, for from what we could see we would be obliged to remain here some time. I ordered the Men to set Nets immediately as we could not touch our Provision during our stay at this place, which they soon did and caught plenty of Fish for our Supper Say Personenconu White Fish, Trout Carp &c.

Wednesday, June 10. Rained for the greatest part of last Night and this day till the afternoon, which has weakened the Ice much. I sent 2 young Men a Hunting to a River 9 Miles from here; where they tell me there used to be many Animals. The Fishery not so good as Yesterday.

Thursday, June 11. Strong Westerly Winds fine clear Weather. The Women went to gather Berries, of which they brought in many (Say Cram-berries) and are very plentiful in this country. Went with one of the Men to a small Island close bye where we picked up some Dozens of Swan, Geese and Duck Eggs, and killed a Brace of Ducks and a Goose. Upon my arrival I was informed that Mr. Leroux had a very serious dispute with his foreman, but as neither of the Parties made any Complaint, I did not think proper to take any Notice of it. In the Evening the young Men returned without finding any large Animals, they killed a swan and a Grey Crain. Caught but 5 Fish to day and only peik (pike), which People in this Country are not fond of, being too common. The Ice moved a little to the Eastward.

Friday, June 12. The Weather as Yesterday. Towards noon our old Companions (the Muskettoes) visit us in greater Numbers than we would wish as they are very troublesome Guests. The Ice moved again in the same Direction. I ascended a Hill close by, but could not perceive that the Ice had been broke in the Middle of the Lake. Hunters killed a Goose and 3 Ducks.

Saturday, June 13. Cloudy Weather, the Wind changeable. About Sun Set it settled in the N.E. and drove back the Ice much broken along the shore, and covered our Netts. One of the Hunters that had been at the Grand River since last Night came back with 3 Beavers and 14 Geese. He was accompanied by 3 Families of Indians who had left Athabasca the same day that we did; they did not bring me a single Fowl, they said that they marched so hard, that they could not kill enough of Provision for their Families. By a Meridian line I found the variation of the Compass to be about 20 Degrees Easterly.

Sunday, June 14. Clear Weather, Wind as last Night. We run a risk of losing our Netts, as there is no getting at them. At sun set appearance of a violent Gust of wind from the Southerd. The Sky in that Quarter of a sudden became the blackest dark blue Colour and lightened much, however it passed away without any wind, but came on very heavy Rain which inevitably must diminish the Ice in its present shattered Condition.

Monday, June 15. In the Morning the Bay still full of Ice and can't get at our Netts. About Noon the wind veered to the Westerd and uncovered our Netts, and cleared a Passage to the opposite Islands. We raise our Netts very much broken and not many Fish. Struck our Tents loaded and embarked at Sun Set made the Traverse in two Hours time, about 8 Miles N.E.b.N. Unloaded upon a small Island and gummed our Canoe at ½ past 11 P.M. being then as clear as to see to write this. We have not seen a star since the second Day (after) we left Athabasca. About 12 o'Clock the Moon made her appearance a little above the Top of the Trees, the under Horn eclipsed and continued so for about 6 minutes; not a Cloud to be seen. I sounded three times in the Traverse, found 6 feet water and a muddy Bottom.

Tuesday, June 16. It blew very hard from the Northerd this morning which prevented our Embarking. A vast quantity of floating Ice. The Men and Indians caught some Trout with Hook and Line. Set a Nett, which we took up again at 12 with three small Fish. I had an Observation which gave 61' 28 North. The Wind moderated and we embarked about one our Course N.W. thro' Islands 10 Miles. We took in much Water making several Traverse. At 5 P.M. we landed and camped, set Netts and Hook and Lines. The Indians kill'd a Goose. N.B. Thundered this Day.

Wednesday, June 17. Rose our Netts &c. Caught but 17 Fish. Stopp'd within a Mile of our Campment by the Ice. The Indians brought us back to a point where we made a very good Fishery, and they went a hunting as well as to look out a Passage (through the ice) amongst the Islands. At 3 P.M. they returned without meeting with any large Animals. They could not observe any Passage, but we expect that the wind blows strong from the N.E. will make a Passage. They killed two Geese. About sun set the weather became much overcast. Thunder, Lightening and Rain.

Thursday, June 18. At 4 this Morning took up our Netts &c. with plenty of Fish, and we steered N.W. 4 Miles, when the Ice stopped us. The Wind S.E. drove the Ice amongst the Islands right in our way, and we could perceive at some distance a Head that it was not much broken. Set our Netts &c. in 4 feet water. Two of our Hunters killed a Rain Deer and a young one. They had seen two Indians with their Families. One of the Indians came to see us about 7 o'Clock. Had nothing. They live upon Fish. They are waiting the Lake being clear to go to the other side of it. He says that the Ice has not yet stirred on the other side of a large Island opposite us. No Fishery.

Friday, June 19. This Morning visited our Netts & Caught but 6 Fish which are very bad. In the forenoon the Indians went ahunting to the Big Island opposite. The Weather cloudy, Wind changeable. Pestered by Muskettoes, tho' we are in a manner surrounded by ice.

Saturday, June 20. Took our Netts up out of the Water, no Fish. Rained very hard last Night and this Morning, notwithstanding which Mr. Leroux and People went back to the point that we left the Day before Yesterday, but I could not think to stir as I watch'd the Ice in hopes of making a Passage. I promised to send for them. Rained at intervals till about 5 o'Clock. We loaded our Canoe and steered for the Big Island W. 6 Miles. When we came to the point of it at the foot [we found] a Traverse which was full of Ice; we set our Netts and soon caught plenty of Fish. I immediately dispatched 2 young Men for Mr. Leroux. Foggy weather. We overtook our Indians on our way here but they had not killed any thing since they left us. I sounded 100 yards from the Island, found 21 fms. There are many Cranberries and Spring onions of which we gathered plenty.

Sunday, June 21. Blew from the Southerd last Night drove the Ice to the Northed. The 2 young Men returned about 8 this Morning. They parted with Mr. Leroux close by, he was obliged to put to shore [as the wind] blew too hard. I try'd to take the Sun's altitude, and by a Glansis (glimpse) of him when it was 12 by my watch the Lat 61° 34 North. At 2 in the afternoon Mr. Leroux and People (arrived). At 5 the Ice was almost all drove past to the Northerd. We embarked, making our way thro' much broken Ice steering W. 15 Miles on the outside of the Traverse, Island and the Ice; the latter seems to be very solid to the N.E. I sounded 3 times in this distance and found 75, 44 and 60 fms water. We camped upon a small Island in the Vicinity of many other of the same Size (threw out some line and Hook) and within 3 Miles of the main Land, which the Ice prevented our getting to. We espied some Rein Deer upon one of the neigh-

bouring Islands. Our Hunters went in pursuit of them and kill'd
5 large and 2 small ones, which was not [a] difficult Matter, the
poor Creatures having no Place to run to for Shelter. In consequence of this Capture the Island were named *Isle de Carribo.* I
sat up all this Night reading to observe the sun's setting and Rising. He was under our Horizon 4 Hrs. 22 Min. Rose N. 20 E. by
Compass. Froze so hard during his absence that the Lake crusted
half a quarter of an Inch thick.

Monday, June 22. Embarked at half past 3 P.M. went round
on the outside of the Islands and steered N.W. 13 Miles along
the Ice edging for the main Land, the wind W. then W. 2 Miles.
Blew too hard obliged us to land upon an Island at ½ past 9
A.M. We could just distinguish Land to the S.E. stretching a
good distance and about 12 leagues from us. We did know not
whether it be the opposite side of the Lake or Islands. I had an
Observation at Noon which gave me 61 53' North, the Variation
of the Compass about 2 pts. Mr. Leroux's People hid 2 Bags
Pemican in the Island (for their return) which occasioned it to be
named *Is la Cach.* The Wind moderating a little we again got
under way by half past two in the afternoon. We steered W.b.N.
5½ Hours 18 Miles chiefly amongst Islands, and at 8 o'Clock
camp'd upon a small one. Have not passed any Ice since 8 this
Morning. Our Indians could not keep up with us, have not seen
them since shortly after we embarked. The Muskettoes are so
numerous tho' the Weather is so far from being warm that we
cannot rest for them.

Tuesday, June 23. Towards Morning our Indians joined us
they paddled all Night. They killed 2 Swans & a Goose. We continued our Route this Morning at half past three, steering W.b.N.
1½ Miles. The Wind North. Came to the foot of a Traverse
across a deep Bay W. 6 Miles. There is a considerable large
River falls in at the Bottom of it about 12 Miles distant. We
found the N.W. of this Bay formed by a No. of small Islands
which were quite full of Ice, but the Wind drove it off the land a
little [so] that we had a clear passage on the inside of it. We steer
S.W. 9 Miles, under Sail then N.W. nearly, thro' Islands we
often carried Sails the wind having veered a little to the Eastard,

this course 16 Miles. Here we landed at half past 2 P.M. at 3 lodges of Redknife Indians (so called from their copper knives) some of those that had given parole to Mr. Leroux. They informed us that there were as many more lodges of their Friends not far off, one of them went immediately (to fetch them). They told us this was all we would see at present. That the Slave and Beaver Indians as well as others of their Tribe will be here by the time that the Swans cast their Feathers. It rained in Torrent upon us this afternoon.

Wednesday, June 24. Traded above 8 packs good Beaver and Muslin (Marten) with those People (in two hours time). They are not above 12 Men able to kill Beaver. The English Chief got upwards of 100 Skins from them (on the score of) old Credit outstanding of which he has many in the country. He gave 40 of them to Mr. Leroux as part payment [for] Credits due him since Winter 86-87 at Slave Lake. With the rest he bought a few Necessaries and some Rum. And some more I gave him and his young Men which made them get Drunk. Had several Councils with these since we arrived, but could learn nothing material regarding our Expedition. They know nothing even of the River (which was the object of my research) but the Entry. I engaged one of their young Men to go and conduct us thither to prevent loss of time in Circumnavigating Bays. Gave him a pair of Leggans Brayet Knife &c., and bought a large new Canoe, that he might embark with the other 2 young Men. I had an Observation this Day at Noon which gave me 62° 24' North Latitude. I look upon it that the variation of the compass is about 26 or 27 Degrees Easterly.

In the afternoon I called the Indians together and informed them that I intended to leave them tomorrow Morning but that Mr. Leroux would remain here till the Indians that they spoke [of] should arrive, and in case they would bring Skins enough to fill his Canoe, that he would send the Frenchmen more foods in order that he might Winter here and build a Fort, which would be continued to them as long as they would deserve it.

They gave me to understand that it would be great encouragement for them to have Frenchmen upon the Land, that they would work hard to kill Beaver, when they would be sure of getting Value for their Skins. That heretofore the Chippiweems always pillaged them where ever they met them (that as they gave them little or nothing in Exchange) which entirely discouraged them from killing Beaver, but when they did it for the Sake of Food and Raiment. Wrote to Messrs. McLeod & McKenzie addressed my Papers to the former to be forwarded by Mr. Leroux to Athabasca.

Thursday, June 25. Parted with Mr. Leroux at 3 this Morning. Our Canoe very deeply laden having embarked some *pieces* that had come in the other Canoe till here. Mr. Leroux got his Men & Indians to salute us with several Vollies, to which we returned a few Shot. We steered S. & b.W. straight across the Bay which is here only 2½ Miles wide – by what I cou'd learn from the Natives it's upwards of 40 Leagues Deep and is much wider than what it is here in many Places & full of Islands. In the Traverse I found 6 Fathoms Water, a Sand Bottom. The Land on this side has quite a different appearance from that where we entered the lake till here. The latter is but one continued View of Mountains & Islands & Solid Rock covered here & there with Moss, Shrubs & Trees, the latter quite stinted in their Growth for want of soil to nourish them; notwithstanding this barren appearance you can hardly land upon those Rocks but you will meet with Gooseberries Cramberries whortle Berries Brow Berries Juniper Berries, Rasberries, what the Men call *Grains a Perdres* Grain a Saccacomis and what the Indians call *Pythagominan* something like a Rasberry but the last grows upon a small Stalk 1½ ft. high in wet Mossy Places. All those are in great plenty tho' they do not all grow in one & the same Place.

Then near the lake the Land is low & sandy tho' it is well covered with wood of a larger Size. It gets gradually higher & at some distance forms a ridge of high Land which appears to run a considerable distance along the Coast & has not much wood on Top appears Rocky and Sandy. We Steer S.S.E. 9 Miles, we are stopped by drifting [ice]. With some difficulty we got to an Island where we landed at 7 oClk A.M. I went to the furthermost End of it to see if we might have any hopes of getting away from here this Day. It's about 5 Miles round. I was much surprized to find that the greatest part of the Wood of the Island had been cut down about 12 or 15 Years since & that no part of it remained on the Ground, but the Stumps which were quite rotten. When I returned I enquired of the Indian Chief what was the meaning of this. He informed me that several Winters ago, that this was the land of the Slave Indians & many of them lived upon the Island round this Bay there being an excellent Fishery all the Year thro' that it was the Cres (Knisteneaux) that drove them away from here by frequently coming to War upon them. If Mr. Leroux winters in this Country he is to build near this Place on account of the Fishery & wood. At 11 oClock A.M. the wind having drove the greatest part of the Ice past the Island, we made our way thro' some Broken Ice tho' at the Risk of damaging our Canoe. Steering S.E. from Point to Point across 5 Bays 21 Miles I sounded several Times & found from 6 to 16 fm. water. I observed that the Inland Country got gradually lower but better covered with Wood than where it was higher. Upon every part of the Land that we came near to were old (deserted) lodges. The Hunters kill'd 2 Swan and a Beaver. We landed at 8 oClk unloaded & gummed our Canoe as usual &c.

Friday, June 26. We landed & continued our Rout (5 oClk) Steering S.E. for 10 Miles across 2 deep Bays. Then S.S.E. Islands in Sight to the Eastward. Travers'd another Bay 3 Miles, then S. 1 Mile to a point which we named the detour, S.S.W. 4½ Miles a heavy Swal (swell) of the Lake. Had an observation here 61° 40 North Lat: S.W. 4 Miles, W.S.W. among Islands. Our Indians kill'd 2 Rein Deer upon one of those Islands, we lost 3 Hours aft Wind going for them. This Course about 9 Miles. Abt. 7 P.M. obliged to Land for the Night the Wind too strong from the S.E. We thought we could observe land in this Direction when the Wind was coming on. From some Distance on the other Side the Detoar the land is low & the lands is very flat & dangerous there being no safe place of landing in case of bad weather except in the Islands we just past. There seems to be plenty of Moos & Rein Deer in this Country. We saw the track every where we landed. Likewise Numbers of White Partridges which are now almost all Grey of the Colour of the Moonfull (moor-fowl). Saw some floating Ice to Day on the lake. The Indians killed 2 Swan.

N.B. My Steersman has a misunderstanding with his Lady last Night & arranged for [her] to remain at the Campmt. but his Cousin (her Furreaux) got her on board & the Husband said nothing to the contrary.

Saturday, June 27. By 3 this Morning we were under Way, after a very restless Night being tormented by Musquittoes. A fine Calm our Course – W.S.W. 9 Miles. Here we came to the foot of a Traverse the opposite Point in *Sight* Bearing S.W. distance 12 Miles. This Bay is at least 8 Miles deep. This Course 2 Miles more. It came on very foggy and as there were so many Bays we landed till it would clear up, which it did in 2 Hours time which we took the advantage of Steering S. 13 Miles past several small Bays; here we came to the point of a very deep one. The land drowned towards the Bottom the opposite Side bearing S. from us distance 10 Miles. Our guides quite at a loss they do not know what course to take, he says its 8 Winters since he has been here, that this Bay is much like the Entrance of the River in consequence we steered down the Bay about W.S.W. Course till we got in amongst Fields of Broken Ice. Still we could not see the Bottom of the Bay nor could we proceed, the Fog coming on made it very difficult for us to get to an Island S.W. of us. It was near dark when we landed upon it & Camp'd.

Sunday, June 28. At a Quarter past 3 this Morning we were on the Water and as we could perceive no Current setting into this Bay, we made the best of our Way to the Point that bore South of us Yesterday Afternoon. S. 3 Miles more, then S.b.W. 7 Miles W. 17 Miles. Had an Observation 61 Degrees N. Lat: W.N.W. 2 Miles here we came to the foot of a Traverse the opposite land bearing S.W. Distance 14 Miles. This being a deep Bay we steered into it about a westerly Course having no Land in *Sight* a head in hopes to find a Passage which the Indian informed us was to be met with before we came to the Grand River. Having a strong aft wind we lost sight of the Indians nor could we put ashore to wait for them without running the Risk of wrecking our Canoe till we came to the bottom of the Bay and ran our Canoe in amongst Bushes, but we found there was no Passage here. In two or three Hours time they join'd us but would not come near our Fire this being not a good Campment. They emptied their Canoe of the water they had taken in & continued their Route & we followed. Did not Camp till Sun Set. The English Chief was in a great Passion with the Red Knif wanted to shoot him for having undertaken to guide us in a Road he did not know, indeed, none of us are well pleased with him, but we don't think with the English Chief that he merits such severe punishment. Besides he gave us some hopes that we are close by the River, that he recollects to have passed from the River thro' the Wood to the Place that we landed at. (In the blowing weather to-day, we were obliged to make use of our large kettle, to keep our canoe from filling, although we did not carry above three feet sail. The Indians very narrowly escaped.)

Monday, June 29. Embarked at 4 oClk this Morning steering along the S.W. side of the Bay. At ½ past 5 we came to the extremity of the point which we doubled & found it to be the Passage we were in search of, occasioned by a very long Island which separated this from the Main Channel of the River. It is about ½ a Mile across not above 6 foot deep. We could observe a vast many Fish in the Water & the Place was almost covered with wild Fowl, Swan, Geese & several kinds of Ducks &c. particularly Black Ducks were very numerous, but we could not get within Gunshot of any of them. The Current set us at S.W.b.W. (though) not very strong. Followed the Course till we passed the Pt. of the long Island (where the River is upwards of 10 Miles across) 14 Miles there is from 1 to 2 ft. water & I suppose when the water is low in the lake the greater part of this Channel must be dry. Now the River turns W. (gradually getting narrower) 24 Miles. Here it is not above a Mile wide but the Current is much stronger. Sounded, found 3½ fms. The Land on the N. Shore from the Lake here is low & well wooded, that on the South appears higher and has plenty of wood on it likewise. The Current is very strong. The Banks are equally high on both Sides, (consisting of) Yellow Clay mix'd with Stones & covered with much Burnt Wood upon the Ground & Young Aspin Trees that have grown since the Fire (that destroyed the larger wood) passed. (It is a very curious and extraordinary circumstance, that land covered with spruce pine, and white birch, when laid waste by fire, should subsequently produce nothing but poplars, where none of that species of tree were previously to be found.

Have a stiff breeze from the Eastward wch drove us on at a great Rate under Sail, our Course about the same tho' winding among Islands. We keep the North Channel where the Current is much stronger. That in the South Channel does not appear to be so much, so of course will be the easiest Road to come up, 10 Miles. Here the River widens. The wind dies away & we have recourse to our Paddles. We keep the North Side of the River our Course N.W. The River is very wide here in form of a small Lake. We cou'd see no opening in any Direction so that we are at a loss what course to take. Our Red Knife Indian has never been further than this. A River falls in from the N. and as he says takes its rise in the Horn Mountain the land of the Beaver Indians. That he and his Relation met with some of them upon this River that there are very extensive Plains on both Sides the Grand River abounding with Buffaloes & Moor Deer. By keeping this Course we came into Shallow water which made us steer to the left, till we came into deeper water, which we followed till the Channel of the River opened to us to the South. We made for the Shore & we Camp'd after Sun Set. Our Course ought to have been W. 15 Miles since we took the Paddle. The Horn Mountain in Sight being N.W. from us & running N.N.E. & S.S.W. I sounded frequently to Day found from 3 to 6 fm. Water. Our Hunters kill'd 2 Geese & a Swan. Vast Nos. of Fowl breeding in those Islands.

Tuesday, June 30. At 4 this Morning we got under way a fine Calm. Our Course S W b S 36 Miles. Upon the South Side of the River is a Ridge of low Mountains running East & west by Compass. The Indians pick'd up a white Brant which appeared to have been Shot with a Bow & Arrow & quite Fresh. S W b W 6 Miles. A Bay upon our left full of small Islands & by appearance the entrance of a River from the South & the ridge of

Mountains terminates here. This Course for 15 Miles. At 6 P.M. appearance of bad weather. We landed for the Night & before we could pitch our Tents it came on a violent Tempest, of Thunder, Lightening, wind & Rain, which ceased in a little Time after giving us a compleat soaking, which the Men and Indians are not so much displeased with it being the Means of their camping a couple of Hours earlier than they would otherwise have done & the latter are very much fatigued having ran much after wild Fowl, which have cast their Feathers. They caught 6 Swans and 5 Geese. I sounded several times today found from 4 to 6 fm water.

Wednesday, July 1. Loaded and push'd off at a quarter before 4 A.M. Soon the River narrows to about ½ Mile our Course W. amongst Islands, a strong Current. The land high on both sides but the Banks are not perpendicular. This course 21 Miles, sounded 9 fms then W.N. 9 Miles. Passed a River upon the S.E. side sounded again 12 fms. N.W.b.W. 3 Miles; here I lost my lead and part of my line it getting fast at the Bottom the Current is too strong to steer'd (in order to get it clear) with 8 Paddles, as a Man could not break it. N.b.W. 5 Miles. A high mountain bearing south from us. N.W.b.N. 4 Miles, pass a small River on the N side then steer'd round a point to W.S.W. At one oClock there came on Thunder, Lightening, Wind, and Rain, which ceased in about ½ an Hour and left us wet to the Skin as we did not land. Great Quantities of Ice along the Banks of the River. Landed upon a small Island where there were the Poles of 4 Lodges, which we concluded to have been Crees [Knisteneaux], upon their War Excursions by appearance 6 or 7 years since. This Course for 15 Miles then W. where the River of the mountain falls in from the southerd. It appears to be a large River upwards of ½ Mile over, at the Entry. About 6 Miles further a small River from the same Direction. This Course (our whole course) 24 Miles. We landed opposite to an Island the Mountains to the Southerd in *sight.* As our Canoe is very deep laden and that we are in daily Expectations of coming to the Rapids, which we have been made to dread, we had 2 Bags of pemican in the opposite Island, which I expect may be of service to us in time to come, tho' our Indians are of a difft. opinion, they having no Expectations of coming back here, this Season, of course it will be lost. Close by are two Indian Campments of last years. By their way of Cutting the Wood they must have had no Iron Works. The Current was very strong all Day. The Indians killed 2 Swans (in the article of provisions), all that the hunters were able to procure).

Tuesday [Thursday], July 2. A very thick Fog this Morning. Embarked at half past 5 P.M. Cleared up at 7. The Water has changed from being limpid to muddy, which we suppose must be owing to some large River falling in from the southerd which the Fog prevented our seeing. At 9 oClock A.M. perceive very high Mountains ahead and upon our nearer approach as a No. of very high Hills. The Tops of them hid in the Clouds ran as far as our view could carry to the southerd. At Noon Lightening, Thunder and Rain. At 1 oClock came a Breast of the Mountains, they appear Barren and Rocky upon Top, but well covered with Wood towards the Bottom. There appears a No. of White Stones upon them which glistens when the Rays of the sun shines upon them. The Indians say they are *Maneloe Aseniah (manetoe aseniah,* or spirit stones), but I think they must be Talk (Talc), tho' they are rather whiter than I have ever seen (on our return, however, these appearances were dissolved, as they were nothing more than patches of snow). Our Course has been W.S.W. 30 Miles. We went on very cautiously here expecting every moment that we would come to some great Rapid or Fall. We were so full of this that every person in his turn thought he heard a Noise &: the falling of water, which only subsisted in our Imaginations. Our Course changes to W.b.N. along the Mountains 12 Miles N.b.W. 21 Miles. At 8 oClock P.M. put on Shore for the Night upon the North side. We saw many of the Native Campments today some of them this Spring and others older. The Hunters killed (only) a swan and a Beaver the (latter was the) first that we have seen since we have been in the River. The Indians complain much of our hard marching, that they are not accustomed to such hard fatigue.

Friday, July 3. Rained all last Night and till 7 this Morning when we embarked and steered N.N.W. for 12 Miles. High mountains on both sides of the River, a strong head wind. Rained hard, obliged us to land at 10 oClock A.M. By my reckoning since my last Observation, we have ran 217 Miles West and 44 Miles N. At a quarter past 2P.M. the Rain subsided, and we got again under way, our Course as before for 5 Miles. Here a River fails in from the N. Soon after the Current became strong and rapid amongst Rocky Islands, the first that we saw in this River, and which we thought a sure indication of soon meeting with Falls and Rapids. Our present Course N.W.b.N. for 10 Miles, then N.W. 3 Miles W.N.W. 12 Miles, N.W. 3 Miles and Camped at 8 oClk at the foot of a high Hill on the North Shore part of it perpendicular with the River. I ascended it accompanied by 2 Men and also Indians, it took us an hour and a quarter hard walking. I was very much surprised to find a Campment on Top of it. The Indians told me that it is the Custom of all the People who have no Arms to make choice of Places of this Kind for their residence, as they could easily make them inaccessible to their Enemies, particularly those who the Crees (Knisteneaux) make War on, they being in continual dread of them. Our view was not so extensive as we had expected it being terminated all round with such Hills as the one we were upon. Between the Hills are Nos. of small Lakes upon which we could perceive many Swans. The Country appeared very thinly wooded, a few Trees of the Pine and Birch, and very small in size. We were obliged to shorten our Stay here on account of the Swarms of Muskettoes that attacked us and were the only Inhabitants of the Place. We saw many of the Natives Encampments the Day, none of them this Years. Since 4 oClk. P.M. the Current has been excessive strong so much so that it makes such a hissing and Ebbilition as a kettle moderately Boiling. The Weather has been cold all Day, which is more sensible to us as it was very Sultry before, since we have been in the River.

Saturday, July 4. At 5 A.M. put off, wind and weather as Yesterday. Steer N.W.b.N. 22 Miles N.W. 6 Miles N.W.b.N. 4 Miles W.N.W. 5 Miles. Pass a small River from the North, turn round a point S.W. 1 Miles N.W. 4 Miles. A River from the south. N.N.W. a Mountain ahead 15 Miles. 2 Rivers opposite one another. W. 4 Miles N.W. 13 Miles. At 8 oClk P.M. Camped upon an Island. The Current as strong all day as it was Yesterday afternoon. A Quantity of Ice along the Banks of ye River. The Indians killed a Goose, and the Men a Beaver which sunk before we could get him (beavers, otters, bears, &c. if shot dead at once, remain like a bladder, but if there remains enough life for them to struggle, they soon fill with water and go to the bottom).

Sunday, July 5. Last Night the sun set at 55 minutes past 9 by my watch, and rose before 2 this morning, We embarked soon after steering N.N.W. thro' Islands for 5 Miles W 4 Miles. The River widens, and the Current slackens a little. N.W. 3 Miles, perceive a ridge of high snowy Mountains ahead. W.S.W. 10 Miles and at ¾ past 7 O'clock we perceived several Smokes, which we made for with all speed. Soon saw the Natives run about in great Confusion, some making [for] the Woods and others to their Canoes. Our Hunters landed before us and spoke to the few that had not been quick enough to run away, in the Chipewean Language which at first they could not understand thro' the confusion they were in, but they saw it was impossible for them to make their Escape as we were all landed they made signs to us for to keep at a Distance, which we did and loaded our Canoe and pitched our Tents before any of us went near them, during which time the English Chief and his young Men were very busy in reconciling them to our Arrival, for when their Flurry was over, and they saw we intended them no hurt, it was found that some of the Men understood our Indians very well, who persuaded them to come down to where we were which they consented to with great Reluctance, and not without evident Signs of Fear, but the Reception they met with partly removed their Terror, and they recalled the rest of their People from their hiding Places. There are five Families of them in all, 26 or 30 Persons, and of two *different* Tribes, Slave and Dog Rib Indians. We made them smoke, tho' it was evident they did not know the use of Tobacco. We likewise gave them some grog to drink, but I believe they accepted of those Civilities more through Fear than Inclination. By the Distribution of Knives, Beads, Awls, Rings, Gartering, Fire Steels, Flints and a couple of Axes, they became more familiar than we expected, for we could not keep them out of our Tents, tho' I did not observe that they tryed to steal anything from us. The Information they gave us respecting the River, seems to me so very *fabulous* that I will not be particular in inserting. Suffice it to say that they would wish to make us believe that we would be several Winters getting to the Sea, and that we all should be old Men by the time we would return. That we would have to encounter many Monsters (which can only exist in their own Imaginations). Besides that there are 2 impracticable Falls or Rapids in the River, the first 30 Days March from us, &c. &c. Tho' I put no faith in those Stories, they had a different Effect upon the English Chief, and his young Men (who were already very tired of their Voyage). It was their Opinion and wish that we should absolutely return, adding to the above Reasons many others – that they were informed that there were very few Animals below this, and the farther we went the fewer there would be, of course that we should Starve, even if no other accident befell us. I with much ado dissuaded them out of their Reasonings and made them to ask one of the Natives to accompany us, which they soon did. One of the others as soon consented to in Consideration of getting a Small Kettles, Axe, Trencher, Knife &c. Altho' it was now 3 oClk in the Afternoon I wanted to make the most of our time. I ordered My Men to reload our Canoe & as soon as we were ready to embark called upon our new Recruit to do the same, which he would rather have declined, however as none of his Friends would take his place, & after the loss of an Hours time we in a manner compelled him to embark. Previous to his departure I observ'd a piece of Ceremony of which I could not learn the meaning. He cut a lock of his Hair separated it into 3 Parts one of which he fastened to the hair of the Crown of his Wifes head, blowing on it three times as hard as he could & repeating some words, the other two he fastened with the same Ceremony on the heads of his two Children. During our short stay with those People they amused us with Dancing to their own Vocal Music, in neither of which there is no great variety, at least as far as we cou'd perceive. They form a Ring Men and Women promiscuously, the former have a Bone Dagger or piece of Stick between the fingers of the Right Hand which they keep extended above the head & in continual Motion, the left they seldom raise so high but keep working backward & forward in a horizontal direction keeping time to their Music. They jump & put themselves into different Antic Shapes, keeping their Heels, close together. At every pause they make the Men give a howl in Imitation of the Wolf, or some other Animal & those that hold out the longest at this strong exercise seem to pass for the best Performers; the Women hang their Arms as if without the Power of Motion. They are all an ugly meagre ill made People particularly about the Legs which are very clumsy & full of Scabs by their frequent roasting them to the Fire. Many of them appear'd very sickly owing as I imagine to their Dirty way of living. They are of the Middle Stature & as far as could be discerned thro' Dust & Grease that cover their whole Body fairer than the generality of Indians, who inhabit warmer Climes. Some of them wear their hair long, others have it long behind & from the Crown down to the two Ears cut quite short, but none of them take any pains to keep it in order. A few of the Old Men had their beards long & the rest had it pulled out by the Roots that not a hair was to be seen. The Men have two double lines Black or Blue Tatoed upon each Cheek from Ear to Nose. The Gristle of the latter is perforated large enough to admit a Goose Quill, which or a piece of Stick some of them had passed in the Orifice. They make their Clothing of the Skin of the Rein or Moos Deer well dressed but the Skin of the first is more Common & they dress many of them in the Hair for winter wear, of either they make Shirts which come down half their Thighs some of which they embroider very neatly with Porcupines Quills & the Hair of the Moos Deer painted Red, Black, Yellow & White (say Col.^{d}). Their Robes are large enough to cover a Man & serve for that purpose asleep or awake. They are fringed round at Bottom their edging comes up half the Thigh & are of a Piece with the Shoes. They are embroidered round the Ancle and upon every Seam; the Women dress the same as the Men. The Men have no covering on their Private Parts except a small Tassel of Parings of Leather, which hang loose by a small Cord, before them in order as I think to keep off the Flies which otherwise wou'd be very troublesome. Both Young & Old Men have the glans of the Penis uncovered, indeed their want of Modesty & their having no Sense of their Nakedness but from the Cold would make a Person think that they were descended from Adam, and probably had he been created at the Arctic Circles he would not have had occasion for Eve, the Serpent, nor the Tree of Knowledge to have given him a Sense of his Nakedness.

Their ornaments consists of Bracelets, Gorgets, Arm & Wrist Bands made of Wood, Horn, or Bone, Belts, Garters & a kind of a Cap which they wear on the Head made of a Piece of Leather 1½ Ins. wide embroidered with Porcupine Quills & stuck round with the Claws of Bears or wild Fowls inverted to each of which hangs a few parings of fine white Ferrit Skins in fashion with a Tassel. The cinctures of Garters are of Porcupine Quills wove with Sinews & are the neatest thing of the kind that ever I saw, some others they make of Common Quills which are not so handsome. To both kinds they fasten a long fringe which are made by working the Hairs of the original of different Colours round strings of Leather. (Their mittens are also suspended from the neck in a position convenient for the reception of the hands.) Their Lodges are as simple as can be imagined, a few Poles laid across one another supported by a Fork & forming a Demi Circle at bottom covered with a few Branches or a Piece or Two of Bark under which they sleep. They make two of those Structures facing one another & make the fire between. Their furniture is of a Piece with their lodgings, two or three dishes of Wood, Bark or horn. The Vessel which serve them to cook their Victuals are something of the Shape of a Gourd wide & bilged below & narrower at Top made of walup Basket work, but so close that it holds Water with any other thing they chuse to put in it. They make it boil by putting a sufficiency of Red hot Stones into it. Those Vessels contain from 2 to 6 Gals. They have a Number of Small Leather Bags to hold their embroidered Work, Lines, Nets, Willow Bark of which they always have a Quantity by them. They work this Bark into Thread upon their Thigh.

Their Nets are from 3 to 40 fm. long 13 to 36 Meshes deep, the short deep ones they set in the Eddy Current in the River & the long ones in the Lakes. They likewise make Lines of the Sinews of Rein Deer, their Hooks of Wood, Horn or Bone. Their Arms & hunting Weapons are Bows & Arrows, Spears, Daggs, & Pogmagans. The Bows are about 5 or 6 ft. long the Strings of Sinew or Green Skin, the Arrows 2½ ft. long including the Point which is of bone, Horn, Stone Iron or Copper. They are feathered at the End with three Feathers. The handle of the Spears are about 6 feet long pointed with a barbed Bone 10 Inches long, with this they spear the Rein Deer in the water; the Daggs are about 12 Inches long flat & sharp pointed made of Bone or Horn. The Pogmagan is made of the Horn of Rein Deer the Branches all cut off but one towards the extremity this is left 4 Inches long. This Machine is upwards of 2 ft. long & serve to them to dispatch their enemies in Battle & such Animals as they catch with Snares. Those Snares are 3 fms. long made of the Green Skin of the Rein or Moos Deer cut so that it requires from 10 to 30 Strand to make this Cord which is no thicker than a Cod Line & strong enough to resist the Strength of any Animal in the Country. They make Snares of Sinews with which they catch Hares & White Partridges which are exceeding numerous in this Country. Their Axes are made of a Piece of brown or Grey Stone 6 or 8 Ins. long 2 Inches Sqr. left flat on the inside rounded on the Outside & tapering to a Point or Edge an Inch wide. They fasten it by the Middle flat Side inward to a handle 2 ft. long with a Cord of Green Skin & altho' a tedious Work cut & split their Wood with this Tool. They make Fire by striking together a Piece of White or Yellow Pirelis (pyrites) & a Flint Stone over a Piece of dry Punk. Young & Old are provided with the materials and in an Instant strike fire. They have small bits of Iron which they get from the next Tribe to them, those from the Red Knives & Chippiweans in barter for Martin Skins & a few

Beaver. They make Knives of those small bits of Iron by fixing them in the End of a small Stick. With those & Beaver Teeth they finish all their Work. They have them in a Sheath hanging on their Neck (which also contains their awls both of iron and horn). Always ready to run their hand into them. Their Canoes are small, pointed at both Ends, flat bottomed cover'd before (in the fore part) all made of the Bark of the Birch Tree & Fir Wood, quite slight & so light that they carry them over Land wherever they go. Seldom more than One Person embarks in them, nor can they carry above two. The Paddles are 6 ft. long half of which is the Blade about 8 Ins. wide.

We learn from those People that we had passed Numbers of Indians who inhabit the Mountains on the East Side of the River. We parted from them at 4 oClk P.M. They promised to remain upon the Banks of the River till the fall in case we should come back. Our Course S.S.W. We soon passed the River of the great Bear Lake which appears to be a fine deep River abt. 100 yds. wide, the Water is quite clear of the colour of Salt Water (Sea). We did not go above 6 Miles when we were obliged to land for the Night by a very heavy Gust of Wind with Rain. Our Campment is under a high Hill or Rock. Our new Conductor told us that it blew every day in the Year on the Top of this Hill. He was very uneasy with us, pretending sickness that we might let him return to his relations to prevent which we be obliged to watch him all Night.

Monday, July 6. Very Cloudy raw Weather this Morning. At 3 oClock A.M. we embarked steering W.S.W. 4 Miles W. 4 Miles, (West-North-West five miles, West eight miles) W.b.S. 16 Miles, W. 27 Miles, S.W. 9 Miles, then W. 6 Miles & camp'd at half past 7 P.M. We passed thro' many Islands to day the Ridge of Snowy Mountains always in Sight. Our Stranger informed us that there are a great Number of Bears and White Buffaloes (small) in the Mountains & that they are inhabited. We camp'd under a high Rocky Hill which I attempted to ascend accompanied by one of the Young Hunters but we were obliged to relinquish our design half way up it being nearly suffocated by Swarms of Musquittoes. I could see that the Mountain terminated here at least as far as we could see & a River falling in from the Westward. Observed a strong Rapling (ripling) Current or rapid close by under the Hill which then was a Precipice.

Tuesday, July y. Embarked at 4 oClock A.M. Crossed to the opposite Side on account of the rapid I mentioned above but we might have saved ourselves the trouble as there was no danger in going straight down it. This proved to be one of the dangerous Rapids we had to pass & convinced me in my Opinion respecting the falsity of the Natives Information. Our Course N.N.W. for three Miles W.N.W. 4 Miles N.W. 10 Miles N. 2 Miles. A small River from the East Side where we landed (at an encampment of) 4 Fires. The People ran off excepting an Old Man & Woman notwithstanding our Conductor called to them but they cou'd neither see nor hear him. The Old Man came down to meet us telling us that he was pitifully worn out with old age & for the time he had to live it was not worth while for him to run away. He began to pull out his Grey Hairs by handfuls distributing it amongst us begging that we should have Mercy on him & his relations. At last our Indian made him listen to him and partly removed his fear he called back his Relations in all 18 People. I made them Presents of Knives, Beads, Awls, &c which pleased them exceedingly. They differed in no respect from those that we had seen and they offered us Fish to eat which was very well boiled and accepted of, with a few they had just caught. We were obliged to force our Guide to embark, he wanted absolutely to return. We learned from those People that we were close by the other great rapid, and that there were several lodges of their Relatives there. 4 Canoes followed us a Man in each to shew us where to take the Road to go down the Rapid. They like the other people told us many discouraging Stories. Our Course from here N.N.E. 2 Miles. The River appeared quite shut up with high perpendicular White Rocks, this did not at all please us. We went ashore to try to visit the Rapid, but there was no possibility of seeing any thing. The Indians made a great Noise about it, but at last we *thought* when they ventured to go down it with their small Canoes, we might venture it with ours, so we followed them at a small distance. We came between the steep Rock I mention as above but did not find the Current stronger than elsewhere. We were still in Expectation of coming to the Rapid till they told us there was no other but what we saw. The River is not above 300 yds overhere (in breadth), I sounded and found 50 fms water. At 2 small Rivulets that fall in between those Rocks, one on each side, we found 6 more Families about 35 persons, who gave us a No. of very excellent Fish of two kinds of white Fish, and another round Green Fish about 14 Inches long. I made them a few Presents and left them, but all the Men in 15 Canoes followed us. This narrow Channel is 3 Miles long and course N.N.E. then we steered N. 3 Miles, landed at 3 more Families of their people 22 Persons. They were camped close by a midling large River. We got Fish Hares and Partridges from them, and made them Presents of some Articles which pleased them much. They regretted that they had not their goods to exchange with us. They had left them at a Lake that this River runs out of, and where some others of their People set Snares for the Rein Deer, but they said that they would go for them and wait our return which we assured them would be in 2 Mos. at farthest. There was a young lad here who our Indians understood better than any that we had yet seen, and was a Slave with those People. He was asked to come along with us, but he took the first Opportunity to slip off with himself, and did not see him afterwards. We steered W. 5 Miles where we again landed at 2 Families 7 People but we imagine that there were others hid in the wood. We had 2 Doz. of Hares here, and they were about boiling a couple which they gave us also. Used them the same as I had done the others and left them steering N.W. 4 Miles 9 oClk camped. One of our Indians killed a Grey Crain. (Our conductor renewed his complaints, not, as he assured us, from any apprehension of our ill-treatment,) but of the Eskmeaux, who he says are very wicked and will kill us all, that it is but two summers since a great Party of them came up this River and killed a Number of his Relations. 2 Indians followed us from the last lodges.

Wednesday, July 8. Embarked at half past 2 A.M. and steered a W. Course. Shortly after we put ashore at 2 lodges of

Indians 9 People. Made them a few (trifling) Presents without debarking and pushed on. We did not go far when we observed several Smoakes on the North Shore under a Hill. When we approached could see the Indians climbing up the Hill into the Wood. The two small Canoes were ahead and (The Indians) spoke to them (assured them of our friendly intentions) upon which they returned to their Fires, and we debarked. Many of those People were clothed in Hair Skins but in everything else they were the same as those we had already seen, tho' we were given to understand that they were a different Tribe and called the Hair (Hare) Indians as Hare (& Fish) are their principal support, large animals being very scarce and only Rein Deer and Bever (frequent this part of the country. They were twenty-five in number; and among them was a woman) who has an Abscess in the Belly and is reduced to a mere Skeleton. There were a No. of old Women singing and howling there, (but whether these noises were to operate as a charm for her cure, or merely to amuse and console her, I do not pretend to determine). I distributed a No. of small Articles among them which made them quite happy, and I changed my Conductor here as he was become very troublesome obliged to watch him Night and Day except when upon the Water. This Fellow had likewise no sooner consented but he repented, alledging that he had not seen much of the River, and that there were more of his Relations close by, who would be willing, to accompany us; but we could not believe him as he told us 10 Minutes before that we should see no more of their Tribe, so that we made him embark and departed. About 3 Hours after a Man overtook us in a small Canoe, which we thought immediately was in order to facilitate our Conductor to desert. About 12 oClk we observed a Man walking along the N.E. shore. The small Canoe made for them and we followed. Found 3 Men 3 Women and 2 Children, they had been a Hunting, they had some Rein Deers (Meat) which they offered to us, but was so rotten and sunk so abominably that we did not accept of it. They and the Men that followed us [told us] that behind the opposite Island that there was a Manitoe (or spirit) in the River, which swallowed every Person that approached him. It would have taken us half a day to have gone to see this Wonder which I did not choose to throw away on an uncertainty. I gave them a Knife and a few Awls and departed. One of them embarked in the small Canoe. Our Course and distance this Day were W. 28 Miles, W.N.W. 23 Miles, W.S.W. 6 Miles, W.b.N. 5 Miles S.W. 4 Miles; and camped at 8 oClock. The most part of this day was Foggy with frequent showers of small Rain.

Thursday, July 9. Thunder and Rain last Night, (and, in the course of it) our Conductor deserted. Could not find him, embarked one of the others against his will, and took his paddles from the one that remained that he might not follow us, at which he that was in our Canoe got quite enraged, jumped at the Paddle threw it on shore, but we embarked it again and pacified him. At half past 3 left our Campment. In a very short time, we saw a Smoak on the East shore which we made for. Our Stranger began to Hallow to them in a very strange manner. He told us that they were not of his Tribe that they were very wicked and would beat us all, and pull out our Hair etc. The Men waited our Arrival, but the Women and Children took to the Woods. They were only 4 in Number and they began to Harangue us all at the same time before we debarked seemingly in a very violent Passion, but our Hunters could not understand what they said. Our Conductor spoke to them and they became quiet. I made them presents of Beads, Knives, Awls etc. The Women and Children came out of the Wood and met with a similar Treatment. In all they were 15 People, and had a better appearance than any of those we had seen, being healthy and full of Flesh and more cleanly. Their language was something different, but I believe only in the accent, for they and our Conductor understood one another very well, and the English Chief understood one of them, tho' he could not understand him. Their Arms and Utensils differ but little from those I have already described. They have no Iron except very small Pieces that serve them for Knives, which they get from the Eskmeaux. Their arrows are made of light wood and have only two Feathers at the End. They had a Bow which is different in Shape from theirs, and say they had it from the Eskmeaux who are their Neighbours. Its of 2 pieces and a very strong Cord of Sinews along the Back of it tied in different places to keep it to the Shape which is this: When this Cord gets wet it requires a good Bow String and a strong arm to draw it. The former must resist the elastic force of the wood and the Cord (I mentioned above) which is very great when it is wet, as it is much contracted, but when it is dry it extends to its common length and is even then a great support to the Bow. The Vessel they cook their victuals is made of a thin frame of wood, oblonged shaped, the Bottom fixed in a Notch, same as a Cask. Their Shirts are not square at Bottom but Tapering to a point from the Belt downwards before and behind and come opposite the Knee embellished with a short Fringe. They have another Fringe the same as I have already described, with the addition of a Stone of a Grey furmacous Berry of the Size and Shape of a large Barley Corn, brown coloured and fluted which they bore thro' the middle and run one on each String of the Fringe with which they decorate their Shirts by sewing one of them on forming a Demy Circle on the Breast and Back and crossing over both Shoulders. The Sleeves are wide and short, but their Mittens supply this Deficiency, as they are long enough to come over part of the Sleeve, and they wear them continually hanging by a Cord over their Necks. Their lygans want nothing but Waistbands to make them Trowsers. They fasten them with a Cord round the Middle so that they are more decent than their Neighbours. Their shoes are sewed to their lygans and garnished on every seam. One of the Men were dressed in Shirt made of Musqural Skins. The Womens dress is the same with the Mens, only their Skirts are longer, and have not a Fringe on the Breast. They have a peculiar way of tying the Hair of the Head, viz the Hair of the Temples or fore part of the Skull is tied in the Fashion of two *Queues* and hanging before the Ears, the Hair of the Scalp or Crown is tied in the same manner down to where People commonly tie their Hair at some distance from the Head and hangs in Balance the whole with a Cord garnished very neatly with original Hair coloured. Some of the Men only dress their Hair in the above manner, the rest and the Women have it hanging loose long or short. Purchased a Couple of very large origi-

nal Skins from them well dressed. I was surprised to see them
have any as I did not think there were any of those Animals in
the Country, and they tell us that they are very scarce. They
don't know what Beaver is. The Men bro.t Skeef from them, and
Careboof Collars or Snares, Bows and arrows etc. We had a
Mess of most delicious fish from them, less than a Herring spot-
ted Black and Yellow very beautifully had a fin from near the
Head to near the Tail, and when stretched was of a Triangular
form & varigated the same as the Fish, had a small head & a
very sharp set of Teeth. We got the Man who our Indian understood to accompany us which his Predecessor was well pleased
at. He says that we will sleep 10 Nights more before we come to
the Sea that close by are some of his Relations & that three
Nights farther we will meet with Eskrneaux who formerly made
War upon them; but are in Friendship with them at present. He
spoke much in derision of the last Indians who we had seen, that
they were all like old Women & great Liars etc. which coincides
with the Opinion I had already entertained of them. As we were
pushing off some of my Men fired a Couple of Guns load with
Powder at the Report of which the Indians were startled, having
never heard or seen any thing of the kind before. This had like to
have prevented our Indian to fulfil his promise, but our Indians
made him understand that what we had done was as a Sign of
Friendship & prevail'd on him to embark in his own small
Canoe tho' he had the offer of a Seat in our. Two others who he
told us were his Brothers followed us in their Canoes. They
amused us with Songs of their own & some in Imitation of the
Eskmeaux, which seemed to enliven our new Guide, so much
that he began to dance upon his Breech in his small Canoe & we
expected every Moment to see him upset but he was not satisfied
with his confined Situation. He paddled up along Side of our
Canoe & asked us to embark him (which a little before he had
refused) we allow'd him & immediately he began to perform an
Eskmeaux Dance upon our Canoe when every Person in the
Canoe called out to him to be quiet which he complied with &
before he sat down pull'd his *Penis* out of his Breeches laying it
on his hand & telling us the Eskmeaux name of it. In short he

took much Pains to shew us that he knew the Eskmeaux & their Customs. We put on shore to leave his Canoe, & he informed us the opposite Hill the Eskmeaux kill'd his Grandfather three winters ago. We saw a Red Fox & a Sifleur on the Hill, the latter our Conductor's Brother kill'd with his Bow & Arrow. About 4 oClk P.M. we saw a Smoke upon the West Shore traversed & landed. The Natives made a terrible uproar speaking quite loud & running up & down like perfect Madmen. The most of the Women & Children had run off with themselves. I was surprized at their appearing in such a Passion, as the two small Canoes that followed us had been there some time before us (landed). (Perceiving the disorder which our appearance occasioned among these people, we waited some time before we quitted the canoe; and I have no doubt, if we had been without people to introduce us, that they would have attempted some violence against us; for when the Indians send away their women and children, it is always with an hostile design.) I made them Presents of some small Articles but they were fonder of the Beads than anything else I gave particularly Blue Ones. One of them to whom I had given a Knife asked me to change it for three Branches of Beads which I did to please him. I bought two Shirts for my Hunters. They made me a present of arrows & some dry fish which I paid them for. There were 5 Families of them but I did not see them all as they kept in their hiding Places. I suppose there might be 40 People Men Women and Children. Here I learned that they were called *Diguthe Dinees* or the Quarrellers. Our Conductor like the others wanted to leave us here, he was afraid that we should not come back this way, & besides that the Eskmeaux would perhaps kill us & take their Women from my Men & Indians, & that he was afraid of them too. Our Indians told him that we were not afraid & that he need not be, that we certainly should come back this way. He embarked & we pushed off & 8 small Canoes follow'd us. Our Course to Day were S.W.b.W. 6 Miles S.W.b.S. 30 Miles S.W. 3 Miles W.b.S. 12 Miles W.b.N. 2 Miles and we encamp'd at 8 oClk on the East Shore. Those Indians told me that from where I met the first of their People this Morning it was not far to go to the Sea over Land on the

East Side & from where I found them it was but a short way to go to it to the Westward that the land on both Sides the River was like a Point. They don't seem to be Thieves, for we cou'd not perceive that they took or wanted to take anything in that way. As soon as we landed they began to dance which differs in no respect from those we had already seen, when this was over they began to jump; and those two seem to be their favourite Amusements. In the height of the Day the weather was Sultry but towards the afternoon became cold. There is a Quantity of Flax lying on the Ground of last Years & the new plant was sprouting up. I observed this no where else.

Friday, July 10. We embarked at 4 oClock A.M. Not far from our Campment the River narrows between high Rocks & our Course from N.N.W. to S.S.W. say N.W. 4 Miles. Here the Banks get low. From the first rapid the Country does not appear so mountainous but the Banks of the River are commonly high and in many Places quite free of Wood & in others well cover'd with Small Trees of the Fir kind & some Birch. We continue our last Course for 2 Miles more, see Snowy Mountains ahead. Here the land appears low on Both Sides except the above mentioned Mountains which are at about 10 Miles distance. The River widens & runs in many Channels amongst Islands some of which are nothing but a Bank of Land & Mud without a Tree, others are covered very thick with a kind of White Spruce & largir Trees than any we have seen this 10 Days. The Banks of those which are abt. 6 ft. above the Surface of the Water shews a face of solid Ice intermix'd with a Black Earth & as the heat of the Sun melts this Ice the Trees are continually tumbling in the River. We were much at a loss what Channel out of some hundreds to take. Our Conductor was for taking the Eastmost, on account as he said that the Eskmeaux were close by on that Road, but I determined upon taking the middle as it was a large piece of Water and running N. & S. I hoped to get an Observation, and that we could always go to the Eastward afterwards; Our Course W.b.N. 6 Miles N.W.b.W. the snowy Mountains W.b.S. from us and running to the Northward as far as we could see. The Indians say they are part of the chain of Mountains we came to the 3d. Inst. At Noon I got an Observation which gave me 67° 47' North Lat. which is farther North than I expected, according to the course I kept, but the difference is partly owing to the Variation of the Compass which is more Easterly than that I thought I am much at a loss here how to act being certain that my going further in this Direction will not answer the Purpose of which the Voyage was intended, as it is evident these Waters must empty themselves into the Northern Ocean (Hyperborean Sea),s but as it is my Opinion as well as my Mens, that as we would not be able to get to the Athabasca this Season by Water, not but the time would permit but our want of Provision would prevent us, therefore I determined to go to the discharge of those Waters, as it would satisfy Peoples Curiosity tho' not their Intentions. My new Conductor is quite discouraged and tired of his Situation, says he never was at the Billhully Toe (which means Lake) that he only was at Eskmeaux lake, which is not far off, that he never had been at it this way, that he went to it over-land from where we found him and to where the Eskmeaux pass the summer. All this discouraged my Hunters and am confident were it in their power would leave me, as they are quite dis-gusted with the Voyage. I satisfied them a little by telling them I would go on but 7 Days more, and that if I did not come to the Sea in that time I should return, and my scarcity of Provisions will make me fulfil this promise, whether I will or not. Our last Course 32 Miles. The Current is stronger than could be expected in such a low Country. N.N.W. 4 Miles N.W. 3 Miles N.E. 2 Miles N.W.b.W. 3 Miles N.E. 2 Miles. At half past 8 P.M. camped close by where three old Campments since the Ice broke up. Our Conductor says they were Eskmeaux. We saw many wild fowl today. The Natives who followed us Yesterday parted with us close by our Campment this Morning.

Saturday, July 11. I sat up last Night to observe at what time the Sun would set, but found that he did not set at all. At half past 12 I called upon one of the Men to see what he never saw before (when, on seeing the sun so high, he thought it was a sig-nal to embark, and began to call the rest of his companions, who would scarcely be persuaded by me, that the sun had not descended nearer to the horizon, and that it was now but a short time past midnight). We took our Rest till ¾ past 3 when we embarked steering about N.W. The River very serpenting. About 7 oClk see a ridge of high land on the N.E. side. Our Conductor says the Road he wanted to bring us runs along this highland. At 12 oClock we landed at a plain where we observed some of the Natives had been lately, I counted the places of upwards of 30 Fires and some of the Men went further where they saw many more. They must have been here some time, tho' they had made no Huts. There are a great No. of Poles stuck in the ground in the River to which they fastened their Nets, and there seems to be an excellent Fishery here. We saw many [fish] jump out of the Water, one of which fell into our Canoe, which was about 10 Inches long and round. We found scattered round their fire places pieces of whalebone, very thick Leather which had been used, pieces of the Frames of their Canoes &c. We could observe where they had spilt Train Oil in several places. Close by was a Spruce Tree branched up to the Top as a Maypole. The Weather cloudy and disagreeably cold. From this place for about 4 Miles the River is wide, then it runs in narrow winding Channels amongst low Islands with hardly a Tree, and the only ones are Willows, very small and low. At 4 oClock we landed at 3 Huts or Houses. The ground plot of them is an Oval Square about 15 feet long 10 feet wide in the middle and about 8 feet at each End, the half of this is dug about a foot below the surface of the Earth, and covered over with Willow Branches, and I suppose serves for a Bed for all the Family. The Middle of the other part is dug a foot deeper in the ground, and is the only part of the House where a Person can stand upright. The space on each side of this is upon a level with the former, one of which is covered in the same manner, and the other is the Fire place, of which they don't make much (use). Tho' close by the Wall the latter is not burnt. The Door is in the middle of the End of the House, its about 2½ feet by 2, and has a covered way (or porch) 5 feet long. To go into the House you must creep on all fours. There is a Hole 18 Inches Square on the Top of the House, which lets in the light. I suppose some times serves there as a

Door and lets out the Smoak, tho' it is not over the Fireplace. What is under ground of the House is lined with split wood. 6 or 8 Stumps of small Trees drove in the Ground, the Root upwards upon which are laid cross pieces, supports (the roof of) the whole Building. The Top of the House or Roof is a long Square 10 feet by 6 feet, the whole is made of drift wood covered with Branches and dry grass, over which is laid Earth a foot deep. Along side of each of these Houses are two or three Square Holes dug 2 feet deep in the ground, and covered over with split wood and Earth, except in the Middle, and I suppose those are Cellars wherein they keep their Winter's provision. In and about the Houses we found Sledge runners &c. Bones, pieces of whale bone, Bark of Poplar cut round which they use as Cork to Buoy up their Nets to which it is fastened with a piece of Whale Bone &c. and before each Hut are a Number of Stumps of Trees (drift wood) stuck in the Ground, upon which it appeared they hung their Fish. We continued our Route, and at 8 oClk we camped. I suppose our Course about N.W., and allowing for the windings that we came 54 Miles. All day we expected that we should meet with some of the Natives. On several Islands we saw the print of their Feet on the Sand, running after wild Fowls, and by appearance not 3 Days ago. Frequent showers of Rain this afternoon, the Weather raw and very disagreeable. Saw a black Fox. Not a Tree to be seen, except a few Willows which are not above 3 feet high. Our Hunters are in a very bad Humour. Our guide has been telling them that will see the lake to morrow, and that it is not a Lake *Sans dessan* that it is not a small one, that he nor his Relations know nothing about it, except that part of it which is opposite to, and not far from their land, only the Eskmeaux live about it that they kill a large Fish in it which they eat, and from the Description must be the whale, and a great many white Bears, and another large animal, but our Hunters could not understand the Description he gave of it, that they have very large Canoes in which 4 or 5 Families embark. Gave one of my Capots to the English Chief and an Original Skin to our Guide.

Sunday, July 12. Rained hard last Night and till 7 o'Clock this Morning, the Weather is Cold. We embarked, our Course winding as Yesterday. The Wind N.N.W. hardly a Shrub to be seen. At 10 oClock A.M. landed at 4 Huts, same as we saw yesterday. Close by the land is high and covered with short Grass and many Plants, which are in Blossom, and has a beautiful appearance, tho' an odd contrast, the Hills covered with Flowers and Verdure, and the Vallies full of Ice and Snow. The Earth is not thawed above 4 Inches from the Surface, below is a solid Body of Ice. The Soil is a Yellow Clay mixed with Stones. Those Huts appear to have been inhabited last Winter. The Natives had lately been here, the Beach was covered with the Track of their feet, many of their Runners and Bars of their Sledges by the Houses, and laid together, as if they intended to come and take them again. Pieces of Net made of Sinews and some of the Bark of the Willow Tree. The Thread of the former was plated (plaited) and must take them much time and pains to plate such a length of Cord. A square Stone Kettle, could contain about 2 Galls., its very surprising how they could have dug it out (of a solid rock into its present form). The Bottom is flat. Small pieces of Flint fixed into a piece of Wood (we supposed a Knife), several wooden Dishes and Troughs, Stern and part of the Keel of a large Canoe very thick Leather we thot the covering of the Canoe, many Bones of large Size Fish and part of two big Heads, we don't know of what animal. I suppose the Sea Horses! After we had satisfied our Curiosity here, we embarked, tho' we did not know what course to steer, our Guide being as ignorant in this Country as any of ourselves. This appeared to be the Entrance of the Lake, tho' the Current was yet very strong, and set West, and we went with it for a high point about 8 Miles distant, which we took to be an Island separate from the plain, where we had last landed, but we found it to be joined by a Neck of low land. I had an Observation which gave me 69° 1' N.L. From the above mentioned Course we continued the same Course for the Westernmost part of the high Island and the most Western land in St. distant 15 Miles. The Lake was quite open to us to the Westward and out of the Canal of the River not above 4 feet Water, and in some places no more than one, the shallowness of the Water makes it impossible to Cost it to the Westward. At 5 o'Clock we came to the Island and during the last 15 Miles 5 feet was the deepest Water. From here we could see the Lake covered with Ice at about 2 Leagues distance and no land ahead, so that we stopped by the Ice ahead and the Shallowness of the Water along shore, and we landed at the limit of our Travels in this Direction. As soon as our Tents were pitched I ordered the Men and Indians to set Nets, and I went with the English Chief to the highest part of the Island from which we could see the Ice in a whole Body extending from S.W. by Compass to the Eastward as far as we could see. To the Southward we could just perceive a Chain of Mountains extending farther to the North than the Edge of the Ice distant upwards of 20 leagues. To the Eastward are a great many Islands. In our Walk we saw many white Partridges (now Brown) very beautiful Plovers, the nest of one of those I found with 4 Eggs, white Owls, and also the Grave of one of the Natives, by which lay a Bow double Paddle Spear &c. The Indians tell me that they landed upon a small Island, about 4 leagues from here, where they saw the Tracks of 2 Men quite fresh, and that they had taken up a *Cache* of Train Oil. Many Bones of white Bears close by where the Oil was hid. The Wind is so high that we can't visit our Nets. My Men express much sorrow that they are obliged to return without seeing the Sea, in which I believe them sincere for we marched exceeding hard coming down the River, and I never heard them grumble; but on the contrary in good Spirits, and in hopes every day that the next would bring them to the *Met d'Ouest,* and declare themselves now and at any time ready to go with me wherever I choose to lead them. Saw several large white Gatts (gulls), another large Bird, the Back and upper parts of the Wings Brown, the Belly and under part of the Wings white.

Monday, July 13. Soon after we went to Bed last Night, (if I may use that expression, in a country where the sun never sinks beneath the horizon) some of them were obliged to get up and move the Baggage on account of the water rising. At 8 o'Clock A.M. we got up. The Men and Indians went to their Nets. Fine calm Weather. Could not find one of them, the Current and Wind drove it from where thay had set it. In the other caught 7 large white Fish, which are not good, a large white Fish of the small Kind, which is excellent. Another Fish about the size of an Herring, which none of us know, except the English Chief, who says, they are very plentiful at Hudson's Bay. Towards Noon Blows hard from the Westward. Have an Observation which gives 69° 14' N. Lat. by a Meridian variation of the Compass 36 Degrees Easterly. This afternoon I ascended the Hill. I could not perceive the Ice had moved, notwithstanding the force of the Wind. Can just distinguish 2 small Islands in the Ice to the N W by Compass. I gave a new Nett to my Men to mount as we must live upon Fish whenever we can catch any, our Provision being reduced to 6 pieces say 510 lbs. among 15 People, which without any other supply would not last us above 12 Days. One of the young Indians found our Net with 3 of the largest kind of white Fish.

Tuesday, July 14. Blew very hard from the N.W. since yesterday evening. Having sat up till 3 o'Clock this morning, I was late getting up. About 8 one of my Men saw a great many animals in the water which he took to be Pieces of Ice, he waken'd all the others to see this Sight. (About nine, however, I was awakened to resolve the doubts which had taken place respecting this extraordinary appearance.) I immediately knew them to be whales, and ordered the Men, to put the Canoe in the Water, we embarked to pursue them but could not come up with any of them. The Weather being Foggy prevented our going far after them. (It was, indeed, a very wild and unreflecting enterprise, and it was a very fortunate circumstance that we failed in our attempt to overtake them, as a stroke from the tail of one of these enormous fish would have dashed the canoe to pieces. We may, perhaps, have been indebted to the foggy weather for our safety...) Our Conductor says it is such Fish as those the Eskmeaux kill, some of them bigger than our Canoe. What appeared out of the Water of those Fish was quite white, but they appeared too large for Porposes. About 12 o'Clock the Fog cleared away and as I had a Curiosity of seeing the Ice, I ordered my Men to load the Canoe. We embarked, and the Indians followed us. We were not above an hour on the Water, when the

Wind of a sudden rose from the N.E. and obliged us to veer about. The Fog prevented our seeing how near we had been to the Ice & we hardly see the Island we came from. We hoisted our Sail tho' the Wind was very near. The Swell augmented & it was as much as two Men could do to bale out the Water. In short we ran a great risk & never was happier than when we got safe to Land. The Indians were still in more danger than we but very lucky for them they had been much farther to windward than we the Swell in a manner drove them on Shore their Canoes full of Water. In all likelihood had they been loaded we should never have seen them. As I did not chuse to run any more risk this way to satisfy my Curiosity, as soon as the Men had rested we continued going on along the Island, which screened us from the Wind, as I intend to lose two or three Days to search for the Natives among the Islands, from whom perhaps I might get some interesting Intelligence tho' my Conductor assures me they are a very unaccountable set of Beings & most likely he says we would see some of them if we went by the Road he wanted us to come down. At 8 oClk we camped upon the East end of the Island (which I called Whale Island) it's abt. 7 Leagues long E. & W. by Compass not above half a Mile wide. We saw several Red Foxes one of which a Young Man Kill'd. There are 5 or 6 very old Huts on this Point. We set our Nets one of them in 5 fathom water, Current Setting at E. by Compass. This Morning I fix'd a Post close by our Campment on which I engraved the latitude of the Place, My own Name & the Number of Men with me & the time we had been here.

Wednesday, July 15. I happened to wake about 4 this Morning. I was surprized to observe the water had come under our Baggage as the Wind had not changed nor blew harder than when we went to Bed. I waken'd my Men to move the Baggage &c. We were all of Opinion that it was the Tide as we had observed at the other End of the Island, that the Water rose & fell, but we thot. that this had been occasioned by the Wind. It continued to rise till about 6, but I could not exactly know the time as the Wind then began to blow very violently. However to put it out of doubt I intend to remain here till next Morning, indeed if I were willing to go off now the Wind would prevent me. Visited our Nets caught but 8 Fish, had an Observation at Noon 69° 7 North. Towards the Evening the Wind augmented, and the Weather cold. The Indians kill'd 2 Swan.

Thursday, July 15 [16]. Rain'd till 7 oClk this Morning the weather Cold & very disagreeable. As near as the inconstancy of the Weather would allow me to observe the Tide rises 16 or 18 Inches. We embarked & steered under Sail among the Islands in hopes of meeting with some of the Natives but all to no purpose. Our Conductor says they are gone to where they fish for Whales, & kill Rein Deer opposite to his Land, & that he & his Relations sees them there every Year that the Water is very deep there, & that we shall see none of them, without it be at a small River that falls into the grand River from the Eastward, & a good way from hence by the Way that he wanted us to come down. As we give up hopes of seeing any of the Natives here abouts we made for the River & stemm'd the Current at 2 oClk P.M. The Water was quite shallow every where we passed cou'd always find bottom with a Paddle. At 7 oClk P.M. we camp'd, set our Nets. The Indians kill'd 2 Geese, 2 Cranes & a White Owl. We find a great change in the Weather since we entered the River being very agreeable but we are much tormented by Musquittoes in consequence.

Friday, July 17. Took up our Nets caught but 6 Fish. Embark'd at 4 oClk A.M. passed several Campments which appeared not to have been long ago. Landed upon a round small Island, close to the Easter Shore on top of which were many Graves. Frame of Small Canoe, Paddles, Sledges, Dishes Troughs, &c. laying about which makes it evident that the living make no use of the Property of those that die. There was not any of the Skins that covered the Canoe remaining. I suppose it must have been eat up by Wild Animals. The Frame was put together with Whalebone sewed in some parts & tied in others, the whole entire. The Sledges are from 4 to 8 ft. long the Bars upwards of 2 ft. long the runners are each 2 Inches thick & 9 Inches deep, the Curve (prow) is 2½ ft. high & of two pieces sewed with Whale Bone. To this and their other thin Spars of Wood which come to the same height & fixed in runner by means of Mortices are sewed two thin Broad Bars length ways at a little distance from one another. Those Frames are fixed together with 3 or 4 (cross) Bars tied tight down upon the Runners. Upon the lower edge of the latter are peg'd with wooden Pegs Pieces of small Bone or Horn, that they may slide the easier. They draw them by Shafts, tho' I only saw one pair among several Sledges. About half past 1 we came opposite to the first Epinettes (spruce trees). Those upon the Main Land are but few & very small, them that are upon the Island are larger and grow quite close to one another, but only in Patches. Indeed it is surprizing that their should be any Wood at all in a Country where the Ground does not thaw 6 Inches from the Surface. Camp'd at 7 oClock P.M. Fine weather.

Saw many Wild Fowl to-day with their Young Ones, but they were so shy that we cou'd not approach them. The Indians kill'd 2 Grey Cranes & a Grey Brant. 2 of them walk'd the most of the Day in hopes of seeing & killing Rein Deer, they were disappointed saw only a few Tracks. I ascended the high Land from which I had a delightful prospect of the River, Hundreds of Streams meandering thro' Islands some cover'd with Wood & others with Grass, the opposite Mountains about 40 Miles distant. The inland view was neither so extensive nor so agreeable, being terminated by Black Barren Hills at no great Distance, between which are small Lakes or Ponds, & the Country around cover'd with Tufts of Moss, not a Tree to be seen. All along the Hill are a kind of Fence made with Branches where the Natives had set Snares to catch White Partridges.

Saturday, July 18. Took up our Nets without a single Fish. Got underway at 3 oClk A.M. the Weather fine & clear. Pass a No. of Campments the print of the Natives feet (were very fresh) on the Sand, so that it can't be a long time since they have been here. We hope to see some of them at the River at which our Conductor says there always are some, which we will pass tomorrow. We observed a Number of Trees Branched to the Top in several Places, it seems the Natives does this close by their Winter Quarters to direct one another. Our Hunters kill'd two

Rein Deer to Day, the first & & only large Animal which we
have seen since we have been in this River, & is a very season-
able Supply. Our pemmican has been mouldy this long time
past, but in our Situation we must eat it & not loose a particle of
it. We did not lose above 3 Hours time going for the above Animals as they were kill'd on the declivity of the Land in sight of
our Canoe. In the Vallies & Low Land close by the River & facing the Sun are plenty of Cramberries. (It is a singular circumstance, that) can gather those of last Year & those of this year
upon the same Shrub. An other Berry of a whitish Yellow
Colour resembling a Rasberry Pathagominan & very well tasted,
& Number of Plants & Herbs which I am not acquainted with.
The Weather became cold towards the Afternoon, appearance of
Rain. Camp'd at 7 oClk P.M. The Young Indian kill'd 8 Geese.
The most part of the Day I walked with the English Chief and
found it very disagreeable & fatiguing; tho' the Country is so
high its nothing but a Morass except the tops of a few Barren
Hills. I had my Hanger in my Hand & tried frequently if any part
of the Ground thaw'd but cou'd never make it enter above 6 or 8
Ins. The face of this high land to the River is in some Places
Rocky in other Places sandy mixt with Stone & Clay, in this are
Veins of Red Earth which the Natives bedaub themselves with.

Sunday, July 19. Rain'd & blew a hard North Wind till 8 this
Morning. When we got up we found that our Conductor had ran
off with himself. I was surprized at the fellow's honesty, he left
a Skin I had given him to cover himself, & went off in his Shirt,
tho' the Weather is very cold. I enquired of the Indians if they
had given him any reason to desert, or if they had perceived that
he wish'd to leave us. They assured me that they had given him
no reason, that some time ago he was saying to them that he was
afraid we should take him away as a Slave; and that they
believed he was frightenedYesterday when he saw them kill the
two Rein Deer with so little trouble. Towards the Afternoon the
Weather became fine & clear. We saw vast flocks of Geese with
their Young, the Hunters kill'd 22 & the Men 2. They have cast
their feathers & can't fly and are of a very small kind not near as
large as those about Athabasca. At 8 oClock we camp'd close to

an Indian Campment where were traces of Whalebone, Rein Deer Horn, & they had work'd Wood here.

Monday, July 20. Embarked at 3 this Morning. Cloudy weather, small Rain, aft wind. About 12 the Rain pour'd down upon us plentifully, and obliged us to Camp at 2 P.M. We saw great Numbers of Fowl, we killed 2 Geese and 4 Swans, the Indians 8 Geese 4 Brant; we could have killed many more had the Weather been favourable. Passed the River where we expected to have met with some of the Natives without seeing any Signs of their being there lately; saw none of their Campments since 10 oClock A.M. Here abouts the land is not high close by the River, the Hills at a distance are covered with Epinette and small Birch to their Tops.

Tuesday, July 21. Embarked this Morning at half past 1 oClock. The Weather disagreeably cold, Wind S.W. At 10 oClock got out from among the Islands, where the River is but one Channel. We find the Current so strong here that we are obliged to Tow our Canoe with a line. The land on both sides of the River is high and almost perpendicular to the River, the Beach under this is not very wide and covered with Grey Free Stone which falls from the Precipice. We make much more way with the Line than Paddle. The Men in the Canoe spells 2 of those on Shore every two Hours, so that there is always one of them that goes in his turn every 4 Hours without resting, by this way we lose little or no time to rest, but it is very hard Duty. At half past 8 o'Clock P.M. we landed at our Campment of the 9th Instant. About 2 hours after 11 of the Natives joined us, they were Camped further up the River. There were 4 or 5 of those we had not seen before. The Brother of our Conductor inquired after him. We informed him of what happened but it did not satisfy him or any of those along with him. They all appeared anxious, and each made his harrangue upon the Occasion, but our Indians said they did not understand them, that they say they spoke ill. His Brother asked me for some blue Beads, and then that he would believe what we said. I paid no attention to him, ordered one of my Men to deliver him his Brother's Bow and Arrow which he had left with us. All hands were putting their

Fusils in order after Yesterday's Rain. The Natives wanted much to know what we were going to do with them. We shewed them a piece of Meat (and a goose) and told them it was to kill such as that, and that we had no Intention of killing them. They begged that we should not fire now. I made the English Chief ask them some Questions which they did not, or pretended not, to understand, so that we could not learn anything from them. My Men and Indians went to rest. I sat up to observe the Natives Motions. They wanted to know why I went not to Bed, and being busy writing this they had a Curiosity to see and know the meaning of it. About 12 oClock I saw four of their women coming along the Shore. As soon as their friends perceived them, two young Men ran to meet them made two of them return, who I suppose were young and the two others were very old accompanied them to our Fire, remained half an hour and went back again. The Men shortly after made a small Fire for themselves, and slept round it like a parcel of whelps, having neither Skins nor Robes to cover themselves, tho' the Weather is cold. My Men had put their Kettle full of Meat on the Fire. I was obliged to prevent the Natives several times from taking it. This was the first instance I saw of any of them wishing to take what was not their own; but I suppose they think provision should be common Property among all People. This is the first time I saw the sun set since I camped here before as it did not before come near the Horizon, except it was last Night the Weather being so cloudy that I could not see it. The water has fallen at this place upwards of three 3 feet since we passed down.

Wednesday, July 23 [22]. We began our March half past 3 this Morning, the Men on the lines (to tow the canoe) I walked with the Indians to their Huts which were further off than what expected. We took 3 Hours hard walking to get to them. Passed a narrow deep River in our way, at the Entrance of which the Natives had Nets set. They had hid their Effects and young Women in the wood, as we saw but few of the former and none of the latter. They have a large Hut built with Drift wood upon the Declivity of the Beach and dug in the Inside to a level. At each End are two Stout Forks, whereon is laid a strong Ridge

Pole, which supports the whole Structure. Its covered with Epinette Bark to keep out the Rain. Number of Spars at different
heights from one end of the Hut to the other covered with Fish,
split open to dry. They make Fires in different parts of the House
that the Fish may dry the sooner. They have Rails on the Outside
of the House which are likewise covered with Fish, but fresher
than those in the Hut. They appear very careful of the Roes or
Sperme (spawn) of the Fish which they dry in like manner. We
got as many Fish from them as we chose to embark, for which I
gave them Beads, as they were fonder of them than of any thing
I possessed, tho' I did not observe they had any of them. Iron
they put little value in. During 2 Hours that I remained here I
kept the English Chief continually questioning them – the result
of which is as follows That their Nation or Tribe is very numerous, that the Eskmeaux are always at variance with them, that
they kill their Relations when they find them weak. Notwithstanding they promise to be always Friends, they of late have
shewn their Treachery by Butchering some of their People in
proof of which some of the Relations of those deceased shewed
us that they had cut off their Hair upon the occasion, & that they
are determined not to believe the Eskmeaux any more; that they
will collect all their Friends to go to revenge the Death of their
Friends. That a strong Party of the Eskmeaux comes up this
River in their large Canoes in search of Flint Stones to point
their Spears and Arrows, that they were now at their Lakes due
East from where we are now, that the distance is not great over
land, where they kill the Rein Deer & that they will begin soon
to kill big fish for their winter stock, that they know nothing
about the Lake in the Direction we were in. To the *Eastward* &
the *Westward* the Ice breaks up but soon freezes again. The Eskmeaux saw large Canoes full of White Men to the Westward 8 or
10 Winters since, from whom they got Iron of which they
exchanged part with them for Leather. Where the big Canoes
came to, they call Belan howlay Tock (Belhoullay Toe) (White
Mens Lake). That the Eskmeaux dress like them wear their Hair
short, have two holes one in each Side of the Mouth in a line
with the under Lip, in which they stick long Beads, which they

find in their Lakes, their Bows differ from theirs they make use of Slings to throw Stones at their Enemies, at which they are very dextrous. They likewise informed us that we should not see any more of their Relations, that they had all left the River to go & kill Rein Deer for their Winters Provision, & that they intended to do the same in a few Days; that Rein Deers, Bears, Carcajeaux (wolvereens), Martin, Foxes, Hares and White Buffaloe, are the only quadrupedes upon their Lands, the latter are only to be met with in the Mountains to the Westward. Went with the Line all Day except 2 Hours Sailing. We camp'd at 8 oClock. From where we started this Morning, the Banks of the River are well covered with Small wood, Epinette, Birch & Willows. We found it very warm travelling.

Thursday, July 23. Got under way at 6 A.M. Very difficult walking along the Beach. Passed several Places where the Natives had camp'd, & set Nets, since we had passed down. Passed a small River at 5 oClock. Here our Indians put on Shore to camp. We passed, which displeased them very much. They were quite fatigued. Camp'd at 8 oClk at our Campment of the 8th Inst. The Weather very fine to Day. All Day upon the Line. Our Hunters join'd us at 10 oClock very sulky. We did not touch our Provision these 6 Days past in which time we have eat 2 Rein Deer, 4 Swans, 45 Geese 1 Brant & a great many Fish, among 10 Men 4 Women & a Boy. I always found North Men bless'd with good appetites but nothing equal to what ours are, & has been since we enter'd the River. I wou'd have thot. it gluttoness in my Men, did I not find that my own Appetite has augmented in proportion to theirs.

Friday, July 24. We embark'd at 5 oClk but shortly after we were obliged to have recourse to our Line, the Stream being too strong to stem it with Paddles. At 8 we passed a small River at each side of wch the Natives and Eskmeaux get Flint. The Bank is a steep high soft Rock variegated Red, Yellow & Green, & water dropping down it. In some Places it tumbled down & broke into small thin Stones like Slate but not hard. Amongst the small Stones were pieces of petrolium like pieces of Yellow Wax but more triable (friable). The English Chief tells me its such Rock as this that are about the Country where the Chippen-weams get Copper behind the Slaves Lake. At 10 oClk A.M. we have an aft wind & the Men (who had been engaged in towing) embark. At 12 oClk we perceiv'd a lodge close by the Waterside the Natives running about in great confusion & making for the Woods. 3 Men waited our Arrival. They kept at a distance from us their Bows & Arrows in their Hands of which they wanted to shew us the use by snapping the Strings, at the same time making Signs to us not to approach them. The English Chief spoke to them, they understood him a little. I shew'd them some Beads they were afraid to come near to take them, (till) I went up to them and gave them to them. When they first preceiv'd our Sails they took us for Eskmeaux who they say have Sails to their larger Canoes. They ask'd us if we had [word illegible] from them, & if we had kill'd any of them. Likewise if we had seen any of *Diguthe Denue* (Duguthee Denees, or Quarrellers). They thought we had kill'd some of them as they saw us have of their Cloaths Bows &c. They appeared to be of the same Tribe tho' they denied it; I suppose through fear. From those questions its evident they had not heard of our being in the Country. They wou'd not own to us that they had any Women, tho' we had seen them run into the Wood. They said they left them with some of their Relations far from the River killing Rein Deer. It was not a long time that they were here their lodge was not finished & they had no fish adrying. They informed us that we should meet with People close by & that there were a great many at the Rapids. They had a Horn Wedge or Chizel with which they split their Canoe Wood. This I purchased gave them a Knife & a few more Beads. One of my Indians having broke his Paddle wanted to take one from those People. When he took it up one of them ran immediately to him & took hold of the Paddle & was resolved not to part with it. I was obliged to interfere to prevent his getting a beating & loosing his Paddle & he appeared very thankful for the Service I had done him. We lost an hour & a half here. The English Chief (& women) were all this time in the Wood. They had found their Property but not their Women. They took several small things which I did not know of till I had embark'd

& left them, or I wou'd have paid for them. The English Chief is quite enraged against them for running away so. He says his heart is ill made (set) against those Bad Slaves that it is hard to have come so far & not see the Natives & get nothing from them, that they hide all their Goods and Young Women. We camp'd at 7 oClock. Sail'd & paddled since 10 this Morning. Soon after we camp'd an Indian whom we had seen before came to us. His family was at a little distance up the River. At 9 oClock he left us. Fine clear Weather.

Saturday, July 25. We embark'd this Morning (at a quarter) past 3. At 7 A.M. passed the Indians lodge. There appears to have been more than one Family. We suppose that he who came to us last Night must have given the others a bad opinion of us which made them run away. Their Fire was still alive & they left a good many Fish scatter'd about their lodge. The Weather very sultry the Current not so strong, (so that the) paddle (was sufficient for our progress) the most part of the Day. The inland Country mountainous the Banks of the River low & well cover'd with Wood among which is the Aspen Tree tho' small & the first I saw coming up: We saw a Pigeon &c. great many Hares. Passed Many Indian Campments which we did not see when we passed down. About 7 oClk the Sky to the westward became of a steel Blue colour with lightening and thunder in consequence we landed at ½ past 7 P.M. to prepare ourselves against the coming Storm. By the time our Canoes were unloaded & secured & that we were busy erecting our Tents it came on with such violence that we expected it would carry every thing before it. Broke the Ridge Pole of my Tent in the Middle where it was sound & 9½ Inches in Circumference. We were obliged to throw ourselves flat upon the ground to escape being hurt by Stones that were hurled about by the Air like Sand. The violence of the Storm subsided in a short Time but the Sky continued to be over cast & appearance of Rain.

Sunday, July 26. Rain'd hard since early afternoon last Night till this Morning. We embark'd at 4 oClk A.M. at 8 we landed, at 3 (large) lodges of Indians. They were all asleep. They were much disturbed & frighten'd by our wakeing them tho' the most of them had seen us before. Their lodges were hanging as thick with fish as they cou'd hold; (but as we wanted some for present use) we sent some of their Young Men to visit their Nets. They brought us plenty, large White Fish (to which the name has been given of *poisson inconnu*) & a round Green Fish, & a few small White Fish, all very good for which I gave them some Beads & made them presents of some more with several other Articles. They were very fond of Iron Work of any kind. My Men bought several Articles for small Pieces of White Iron (Cannister). There are 5 or 6 Men here that we did not see before, among which is a Dog Rib Indian who left his own Lands on account of some Quarrals. The English Chief understood this Man as well as one of his own Nation. He informed us that he understood from the People with whom he now lives (Hare Indians) that there is another large River on the other Side of the Mountains to the S.W. which falls into the *Belhowlay Toe* (Belhoullay Toe, or White-man's Lake) in comparison to which this is but a small River that the Natives are Big and very wicked kill Common Men with their Eyes, that they make Canoes larger than Ours, that those at the Entry kill a kind of a large Beaver the Skin of which is almost Red, that there has been by Canoes say Ships there often. He knows of no Communication by Water to the above River, those of the Natives who saw it went over the Mountains on Foot. He says that there are a few Beaver on this land which I told him to work & advise the others to do the same & likewise the Martins, Foxes, Beaver, Elic [Elk?] &c. which they might carry to barter for Iron with his own Nation, who are now supplied with Goods by French People near their Land. He was very inquisitive to know if we intend to come back this way again, we told him we did not know. He told us that it is but few of the Natives who are to be seen along the River, that their Young People were killing Rein Deer close by the Eskmeaux Lake where the latter have lately killed one of their Tribe. They say they are very treacherous, that they frequently promise to be Friends which they do not keep longer than they think convenient. They intend to be revenged of them for their last act of Treachery without they pay for the Body of the Person murdered. They say the Eskmeaux Lakes not far off. My Indians wanted to get a young girl that was here. I inquired if they were willing to part with her, but I found that they would not by fair Means, upon no Consideration. Had I not prevented my Indians were going to take her by Force. I am obliged to be very watchful over them, for they are always ready to take things from the Natives without giving them anything in return. About 12 o'Clock we passed a Middling large River from the Eastwards, one of the Natives who followed us told us it was called the *Winter Road River.* We did not find the stream strong to day along shore there being many Eddy Currents. We sailed part of the Day. Camp'd at ½ past 7 o'Clock.

Monday, July 27. Fine Weather, embarked at 20 Minutes past 2 of the Clock A.M. At 7 landed at 3 Families of Natives close by the Rapid. The Indians that followed us Yesterday arrived here some time before us. We found but few People, we supposed that they hid themselves upon the News of our approach. We remained here about 2 hours. Some of the People we had seen before who told us then they had left their Property at a lake close by and had promised to go for them; but they were now no nearer than what they were at that time. They had plenty of Fish, some of which was tied up in Birch Bark. During our stay with them I endeavoured to get some further Intelligence respecting the River I heard of yesterday. They declared to us they knew nothing of it but from hearsay, that none of them were further than the Mountains on the other side of this River, that they were told it was a much larger River than this, that it ran towards the Midday Sun, and that there were People a little further up the River who inhabit the opposite Mountain and had lately come down from them to fish, and who knew the other River very well. I promised some Beads to one of them if he would describe the Country round upon the Land, this he immediately undertook & perform'd. Without paying any regard to Courses, he drew a very long point of Land between the River running into the Great Lake, at the Extremity of which he said there was a *Belahoulay Couin* White Mens Fort, that he did not see but was told of it by other Nations. This I take to be *Unal-*

aschka Fort & of course, the River to the West to be Cooks River & this to fall into or join with Norta Sound not as a River but a Body of dead water. I ask'd this Man if he would go with me across the Mountains to the other River, this he would by no means consent to, alledging that he did not know the Road & that I wou'd get some of the People close by to accompany me as they knew the Road very well, but I believed this more as an excuse than as a truth. I gave him what I promised him & left them. Their is a Man of them who has several Ulcers on his Back, they did not seem to take the least Care of them, only that a Woman was close by him with a Bunch of Branches in her hand keeping off the Flies. We landed at the other lodges at 10 oClk A.M. I ordered my Men to unload as I intended to pass the rest of the Day here, in order to get more familiar with the Natives, that they might answer with less reserve any Questions put to them. (This object, however, was in danger of being altogether frustrated...) My young Indians having arrived here before me, they had some Misunderstanding with the Natives, who upon their Arrival & before they debark'd took hold of their Canoe pull'd it on the Shore. The weight of the People in it Broke it. This they took as an assault & was going to avenge it as such, had I not come up to prevent it. I find the variation of the Compass to be abt. 29 degrees Easterly. At 4 P.M. I ordered my Interpreter to harangue them in Council. After a long discourse cou'd learn very little satisfactory Intelligence. What they said regarding the River to the Westward agreed with what we had already heard but what they say of the Inhabitants is still more absurd; that they are very big, have Wings but don't fly, that they live upon large Birds which they kill with ease, tho' those Birds would kill common Men if they would approach them, that the People at the Entry of the River kill Men with their Eyes & live upon large Beaver one of which they devour at a Meal, that large Canoes come to this Place &c. &c. All this they heard from other People, they were never further than the first Mountains to kill the small white Buffaloe. That the Sources of the River which comes into this River & those that fall into the other are separated by the Mountains, & that they are all very small, that the People on the other Side of the Mountains kill them where they meet. Its very certain that those People know more about the Country than they chuse to tell me at least than what comes to my Ears. I am obliged to depend upon my Interpreter for all News, his being now & long since tired of the Voyage may occasion him to conceal from me part of what the Natives tell him for fear he should be obliged to undergo more fatigues, tho' he has always declared to me that he would not abandon me wherever I went. As soon as we left them they began their fav'rite & only Amusement (except Jumping) Dancing in which Young & Old, Male & Female join'd & continued as they could hold out. They try to imitate the Rein Deer Bear & Wolf in their Pranks or howling. When this Pastime was over I made the English Chief again begin a discourse with them on the former Topic, but with no better success than before. I appeared to be quite angry with [them] and made him tell them, that I thought they did not tell me the Truth, and that if they did not tell me every thing they knew, that one of them must come along with me tomorrow to shew me the road to the other River, for which I would give him Iron Work and Beads for his pains, upon which they all to a man became sick and answered in a very sickly Tone, that they knew no more than what they had already told, that they would die if I took any of them, that they knew nothing of the Road. They began to dissuade my Interpreter from going by telling him that they loved him like themselves, and if he should go he should be killed &c. This and the solicitation of his woman seemed to have the desired effect upon him, tho' he hid from me. I can expect no other account of the Country or the other great River, till I get to the River of the Bear Lake, where I expect to find some of the Natives who promised to wait us there, and who had mentioned this River to me when we passed them, which I paid no Attention to then, as I thot it was a misunderstanding of my Interpreters, or what they might have invented along with their other lies to prevent my proceeding down this River. We are well supplied with Fish, dry and fresh, by the People, they likewise gathered as many *buck* or whurtle Berries for us as we chose, all which accepted Beads,

Awls Knives and pieces of white Iron. I traded a few Beaver Skins from them, they say that they are not very numerous on their lands, that there are likewise a few Moor Deer and Buffaloes. They begged of us not to hurt some of their young Men who were killing Geese upon Islands above here. I made all the Men presents of a few trifling Articles. At Sun Set I was obliged to shoot one of their Dogs, all day we could not keep them away from our Baggage. I had told them before to keep them away but they paid no attention to me. When they heard the Report of the Pistol and saw the Dog dead, they got terribly frighted the women took their Children on their Backs to run into the Woods. I made the English Chief tell them that the Dog was kill'd because he stole our provisions, and to tie all the rest of their Dogs if they did not chose they should be used in the same manner, but that they need not be afraid themselves that we should do them no hurt. The woman to whom the Dog belonged to was crying bitterly, and said she had lost 5 Children last winter for whom she was not so sorry as for the Dog. I gave her a few Beads and an Awl, and all was over. It does not require much Reason to make the Men or Women cry or feign Sickness. When we arrived this day the latter were all in Tears, and we since learn'd that it was for fear that we should take any of them away with us. Indeed they are not very tempting objects, for they are as ugly and disagreeable Beings as can be, notwithstanding which one of our married Men and one of the Hunters got the better of their feelings, and prevailed with two of the above objects to accept of a share of their Bed for the Night, the Reward a small knife, but in place of a Farrian each they had three, the young Men having invited their Companions to partake of their favours, however the Recompence was augmented in proportion. One of the upper part of the Beach here grow plenty of Liquorice & its now in Blossom. I pulled up some of the Roots and eat them. I asked the Natives if they made use of it; [they] told me not, some of the Roots very large and long.

Tuesday, July 28. At 4 this Morning, I ordered my Men to load our Canoe, during which time I went with the English Chief up to the lodges, and found that the most of them had decamp'd in the Night. Those that were remaining were all so sick that they could not rise for fear that I should take any of them along with me. They all said that they would kill Beaver and Martins plenty because the French People were fond of their Skins. They were quite happy when they saw we did not take any of them with us. After we got into our Canoe they came out of their lodges and told us to visit their Nets that were a little way up the River and take all the Fish in them. We took as many as we wanted. We debarked shortly after at 2 lodges full of Fish. There were no people there, we supposed they were amongst those we had just left. My Indians rumaged both lodges and found several small Articles which they took a liking to. I gave them Beads and Awls to put in their place, but they did not understand why this should be left as the Owners were not present. They wanted to keep both. I took up a Net out of the Water and left a Big Knife in place of it. It is not above 4 fms. long and it is 32 Meshes deep. These Nets are much more convenient to set in the Eddy Country than our long ones. This is the place that the Indians call the Rapid. We came up it all the way with the Paddle, so that the Current is not near so strong here as in many other parts of the River, and it is well it is so, for it would be very difficult coming up with line & there being no Beach in many places and the Rocks high and perpendicular, rather hanging over the Water; hundreds of Swallows nests in those Rocks. Very Sultry Weather. At 11 oClk obliged to land to gum our Canoe. This is the first time we landed for this purpose since we left Athabasca. In less than an hour we got ready for marching. At 1 oClk we put on Shore at a Fire which we suppos'd had been kindled by the young Men that were hunting Geese. Our Hunters found their Canoe and Fowl hid in the Wood. They shortly after discovered their Owners and brought them to the waterside. Out of upwards of 200 Geese we picked 36 which were eatable. The rest were quite green and stunk abominably, it was some time since they had killed them, and not gutted them. We could not imagine that any people would eat Rotteness were we not persuaded they do. I paid for those we had taken and departed. At 7 P.M. the Weather became cloudy and overcast, at 8 we camp'd, at 9 it began to lighten and thunder very severely. Soon after came on a perfect Hurricane and heavy Rain, blew down our Tents, and was like to carry away our Canoe, which was fasten'd down to Trees with a Cod line. It lasted 2 Hours and soaked us completely. We were obliged to throw away part of the Fowls, we embarked today.

Wednesday, July 29. The Weather cloudy. Yesterday the Heat was insupportable, and today we cant put clothes enough on to keep us warm. Embarked at a quarter past 4 afterward which drove us on at a great Rate (though) the Current is very strong. About 10 oClk we came to the other Rapid, which we came up with the Line. On the West side found it much stronger than when we went down. The Water has fallen at least 6 feet and has uncovered many Beaches in the River, which we had not seen. One of my young Hunters was liked to get drown'd crossing a River that falls in here from the Westward, its the most considerable one except the River of the Mountains that comes from this Direction. A strong North wind all day and cold. Camp'd at a quarter past 8. We killed a Goose and catched some young ones.

Saturday [Thursday], July 30. Embark'd at 4 oClock this Morning. Rained hard last night, cloudy Weather, but not so cold as Yesterday Wind N.W. Sailed part of the Day, camp'd at half past P.M. We killed 5 old Geese and 30 young ones (which had just begun to fly). The Indians killed 6 old and 10 young Geese. The English Chief had a dispute with one of his young Men. He discovered that he was too intimate with his young Wife, and that she was to run away with him when they would get to their own Country. This is all I could learn of their Discourse. This 2 or 3 Days past we have eat a good deal of the liquorice Root, plenty of which is along the River. We find it a good astringent.

Friday, July 31. Rained all Night and till 9 this Morning when we embark'd. The Wind and Weather as Yesterday. About 3 P.M. clear'd up the wind died away and became warm. At 5 Easterly Wind and cold. Plenty of whurtle Berries, Rasberries &c (and a berry called *Poire*, which grows in the greatest abun-

dance) along the Bank. We are much impeded in our March by
Banks of sand and small Stones, which renders the Water shallow at a distance from the shore. In other Places the Bank of the
River is high of black Earth and Sand continually tumbling, in
some part shews a face of solid Ice, to within a foot of the Surface. We camp'd at a Quarter before 8.7 We killed 5 Geese, our
Indians 2. My foreman had some words with the latter for mim-
icking his way of Paddling. Tonight we begin upon our Corn.
We ate only 3 Days upon our Provision since we began to mount
the Current. It was my Intention to have gone up the River on
the South Side from the last rapid to see if there are any Rivers
of consequence coming in from the westward, but the No. of
Sand Banks & the Current being too strong obliges me to
Traverse to the old Side where the Eddy Currents are very frequent wherein we can set our Nets & make much more head-
way.

Saturday, August 1. Embark'd at 3 this Morning weather
clear & cold wind S.E. At 3 P.M. we travers'd & landed to take
the Line. Here is a Campment of the Natives apparently as if
they had left it Yesterday. At 5 oClk we found a Man, 2 Women,
& 2 Children camp'd close by the Water side. We had not seen
them before. They have but few fish. We enquired if there were
any of their Friends close by, [they] say not, except a Lodge on
the other side & a Man from this ahunting. I find my Interpreter
rather averse to ask such Questions as I desire him. I believe that
he is afraid that I might get some intelligence which wou'd prevent his seeing Athabasca this Season, if he would act as he
ought. We left him with the Indian. We camp'd at ½ past 7 at
our Campmt. of the 5th Ulto. The Indian came along with the
English Chief to our Fire. He says that it is not many Nights
since the Indian who went down part of the River with us had
passed here; that he wou'd meet with 3 lodges of his People
above the River of the Bear Lake, that he knows nothing of the
River to The Westward, only that he heard his Friends say there
was such a Thing. Tonight is the first Time it had been dark
enough to see a Star since we left Athabasca.

Sunday, August 2. We got under weigh with the line at 3 this Morning I walk'd along with the Indians as they went faster than my Men particularly today as (I suspected that) they wanted to arrive at the Natives before us. I observ'd several small Springs of Mineral Water running from under the Mountain, & along the Beach many lumps of Iron Ore. When we came to the River of the Bear Lake I made one of the young Indians remain for my Canoe & took his Place in the Small Canoe. This River is abt. 250 Yds. wide here, the Water quite clear of a (greenish) Sea Colour. Where I landed on the opposite Shore found that the Natives had been lately here from the print of their feet in the Sand. We continued walking on till 6 oClk A.M. when we saw several Smokes along the Shore. We made ourselves sure those were the Natives we were to meet with, therefore hasten'd our Pace. As we approach'd we found a sulpherous Smell & upon our coming to the first found that the whole Bank was on Fire for a considerable Distance; that it is a Coal Mine. The Fire had communicated to it from an old Indian Campmt. The Beach is cover'd with Coals. The English Chief gather'd some of the softest he cou'd find to dye Black. He says it is with this the Natives colour their Quills Black. Here we waited for the big Canoe which arrived an hour afterwards. At half past 10 oClk we saw several Indians Marks (which consisted of pieces of bark fixed on poles), which pointed to the Woods opposite to which is an old Beaten Road & it appear'd People had lately passed in it. The Beach is cover'd with Tracks. A little further were the Poles of 5 lodges standing. Here we landed & unloaded our Canoe. I dispatch'd a Frenchman to see if he could find any Natives within a Days March of us. I wanted the English Chief to go, but he wou'd not, saying that he was too much fatigued & the Young Men wou'd Answer the same Purpose, as we had already seen those People that they wou'd not hesitate coming to see us. This is the first time he refus'd me & I believe its from Jealousy, tho' I have taken every precaution it shou'd not be of the Frenchmen (Canadians). No appearance of Snow on the opposite Mountains, tho' they were almost covered with it when we passed before. Set 2 Nets. At 11 oClk at Night the Frenchman & Indian return'd. They had been to the first Campment where there were 4 Fires, its not long since the natives had left it. They were obliged to make the Tour of several small Lakes which the Natives cross with their small Canoes. The *Encampment* was on the Border of a Lake which was too large to go round & prevented their going any further. They saw several Beavers & Beaver lodges in those small Lakes. They kill'd one, its Furs begin to get long, which is a sure sign of the approach of the Fall. They likewise saw the track of Moor & Rein Deer plenty but old. This being the Time that the Rein Deer leaves the Plains to come to the Wood as the Musquittoes time is almost over, makes me apprehensive that we will not find a single Indian on the River Side as they will be in or about the Mountains setting Snares to catch Careboeuff.

Monday, August 3. We got underway at 4 this Morning. Strong westerly Wind. Cloudy cold Weather. At 12 oClk the weather clear'd up & became fine. The Current very strong. The Water has fallen much since we passed, discover'd many Banks which were not visible. Kill'd 4 Geese of a larger kind than usual. Saw several Indian Campments along the River. Landed for the Night 8 oClkP.M.

Tuesday, August 4. At 4 oClk this Morning we got underway. Fine Calm. There fell a very heavy Dew last Night & was cold. Unloaded our Canoe at 9 oClk A.M. to gum lost about an Hours time. The Weather (became extremely) warm. Saw many tracks of Rein Deer along the Water Side. Camp'd at half past 6 to set our Nets. The Current very strong all Day & difficult walking along the Beach.

Tuesday [Wednesday], August 5. Rose our Nets without a single Fish. The Water is so low that there is not Room in the Eddy Current to set Nets. Current strong as Yesterday bad walking. The Beach is large Stones. It is so cold to day that our marching don't keep us warm with all our Cloaths on. At noon Yesterday we found our Shirt too heavy. Past several Points to day, had we been loaded we shou'd have been obliged to unload to have come up them. Camp'd at 6 oClk very much fatigued. The Indians kill'd 4 Geese. The Mens two Women are continually employ'd making Shoes (of moose-skin), as a pair does not last us above one Day. Of course don't debark out of the Canoe.

Thursday, August 6. Rain'd last Night & this Morning which prevented our getting on our way till ½ past 6 A.M. A strong aft Wind which with the help of our Paddles drove us on at a good rate. We landed at 6 oClk &camp'd to wait our Indians who we have not seen since Morning. At ½ past 7 they arriv'd in a very ill humour. We have not seen the least appearance of Indian Campments since the Day before Yesterday.

Tuesday [Friday], August 7. Commenced our Day at ½ past 3 this Morning. Shortly after we saw two Rein Deer on the Beach a head. We stopp'd & our Indians went to approach them, but they were too ambitious who shou'd first get near them, that they rais'd the Animals, of course lost them. At the same time we saw an Animal traversing, we immediately made for it & killed it. It proved to be a Rein Deer Female, & from the Number of cuts she had in the hind Legs, we judged she had been pursued by Wolves & that they had destroy'd her Young Ones. Her Udder was full of Milk, one of the Young Indians cut it up & emptied the Milk among some boiled Corn & ate it declaring it was (*Wicazen*) delicious. At 5 P.M. we saw an Animal running along the Beach which some said was a Dog & others said was a Grey Fox. Soon after I put a Shore for the Night at the Entrance of a small River, as I thot. there might be some Natives not far off. I order my Hunters to arange their Fuzees & gave them Ammunition to go a hunting To-morrow & at the same Time to look out for Natives in the Neighbouring Mountains. I found a small Canoe in the Edge of the Wood, had a Paddle & Bow in it. It had been mended this Spring, the Bark was much neater sewed than any I had yet seen. We saw many old Campmts. in the Course of the Day. The Current very strong & point (along the points) equal to rapids.

Saturday, August 8. Rain'd exceeding hard all last Night & this Day till past Noon when it clear'd up a little. Strong westerly Wind & cold. At 3 oClk the Indians went a Hunting at 8 they returned without having kill'd anything. They saw plenty Rein Deer Tracks. They fell upon an old Beaten Path which one of them follow'd for some time. He said it did not appear that any of the Natives had passed it for some time past. It began again to rain & continued till the Morning.

Sunday, August 9. We embark'd at half past 3 A.M. the weather Cloudy & cold at 10 it clear'd up. Weather calm & moderate. Saw a small Canoe in the Edge of the Woods. One of the Indians kill'd a Dog very poor. Saw a Number of Places where the Natives had made Fire, by which it appear'd that they do not remain a long time along the River, that they cross from one Side to the other. We saw some Roads which were cut upon each Side opposite to one another. We perceiv'd that the Water rose considerably since last Night. Found the Current strong all Day. We camp'd at 7 oClk.

Monday, August 10. Embark'd at 3 this morning fine clear weather a slight Wind from the S.E. The Indians went ahead ahunting. Loaded (landed) at 10 oClck opposite to the Mountains we had passed the 2d. Ults. to try to ascertain the variation of the Compass at this Place which I cou'd do but imperfectly as I cannot depend on my watch. I find it about 27 degrees Easterly. One of my Hunters join'd us here he had walked all Day not kill'd anything. As this opposite Mountains are the last considerable ones on the S.W. Side of the River I ordered my Men to Traverse the River that I wanted to ascend one of the Mountains. It was near 4 before we landed. I immediately set off accompanied by the Young Indian my Men being more fatigued than curious: & we soon began to experience that we wou'd pay for ours. The Wood which is chiefly Epinettes was so thick that it was with much ado we cou'd make our Way thro' it. After we had walked upwards of an Hours time, the Wood became thinner of the White Birch & Aspen Kind, the former was the largest and the tallest that I had ever seen. When we had travers'd this the Ground began to rise & cover'd with small Pines. Here we got the first View of the Mountains since we left the Canoe upwards of 3 Hours walking, and they appear'd as far from us as when we had seen them from the River. My Companion wanted absolutely to return, his Shoes & Leggins were all torn to Pieces, besides he said that we wou'd not be able to return thro' such bad Road in the Night, however I persisted in proceeding & that we wou'd pass the Night in the Mountains & return in the Morning. As we approach'd them the Ground became quite Marshy & we waded in Water & Grass up to the Middle till we came within a Mile of the Foot of the Mountains, where I fell in up to the Arm Pits & with some difficulty extricated myself. I found it impossible to proceed in a Straight Line & the Marsh extended as far as I could see, so that I did not attempt to make the Circuit, so therefore thought it most prudent to make the best of my Way back to my Canoe (tho' it was Night) when I arriv'd after 12 oClk very much fatigued.

Tuesday, August 11. We observed several Tracks along the Beach & a Campment in the Edge of the Wood which appeared to be 5 or 6 Days old. We would have continued our Rout along this Side the River were it not that we have not seen our Hunters since Yesterday Morning. We embark'd before 3 A.M. & travers'd. At 5 we see two of them coming down the River in search of us, as they were surprized what detained us. They kill'd no large Animals, only one Beaver & a few Hares, & they said that the Wood was so thick near the River that it was impossible to hunt. They had seen several of the Natives Campments not far from the River, & they were of Opinion that they were here when we passed downwards, & their having discovered us is the Reason that we meet with none of them now. I asked the English Chief to return with me to the other Side to endeavour to find those whose Track & Campments we had seen, which he was not willing to do, he wanted to send the Young Men but I cou'd not trust them & am very doubtful me himself. They are still afraid that I may meet with the Natives who might give me Accounts of the other River & that I should go over Land to it, & bring them along with me. I was told to Day by one of my Men that the English Chief his wives & Brother were to leave me, this Side of the Slave Lake to go to the Land of the Beaver Indians, & again the Middle of the Winter wou'd be back to the Slave Lake where he was to meet some of his Relations who went to War last Spring to whom he had given Rendezvous. This he learn'd from one of the young Men. We traversed and continued tracking the Indians till past 12 o'Clock when we lost their Tracks. We supposed they must have crossed to the East side. We saw several Dogs on each side of the River. The young Indians killed a Wolf, which is fat, the Men eat it and declared it to be very good. Killed 15 young Geese which are big and begin to fly. It was 8 o'Clock when we camp'd. Lost upwards of 4 Hours to day traversing, fine Weather all Day.

Wednesday, August 12. All embarked at 3 this Morning. Sent the young Indians across, that we might not miss any of the Natives should there be any along the River. We saw many places where they had made Fire along the Beach, none of them old and fire running in the Wood in many places. At 4 oClock we came to a Campment which the People had left this Morning, we found there Tracks in several Places in the Wood. As I thought they could not be far off, I asked the English Chief to go and try, if he could find them which he seemed loath to do. I told him I intended to go with him, and he could not be off, we parted and went several Miles into the wood but we could not find any thing of them. The fire had ran all over the country, burnt about 3 Ins. of black light soil, which covered a cold body of Clay and which was so hard that the Feet left no Track. At 10 o'Clock we returned from our fruitless Excursion. The young Men kill'd 7 Geese. Had several Showers of Rain with Gusts of Wind and Thunder. The Men set Nets during my Absence.

Thursday, August 13. Rose our Nets without a single Fish and embark'd at half past 3 A.M. Fine weather. Pass a No. of Places where the Natives had made Fires, and many Tracks along the Beach. At 7 o'Clk we came opposite the Island where we had hid our Pemmican, 2 of the young Indians went for it, and found it as we had left it, and is very acceptable to us, as it will enable us to get out of the River without losing much time to hunt. Shortly after we perceived a smoak on the S.W. Shore, 3 Leagues distant, it did not appear to be a running fire. The Indians were a little way ahead of us, and paid no attention to this smoak. They saw a flock of Geese ahead which they fired several Shot on, and we immediately perceived that the smoak disappeared, and soon after saw the Natives run along the Shore and soon embarking in their small Canoes. Tho' we were almost opposite to them, we could not think of traversing without going further upon account of the Strength of the Current. I ordered the Indians to make all the haste they could to go and speak with and make them wait our arrival. As soon as our small Canoe struck off we could see the Natives that were in their Canoes landing, drawing their Canoes on the Beach and making for the Wood. It was past 10 A.M. before we landed at where they left their Canoes which were 4 in Number. They were in such Terror that they left a Number of their Things on the Beach. They did not wait the arrival of our Indians, the latter I found busy running among the things and looking for more in the Wood. I was very vex'd at them, that instead of looking for the Natives, they were separating (dividing) their Property for which I severely rebuked the English Chief. I ordered him, his young Men and my own Men to go and look out for the Indians. I went also, but they were too much frightened and had too much the Start of us to over take them. We saw several Dogs in the Woods, some of which followed us to the Water side. The English Chief was very much displeased that I had reproach'd him, and told me so. I waited such an Opportunity to tell him [what I thought of] his Behaviour to me for some time past, told him that I had more reason to be angry than he, that I had come a great way at great Expence to no Purpose, and that I thot. he hid from me (a principal) part of what the Natives told him respecting the Country &c. for fear that he should have to follow me, and that his Reason for not killing (game, &c.) was his Jealousy, which likewise kept him from looking for the Natives. as he ought, and that we never had given him any reason for such Suspicion.

He got into a most violent Passion, and said, we spoke ill, that he was not jealous, that he had not concealed any thing from us, and that till now there were no Animals, and that he would not accompany us any further tho' he was without Ammunition, he cou'd live the same as the Slaves (the name given to the inhabitants of that part of the country), and that he would remain among them &c. &c. As soon as he was done his Harrangue he began to cry bitterly, and his Relations help'd him. They said

they cried (for their) dead Friend. I did not interrupt them in
their Grief for two Hours. As I could not well [do] without them,
I was obliged to use every method to make the English Chief
change his mind. At last he consented with a great (apparent)
Reluctance, and we embark'd. I sent the young Men across the
River in case we should meet with any more of the Natives they
could not escape from us so easily. What the Natives left behind
were Bows, Arrows, Snares for Moor and Rein Deer, and for
Hares, Fishing Hooks and lines, Nets, a few Bark Dishes, a few
Martin and Beaver, old Beaver Robes, and a small Robe made of
Loopserviers (the skin of the lynx). Their Canoes are curiously
made of the Bark of the Epinette, and can carry two or three
People. I ordered my Men to put their Canoes into the Shade,
gave the most of other things to the Indians (young). The
English Chief would not accept of any of them. I left in place
(and as the purchase) of them fastened upon 3 high Poles, 2
small Pieces of Cloth, small Knives, a File, Beads, Awls, 2 Fire
Steeles, a Comb, Rings. Got a Martin put upon a proper Mould,
as they were not properly moulded, and a Beaver Skin stretched
upon a Frame, to which I tied a Scraper. The Indians are of opinion that the above Articles will be lost as the Natives are so
frightened that they will not [come] back here any more. We lost
6 Hours at this Place. 3 of the Dogs followed us along the Beach.
Camp'd at half past 8 close by the Entrance of the River of the
Mountains: While the Men were unloading I took a Walk along
the Beach and on Banks which were uncovered since we past
down by the Water falling were all over white with fine Particles
of Salt. I invited the English Chief to sup with me. I gave him a
Dram or two and [we] were as good friends as ever. He told me
that it was the Custom of the Chipewean Chiefs to go to War
after the Crees (after they had shed tears, in order to wipe away
the disgrace attached to such a feminine weakness), and that
next Spring he should go for certain, that he would remain and
do as he used to do for the French people till that time. Gave him
a little grog to carry to his Tent to drown his chagrine. The Indians killed 3 Geese today, fair Weather.

Friday, August 14. We embarked at a Quarter before 4 A.M. We went about 2 Miles into the River of the Mountains. Fire on each side of it in the Ground. In traversing I sounded it and found 5, 4½ and 3½ fm Water which is quite Muddy and keeps [distinct from the water] of the Grand River on the West side down to what we call the last rapid where it meets together. Passed several of the Natives Campments. A River on the North side which appeared to be navigable. We camp'd at ½ past 6 P.M. Plenty of Berries which the Men call *Poires,* they are purple (somewhat) bigger than a Pea, very well Tasted, some Goose Berries and a few Strawberries.

Saturday, August 15. We embark'd at 3 oClk this Morning. Till 2 P.M. saw many Campments, along the Water side, since which time very little Beach. Banks of the River high and no Eddy Current. We camp'd at ½ past 5 P.M. The Indians killed 12 Geese (and berries were collected in great abundance). Very sultry all Day.

Sunday, August 14 [16]. Embarked at a Quarter before 4 A.M. Past our Campment of the 30th. June 9 oClk A.M. Here the River is wide and flat along shore, the land on the North side low, soil black, mixt with Stone well covered with Aspin, Poplar, White Birch, Epinette &c. The Current is not strong, we go up it nearly as fast as in dead water. At 12 passed a Campment of 3 Fires, the only one we saw this Day. The Weather as Yesterday.

Monday, August 17. Embarked at half past 3 A.M. We passed 3 Campments. By the manner their *Shude* were made we think that some of the Red Knives must have come down this length and seen some of the Natives tho' it is not customary with them to come this way. I arranged the young Indians late last Night to go ahead to hunt, overtook them at 10 oClk. They had killed some 5 young Swans. The English Chief killed an Eagle, 3 Cranes, a small Beaver, and 2 Geese. We camped at our Camp of the 29th June last 7 oClk P.M. My foreman who lead the March had some words with one of my Steersmen for hard marching, that he did not give them time to eat or smoak &c. They wanted to land to see who was the best Man, but it was not deemed necessary to comply with their request. I interfered and all was over. This is the first and only dispute of the kind that we have had since we commenced our Voyage. One of the young Indians lost a gun belonging to one of the Men, it fell over board out of his Canoe.

Tuesday, August 18. At 4 this Morning I equipped all the Indians to go ahunting and sent them ahead, as our Stock of Provisions is nearly out. We embarked at half past 6 and we traversed to the North Shore where the land was low and almost out of sight. It was near 12 when we arrived. We were 6 Miles to the N of the Main Channel of the River. There were the Tracks and Beds of a Number of Buffaloes here fresh. A River close by which comes from the Horn Mountains, not far off. At 5 oClk P.M. we landed when the Indians had gone ahunting. Before the Canoe was unloaded the English arrived with the Tongue of a Cow (or female buffalo). 4 Men and 2 Indians went for the Meat. It was dark before they came back. The Indians tell me they saw several (human) Tracks in the Sand on the opposite Island. They killed 5 Geese. We came the value of 8 Hours good Marching today.

Wednesday, August 19. Sent the Indians again ahead, to go ahunting when they choosed. The Men gummed their Canoe, having had no time to do it last Night, and we embarked at half past 5 A.M. and at 9 A.M. landed where the Indians went ahunting to wait their return. I found the Variation of the Compass here to be about 20 Degrees Easterly. The Men made themselves Paddles and repaired the Canoes. I observe that the Mens Paddles row very fast in the Water of this River. I do not know what this may be owing to – its some Quality in the Water. The Hunters arrived late without meeting with any large Animals, they killed 3 Swans and 3 Geese. The Woman gathered plenty of small Cramberrries (and crowberries).

Thursday, August 20. We embarked at 4 oClk A.M. Made the Men follow the North Side of the River, tho' the Current is much stronger, to see the River, which the Indians had mentioned to me when going down as coming from the Land of the Beaver Indians and falling in here about, but there proved to be none here, and that he meant the River which we passed the Day before Yesterday (on the line). The Current very strong. Traversed to a Island opposite. Here the Current is still stronger, like a Rapid. Found a Paddle and an Awl on the waterside. The former we knew to be the Crees (Knisteneaux). I suppose it must be the *Mirde Dours* (the chief Merde-d'ours) and his Party who went to War last Year, and has taken this Route on their return to Athabasca, and probably they must have been the Cause of our not seeing many Natives along the River. The Weather Raw and Cloudy which we find very disagreeable It having been so fine and warm several Days before. We camped at half past 7 P.M. on the North side where the land is very low and flat to come near the Shore. The Indians killed 5 young Swan and missed a Bear. Appearance of Rain.

Friday, August 21. Weather cold, a very strong easterly wind, frequent showers of Rain which detained us in our Campment all Day. In the Afternoon the Indians went on the Track of a Moose Deer, had no luck.

Saturday, August 22. The Wind veered round to the Westward, still very strong and cold, as Yesterday. We embarked and in 3 hours time came to the Entrance of the Slave Lake under half sail. With the Paddle, it would have taken us at least 8 hours to come [to] it. The Indians did not arrive till 4 hours after us. The Wind is too strong to attempt going in the Lake. Set a Net, and camp'd for the Night. The Women gather plenty of Berries viz. *Quiei de Pouilles* Cramberries, Crow Berries, and original Berries. The Indians killed 2 Swans, 1 Geese, the Men 2 Geese.

Sunday, August 23. Embarked at 5 A.M. Rose our Nets, caught 5 small Pike. Entered the Lake thro' the same Entrance we came out of it, tho' the South side of the Lake would be the shortest road, but we are not sure of there being a good Fishery along the Coast, and we are certain of catching plenty the way we came, besides I expect to find Mr. Leroux where I left him, having given him orders to remain there till the Fall, and I can leave what goods I have left with him, if I find it necessary he should Winter. We paddled a long way into a deep Bay to take the wind. When we came to hoist sail we found we had forgot our Mast at our Campment. Landed and cut another. Hoisted half sail which drove us on at a great rate. At 12 the wind and Swell augmented much, our underyard broke, but luckily our Mast Top resisted till we had time to fasten down the Yard with a Pole without lowering sail. Took in much Water, and had our Mast given in all probability we should have filled and sunk. We went on with great Danger, being along a flat lee shore, not able to land till 3 O'Clock P.M. 2 Men continually Bailing out the Water which we took in on every side. Doubled a Point which screened us from the Wind and swell. Camped for the Night, and to wait for our Indians, set Nets, made a Yard and Mast. Gummed our Canoe, visited our Nets, caught 6 small white Fish, and 2 pike, gathered plenty Cramberries and Crow Berries. Towards Night the weather became moderate.

Monday, August 24. Rose our Nets, caught 14 white Fish, 10 pike, and 2 trout. Embarked at 5 A.M. Small Breezes from the southward, hoisted sail, went on slowly as our Indians are behind. At 11 A.M. landed, to boil Kettle and dry our Nets that they may be ready for to set to Night. At one we again got under way. At 4 we perceived a (large) Canoe with a sail and two small ones ahead. We soon came up with them, and found them Mr. Leroux, his Father in Law and Family on ahunting Party, 26 Days since he left his House. It was his Intention to have gone as far as the Entrance of the River to leave a Letter for me in case I should pass. He had seen no more Indians where I had left him. Had made a Voyage to *Lac la Merde* (Lac la Marte), where he found 18 small Canoes, of the Slave Indians of whom he got 5 Pack chiefly Martins. There were 4 Beaver Indians among them, who had traded the greatest part of the above with the Slaves before his arrival. They informed him that their Relations had more Skins but that they were afraid to come with them, tho' they had heard French People were to come with Goods to meet them. He gave them a pair of Trenches (ice chisels) each and other Trifles, sent them back to conduct their Friends to the Slave Lake, where he told them he was to remain next Winter. The Red Knives and Slaves were almost all gone to the *Carabouf* Country he sent them Pawles. He has sent 16 ½ Packs to

Athabasca, wrote for more Goods which I had ordered him only to do in case he made 30 Packs, as I thot. it hardly worth while to establish a Post at such a distance without it produced that Number, but it was the above reasons and his hopes of seeing them on the first Ice, which induced him to ask for Goods. As soon as we landed my Men and Mr. Leroux's Men set 3 Nets, soon after caught 20 Fish of different sorts. About Dusk the English Chief arrived, came to my Tent with a most pitiful look, that he had like to have got drowned following us, that his Brother and other young Men had a very narrow Escape. Their Canoes broke at a distance from the Shore, but as it was flat they made their Escape by his help. He left them crying to overtake me, that I might wait for them; that he is afraid they will not be able to mend their Canoe, &c. &c.

Tuesday, August 25. It was late this Morning before we got up. Gave some Rum to my Men last Night to divert themselves. Visited our Nets, caught but few Fish. My Men live upon Leroux's Stores. At 11 A.M. the young Men arrived and reproached me for having left them so far behind. They had killed 2 Swans, and brought me one of them. The Wind southerly all Day, and too strong for us, are we at the Foot of a Grand Traverse. At Noon I had an Observation 61° 29' North. Can't visit our Nets. In the afternoon the Sky became overcast, lightening and loud Claps of Thunder. The Wind veered round to the Westward and blew a Hurricane.

Wednesday, August 22 [26]. Rained all last Night and till 8 this morning, the wind as yesterday. The Indians went ahunting, came back in the evening without killing anything. The English Chief missed an original. In the Afternoon heavy showers thunder &c.

Thursday, August 27. Embarked before 4 A.M., hoisted sail at 9 A.M., landed to Cook Kettle (to dress victuals) and wait for Mr. Leroux and Indians. The former joined us at 11 o'Clock and we got under way. Fine calm. At 4 P.M. Mr. Leroux broke his Canoe, landed to mend it. A little Breeze from the southward, which we took the advantage of. At ½ past 5 P.M. camp'd, set our Nets. No word of Mr. Leroux or the Indians, heard them

Fire. The English Chief and People are quite exhausted with fatigue. He wanted to remain this morning to go to the Land of the Beaver Indians, and that he would be back to Athabasca in the course of the Winter.

Friday, August 28. Blew hard all last Night and this Morning, had much difficulty to go to our Nets. Caught plenty white Fish, Trout, &c. Towards the Afternoon the wind augmented. 2 of the Men who were gathering Berries saw 2 original (moosedeer), the Tracks of Buffaloes and Rein Deer. At Sun Set we heard 2 shot, saw a fire on the opposite side of the Bay. We made a great fire that they might see where we are. After we all had gone to Bed heard the Report of a Gun. Soon after the English Chief made his appearance in a great flurry and quite wet, informed us that he believed the Frenchmen were drowned, and that his Brother and Companions had got their Canoe broke to Pieces, lost their Guns and the Meat of a Rein Deer which they had killed this morning, that they were close by, asked a Frenchman to go and carry (fire... to) them as they were starving with cold however they and his women joined us. We gave them dry clothes to put on. It was so dark that it was impossible for us to go and look out for Mr. Leroux who they said had taken the Traverse along with them.

Saturday, August 29. By the Break of Day I got up and went to see if I could learn anything of Mr. Leroux. Before I came to where the Indians had landed, I saw a man coming along the Beach. It was an Indian who Mr. Leroux sent to tell me to send Men for the Meat of a Carrabouf, which he got from the Indian who had left him some time ago. He says their Canoe was full of Water when they landed last Night. Sent Men for the Meat. My Indians went ahunting. At 11 oClk A.M. Mr. Leroux and his Indians arrived. The Hunters without killing anything. They are determined not to follow me any more, because they already ran so much risk and they are afraid of getting drowned. In the Afternoon it became Calm, and I sent Mr. Leroux and all the Indians off and told them I should leave them all when Mr. Leroux had built, and that I would follow, tonight. Set our Nets.

Sunday, August 30. Embarked at 1 this morning. Rose our Nets with a large Trout and 20 white Fish. At Sun rise passed Mr. Leroux and Indians where they had landed to rest a few Hours. About this time a smart aft Breeze arose which wafted us to Mr. Leroux's House, by 2 P.M. It was late before the Indians arrived. According to promise I gave my Indians a good Equipment of Iron work, ammunition Tobacco &c. &c. as a recompence for the misery they underwent along with me. I ordered the English Chief to go to the land of the Beaver Indians to bring them to Trade their Piltras (peltries) with Mr. Leroux who I leave here to Winter. Gave the latter what Goods I had remaining, and promised to send him a few more Pieces, Should I not meet them after my arrival at Athabasca, as it will be the same Expence sending them now or next Spring, and by remaining here will be sure of what the Country is able to produce. The English Chief is to be at Athabasca in the Month of March next with plenty of Beaver and Martins.

Monday, August 31. I did not go to Bed all last Night, getting everything in order to embark this Morning (and to prepare instructions for Mr. Le Roux). Got a Bag of pounded Meat and a little Grease from Mr. Leroux suppose 80 lbs. Parted with them at 5 A.M. Fine calm. At 10 A.M. we were obliged to land upon a small Island our Canoe taking in more Water than common. We found that the Indian children had shot an Arrow throw her under Water Mark. Cooked a Kettle of Fish here lost 1½ Hour. At 12 the Wind rose from the S E this being the Direction we went in, impeded our March considerably. I had an Observation 62° 15 North. Camped at 7 oClock.

Tuesday, September 1. We embarked at 5 A.M., fine Calm Weather, passed the Isles *la Cache* at 12 could not perceive the land which we saw to the south when we passed here before. Passed the Carabouf Island at 5P.M. See land to the S and b.W, which we think is the opposite (side) of the lake extending a great distance. Camp'd at half past 6 P.M. Thunder and appearance of a change of Weather.

Thursday [Wednesday]. September 2. Rained and blew hard the latter part of the last Night. The Rain subsided at half past 6

A.M. when we embarked. In a Traverse of 12 Miles took a good deal of Water. At 12 it became Calm, had an observation 61° 36 North. At 3 P.M. a slight Breeze from the Westward, it soon encreased. We hoisted sail and took a Traverse of 24 Miles for the point of the old Fort where we arrived and landed for the Night at 7 o'Clock. Our taking this Traverse shortened our Road 3 Leagues, we did not expect to have got clear of the lake in such a situation.

Thursday, September 3. Blew exceeding hard all Night. We embarked at 4 A.M. and took us 3 hours to go 5 Miles without stopping, notwithstanding we were screened from the Swell by a large Bank. Here we enter the (small) River where the Wind has no effect upon us. Frequent showers today. Camp'd at 6P.M.

Friday, September 4. Dark and Cloudy weather at 5 A.M. At 10 A.M. we embarked. Cleared up, see (a) few Fowl. Camped at 7.

Saturday, September 5. Cloudy weather, embarked at 5 A.M. At 8 began to rain very hard, put on shore and camp'd half an hour after. Detained all day.

Sunday, September 6. Rained all last Night. A strong North Wind. Many numerous Flocks of wild fowl, pass to the Southward. At 6 A.M. the rain subsided a little, we embarked but it soon began again to pour down in Streams on us. An aft wind which we took the advantage of at the Expence of a complete Soaking. Killed 7 Geese today. Camped at ½ past 6P.M.

Monday, September 7. Embarked at half past 5 this morning, a hard wind, frequent showers of small Rain. At 3 oClkP.M. ran our Canoe upon a Stump, and before we could land she filled with Water. We took 2 Hours to repair her. We camped at 7 oClk P.M.

Tuesday, September 8. Embarked at ½ past 4 A.M. A thick Mist till 9 A.M. when it cleared away, fine weather. At 3 P.M. came to the first carrying place (Portage la Noyz) *(Portage des Noyes).* We camped at the upper end of it to dry our things, some of which are almost rotten.

Wednesday, September 9. At 5 A.M. the Canoe broke on the Mens shoulders in Portage De Chilique *(Portage du Chetique).*

The guide mended her while the others carried the Baggage. Gummed our Canoe at Portage *La Montagne.* Passed Portages De Epinette De Barrel De Embarass and De Casette and camped at Riviere au Chien (Dog River) at ½ past 4 P.M. Men much fatigued. Gummed our Canoe, made Paddles to replace some broke coming up the Rapids, killed a Swan.

Tuesday [Thursday], September 10. Embarked at ½ past 5 A.M. Rained and blew hard last Night. This Morning the former subsided and the latter augmented. Wind N.W. At 7 A.M. hoisted sail. In the afternoon frequent Showers of Rain and Hail, in the afternoon 2 Showers of Snow the wind very strong. At 6 oClock landed at a lodge of Crees (Knisteneaux), 3 Men and Women (children) they are on their return from War, one of them very sick. They parted with the rest of their Party in the Enemies Country thro' Hunger (say 2 Men and their Families). After they had separated they met with a Family of the Enemy and destroyed them. They do not know what is become of their Friends, they suppose they have returned from the Peace River or starved. I gave Medicine to the Sick, and a little ammunition to the healthy which they were much in Need of, having lived by their Bows and arrows this 6 Months, they have suffered very much.

Friday, September 11. Embarked at half past 4 A.M. Froze hard last Night, cold weather throughout the Day, appearance of Snow. At 6 oClkP.M. landed for the Night at our Campment (of the third of June), the wind at N E and cold.

At 8 oClock entered the lake of the Hills, at 10 the Wind veered to the Westward, and as strong as we could bear it with high sail, which wafted us to Fort Chipewean by 3 oClk P.M. Here we found Mr. McLeod with 5 Men busy building a new House.

102 Days since we had left this Place.

PART 3

JOURNAL OF A VOYAGE
FROM
FORT CHIPEWYAN
TO THE
PACIFIC OCEAN
IN 1793

Chapter 1

PEACE RIVER

Wednesday, October 10, 1792. Having made every necessary preparation, I left Fort Chepewyan, to proceed up the Peace River. I had resolved to go as far as our most distant settlement, which would occupy the remaining part of the season, it being the route by which I proposed to attempt my next discovery, across the mountains from the source of that river; for whatever distance I could reach this fall, would be a proportionate advancement of my voyage.

In consequence of this design, I left the establishment of Fort Chepewyan, in charge of Mr. Roderic Mackenzie, accompanied by two canoes laden with the necessary articles for trade: we accordingly steered West for one of the branches that communicates with the Peace River, called the Pine River; at the entrance of which we waited for the other canoes, in order to take some supplies from them, as I had reason to apprehend they would not be able to keep up with us. We entered the Peace River at seven in the morning of the 12th, taking a Westerly course. It is evident, that all the land between it and the Lake of the Hills, as far as the Elk River, is formed by the quantity of earth and mud, which is carried down by the streams of those two great rivers. In this space there are several lakes. The lake, Clear Water, which is the deepest, Lake Vassieu, and the Athabasca Lake, which is the largest of the three, and whose denomination in the Knistineaux language, implies, a flat low, swampy country, subject to inundations. The two last lakes are now so shallow, that, from the cause just mentioned, there is every reason to expect, that in a few years, they will have exchanged their character and become extensive forests.

This country is so level, that, at some seasons, it is entirely overflowed, which accounts for the periodical influx and reflux of the waters between the Lake of the Hills and the Peace River.

On the 13th at noon we came to the Peace Point; from which, according to the report of my interpreter, the river derives its name; it was the spot where the Knisteneaux and Beaver Indians settled their dispute; the real name of the river and point being that of the land which was the object of contention.

When this country was formerly invaded by the Knisteneaux, they found the Beaver Indians inhabiting the land about Portage la Loche; and the adjoining tribe were those whom they called slaves. They drove both these tribes before them; when the latter proceeded down the river from the Lake of the Hills, in consequence of which that part of it obtained the name of the Slave River. The former proceeded up the river; and when the Knisteneaux made peace with them, this place was settled to be the boundary.

We continued our voyage, and I did not find the current so strong in this river as I had been induced to believe, though this, perhaps, was not the period to form a correct notion of that circumstance, as well as of the breadth, the water being very low; so that the stream has not appeared to me to be in any part that I have seen, more than a quarter of a mile wide.

The weather was cold and raw, so as to render our progress unpleasant; at the same time we did not relax in our expedition, and, at three on the afternoon of the 17th we arrived at the falls. The river at this place is about four hundred yards broad, and the fall about twenty feet high: the first carrying place is eight hundred paces in length, and the last, which is about a mile onwards, is something more than two thirds of that distance. Here we found several fires, from which circumstance we concluded, that the canoes destined for this quarter, which left the fort some days before us, could not be far a-head. The weather continued to be very cold, and the snow that fell during the night was several inches deep.

On the morning of the 18th, as soon as we got out of the draught of the fall, the wind being at North-East, and strong in our favour, we hoisted sail, which carried us on at a considerable rate against the current, and passed the Loon River before twelve o'clock; from thence we soon came along the Grande Isle, at the upper end of which we encamped for the night. It now froze very hard: indeed, it had so much the appearance of winter, that I began to entertain some alarm lest we might be stopped by the ice: we therefore set off at three o'clock in the morning of the 19th, and about eight we landed at the Old Establishment.

The passage to this place from Athabasca having been surveyed by M. Vandrieul, formerly in the Company's service, I did not think it necessary to give any particular attention to it; I shall, however, just observe, that the course in general from the Lake of the Hills to the falls, is Westerly, and as much to the North as the South of it, from thence it is about West-South-West to this fort.

The country in general is low from our entrance of the river to the falls, and with the exception of a few open parts covered with grass, it is clothed with wood. Where the banks are very low the soil is good, being composed of the sediment of the river and putrefied leaves and vegetables. Where they are more elevated, they display a face of yellowish clay, mixed with small stones. On a line with the falls, and on either side of the river, there are said to be very extensive plains, which afford pasture to numerous herds of buffaloes. Our people a-head slept here last night, and, from their carelessness, the fire was communicated to and burned down, the large house, and was proceeding fast to the smaller buildings when we arrived to extinguish it.

We continued our voyage, the course of the river being South-West by West one mile and a quarter, South by East one mile, South-West by South three miles, West by South one mile, South-South-West two miles, South four miles, South-West seven miles and an half, South by West one mile, North-North-West two miles and an half, South five miles and a quarter,

South-West one mile and an half, North-East by East three miles and an half, and South-East by East one mile.

We overtook Mr. Finlay, with his canoes, who was encamped near the fort of which he was going to take the charge, during the ensuing winter, and made every necessary preparative for a becoming appearance on our arrival the follow-ing morning. Although I had been since the year 1787 in the Athabasca country, I had never yet seen a single native of that part of it which we had now reached.

At six o'clock in the morning of the 20th, we landed before the houses amidst the rejoicing and firing of the people, who were animated with the prospect of again indulging themselves in the luxury of rum, of which they had been deprived since the beginning of May; as it is a practice throughout the North-West, neither to sell or give any rum to the natives during the summer. There was at this time only one chief with his people, the other two being hourly expected with their bands; and on the 21st and 22nd they all arrived except the war chief and fifteen men. As they very soon expressed their desire of the expected regale, I called them together, to the number of forty-two hunters, or men capable of bearing arms, to offer some advice, which would be equally advantageous to them and to us, and I strengthened my admonition with a nine gallon cask of reduced rum and a quan-tity of tobacco. At the same time I observed, that as I should not often visit them, I had instanced a greater degree of liberality than they had been accustomed to.

The number of people belonging to this establishment amounts to about three hundred, of which, sixty are hunters. Although they appear from their language to be of the same stock as the Chepewyans, they differ from them in appearance, manners, and customs, as they have adopted those of their former enemies, the Knisteneaux: they speak their language, as well as cut their hair, paint, and dress like them, and possess their immoderate fondness for liquor and tobacco. This descrip-tion, however, can be applied only to the men, as the women are less adorned even than those of the Chepewyan tribes. We could not observe, without some degree of surprize, the contrast between the neat and decent appearance of the men, and the nastiness of the women. I am disposed, however, to think that this circumstance is generally owing to the extreme submission and abasement of the latter: for I observed, that one of the chiefs allowed two of his wives more liberty and familiarity than were accorded to the others, as well as a more becoming exterior, and their appearance was proportionably pleasing. I shall, however, take a future opportunity to speak more at large on this subject.

There were frequent changes of the weather in the course of the day, and it froze rather hard in the night. The thickness of the ice in the morning was a sufficient notice for me to proceed. I accordingly gave the natives such good counsel as might influence their behaviour, communicated my directions to Mr. Finlay for his future conduct, and took my leave under several vollies of musketry, on the morning of the 23d. I had already dispatched my loaded canoes two days before, with directions to continue their progress without waiting for me. Our course was South-South-East one mile and an half, South three quarters; East seven miles and an half, veering gradually to the West four miles and an half. South-East by South three miles, South-East three miles and an half, East-South-East to Long Point three miles, South-West one mile and a quarter, East by North four miles and three quarters, West three miles and an half, West-South-West one mile, East by South five miles and an half, South three miles and three quarters, South-East by South three miles, East-South-East three miles, East-North-East one mile, when there was a river that flowed in on the right, East two miles and an half, East-South-East half a mile, South-East by South seven miles and an half, South two miles, South-South-East three miles and an half; in the course of which we passed an island South by West, where a rivulet flowed in on the right, one mile, East one mile and an half, South five miles, South-East by South four miles and an half, South-West one mile, South-East by East four miles and an half, West-South-West half a mile, South-West six miles and three quarters, South-East by South one mile and an half, South one mile and an half, South-East by South two miles, South-West three quarters of a mile, South-

East by South two miles and an half, East by South one mile and three quarters, South two miles, South-East one mile and an half, South-South-East half a mile, East by South two miles and an half, North-East three miles, South-West by West short distance to the establishment of last year, East-North-East four miles, South-South-East one mile and three quarters, South half a mile, South-East by South three quarters of a mile, North-East by East one mile, South three miles, South-South-East one mile and three quarters, South by East four miles and an half, South-West three miles, South by East two miles, South by West one mile and an half, South-West two miles, South by West four miles and an half, South-West one mile and an half, and South by East three miles. Here we arrived at the forks of the river; the Eastern branch appearing to be not more than half the size of the Western one. We pursued the latter, in a course South-West by West six miles, and landed on the first of November at the place which was designed to be my winter residence: indeed, the weather had been so cold and disagreeable, that I was more than once apprehensive of our being stopped by the ice, and, after all, it required the utmost exertions of which my men were capable to prevent it; so that on their arrival they were quite exhausted. Nor were their labours at an end, for there was not a single hut to receive us: it was, however, now in my power to feed and sustain them in a more comfortable manner.

We found two men here who had been sent forward last spring, for the purpose of squaring timber for the erection of an house, and cutting pallisades, &c. to surround it. With them was the principal chief of the place, and about seventy men, who had been anxiously waiting for our arrival, and received us with every mark of satisfaction and regard which they could express. If we might judge from the quantity of powder that was wasted on our arrival, they certainly had not been in want of ammunition, at least during the summer.

The banks of the river, from the falls, are in general lofty, except at low woody points, accidentally formed in the manner I have already mentioned: they also displayed, in all their broken parts, a face of clay, intermixed with stone; in some places there likewise appeared a black mould.

In the summer of 1788, a small spot was cleared at the Old Establishment, which is situated on a bank thirty feet above the level of the river, and was sown with turnips, carrots, and parsnips. The first grew to a large size, and the others thrived very well. An experiment was also made with potatoes and cabbages, the former of which were successful; but for want of care the latter failed. The next winter the person who had undertaken this cultivation, suffered the potatoes, which had been collected for seed, to catch the frost, and none had been since brought to this place. There is not the least doubt but the soil would be very productive, if a proper attention was given to its preparation. In the fall of the year 1787, when I first arrived at Athabsaca, Mr. Pond was settled on the banks of the Elk River, where he remained for three years, and had formed as fine a kitchen garden as I ever saw in Canada.

In addition to the wood which flourished below the fall, these banks produce the cypress tree, arrow-wood, and the thorn. On either side of the river, though invisible from it, are extensive plains, which abound in buffaloes, elks, wolves, foxes, and bears. At a considerable distance to the Westward, is an immense ridge of high land or mountains, which take an oblique direction from below the falls, and are inhabited by great numbers of deer, who are seldom disturbed, but when the Indians go to hunt the beaver in those parts; and, being tired of the flesh of the latter, vary their food with that of the former. This ridge bears the name of the Deer Mountain. Opposite to our present situation, are beautiful meadows, with various animals grazing on them, and groves of poplars irregularly scattered over them.

My tent was no sooner pitched, than I summoned the Indians together, and gave each of them about four inches of Brazil tobacco, a dram of spirits, and lighted the pipe. As they had been very troublesome to my predecessor, I informed them that I had heard of their misconduct, and was come among them to inquire into the truth of it. I added also that it would be an established rule with me to treat them with kindness, if their behaviour should be such as to deserve it; but, at the same time, that I should be equally severe if they failed in those returns which I had a right to expect from them. I then presented them with a quantity of rum, which I recommended to be used with discretion; and added some tobacco, as a token of peace. They, in return, made me the fairest promises; and, having expressed the pride they felt on beholding me in their country, took their leave.

I now proceeded to examine my situation; and it was with great satisfaction I observed that the two men who had been sent hither some time before us, to cut and square timber for our future operations, had employed the intervening period with activity and skill. They had formed a sufficient quantity of pallisades of eighteen feet long, and seven inches in diameter, to inclose a square spot of an hundred and twenty feet; they had also dug a ditch of three feet deep to receive them; and had prepared timber, planks &c. for the erection of an house.

I was, however, so much occupied in settling matters with the Indians, and equipping them for their winter hunting, that I could not give my attention to any other object, till the 7th, when I set all hands at work to construct the fort, build the house, and form store-houses. On the preceding day the river began to run with ice, which we call the last of the navigation. On the 11th we had a South-West wind, with snow. On the 16th the ice stopped in the other fork, which was not above a league from us across the intervening neck of land. The water in this branch continued to flow till the 22d, when it was arrested also by the frost, so that we had a passage across the river, which would last to the latter end of the succeeding April. This was a fortunate circumstance, as we depended for our support upon what the hunters could provide for us, and they had been prevented by the running of the ice from crossing the river. They now, however, very shortly procured us as much fresh meat as we required, though it was for some time a toilsome business to my people, for as there was not yet a sufficient quantity of snow to run sledges, they were under the necessity of loading themselves with the spoils of the chase.

On the 27th the frost was so severe that the axes of the workmen became almost as brittle as glass. The weather was very various until the 2d of December, when my Farenheit's thermometer was injured by an accident, which rendered it altogether useless. The following table, therefore, from the 16th of November, to this unfortunate circumstance, is the only correct account of the weather which I can offer.

In this situation, removed from all those ready aids which add so much to the comfort, and indeed is a principal characteristic of civilized life, I was under the necessity of employing my judgment and experience in accessory circumstances, by no means connected with the habits of my life, or the enterprise in which I was immediately engaged. I was now among a people who had no knowledge whatever of remedial application to those disorders and accidents to which man is liable in every part of the globe, in the distant wilderness, as in the peopled city. They had not the least acquaintance with that primitive medicine which consists in an experience of the healing virtues of herbs and plants, and is frequently found among uncivilised and savage nations. This circumstance now obliged me to be their physician and surgeon, as a woman with a swelled breast, which had been lacerated with flint stones for the cure of it, presented herself to my attention, and by cleanliness, poultices, and healing salve, I succeeded in producing a cure. One of my people also, who was at work in the woods, was attacked with a sudden pain near the first joint of his thumb, which disabled him from holding an axe. On examining his arm, I was astonished to find a narrow red stripe, about half an inch wide, from his thumb to his shoulder; the pain was violent, and accompanied with chilliness and shivering. This was a case that appeared to be beyond my skill, but it was necessary to do something towards relieving the mind of the patient, though I might be unsuccessful in removing his complaint. I accordingly prepared a kind of volatile liniment of rum and soap, with which I ordered his arm to be rubbed, but with little or no effect. He was in a raving state throughout the night, and the red stripe not only increased, but was also accompanied with the appearance of several blotches on his body, and pains in his stomach: the propriety of taking some blood from him now occurred to me, and I ventured, from absolute necessity, to perform that operation for the first time, and with an effect that justified the treatment. The following night afforded him rest, and in a short time he regained his former health and activity.

I was very much surprised on walking in the woods at such an inclement period of the year, to be saluted with the singing of birds, while they seemed by their vivacity to be actuated by the invigorating power of a more genial season. Of these birds the male was something less than the robin; part of his body is of a delicate fawn colour, and his neck, breast, and belly, of a deep scarlet; the wings are black, edged with fawn colour, and two white stripes running across them; the tail is variegated, and the head crowned with a tuft. The female is smaller than the male, and of a fawn colour throughout, except on the neck, which is enlivened by an hue of glossy yellow. I have no doubt but they are constant inhabitants of this climate, as well as some other small birds which we saw, of a grey colour.

Chapter 2

RAINY LAKE

Sunday, December 23. I this day removed from the tent into the house which had been erected for me, and set all the men to begin the buildings intended for their habitation. Materials sufficient to erect a range of five houses for them, of about seventeen by twelve feet, were already collected. It would be considered by the inhabitants of a milder climate, as a great evil, to be exposed to the weather at this rigorous season of the year, but these people are inured to it, and it is necessary to describe in some measure the hardships which they undergo without a murmur, in order to convey a general notion of them.

The men who were now with me, left this place in the beginning of last May, and went to the Rainy Lake in canoes, laden with packs of fur, which, from the immense length of the voyage, and other concurring circumstances, is a most severe trial of patience and perseverance: there they do not remain a sufficient time for ordinary repose, when they take a load of goods in exchange, and proceed on their return, in a great measure, day and night. They had been arrived near two months, and, all that time, had been continually engaged in very toilsome labour, with nothing more than a common shed to protect them from the frost and snow. Such is the life which these people lead; and is continued with unremitting exertion, till their strength is lost in premature old age.

The Canadians remarked, that the weather we had on the 25th, 26th and 27th of this month, denoted such as we might expect in the three succeeding months. On the 29th, the wind being at North-East, and the weather calm and cloudy, a rumbling noise was heard in the air like distant thunder, when the sky cleared away in the South-West; from whence there blew a perfect hurricane, which lasted till eight. Soon after it commenced, the atmosphere became so warm that it dissolved all the snow on the ground; even the ice was covered with water, and had the same appearance as when it is breaking up in the spring. From eight to nine the weather became calm, but immediately after a wind arose from the North-East with equal violence, with clouds, rain, and hail, which continued throughout the night and till the evening of the next day, when it turned to snow. One of the people who wintered at Fort Dauphin in the year 1780, when the small-pox first appeared there, informed me, that the weather there was of a similar description.

Thursday, January 1, 1793. On the first day of January, my people, in conformity to the usual custom, awoke me at the break of day with the discharge of fire-arms, with which they congratulated the appearance of the new year. In return, they were treated with plenty of spirits, and when there is any flour, cakes are always added to their regales, which was the case on the present occasion.

On my arrival here last fall, I found that one of the young Indians had lost the use of his right hand by the bursting of a gun, and that his thumb had been maimed in such a manner as to hang only by a small strip of flesh. Indeed, when he was brought to me, his wound was in such an offensive state, and emitted such a putrid smell, that it required all the resolution I possessed to examine it. His friends had done every thing in their power to relieve him; but as it consisted only in singing about him, and blowing upon his hand, the wound, as may be well imagined, had got into the deplorable state in which I found it. I was rather alarmed at the difficulty of the case, but as the young man's life was in a state of hazard, I was determined to risk my surgical reputation, and accordingly took him under my care. I immediately formed a poultice of bark, stripped from the roots of the spruce-fir, which I applied to the wound, having first washed it with the juice of the bark; this proved a very painful dressing: in a few days, however, the wound was clean, and the proud flesh around it destroyed. I wished very much in this state of the business to have separated the thumb from the hand, which I well knew must be effected before the cure could be performed; but he would not consent to that operation, till, by the application of vitriol, the flesh by which the thumb was suspended, was shrivelled almost to a thread. When I had succeeded in this object, I perceived that the wound was closing rather faster than I desired. The salve I applied on the occasion was made of the Canadian balsam, wax, and tallow dropped from a burning candle into water. In short, I was so successful, that about Christmas my patient engaged in an hunting party, and brought me the tongue of an elk: nor was he finally ungrateful. When he left me I received the warmest acknowledgments, both from himself, and his relations with whom he departed, for my care of him. I certainly did not spare my time or attention on the occasion, as I regularly dressed his wound three times a day, during the course of a month.

On the 5th in the morning the weather was calm, clear, and very cold; the wind blew from the South-West, and in the course of the afternoon it began to thaw. I had already observed at Athabasca, that this wind never failed to bring us clear mild weather, whereas, when it blew from the opposite quarter, it produced snow. Here it is much more perceptible, for if it blows hard South-West for four hours, a thaw is the consequence, and if the wind is at North-East it brings sleet and snow. To this cause it may be attributed, that there is now so little snow in this part of the world. These warm winds come off the Pacific Ocean, which cannot, in a direct line, be very far from us; the distance being so short, that though they pass over mountains covered with snow, there is not time for them to cool.

There being several of the natives at the house at this time, one of them, who had received an account of the death of his father, proceeded in silence to his lodge, and began to fire off his gun. As it was night, and such a noise being so uncommon at such an hour, especially when it was so often repeated, I sent my interpreter to inquire into the cause of it, when he was informed by the man himself, that this was a common custom with them on the death of a near relation, and was a warning to their friends not to approach, or intrude upon them, as they were, in consequence of their loss, become careless of life. The chief, to whom the deceased person was also related, appeared with his war-cap on his head, which is only worn on these solemn occasions, or when preparing for battle, and confirmed to me this singular custom of firing guns, in order to express their grief for the death of relations and friends.[21] The women alone indulge in tears on such occasions; the men considering it as a mark of pusillanimity and a want of fortitude to betray any personal tokens of sensibility or sorrow.

The Indians informed me, that they had been to hunt at a large lake, called by the Knisteneaux, the Slave Lake, which derived its name from that of its original inhabitants, who were called Slaves. They represented it as a large body of water, and that it lies about one hundred and twenty miles due East from this place. It is well known to the Knisteneaux, who are among the inhabitants of the plains on the banks of the Saskatchiwine river; for formerly, when they used to come to make war in this country, they came in their canoes to that lake, and left them there; from thence there is a beaten path all the way to the Fork, or East branch of this river, which was their war-road.

Thursday, January 10. Among the people who were now here, there were two Rocky Mountain Indians, who declared, that the people to whom we had given that denomination, are by no means entitled to it, and that their country has ever been in the vicinity of our present situation. They said, in support of their assertion, that these people were entirely ignorant of those parts which are adjacent to the mountain, as well as the navigation of the river; that the Beaver Indians had greatly encroached upon them, and would soon force them to retire to the foot of these mountains. They represented themselves as the only real natives of that country then with me: and added, that the coun-

---

21. When they are drinking together, they frequently present their guns to each other, when any of the parties have not other means of procuring rum. On such an occasion they always discharge their pieces, as a proof, I imagine, of their being in good order, and to determine the quantity of liquor they may propose to get in exchange for them.

try, and that part of the river that intervenes between this place and the mountains, bear much the same appearance as that around us; that the former abounds with animals, but that the course of the latter is interrupted, near, and in the mountains, by successive rapids and considerable falls. These men also informed me, that there is another great river towards the midday sun, whose current runs in that direction, and that the distance from it is not great across the mountains.

The natives brought me plenty of furs. The small quantity of snow, at this time, was particularly favourable for hunting the beaver, as from this circumstance, those animals could, with the greater facility, be traced from their lodges to their lurking-places.

On the 12th our hunter arrived, having left his mother-in-law, who was lately become a widow with three small children, and in actual labour of a fourth. Her daughter related this circumstance to the women here, without the least appearance of concern, though she represented her as in a state of great danger, which probably might proceed from her being abandoned in this unnatural manner. At the same time without any apparent consciousness of her own barbarous negligence; if the poor abandoned woman should die, she would most probably lament her with great outcries, and, perhaps, cut off one or two joints of her fingers as tokens of her grief. The Indians, indeed, consider the state of a woman in labour as among the most trifling occurrences of corporal pain to which human nature is subject, and they may be, in some measure, justified in this apparent insensibility from the circumstances of that situation among themselves. It is by no means uncommon in the hasty removal of their camps from one position to another, for a woman to be taken in labour, to deliver herself in her way, without any assistance or notice from her associates in the journey, and to overtake them before they complete the arrangements of their evening station, with her new-born babe on her back.

I was this morning threatened with a very unpleasant event, which, however, I was fortunately enabled to control. Two young Indians being engaged in one of their games, a dispute ensued, which rose to such an height, that they drew their knives, and if I had not happened to have appeared, they would, I doubt not, have employed them to very bloody purposes. So violent was their rage, that after I had turned them both out of the house, and severely reprimanded them, they stood in the fort for at least half an hour, looking at each other with a most vindictive aspect, and in sullen silence.

The game which produced this state of bitter enmity, is called that of the Platter, from a principal article of it. The Indians play at it in the following manner.

The instruments of it consist of a platter, or dish, made of wood or bark, and six round, or square, but flat pieces of metal, wood, or stone, whose sides or surfaces are of different colours. These are put into the dish, and after being for some time shaken together, are thrown into the air, and received again in the dish with considerable dexterity; when, by the number that are turned up of the same mark or colour, the game is regulated. If there should be equal numbers, the throw is not reckoned; if two or four, the platter changes hands.

On the 13th, one of these people came to me, and presented in himself a curious example of Indian superstition. He requested me to furnish him with a remedy that might be applied to the joints of his legs and thighs, of which he had, in a great measure lost the use for five winters. This affliction he attributed to his cruelty about that time, when having found a wok with two whelps in an old Beaver lodge, he set fire to it and consumed them.

The winter had been so mild, that the swans had but lately left us, and at this advanced period there was very little snow on the ground: it was, however, at this time a foot and a half in depth, in the environs of the establishment below this, which is at the distance of about seventy leagues.

On the 28th the Indians were now employed in making their snow-shoes, as the snow had not hitherto fallen in sufficient quantity to render them necessary.

Sunday, February 2. The weather now became very cold, and it froze so hard in the night that my watch stopped; a circumstance that had never happened to this watch since my residence in the country.

There was a lodge of Indians here, who were absolutely starving with cold and hunger. They had lately lost a near relation, and had, according to custom, thrown away every thing belonging to them, and even exchanged the few articles of raiment which they possessed, in order, as I presume, to get rid of every thing that may bring the deceased to their remembrance. They also destroy every thing belonging to any deceased person, except what they consign to the grave with the late owner of them. We had some difficulty to make them comprehend that the debts of a man who dies should be discharged, if he left any furs behind him: but those who understand this principle of justice, and profess to adhere to it, never fail to prevent the appearance of any skins beyond such as may be necessary to satisfy the debts of their dead relation.

On the 8th I had an observation for the longitude. In the course of this day one of my men, who had been some time with the Indians, came to inform me that one of them had threatened to stab him; and on his preferring a complaint to the man with whom he now lived, and to whom I had given him in charge, he replied, that he had been very imprudent to play and quarrel with the young Indians out of his lodge, where no one would dare to come and quarrel with him; but that if he had lost his life where he had been, it would have been the consequence of his own folly. Thus, even among these children of nature, it appears that a man's house is his castle, where the protection of hospitality is rigidly maintained.

The hard frost which had prevailed from the beginning of February continued to the 16th of March, when the wind blowing from the South-West, the weather became mild.

On the 22d a wolf was so bold as to venture among the Indian lodges, and was very near carrying off a child.

I had another observation of Jupiter and his satellites for the longitude. On the 13th some geese were seen, and these birds are always considered as the harbingers of spring. On the 1st of April my hunters shot five of them. This was a much earlier period than I ever remember to have observed the visits of wild fowl in this part of the world. The weather had been mild for the last fortnight, and there was a promise of its continuance. On the 5th the snow had entirely disappeared.

At half past four this morning I was awakened to be informed that an Indian had been killed. I accordingly hastened to the camp, where I found two women employed in rolling up the dead body of a man, called the White Partridge, in a beaver robe, which I had lent him. He had received four mortal wounds from a dagger, two within the collar-bone, one in the left breast, and another in the small of the back, with two cuts across his head. The murderer, who had been my hunter throughout the winter, had fled; and it was pretended that several relations of the deceased were gone in pursuit of him. The history of this unfortunate event is as follows: –

These two men had been comrades for four years; the murderer had three wives; and the young man who was killed, becoming enamoured of one of them, the husband consented to yield her to him, with the reserved power of claiming her as his property, when it should be his pleasure. This connection was uninterrupted for near three years, when, whimsical as it may appear, the husband became jealous, and the public amour was suspended. The parties, however, made their private assignations, which caused the woman to be so ill treated by her husband, that the paramour was determined to take her away by force; and this project ended in his death. This is a very common practice among the Indians, and generally terminates in very serious and fatal quarrels. In consequence of this event all the Indians went away in great apparent hurry and confusion, and in the evening not one of them was to be seen about the fort.

The Beaver and Rocky Mountain Indians, who traded with us in this river, did not exceed an hundred and fifty men, capable of bearing arms; two thirds of whom call themselves Beaver Indians. The latter differ only from the former, as they have, more or less, imbibed the customs and manners of the Knisteneaux. As I have already observed, they are passionately fond of liquor, and in the moments of their festivity will barter any thing they have in their possession for it.

Though the Beaver Indians made their peace with the Knisteneaux, at Peace Point, as already mentioned, yet they did not secure a state of amity from others of the same nation, who had driven away the natives of the Saskatchiwine and Missinipy Rivers, and joined at the head water of the latter, called the Beaver River: from thence they proceeded West by the Slave Lake just described, on their war excursions, which they often repeated, even till the Beaver Indians had procured arms, which was in the year 1782. If it so happened that they missed them, they proceeded Westward till they were certain of wreaking their vengeance on those of the Rocky Mountain, who being without arms, became an easy prey to their blind and savage fury. All the European articles they possessed, previous to the year 1780, were obtained from the Knisteneaux and Chepewyans, who brought them from Fort Churchill, and for which they were made to pay an extravagant price.

As late as the year 1786, when the first traders from Canada arrived on the banks of this river, the natives employed bows and snares, but at present very little use is made of the former, and the latter are no longer known. They still entertain a great dread of their natural enemies, but they are since become so well armed, that the others now call them their allies. The men are in general of a comely appearance, and fond of personal decoration. The women are of a contrary disposition, and the slaves of the men: in common with all the Indian tribes polygamy is allowed among them. They are very subject to jealousy, and fatal consequences frequently result from the indulgence of that passion. But notwithstanding the vigilance and severity which is exercised by the husband, it seldom happens that a woman is without her favourite, who, in the absence of the husband, exacts the same submission, and practices the same tyranny. And so premature is the tender passion, that it is sometimes known to invigorate so early a period of life as the age or eleven or twelve years. The women are not very prolific; a circumstance which may be attributed, in a great measure, to the hardships that they suffer, for except a few small dogs, they alone perform that labour which is allotted to beasts of burthen in other countries. It is not uncommon, while the men carry nothing but a gun, that their wives and daughters follow with such weighty burdens, that if they lay them down they cannot replace them, and that is a kindness which the men will not deign to perform; so that during their journeys they are frequently obliged to lean against a tree for a small portion of temporary relief. When they arrive at the place which their tyrants have chosen for their encampment, they arrange the whole in a few minutes, by forming a curve of poles, meeting at the top, and expanding into circles of twelve or fifteen feet diameter at the bottom, covered with dressed skins of the moose sewed together. During these preparations, the men sit down quietly to the enjoyment of their pipes, if they happen to have any tobacco. But notwithstanding this abject state of slavery and submission, the women have a considerable influence on the opinion of the men in every thing except their own domestic situation.

These Indians are excellent hunters, and their exercise in that capacity is so violent as to reduce them in general to a very meagre appearance. Their religion is of a very contracted nature, and I never witnessed any ceremony of devotion which they had not borrowed from the Knisteneaux, their feasts and fasts being in imitation of that people. They are more vicious and warlike than the Chepewyans, from whence they sprang, though they do not possess their selfishness, for while they have the means of purchasing their necessaries, they are liberal and generous, but when those are exhausted they become errant beggars: they are, however, remarkable for their honesty, for in the whole tribe there were only two woman and a man who had been known to have swerved from that virtue, and they were considered as objects of disregard and reprobation. They are afflicted with but few diseases, and their only remedies consist in binding the temples, procuring perspiration, singing, and blowing on the sick person, or affected part. When death overtakes any of them, their property, as I have before observed, is sacrificed and destroyed; nor is there any failure of lamentation or mourning on such occasion: they who are more nearly related to the departed person, black their faces, and sometimes cut off their hair; they also pierce their arms with knives and arrows. The grief of the females is carried to a still greater excess; they not only cut their hair, and cry and howl, but they will sometimes, with the utmost deliberation, employ some sharp instrument to separate the nail from the finger, and then force back the flesh beyond the first joint, which they immediately amputate. But this extraordinary mark of affliction is only displayed on the death of a favourite son, an husband, or a father. Many of the old women have so often repeated this ceremony, that they have not a complete finger remaining on either hand. The women renew their lamentations at the graves of their departed relatives for a long succession of years. They appear, in common with all the Indian tribes, to be very fond of their children, but they are as careless in their mode of swadling them in their infant state, as they are of their own dress: the child is laid down on a board, of about two feet long, covered with a bed of moss, to which it is fastened by bandages, the moss being changed as often as the occasion requires. The chief of the nation had no less than nine wives, and children in proportion.

When traders first appeared among these people, the Canadians were treated with the utmost hospitality and attention; but they have, by their subsequent conduct, taught the natives to withdraw that respect from them, and sometimes to treat them with indignity. They differ very much from the Chepewyans and Knisteneaux, in the abhorrence they profess of any carnal communication between their women and the white people. They carry their love of gaming to excess; they will pursue it for a succession of days and nights, and no apprehension of ruin, nor influence of domestic affection, will restrain them from the indulgence of it. They are a quick, lively, active people, with a keen, penetrating, dark eye; and though they are very susceptible of anger, are as easily appeased. The males eradicate their beards, and the females their hair in every part, except their heads, where it is strong and black, and without a curl. There are many old men among them, but they are in general ignorant of the space in which they have been inhabitants of the earth, though one of them told me that he recollected sixty winters.

An Indian in some measure explained his age to me, by relating that he remembered the opposite hills and plains, now interspersed with groves of poplars, when they were covered with moss, and without any animal inhabitant but the rein-deer. By degrees, he said, the face of the country changed to its present appearance, when the elk came from the East, and was followed by the buffalo; the rein-deer then retired to the long range of high lands that, at a considerable distance, run parallel with this river.

On the 20th of April I had an observation of Jupiter and his satellites, for the longitude, and we were now visited by our summer companions the gnats and mosquitoes. On the other side of the river, which was yet covered with ice, the plains were delightful; the trees were budding, and many plants in blossom. Mr. Mackay brought me a bunch of flowers of a pink colour, and a yellow button, encircled with six leaves of a light purple. The change in the appearance of nature was as sudden as it was pleasing, for a few days only were passed away since the ground was covered with snow. On the 25th the river was cleared of the ice.

I now found that the death of the man called the White Partridge, had deranged all the plans which I had settled with the Indians for the spring hunting. They had assembled at some distance from the fort, and sent an embassy to me, to demand rum to drink, that they might have an opportunity of crying for their deceased brother. It would be considered as an extreme degradation in an Indian to weep when sober, but a state of intoxication sanctions all irregularities. On my refusal, they threatened to go to war, which, from motives of interest as well as humanity, we did our utmost to discourage; and as a second message was brought by persons *of* some weight among these people, and on whom I could depend, I thought it prudent to comply with the demand, on an express condition, that they would continue peaceably at home.

The month of April being now past, in the early part of which I was most busily employed in trading with the Indians, I ordered our old canoes to be repaired with bark, and added four new ones to them, when with the furs and provisions I had purchased, six canoes were loaded and dispatched on the 8th of May for Fort Chepewyan. I had, however, retained six of the men who agreed to accompany me on my projected voyage of discovery. I also engaged my hunters, and closed the business of the year for the company by writing my public and private dispatches.

Having ascertained, by various observations, the latitude of this place to be 56.9 North, and longitude 117.35.15 West: – on the 9th day of May, I found, that my acrometer was one hour forty-six minutes slow to apparent time; the mean going of it I had found to be twenty-two seconds slow in twenty-four hours. Having settled this point, the canoe was put into the water: her dimensions were twenty-five feet long within, exclusive of the curves of stem and stern, twenty six inches hold, and four feet nine inches beam. At the same time she was so light, that two men could carry her on a good road three or four miles without resting. In this slender vessel, we shipped provisions, goods for presents, arms, ammunition, and baggage, to the weight of three thousand pounds, and an equipage of ten people; viz. Alexander Mackay, Joseph Landry, Charles Ducette,[22] François Beaulieux, Baptist Bisson, François Courtois, and Jacques Beauchamp, with two Indians as hunters and interpreters. One of them, when a boy, was used to be so idle, that he obtained the reputable name of Cancre, which he still possesses. With these persons I embarked at seven in the evening. My winter interpreter, with another person, whom I left here to take care of the fort, and supply the natives with ammunition during the summer, shed tears on the reflection of those dangers which we might encounter in our expedition, while my own people offered up their prayers that we might return in safety from it.

---

22. Joseph Landry and Charles Ducette were with me in my former voyage.

Chapter 3

SOUTH BY WEST

Thursday, May 9. We began our voyage with a course South by West against a strong current one mile and three quarters, South-West by South one mile, and landed before eight on an island for the night.

Friday, May 10. The weather was clear and pleasant, though there was a keenness in the air; and at a quarter past three in the morning we continued our voyage, steering South-West three quarters of a mile, South-West by South one mile and a quarter, South three quarters of a mile, South-West by South one quarter of a mile, South-West by West one mile, South-West by South three miles, South by West three quarters of a mile, and South-West one mile. The canoe being strained from its having been very heavily laden, became so leaky, that we were obliged to land, unload, and gum it. As this circumstance took place about twelve, I had an opportunity of taking an altitude, which made our latitude 55.58.48.

When the canoe was repaired we continued our course, steering South-West by West one mile and an half, when I had the misfortune to drop my pocket-compass into the water; West half a mile, West-South-West four miles and an half. Here, the banks are steep and hilly, and in some parts undermined by the river. Where the earth has given way, the face of the cliffs discovers numerous strata, consisting of reddish earth and small stones, bitumen, and a greyish earth, below which, near the water-edge, is a red stone. Water issues from most of the banks, and the ground on which it spreads is covered with a thin white scurf, or particles of a saline substance: there are several of these salt springs. At half past six in the afternoon the young men landed, when they killed an elk and wounded a buffalo. In this spot we formed our encampment for the night.

From the place which we quitted this morning, the West side of the river displayed a succession of the most beautiful scenery I had ever beheld. The ground rises at intervals to a considerable height, and stretching inwards to a considerable distance: at every interval or pause in the rise, there is a very gently-ascending space or lawn, which is alternate with abrupt precipices to the summit of the whole, or, at least as far as the eye could distinguish. This magnificent theatre of nature has all the decorations which the trees and animals of the country can afford it: groves of poplars in every shape vary the scene; and their intervals are enlivened with vast herds of elks and buffaloes; the former choosing the steeps and uplands, and the latter preferring the plains. At this time the buffaloes were attended with their young ones who were frisking about them; and it appeared that the elks would soon exhibit the same enlivening circumstance. The whole country displayed an exuberant verdure; the trees that bear a blossom were advancing fast to that delightful appearance, and the velvet rind of their branches reflecting the oblique rays of a rising or setting sun, added a splendid gaiety to the scene, which no expressions of mine are qualified to describe. The East side of the river consists of a range of high land covered with the white spruce and the soft birch, while the banks abound with the alder and the willow. The water continued to rise, and the current being proportionably strong, we made a greater use of setting poles than paddles.

Saturday, May 11. The weather was overcast. With a strong wind a-head, we embarked at four in the morning, and left all the fresh meat behind us, but the portion which had been assigned to the kettle; the canoe being already too heavily laden. Our course was West-South-West one mile, where a small river flowed in from the East, named *Quiscatina Sepy,* or River with the High Banks; West half a mile, South half a mile, South-West by West three quarters of a mile, West one mile and a quarter, South-West a quarter of a mile, South-South-West half a mile, and

West by South a mile and an half. Here I took a meridian altitude, which gave 55.56.3 North latitude. We then proceeded West three miles and an half, West-South-West, where the whole plain was on fire, one mile, West one mile, and the wind so strong a-head, that it occasioned the canoe to take in water, and otherwise impeded our progress. Here we landed to take time, with the mean of three altitudes, which made the watch slow, 1.42.10 apparent time.

We now proceeded West-South-West, one mile and a quarter, where we found a chief of the Beaver Indians on an hunting party. I remained, however, in my canoe and though it was getting late, I did not choose to encamp with these people, lest the friends of my hunters might discourage them from proceeding on the voyage. We, therefore, continued our course, but several Indians kept company with us, running along the bank and conversing with my people, who were so attentive to them, that they drove the canoe on a stony flat, so that we were under the necessity of landing to repair the damages, and put up for the night, though very contrary to my wishes. My hunters obtained permission to proceed with some of these people to their lodges, on the promise of being back by the break of day; though I was not without some apprehension respecting them. The chief, however, and another man, as well as several people from the lodges, joined us, before we had completed the repair of the canoe; and they made out a melancholy story, that they had neither ammunition or tobacco sufficient for their necessary supply during the summer. I accordingly referred him to the Fort, where plenty of those articles were left in the care of my interpreter, by whom they would be abundantly furnished, if they were active and industrious in pursuing their occupations. I did not fail, on this occasion, to magnify the advantages of the present expedition; observing, at the same time, that its success would depend on the fidelity and conduct of the young men who were retained by me to hunt. The chief also proposed to borrow my canoe, in order to transport himself and family across the river: several plausible reasons, it is true, suggested themselves for resisting his proposition; but when I stated to him, that, as the canoe was intended for a voyage of such consequence, no woman could be permitted to be embarked in it, he acquiesced in the refusal. It was near twelve at night when he took his leave, after I had gratified him with a present of tobacco.

Sunday, May 12. Some of the Indians passed the night with us, and I was informed by them, that, according to our mode of proceeding, we should, in ten days, get as far as the rocky mountains. The young men now returned, to my great satisfaction, and with the appearance of contentment: though I was not pleased when they dressed themselves in the clothes which I had given them before we left the Fort, as it betrayed some latent design.

At four in the morning we proceeded on our voyage, steering West three miles, including one of our course yesterday, North-West by North four miles, West two miles and an half, North-West by West a mile and an half, North by East two miles, North-West by West one mile, and North-North-West three miles. After a continuation of our course to the North for a mile and an half, we landed for the night on an island where several of the Indians visited us, but unattended by their women, who remained in their camp, which was at some distance from us.

The land on both sides of the river, during the last two days, is very much elevated, but particularly in the latter part of it, and, on the Western side, presents in different places, white, steep, and lofty cliffs. Our view being confined by these circumstances, we did not see so many animals as on the 10th. Between these lofty boundaries, the river becomes narrow, and in a great measure free from islands; for we had passed only four: the stream, indeed, was not more than from two hundred to three hundred yards broad; whereas before these cliffs pressed upon it, its breadth was twice that extent and besprinkled with islands. We killed an elk, and fired several shots at animals from the canoe.

The greater part of this band being Rocky Mountain Indians, I endeavoured to obtain some intelligence of our intended route, but they all pleaded ignorance, and uniformly declared, that they knew nothing of the country beyond the first mountain: at the same time they were of opinion, that, from the strength of the current and the rapids, we should not get there by water; though they did not hesitate to express their surprise at the expedition we had already made.

I inquired, with some anxiety, after an old man who had already given me an account of the country beyond the limits of his tribe, and was very much disappointed at being informed, that he had not been seen for upwards of a moon. This man had been at war on another large river beyond the Rocky Mountain, and described to me a fork of it between the mountains; the Southern branch of which he directed me to take: from thence, he said, there was a carrying-place of about a day's march for a young man to get to the other river. To prove the truth of his relation, he consented, that his son, who had been with him in those parts, should accompany me; and he accordingly sent him to the Fort some days before my departure; but the preceding night he deserted with another young man, whose application to attend me as a hunter, being refused, he persuaded the other to leave me. I now thought it right to repeat to them what I had said to the chief of the first band, respecting the advantages which would be derived from the voyage, that the young men might be encouraged to remain with me; as without them I should not have attempted to proceed.

Monday, May 13. The first object that presented itself to me this morning was the young man whom I have already mentioned, as having seduced away my intended guide. At any other time or place I should have chastised him for his past conduct, but in my situation it was necessary to pass over his offence, lest he should endeavour to exercise the same influence over those who were so essential to my service. Of the deserter he gave no satisfactory account, but continued to express his wish to attend me in his place, for which he did not possess any necessary qualifications.

The weather was cloudy, with an appearance of rain; and the Indians pressed me with great earnestness to pass the day with them, and hoped to prolong my stay among them by assuring me that the winter yet lingered in the rocky mountains: but my object was to lose no time, and having given the chief some tobacco for a small quantity of meat, we embarked at four, when my young men could not conceal their chagrin at parting with their friends, for so long a period as the voyage threatened to occupy. When I had assured them that in three moons we should return to them, we proceeded on our course, West-North-West half a mile, West-South-West one mile and an half, West by North three miles, North-West by West two miles and an half, South-West by West half a mile, South-South-West a mile and an half, and South-West a mile and a half. Here I had a meridian altitude, which gave 56.17.44 North latitude.

The last course continued a mile and an half, South by West three quarters of a mile, South-West by South three miles and an half, and West-South-West two miles and an half. Here the land lowered on both sides, with an increase of wood, and displayed great numbers of animals. The river also widened from three to five hundred yards, and was full of islands and flats. Having continued our course three miles, we made for the shore at seven, to pass the night.

At the place from whence we proceeded this morning, a river falls in from the North; there are also several islands, and many rivulets on either side, which are too small to deserve particular notice. We perceived along the river tracks of large bears, some of which were nine inches wide, and of a proportionate length. We saw one of their dens, or winter quarters, called *watee,* in an island, which was ten feet deep, five feet high, and six feet wide; but we had not yet seen one of those animals. The Indians entertain great apprehension of this kind of bear, which is called the grisly bear, and they never venture to attack it but in a party of at least three or four. Our hunters, though they had been much higher than this part of our voyage, by land, knew nothing of the river. One of them mentioned, that having been engaged in a war expedition, his party on their return made their canoes at some distance below us. The wind was North throughout the day, and at times blew with considerable violence.

The apprehensions which I had felt respecting the young men were not altogether groundless, for the eldest of them told me that his uncle had last night addressed him in the following manner: – "My nephew, your departure makes my heart painful. The white people may be said to rob us of you. They are about to conduct you into the midst of our enemies, and you may never more return to us. Were you not with the Chief,[23] I know not what I should do, but he requires your attendance, and you must follow him."

Tuesday, May 14. The weather was clear, and the air sharp, when we embarked at half past four. Our course was South by West one mile and an half, South-West by South half a mile, South-West. We here found it necessary to unload, and gum the canoe, in which operation we lost an hour; when we proceeded on the last course one mile and an half. I now took a meridian altitude, which gave 56.11.19 North latitude, and continued to proceed West-South-West two miles and an half. Here the Bear River, which is of a large appearance, falls in from the East; West three miles and an half, South-South-West one mile and an half, and South-West four miles and an half, when we encamped upon an island about seven in the evening.

During the early part of the day, the current was not so strong as we had generally found it, but towards the evening it became very rapid, and was broken by numerous islands. We were gratified, as usual, with the sight of animals. The land on the West side is very irregular, but has the appearance of being a good beaver country; indeed we saw some of those animals in the river. Wood is in great plenty, and several rivulets added their streams to the main river. A goose was the only article of provision which we procured to day. Smoke was seen, but at a great distance before us.

Wednesday, May 15. The rain prevented us from continuing our route till past six in the morning, when our course was South-West by West three quarters of a mile; at which time we

---

23. These people, as well as all the natives on this side of Lake Winipic, give the mercantile agent that distinguished appellation.

passed a river on the left, West by South two miles and an half. The bank was steep, and the current strong. The last course continued one mile and an half, West-South-West two miles, where a river flowed in from the right, West by South one mile and an half, West-North-West one mile, and West by North two miles. Here the land takes the form of an high ridge, and cut our course, which was West for three miles, at right angles. We now completed the voyage of this day.

In the preceding night the water rose upwards of two inches, and had risen in this proportion since our departure. The wind, which was West-South-West, blew very hard throughout the day, and with the strength of the current, greatly impeded our progress. The river, in this part of it, is full of islands; and the land, on the South or left side, is thick with wood. Several rivulets also fall in from that quarter. At the entrance of the last river which we passed, there was a quantity of wood, which had been cut down by axes, and some by the beaver. This fall, however, was not made, in the opinion of my people, by any of the Indians with whom we were acquainted.

The land to the right is of a very irregular elevation and appearance, composed in some places of clay, and rocky cliffs, and others exhibiting stratas of red, green, and yellow colours. Some parts, indeed, offer a beautiful scenery, in some degree similar to that which we passed on the second day of our voyage, and equally enlivened with the elk and the buffalo, who were feeding in great numbers, and unmolested by the hunter. In an island which we passed, there was a large quantity of white birch, whose bark might be employed in the construction of canoes.

Thursday, May 16. The weather being clear, we reimbarked at four in the morning, and proceeded West by North three miles. Here the land again appeared as if it run across our course, and a considerable river discharged itself by various streams. According to the Rocky Mountain Indian, it is called the Sinew River. This spot would an excellent situation for a fort or factory, as there is plenty of wood, and every reason to believe that the country abounds in beaver. As for the other animals, they are in evident abundance, as in every direction the elk and the buffalo are seen in possession of the hills and the plains. Our course continued West-North-West three miles and an half, North-West one mile and an half, South-West by West two miles; (the latitude was by observation 56.16.54) North, West by North half a mile, West-North-West three quarters of a mile; a small river appearing on the right, North-West one mile and an half, West by North half a mile, West by South one mile and an half, West one mile; and at seven we formed our encampment.

Mr. Mackay, and one of the young men, killed two elks, and mortally wounded a buffalo, but we only took a part of the flesh of the former. The land above the spot where we encamped, spreads into an extensive plain, and stretches on to a very high ridge, which, in some parts, presents a face of rock, but is principally covered with verdure, and varied with the poplar and white birch tree. The country is so crowded with animals as to have the appearance, in some places, of a stall-yard, from the state of the ground, and the quantity of dung which is scattered over it. The soil is black and light. We this day saw two grisly and hideous bears.

Friday, May 17. It froze during the night, and the air was sharp in the morning, when we continued our course West-North-West three miles and an half, South-West by South two miles and an half, South-West by West one mile and an half, West three quarters of a mile, West-South-West one mile and a quarter, and South-West by South one mile and an half. At two in the afternoon the rocky mountains appeared in sight, with their summits covered with snow, bearing South-West by South: they formed a very agreeable object to every person in the canoe, as we attained the view of them much sooner than we expected. A small river was seen on our right, and we continued our progress South-West by South six miles, when we landed at seven, which was our usual hour of encampment.

Mr. Mackay, who was walking along the side of the river, discharged his piece at a buffalo, when it burst near the muzzle, but without any mischievous consequences. On the high grounds, which were on the opposite side of the river, we saw a buffalo tearing up and down with great fury, but could not discern the cause of his impetuous motions; my hunters conjectured that he had been wounded with an arrow by some of the natives. We ascended several rapids in the course of the day, and saw one bear.

Saturday, May 18. It again froze very hard during the night, and at four in the morning we continued our voyage, but we had not proceeded two hundred yards, before an accident happened to the canoe, which did not, however, employ more than three quarters of an hour to complete the repair. We then steered South by West one mile and three quarters, South-West by South three miles, South-West by West one mile and a quarter, West by South three quarters of a mile, South-West half a mile, West by South one mile, South by West one mile and an half, South-South-West, where there is a small run of water from the right, three miles and an half, when the canoe struck on the stump of a tree, and unfortunately where the banks were so steep that there was no place to unload, except a small spot, on which we contrived to dispose the lading in the bow, which lightened the canoe so as to raise the broken part of it above the surface of the water; by which contrivance we reached a convenient situation. It required, however, two hours to complete the repair, when the weather became dark and cloudy, with thunder, lightning, and rain; we, however, continued the last course half a mile, and at six in the evening we were compelled by the rain to land for the night.

About noon we had landed on an island where there were eight lodges of last year. The natives had prepared bark here for five canoes, and there is a road along the hills where they had passed. Branches were cut and broken along it; and they had also stripped off the bark of the trees, to get the interior rind, which forms a part of their food.

The current was very strong through the whole of the day, and the coming up along some of the banks was rendered very dangerous, from the continual falling of large stones, from the upper parts of them. This place appears to be a particular pass for animals across the river, as there are paths leading to it on both sides, every ten yards.

In the course of the day we saw a ground hog, and two cormorants. The earth also appeared in several places to have been turned up by the bears, in search of roots.

Sunday, May 19. It rained very hard in the early part of the night, but the weather became clear towards the morning, when we embarked at our usual hour. As the current threatened to be very strong, Mr. Mackay, the two hunters, and myself, went on shore, in order to lighten the canoe, and ascended the hills, which are covered with cypress, and but little encumbered with underwood. We found a beaten path, and before we had walked a mile fell in with an herd of buffaloes, with their young ones; but I would not suffer the Indians to fire on them, from an apprehension that the report of their fowling pieces would alarm the natives that might be in the neighbourhood; for we were at this time so near the mountains, as to justify our expectation of seeing some of them. We, however, sent our dog after the herd, and a calf was soon secured by him. While the young men were skinning the animal, we heard two reports of firearms from the canoe, which we answered, as it was a signal for my return: we then heard another, and immediately hastened down the hill, with our veal, through a very close wood. There we met one of the men, who informed us that the canoe was at a small distance below, at the foot of a very strong rapid, and that as several waterfalls appeared up the river, we should be obliged to unload and carry. I accordingly hastened to the canoe, and was greatly displeased that so much time had been lost, as I had given previous directions that the river should be followed as long as it was practicable. The last Indians whom we saw had informed us that at the first mountain there was a considerable succession of rapids, cascades, and falls, which they never attempted to ascend; and where they always passed over land the length of a day's march. My men imagined that the carrying place was at a small distance below us, as a path appeared to ascend an hill, where there were several lodges, of the last year's construction. The account which had been given me of the rapids, was perfectly correct: though by crossing to the other side, I must acknowledge with some risk, in such an heavy-laden canoe, the river appeared to me to be practicable, as far as we could see: the traverse, therefore, was attempted, and proved successful. We now towed the canoe along an island, and proceeded without any considerable difficulty till we reached the extremity of it, when the line could be no longer employed; and in endeavouring to clear the point of the island, the canoe was driven with such violence on a stony shore, as to receive considerable injury. We now employed every exertion in our power to repair the breach that had been made, as well as to dry such articles of our loading as more immediately required it: we then transported the whole across the point, when we reloaded, and continued our course about three quarters of a mile. We could now proceed no further on this side of the water, and the traverse was rendered extremely dangerous, not only from the strength of the current, but by the cascades just below us, which, if we had got among them, would have involved us and the canoe in one common destruction. We had no other alternative than to return by the same course we came, or to hazard the traverse, the river on this side being bounded by a range of steep, over-hanging rocks, beneath which the current was driven on with resistless impetuosity from the cascades. Here are several islands of solid rock, covered with a small portion of verdure, which have been worn away by the constant force of the current, and occasionally, as I presume, of ice, at the water's edge, so as to be reduced in that part to one fourth the extent of the upper surface; presenting, as it were, so many large tables, each of which was supported by a pedestal of a more circumscribed projection. They are very elevated for such a situation, and afford an asylum for geese, which were at this time breeding on them. By crossing from one to the other of these islands, we came at length to the main traverse, on which we ventured, and were successful in our passage. Mr. Mackay, and the Indians, who observed our manoeuvres from the top of a rock, were in continual alarm for our safety, with which their own, indeed, may be said to have been nearly connected: however, the dangers that we encountered were very much augmented by the heavy loading of the canoe.

When we had effected our passage, the current on the West side was almost equally violent with that from whence we had just escaped, but the craggy bank being somewhat lower, we were enabled, with a line of sixty fathoms, to tow the canoe, till we came to the foot of the most rapid cascade we had hitherto seen. Here we unloaded, and carried every thing over a rocky point of an hundred and twenty paces. When the canoe was reloaded, I, with those of my people who were not immediately employed, ascended the bank, which was there, and indeed, as far as we could see it, composed of clay, stone, and a yellow gravel. My present situation was so elevated, that the men, who were coming up a strong point could not hear me, though I called to them with the utmost strength of my voice, to lighten the canoe of part of its lading. And here I could not but reflect, with infinite anxiety, on the hazard of my enter-prize: one false step of those who were attached to the line, or the breaking of the line itself, would have at once consigned the canoe, and every thing it contained, to instant destruction: it, however, ascended the rapid in perfect security, but new dangers immediately presented themselves, for stones, both small and great, were continually rolling from the bank, so as to render the situation of those who were dragging the canoe beneath it extremely perilous; besides, they were at every step in danger, from the steepness of the ground, of falling into the water: nor was my solicitude diminished by my being necessarily removed at times from the sight of them.

In our passage through the woods, we came to an inclosure, which had been formed by the natives for the purpose of setting snares for the elk, and of which we could not discover the extent. After we had travelled for some hours through the forest, which consisted of the spruce, birch, and the largest poplars I had ever seen, we sunk down upon the river, where the bank is low, and near the foot of a mountain; between which, and an high ridge, the river flows in a channel of about one hundred yards broad; though, at a small distance below, it rushes on between perpendicular rocks, where it is not much more than half that breadth. Here I remained, in great anxiety, expecting the arrival of the canoe, and after some time I sent Mr. Mackay with one of the Indians down the river in search of it, and with the other I went up it to examine what we might expect in that quarter. In about a mile and a half I came to a part where the river washes the feet of lofty precipices, and presented, in the form of rapids and cascades, a succession of difficulties to our navigation. As the canoe did not come in sight we returned, and from the place where I had separated with Mr. Mackay, we saw the men carrying it over a small rocky point. We met them at the entrance of the narrow channel already mentioned; their difficulties had been great indeed, and the canoe had been broken, but they had persevered with success, and having passed the carrying-place, we proceeded with the line as far as I had already been, when we crossed over and encamped on the opposite beach; but there was no wood on this side of the water, as the adjacent country had been entirely overrun by fire. We saw several elks feeding on the edge of the opposite precipice, which was upwards of three hundred feet in height.

Our course to-day was about South-South-West two miles and an half, South-West half a mile, South-West by South one mile and an half, South-by West half a mile, South-West half a mile, and West one mile and an half. There was a shower of hail, and some rain from flying clouds. I now dispatched a man with an Indian to visit the rapids above, when the latter soon left him to pursue a beaver, which was seen in the shallow water on the inside of a stony island; and though Mr. Mackay, and the other Indian joined him, the animal at length escaped from their pursuit. Several others were seen in the course of the day, which I by no means expected, as the banks are almost every where so much elevated above the channel of the river. Just as the obscurity of the night drew on, the man returned with an account that it would be impracticable to pass several points, as well as the super-impending promontories.

Monday, May 20. The weather was clear with a sharp air, and we renewed our voyage at a quarter past four, on a course

South-West by West three quarters of a mile. We now, with infinite difficulty passed along the foot of a rock, which, fortunately, was not an hard stone, so that we were enabled to cut steps in it for the distance of twenty feet; from which, at the hazard of my life, I leaped on a small rock below, where I received those who followed me on my shoulders. In this manner four of us passed and dragged up the canoe, in which attempt we broke her. Very luckily, a dry tree had fallen from the rock above us, without which we could not have made a fire, as no wood was to be procured within a mile of the place. When the canoe was repaired, we continued towing it along the rocks to the next point, when we embarked, as we could not at present make any further use of the line, but got along the rocks of a round high island of stone, till we came to a small sandy bay. As we had already damaged the canoe, and had every reason to think that she soon would risk much greater injury, it became necessary for us to supply ourselves with bark, as our provision of that material article was almost exhausted; two men were accordingly sent to procure it, who soon returned with the necessary store.

Mr. Mackay, and the Indians who had been on shore, since we broke the canoe, were prevented from coming to us by the rugged and impassable state of the ground. We, therefore, again resumed our course with the assistance of poles, with which we pushed onwards till we came beneath a precipice, where we could not find any bottom; so that we were again obliged to have recourse to the line, the management of which was rendered not only difficult but dangerous, as the men employed in towing were under the necessity of passing on the outside of trees that grew on the edge of the precipice. We, however, surmounted this difficulty, as we had done many others, and the people who had been walking over land now joined us. They also had met with their obstacles in passing the mountain.

It now became necessary for us to make a traverse, where the water was so rapid, that some of the people stripped themselves to their shirts that they might be the better prepared for swimming, in case any accident happened to the canoe, which they seriously apprehended; but we succeeded in our attempt without any other inconvenience, except that of taking in water. We now came to a cascade, when it was thought necessary to take out part of the lading. At noon we stopped to take an altitude, opposite to a small river that flowed in from the left: while I was thus engaged, the men went on shore to fasten the canoe, but as the current was not very strong, they had been negligent in performing this office; it proved, however, sufficiently powerful to sheer her off, and if it had not happened that one of the men, from absolute fatigue had remained and held the end of the line, we should have been deprived of every means of prosecuting our voyage, as well as of present subsistence. But notwithstanding the state of my mind on such an alarming circumstance, and an intervening cloud that interrupted me, the altitude which I took has been since proved to be tolerably correct, and gave 56 North latitude. Our last course was South-South-West two miles and a quarter.

We now continued our toilsome and perilous progress with the line West by North, and as we proceeded the rapidity of the current increased, so that in the distance of two miles we were obliged to unload four times, and carry every thing but the canoe: indeed, in many places, it was with the utmost difficulty that we could prevent her from being dashed to pieces against the rocks by the violence of the eddies. At five we had proceeded to where the river was one continued rapid. Here we again took every thing out of the canoe, in order to tow her up with the line, though the rocks were so shelving as greatly to increase the toil and hazard of that operation. At length, however, the agitation of the water was so great, that a wave striking on the bow of the canoe broke the line, and filled us with inexpressible dismay, as it appeared impossible that the vessel could escape from being dashed to pieces, and those who were in her from perishing. Another wave, however, more propitious than the former, drove her out of the tumbling water, so that the men were enabled to bring her ashore, and though she had been carried over rocks by these swells which left them naked a moment after, the canoe had received no material injury. The men were, however, in such a state from their late alarm, that it would not only have been unavailing but imprudent to have proposed any further progress at present, particularly as the river above us, as far as we could see, was one white sheet of foaming water.

Chapter 4

FOUL WEATHER

That the discouragements, difficulties, and dangers, which had hitherto attended the progress of our enterprize, should have excited a wish in several of those who were engaged in it to discontinue the pursuit, might be naturally expected; and indeed it began to be muttered on all sides that there was no alternative but to return.

Instead of paying any attention to these murmurs, I desired those who had uttered them to exert themselves in gaining an ascent of the hill, and encamp there for the night. In the mean time I set off with one of the Indians, and though I continued my examination of the river almost as long as there was any light to assist us, I could see no end of the rapids and cascades: I was, therefore, perfectly satisfied, that it would be impracticable to proceed any further by water. We returned from this reconnoitring excursion very much fatigued, with our shoes worn out and wounded feet; when I found that, by felling trees on the declivity of the first hill, my people had contrived to ascend it.

From the place where I had taken the altitude at noon, to the place where we made our landing, the river is not more than fifty yards wide, and flows between stupendous rocks, from whence huge fragments sometimes tumble down, and falling from such an height, dash into small stones, with sharp points, and form the beach between the rocky projections. Along the face of some of these precipices, there appears a stratum of a bitumenous substance which resembles coal; though while some of the pieces of it appeared to be excellent fuel, others resisted, for a considerable time, the action of fire, and did not emit the least flame. The whole of this day's course would have been altogether impracticable, if the water had been higher, which must be the case at certain seasons. We saw also several encampments of the Knisteneaux along the river, which must have been formed by them on their war excursions: a decided proof of the savage, bloodthirsty disposition of that people; as nothing less than such a spirit could impel them to encounter the difficulties of this almost inaccessible country, whose natives are equally unoffending and defenceless.

Mr. Mackay informed me, that in passing over the mountains, he observed several chasms in the earth that emitted heat and smoke, which diffused a strong sulphureous stench. I should certainly have visited this phenomenon, if I had been sufficiently qualified as a naturalist, to have offered scientific conjectures or observations thereon.

Tuesday, May 21. It rained in the morning, and did not cease till about eight, and as the men had been very fatigued and disheartened, I suffered them to continue their rest till that hour. Such was the state of the river, as I have already observed, that no alternative was left us; nor did any means of proceeding present themselves to us, but the passage of the mountain over which we were to carry the canoe as well as the baggage. As this was a very alarming enterprize, I dispatched Mr. Mackay with three men and the two Indians to proceed in a straight course from the top of the mountain, and to keep the line of the river till they should find it navigable. If it should be their opinion, that there was no practicable passage in that direction, two of them were instructed to return in order to make their report; while the others were to go in search of the Indian carrying-place. While they were engaged in this excursion, the people who remained with me were employed in gumming the canoe, and making handles for the axes. At noon I got an altitude, which made our latitude 56.0.8. At three o'clock had time, when my watch was slow 1.31.32 apparent time.

At sun-set, Mr. Mackay returned with one of the men, and in about two hours was followed by the others. They had penetrated thick woods, ascended hills and sunk into vallies, till they got beyond the rapids, which, according to their calculation, was a distance of three leagues. The two parties returned by different routes, but they both agreed, that with all its difficulties, and they were of a very alarming nature, the outward course was that which must be preferred. Unpromising, however, as the account of their expedition appeared, it did not sink them into a state of discouragement; and a kettle of wild rice, sweetened with sugar, which had been prepared for their return, with their usual regale of rum, soon renewed that courage which disdained all obstacles that threatened our progress: and they went to rest, with a full determination to surmount them on the morrow. I sat up, in the hope of getting an observation of Jupiter and his first satellite, but the cloudy weather prevented my obtaining it.

Wednesday, May 22. At break of day we entered on the extraordinary journey which was to occupy the remaining part of it. The men began, without delay, to cut a road up the mountain, and as the trees were but of small growth, I ordered them to fell those which they found convenient, in such a manner, that they might fall parallel with the road, but, at the same time, not separate them entirely from the stumps, so that they might form a kind of railing on either side. The baggage was now brought from the waterside to our encampment. This was likewise from the steep shelving of the rocks, a very perilous undertaking, as one false step of any of the people employed in it, would have been instantly followed by falling headlong into the water. When this important object was attained, the whole of the party proceeded with no small degree of apprehension, to fetch the canoe, which, in a short time, was also brought to the encampment; and, as soon as we had recovered from our fatigue, we advanced with it up the mountain, having the line doubled and fastened successively as we went on to the stumps; while a man at the end of it, hauled it round a tree, holding it on and shifting it as we proceeded; so that we may be said, with strict truth, to have warped the canoe up the mountain: indeed by a general and most laborious exertion, we got every thing to the summit by two in the afternoon. At noon, the latitude was 56.0.47 North. At five, I sent the men to cut the road onwards, which they effected for about a mile, when they returned.

The weather was cloudy at intervals, with showers and thunder. At about ten, I observed an emersion of Jupiter's second satellite; time by the achrometer 8.32.20 by which I found the longitude to be 120.29.30 West from Greenwich.

Thursday, May 23. The weather was clear at four this morning, when the men began to carry. I joined Mr. Mackay, and the two Indians in the labour of cutting a road. The ground continued rising gently till noon, when it began to decline; but though on such an elevated situation, we could see but little, as mountains of a still higher elevation and covered with snow, were seen far above us in every direction. In the afternoon the ground became very uneven; hills and deep defiles alternately presented themselves to us. Our progress, however, exceeded my expectation, and it was not till four in the afternoon that the carriers overtook us. At five, in a state of fatigue that may be more readily conceived than expressed, we encamped near a rivulet or spring that issued from beneath a large mass of ice and snow.

Our toilsome journey of this day I compute at about three miles; along the first of which the land is covered with plenty of wood, consisting of large trees, encumbered with little underwood, through which it was by no means difficult to open a road, by following a well-beaten elk path; for the two succeeding miles we found the country overspread with the trunks of trees, laid low by fire some years ago; among which large copses had sprung up of a close growth, and intermixed with briars, so as to render the passage through them painful and tedious. The soil in the woods is light and of a dusky colour; that in the burned country is a mixture of sand and clay with small stones. The trees are spruce, red-pine, cypress, poplar, white birch, willow, alder, arrow-wood, red-wood, liard, service-tree, bois-picant, &c. I never saw any of the last kind before. It rises to about nine feet in height, grows in joints without branches, and is tufted at the extremity. The stem is of an equal size from the bottom to the top, and does not exceed an inch in diameter; it is covered with small prickles, which caught our trowsers, and working through them, sometimes found their way to the flesh. The shrubs are, the gooseberry, the currant and several kinds of briars.

Friday, May 24. We continued our very laborious journey, which led us down some steep hills, and through a wood of tall pines. After much toil and trouble in bearing the canoe through the difficult passages which we encountered, at four in the afternoon we arrived at the river, some hundred yards above the rapids or falls, with all our baggage. I compute the distance of this day's progress to be about four miles; indeed I should have measured the whole of the way, if I had not been obliged to engage personally in the labour of making the road. But after all, the Indian carrying way, whatever may be its length, and I think it cannot exceed ten miles, will always be found more safe and expeditious than the passage which our toil and perseverance formed and surmounted.

Those of my people who visited this place on the 21st, were of opinion that the water had risen very much since that time. About two hundred yards below us the stream rushed with an astonishing but silent velocity, between perpendicular rocks, which are not more than thirty-five yards asunder: when the water is high, it runs over those rocks, in a channel three times that breadth, where it is bounded by far more elevated precipices. In the former are deep round holes, some of which are full of water, while others are empty, in whose bottom are small round stones, as smooth as marble. Some of these natural cylinders would contain two hundred gallons. At a small distance below the first of these rocks, the channel widens in a kind of zig-zag progression; and it was really awful to behold with what infinite force the water drives against the rocks on one side, and with what impetuous strength it is repelled to the other: it then falls back, as it were, into a more strait but rugged passage, over which it is tossed in high, foaming, half-formed billows, as far as the eye could follow it.

The young men informed me that this was the place where their relations had told me that I should meet with a fall equal to that of Niagara: to exculpate them, however, from their apparent

misinformation, they declared that their friends were not accustomed to utter falsehoods, and that the fall had probably been
destroyed by the force of the water. It is, however, very evident
that those people had not been here, or did not adhere to the
truth. By the number of trees which appeared to have been felled
with axes, we discovered that the Knisteneaux, or some tribes
who are known to employ that instrument, had passed this way.
We passed through a snare enclosure, but saw no animals,
though the country was very much intersected by their tracks.

Saturday, May 25. It rained throughout the night, and till
twelve this day; while the business of preparing great and small
poles, and putting the canoe in order, &c. caused us to remain
here till five in the afternoon. I now attached a knife, with a
steel, flint, beads, and other trifling articles to a pole, which I
erected, and left as a token of amity to the natives. When I was
making this arrangement, one of my attendants, whom I have
already described under the title of the Cancre, added to my
assortment a small round piece of green wood, chewed at one
end in the form of a brush, which the Indians use to pick the
marrow out of bones. This he informed me was an emblem of a
country abounding in animals. The water had risen during our
stay here one foot and an half perpendicular height.

We now embarked, and our course was North-West one
mile and three quarters. There were mountains on all sides of us,
which were covered with snow: one in particular, on the South
side of the river, rose to a great height. We continued to proceed
West three quarters of a mile, North-West one mile, and West-
South-West a quarter of a mile, when we encamped for the
night. The Cancre killed a small elk.

Sunday, May 26. The weather was clear and sharp, and
between three and four in the morning we renewed our voyage,
our first course being West by South three miles and an half,
when the men complained of the cold in their fingers, as they
were obliged to push on the canoe with the poles. Here a small
river flowed in from the North. We now continued to steer
West-South-West a quarter of a mile, West-North-West a mile
and an half, and West two miles, when we found ourselves on a

parallel with a chain of mountains on both sides of the river, running South and North. The river, both yesterday and the early part of to-day, was from four to eight hundred yards wide, and full of islands, but was at this time diminished to about two hundred yards broad, and free from islands, with a smooth but strong current. Our next course was South-West two miles, when we encountered a rapid, and saw an encampment of the Knisteneaux. We now proceeded North-West by West one mile, among islands, South-West by West three quarters of a mile, South-South-East one mile, veered to South-West through islands three miles and an half, and South by East half a mile. Here a river poured in on the left, which was the most considerable that we had seen since we had passed the mountain. At seven in the evening we landed and encamped.

Though the sun had shone upon us throughout the day, the air was so cold that the men, though actively employed, could not resist it without the aid of their blanket coats. This circumstance might in some degree be expected from the surrounding mountains, which were covered with ice and snow; but as they are not so high as to produce the extreme cold which we suffered, it must be particularly attributed to the high situation of the country itself, rather than to the local elevation of the mountains, the greatest height of which does not exceed fifteen hundred feet; though in general they do not rise to half that altitude. But as I had not been able to take an exact measurement, I do not presume upon the accuracy of my conjecture. Towards the bottom of these heights, which were clear of snow, the trees were putting forth their leaves, while those in their middle region still retained all the characteristics of winter, and on their upper parts there was little or no wood.

Monday, May 27.[24] The weather was clear, and we continued our voyage at the usual hour, when we successively found

24. From this day, to the 4th of June the courses of my voyage are omitted, as I lost the book that contained them. I was in the habit of sometimes indulging myself with a short doze in the canoe, and I imagine that the branches of the trees brushed my book from me, when I was in such a situation, which renders the account of these few days less distinct than usual.

several rapids and points to impede our progress. At noon our latitude was 56.5.54 North. The Indians killed a stag; and one of the men who went to fetch it was very much endangered by the rolling down of a large stone from the heights above him.

Tuesday, May 28. The day was very cloudy. The mountains on both sides of the river seemed to have sunk, in their elevation, during the voyage of yesterday. To-day they resumed their former altitude, and run so close on either side of the channel, that all view was excluded of every thing but themselves. This part of the current was not broken by islands; but in the afternoon we approached some cascades, which obliged us to carry our canoe and its lading for several hundred yards. Here we observed an encampment of the natives, though some time had elapsed since it had been inhabited. The greater part of the day was divided between heavy showers and small rain; and we took our station on the shore about six in the evening, about three miles above the last rapid.

Wednesday, May 29. The rain was so violent throughout the whole of this day, that we did not venture to proceed. As we almost expended the contents of a rum-keg, and this being a day which allowed of no active employment, I amused myself with the experiment of enclosing a letter in it, and dispatching it down the stream, to take its fate. I accordingly introduced a written account of all our hardships, &c. carefully enclosed in bark, into the small barrel by the bung-hole, which being carefully secured, I consigned this epistolatory cargo to the mercy of the current.

Thursday, May 30. We were alarmed this morning at break of day, by the continual barking of our dog, who never ceased from running backwards and forwards in the rear of our situation: when, however, the day advanced, we discovered the cause of our alarm to proceed from a wolf, who was parading a ridge a few yards behind us, and had been most probably allured by the scent of our small portion of fresh meat. The weather was cloudy, but it did not prevent us from renewing our progress at a very early hour. A considerable river appeared from the left, and we continued our course till seven in the evening, when we landed at night where there was an Indian encampment.

Friday, May 31. The morning was clear and cold, and the current very powerful. On crossing the mouth of a river that flowed in from the right of us, we were very much endangered; indeed all the rivers which I have lately seen, appear to overflow their natural limits, as it may be supposed, from the melting of the mountain snow. The water is almost white, the bed of the river being of lime-stone. The mountains are one solid mass of the same materials, but without the least shade of trees, or decoration of foliage. At nine the men were so cold that we landed, in order to kindle a fire, which was considered as a very uncommon circumstance at this season; a small quantity of rum, however, served as an adequate substitute; and the current being so smooth as to admit of the use of paddles, I encouraged them to proceed without any further delay. In a short time an extensive view opened upon us, displaying a beautiful sheet of water, that was heightened by the calmness of the weather, and a splendid sun. Here the mountains, which were covered with wood, opened on either side, so that we entertained the hope of soon leaving them behind us. When we had got to the termination of this prospect, the river was barred with rocks, forming cascades and small islands. To proceed onwards, we were under the necessity of clearing a narrow passage of the drift wood, on the left shore. Here the view convinced us that our late hopes were without foundation, as there appeared a ridge or chain of mountains, running South and North as far as the eye could reach.

On advancing two or three miles, we arrived at the fork, one branch running about West-North-West, and the other South-South-East. If I had been governed by my own judgment, I should have taken the former, as it appeared to me to be the most likely to bring us nearest to the part where I wished to fall on the Pacific Ocean, but the old man whom I have already mentioned as having been frequently on war expeditions in this country, had warned me not, on any account, to follow it, as it was soon lost in various branches among the mountains, and that there was no great river that ran in any direction near it; but by following the latter, he said, we should arrive at a carrying-place to another large river, that did not exceed a day's march, where the inhabitants build houses, and live upon islands. There was so much apparent truth in the old man's narrative, that I determined to be governed by it; for I did not entertain the least doubt, if I could get into the other river, that I should reach the ocean.

I accordingly ordered my steersman to proceed at once to the East branch, which appeared to be more rapid than the other, though it did not possess an equal breadth. These circumstances disposed my men and Indians, the latter in particular being very tired of the voyage, to express their wishes that I should take the Western branch, especially when they perceived the difficulty of stemming the current, in the direction on which I had determined. Indeed the rush of water was so powerful, that we were the greatest part of the afternoon in getting two or three miles – a very tardy and mortifying progress, and which, with the voyage, was openly execrated by many of those who were engaged in it: and the inexpressible toil these people had endured, as well as the dangers they had encountered, required some degree of consideration; I therefore employed those arguments which were the best calculated to calm their immediate discontents, as well as to encourage their future hopes, though, at the same time, I delivered my sentiments in such a manner as to convince them that I was determined to proceed.

Saturday, June 1. On the 1st of June we embarked at sunrise, and towards noon the current began to slacken; we then put to shore, in order to gum the canoe, when a meridian altitude gave me 55.42.16 North latitude. We then continued our course, and towards the evening the current began to recover its former strength. Mr. Mackay and the Indians had already disembarked, to walk and lighten the boat. At sun-set we encamped on a point, being the first dry land which had been found on this side the river, that was fit for our purpose, since our people went on shore. In the morning we passed a large rapid river, that flowed in from the right.

In no part of the North-West did I see so much beaver-work, within an equal distance, as in the course of this day. In some places they had cut down several acres of large poplars; and we saw also a great number of these active and sagacious animals. The time which these wonderful creatures allot for their labours, whether in erecting their curious habitations, or providing food, is the whole of the interval between the setting and the rising sun.

Towards the dusky part of the evening we heard several discharges from the fowling pieces of our people, which we answered, to inform them of our situation; and some time after it was dark, they arrived in an equal state of fatigue and alarm: they were also obliged to swim across a channel in order to get to us, as we were situated on an island, though we were ignorant of the circumstances, till they came to inform us. One of the Indians was positive that he heard the discharge of firearms above our encampment; and on comparing the number of our discharges with theirs, there appeared to be some foundation for his alarm, as we imagined that we had heard two reports more than they acknowledged; and, in their turn, they declared that they had heard twice the number of those which we knew had proceeded from us. The Indians were therefore certain, that the Knisteneaux must be in our vicinity, on a war expedition, and consequently, if they were numerous, we should have had no reason to expect the least mercy from them in this distant country. Though I did not believe that circumstance, or that any of the natives could be in possession of fire-arms, I thought it right, at all events, we should be prepared. Our fusees were, therefore, primed and loaded, and having extinguished our fire, each of us took his station at the foot of a tree, where we passed an uneasy and restless night.

Sunday, June 2. The succeeding morning being clear and pleasant, we proceeded at an early hour against a rapid current, intersected by islands. About eight we passed two large trees, whose roots having been undermined by the current, had recently fallen into the river; and, in my opinion, the crash of their fall had occasioned the noise which caused our late alarm. In this manner the water ravages the islands in these rivers, and by driving down great quantities of wood, forms the foundations of others. The men were so oppressed with fatigue, that it was necessary they should encamp at six in the afternoon. We, therefore, landed on a sandy island, which is a very uncommon object, as the greater part of the islands consist of a bottom of round stones and gravel, covered from three to ten feet with mud and old driftwood. Beaver-work was as frequently seen as on the preceding day.

Monday, June 3. On the 3d of June we renewed our voyage with the rising sun. At noon I obtained a meridian altitude, which gave 55.22.3 North latitude. I also took time, and the watch was slow 1.30.14 apparent time. According to my calculation, this place is about twenty-five miles South-East of the fork.[25]

---

25. I shall now proceed with my usual regularity, which, as I have already mentioned, has been, for some days, suspended, from the loss of my book of observation.

Chapter 5

RISING WATER

Tuesday, June 4. We embarked this morning at four in a very heavy fog. The water had been continually rising, and, in many places, overflowed its banks. The current also was so strong, that our progress was very tedious, and required the most laborious exertions. Our course was this day, South-South-East one mile, South-South-West half a mile, South-East three quarters of a mile, North-East by East three quarters of a mile, South-East half a mile, South-East by South one mile, South-South-East one mile three quarters, South-East by South half a mile, East by South a quarter of a mile, South-East three quarters of a mile, North-East by East half a mile, East by North a quarter of a mile, South-East half a mile, South-East by South a quarter of a mile, South-East by East half a mile, North-East by East half a mile, North-North-East three quarters of a mile, to South by East one mile and an half. We could not find a place fit for an encampment, till nine at night, when we landed on a bank of gravel, of which little more appeared above the water than the spot we occupied.

Wednesday, June 5. This morning we found our canoe and baggage in the water, which had continued rising during the night. We then gummed the canoe, as we arrived at too late an hour to perform that operation on the preceding evening. This necessary business being completed, we traversed to the North shore, where I disembarked with Mr. Mackay, and the hunters, in order to ascend an adjacent mountain, with the hope of obtaining a view of the interior part of the country. I directed my people to proceed with all possible diligence, and that, if they met with any accident, or found my return necessary, they should fire two guns. They also understood, that when they should hear the same signal from me, they were to answer, and wait for me, if I were behind them.

When we had ascended to the summit of the hill, we found that it extended onwards in an even, level country; so that, encumbered as we were, with the thick wood, no distant view could be obtained; I therefore climbed a very lofty tree, from whose top I discerned on the right a ridge of mountains covered with snow, bearing about North-West; from thence another ridge of high land, whereon no snow was visible, stretched towards the South; between which and the snowy hills on the East side, there appeared to be an opening, which we determined to be the course of the river.

Having obtained all the satisfaction that the nature of the place would admit, we proceeded forward to overtake the canoe, and after a warm walk came down upon the river, when we discharged our pieces twice, but received no answering signal. I was of opinion, that the canoe was before us, while the Indians entertained an opposite notion. I, however, crossed another point of land, and came again to the waterside about ten. Here we had a long view of the river, which circumstance excited in my mind, some doubts of my former sentiments. We repeated our signals, but without any return; and as every moment now increased my anxiety, I left Mr. Mackay and one of the Indians at this spot to make a large fire, and send branches adrift down the current as notices of our situation, if the canoe was behind us; and proceeded with the other Indian across a very long point, where the river makes a considerable bend, in order that I might be satisfied if the canoe was a-head. Having been accustomed, for the last fortnight to very cold weather, I found the heat of this day almost insupportable, as our way lay over a dry land, which was relieved by no shade, but such as a few scattered cypresses could afford us. About twelve we arrived once more at the river, and the discharge of our pieces was as unsuccessful as it had hitherto been. The water rushed before us with uncommon velocity; and we tried the experiment of sending fresh branches down it. To add to the disagreeableness of our situation, the gnats and musquitoes appeared in swarms to torment us. When we returned to our companions, we found that they had not been contented with remaining in the position where I had left them, but had been three or four miles down the river, but were come back to their station, without having made any discovery of the people on the water.

Various very unpleasing conjectures at once perplexed and distressed us: the Indians, who are inclined to magnify evils of any and every kind, had at once consigned the canoe and every one on board it to the bottom; and were already settling a plan to return upon a raft, as well as calculating the number of nights that would be required to reach their home. As for myself, it will be easily believed, that my mind was in a state of extreme agitation; and the imprudence of my conduct in leaving the people, in such a situation of danger and toilsome exertion, added a very painful mortification to the severe apprehensions I already suffered: it was an act of indiscretion which might have put an end to the voyage that I had so much at heart, and compelled me at length to submit to the scheme which my hunters had already formed for our return.

At half past six in the evening, Mr. Mackay and the Cancre set off to proceed down the river, as far as they could before the night came on, and to continue their journey in the morning to the place where we had encamped the preceding evening. I also proposed to make my excursion upward; and, if we both failed of success in meeting the canoe, it was agreed that we should return to the place where we now separated.

In this situation we had wherewithal to drink in plenty, but with solid food we were totally unprovided. We had not seen even a partridge throughout the day, and the tracks of rein-deer that we had discovered, were of an old date. We were, however, preparing to make a bed of the branches of trees, where we should have had no other canopy than that afforded us by the heavens, when we heard a shot, and soon after another, which was the notice agreed upon, if Mr. Mackay and the Indian should see the canoe: that fortunate circumstance was also confirmed by a return of the signal from the people. I was, however, so fatigued from the heat and exercise of the day, as well as incommoded from drinking so much cold water, that I did not wish to remove till the following morning; but the Indian made such bitter complaints of the cold and hunger which he suffered, that I complied with his solicitations to depart; and it was almost dark when we reached the canoe, barefooted, and drenched with rain. But these inconveniences affected me very little, when I saw myself once more surrounded with my people. They informed me, that the canoe had been broken; and that they had this day experienced much greater toil and hardships than on any former occasion. I thought it prudent to affect a belief of every representation that they made, and even to comfort each of them with a consolatory dram: for, however difficult the passage might have been, it was too short to have occupied the whole day, if they had not relaxed in their exertions. The rain was accompanied with thunder and lightning.

It appeared from the various encampments which we had seen, and from several paddles we had found, that the natives frequent this part of the country at the latter end of the summer and the fall. The course to day was nearly East-South-East two miles and an half, South by West one mile, South-South-East one mile and an half, East two miles, and South-East by South one mile.

Thursday, June 6. At half past four this morning we continued our voyage, our courses being South-East by South one mile, East by South three quarters of a mile, South-East by East two miles. The whole of this distance we proceeded by hauling the canoe from branch to branch. The current was so strong, that it was impossible to stem it with the paddles; the depth was too great to receive any assistance from the poles, and the bank of the river was so closely lined with willows and other trees, that it was impossible to employ the line. As it was past twelve before we could find a place that would allow of our landing, I could not get a meridian altitude. We occupied the rest of the day in repairing the canoe, drying our cloaths, and making paddles and poles to replace those which had been broken or lost.

Friday, June 7. The morning was clear and calm; and since we had been at this station the water had risen two inches; so that the current became still stronger; and its velocity had already been so great as to justify our despair in getting up it, if we had not been so long accustomed to surmount it. I last night observed an emersion of Jupiter's first satellite, but inadvertently went to bed, without committing the exact time to writing: if my memory is correct, it was 8.18.10 by the time-piece. The canoe, which had been little better than a wreck, being now repaired, we proceeded East two miles and a quarter, South-South-East half a mile, South-East a quarter of a mile, when we landed to take an altitude for time. We continued our route at South-East by East three quarters of a mile, and landed again to determine the latitude, which is 55.2.51. To this I add, 2.45 Southing, which will make the place of taking altitude for time 55.5.36 with which I find that my time-piece was slow, 1.32.23 apparent time; and made the longitude obtained 122.35.50 West of Greenwich.

From this place we proceeded East by South four miles and an half, East-South-East one mile and an half, in which space there falls in a small river from the East; East half a mile, South-East a mile and an half, East a quarter of a mile, and encamped at seven o'clock. Mr. Mackay and the hunters walked the greatest part of the day, and in the course of their excursion killed a porcupine.[26] Here we found the bed of a very large bear quite fresh. During the day several Indian encampments were seen, which were of a late erection. The current had also lost some of its impetuosity during the greater part of the day.

Saturday, June 8. It rained and thundered through the night, and at four in the morning we again encountered the current. Our course was East a quarter of a mile, round to South by East along a very high white sandy bank on the East shore, three quarters of a mile, South-South-East a quarter of a mile, South-

---

26. We had been obliged to indulge our hunters with sitting idle in the canoe, lest their being compelled to share in the labour of navigating it should disgust and drive them from us. We, there fore, employed them as much as possible on shore, as well to procure provisions as to lighten the canoe.

South-West a quarter of a mile, South-South-East one mile and a quarter, South-East two miles, with a slack current; South-East by East two miles and a quarter, East a quarter of a mile, South-East a quarter of a mile, South-East by South four miles and an half, South-East one mile and an half, South-South-West half a mile, East-North-East half a mile, East-South-East a quarter of a mile, South-East by South one mile, South-East by East half a mile, East by South three quarters of a mile, when the mountains were in full view in this direction, and Eastward. For the three last days we could only see them at short intervals and long distances; but till then, they were continually in sight on either side, from our entrance into the fork. Those to the left were at no great distance from us.

For the last two days we had been anxiously looking out for the carrying-place, but could not discover it, and our only hope was in such information as we should be able to procure from the natives. All that remained for us to do, was to push forwards till the river should be no longer navigable: it had now, indeed, overflowed its banks, so that it was eight at night before we could discover a place to encamp. Having found plenty of wild parsneps, we gathered the tops, and boiled them with pemmican for our supper.

Sunday, June 9. The rain of this morning terminated in an heavy mist at half past five, when we embarked and steered South-East one mile and an half, when it veered North-North-East half a mile, South-East three quarters of a mile, East by South three quarters of a mile, East-South-East a quarter of a mile, South-South-East a quarter of a mile, South-East by East one mile, North-East by East half a mile, South-East by East half a mile, South-East by South three quarters of a mile, South-East three quarters of a mile, East by South half a mile, South-East by East half a mile, East-North-East three quarters of a mile, when it veered to South-South-East half a mile, then back to East (when a blue mountain, clear of snow, appeared a-head) one mile and an half; North-East by East half a mile, East by North one mile, when it veered to South-East half a mile, then on to North-West three quarters of a mile, and back to North-East by

East half a mile, South by West a quarter of a mile, North-East by East to North-North-East half a mile, South-South-East a quarter of a mile, and East by North half a mile: here we perceived a smell of fire; and in a short time heard people in the woods, as if in a state of great confusion, which was occasioned, as we afterwards understood, by their discovery of us. At the same time this unexpected circumstance produced some little discomposure among ourselves, as our arms were not in a state of preparation, and we were as yet unable to ascertain the number of the party. I considered, that if there were but few it would be needless to pursue them, as it would not be probable that we should overtake them in these thick woods; and if they were numerous, it would be an act of great imprudence to make the attempt, at least during their present alarm. I therefore ordered my people to strike off to the opposite side, that we might see if any of them had sufficient courage to remain; but, before we were half over the river, which, in this part, is not more than an hundred yards wide, two men appeared on a rising ground over against us, brandishing their spears, displaying their bows and arrows, and accompanying their hostile gestures with loud vociferations. My interpreter did not hesitate to assure them, that they might dispel their apprehensions, as we were white people, who meditated no injury, but were, on the contrary, desirous of demonstrating every mark of kindness and friendship. They did not, however, seem disposed to confide in our declarations, and actually threatened, if we came over before they were more fully satisfied of our peaceable intentions, that they would discharge their arrows at us. This was a decided kind of conduct which I did not expect; at the same time I readily complied with their proposition, and after some time had passed in hearing and answering their questions, they consented to our landing, though not without betraying very evident symptoms of fear and distrust. They, however, laid aside their weapons, and when I stepped forward and took each of them by the hand, one of them, but with a very tremulous action, drew his knife from his sleeve, and presented it to me as a mark of his submission to my will and pleasure. On our first hearing the noise of these people in the woods, we displayed our flag, which was now shewn to them as a token of friendship. They examined us, and every thing about us, with a minute and suspicious attention. They had heard, indeed, of white men, but this was the first time that they had ever seen an human being of a complexion different from their own. The party had been here but a few hours; nor had they yet erected their sheds; and, except the two men now with us, they had all fled, leaving their little property behind them. To those which had given us such a proof of their confidence, we paid the most conciliating attentions in our power. One of them I sent to recal his people, and the other, for very obvious reasons, we kept with us. In the mean time the canoe was unloaded, the necessary baggage carried up the hill, and the tents pitched.

Here I determined to remain till the Indians became so familiarized with us, as to give all the intelligence which we imagined might be obtained from them. In fact, it had been my intention to land where I might most probably discover the carrying-place, which was our more immediate object, and undertake marches of two or three days, in different directions, in search of another river. If unsuccessful in this attempt, it was my purpose to continue my progress up the present river, as far as it was navigable, and if we did not meet with natives to instruct us in our further progress, I had determined to return to the fork, and take the other branch, with the hope of better fortune.

It was about three in the afternoon when we landed, and at five the whole party of Indians were assembled. It consisted only of three men, three women, and seven or eight boys and girls. With their scratched legs, bleeding feet, and dishevelled hair, as in the hurry of their flight they had left their shoes and leggins behind them, they displayed a most wretched appearance: they were consoled, however, with beads, and other trifles, which seemed to please them; they had pemmican also given to them to eat, which was not unwelcome, and in our opinion, at least, superior to their own provision, which consisted entirely of dried fish.

When I thought that they were sufficiently composed, I sent for the men to my tent, to gain such information respecting the country as I concluded it was in their power to afford me. But my expectations were by no means satisfied: they said that they were not acquainted with any river to the Westward, but that there was one from whence they were just arrived, over a carrying-place of eleven days march, which they represented as being a branch only of the river before us. Their iron-work they obtained from the people who inhabit the bank of that river, and an adjacent lake, in exchange for beaver skins, and dressed moose skins. They represented the latter as travelling, during a moon, to get to the country of other tribes, who live in houses, with whom they traffic for the same commodities; and that these also extend their journies in the same manner to the sea coast, or, to use their expression, the Stinking Lake, where they trade with people like us, that come there in vessels as big as islands. They added, that the people to the Westward, as they have been told, are very numerous. Those who inhabit the other branch they stated as consisting of about forty families, while they themselves did not amount to more than a fourth of that number; and were almost continually compelled to remain in their strong holds, where they sometimes perished with cold and hunger, to secure themselves from their enemies, who never failed to attack them whenever an opportunity presented itself.

This account of the country, from a people who I had every reason to suppose were well acquainted with every part of it, threatened to disconcert the project on which my heart was set, and in which my whole mind was occupied. It occurred to me, however, that from fear, or other motives, they might be tardy in their communication; I therefore assured them that, if they would direct me to the river which I described to them, I would come in large vessels, like those that their neighbours had described, to the mouth of it, and bring them arms and ammunition in exchange for the produce of their country; so that they might be able to defend themselves against their enemies, and no longer remain in that abject, distressed, and fugitive state in which they then lived. I added also, that in the mean time, if they would, on my return, accompany me below the mountains, to a country which was very abundant in animals, I would furnish them, and their companions, with every thing they might want; and make peace between them and the Beaver Indians. But all these promises did not appear to advance the object of my inquiries, and they still persisted in their ignorance of any such river as I had mentioned, that discharged itself into the sea.

In this state of perplexity and disappointment, various projects presented themselves to my mind, which were no sooner formed than they were discovered to be impracticable, and were consequently abandoned. At one time I thought of leaving the canoe, and every thing it contained, to go over land, and pursue that chain of connexion by which these people obtain their ironwork; but a very brief course of reflection convinced me that it would be impossible for us to carry provisions for our support through any considerable part of such a journey, as well as presents, to secure us a kind reception among the natives, and ammunition for the service of the hunters, and to defend ourselves against any act of hostility. At another time my solicitude for the success of the expedition incited a wish to remain with the natives, and go to the sea by the way they had described; but the accomplishment of such a journey, even if no accident should interpose, would have required a portion of time which it was not in my power to bestow. In my present state of information, to proceed further up the river was considered as a fruitless waste of toilsome exertion; and to return unsuccessful, after all our labour, sufferings, and dangers, was an idea too painful to indulge. Besides, I could not yet abandon the hope that the Indians might not yet be sufficiently composed and confident, to disclose their real knowledge of the country freely and fully to me. Nor was I altogether without my doubts respecting the fidelity of my interpreter, who being very much tired of the voyage, might be induced to withhold those communications which would induce me to continue it. I therefore continued my attentions to the natives, regaled them with such provisions as I had, indulged their children with a taste of sugar, and determined to suspend my conversation with them till the following morning. On my expressing a desire to partake of their fish, they brought me a few dried trout, well cured, that had been taken in the river which they lately left. One of the men also brought me five beaver skins, as a present.

Monday, June 10. The solicitude that possessed my mind interrupted my repose; when the dawn appeared I had already quitted my bed, and was waiting with impatience for another conference with the natives. The sun, however, had risen before they left their leafy bowers, whither they had retired with their children, having most hospitably resigned their beds, and the partners of them, to the solicitations of my young men.

I now repeated my inquiries, but my perplexity was not removed by any favourable variation in their answers. About nine, however, one of them, still remaining at my fire, in conversation with the interpreters, I understood enough of his language to know that he mentioned something about a great river, at the same time pointing significantly up that which was before us. On my inquiring of the interpreter respecting that expression, I was informed that he knew of a large river that runs towards the midday sun, a branch of which flowed near the source of that which we were now navigating; and that there were only three small lakes, and as many carrying-places, leading to a small river, which discharges itself into the great river, but that the latter did not empty itself into the sea. The inhabitants, he said, built houses, lived on islands, and were a numerous and warlike people. I desired him to describe the road to the other river, by delineating it with a piece of coal, on a strip of bark, which he accomplished to my satisfaction. The opinion that the river did not discharge itself into the sea, I very confidently imputed to his ignorance of the country.

My hopes were now renewed, and an object presented itself which awakened my utmost impatience. To facilitate its attainment, one of the Indians was induced, by presents, to accompany me as a guide to the first inhabitants, which we might expect to meet on the small lakes in our way. I accordingly resolved to depart with all expedition, and while my people were making every necessary preparation, I employed myself in writing the following description of the natives around me.

They are low in stature, not exceeding five feet six or seven inches; and they are of that meagre appearance which might be expected in a people whose life is one succession of difficulties, in procuring subsistence. Their faces are round, with high cheek bones; and their eyes, which are small, are of a dark brown colour; the cartilage of their nose is perforated, but without any ornaments suspended from it; their hair is of a dingy black, hanging loose and in disorder over their shoulders, but irregularly cut in the front, so as not to obstruct the sight; their beards are eradicated, with the exception of a few straggling hairs, and their complexion is a swarthy yellow.

Their dress consists of robes made of the skins of the beaver, the ground hog, and the rein-deer, dressed in the hair, and of the moose-skin without it. All of them are ornamented with a fringe, while some of them have tassels hanging down the seams; those of the ground hog are decorated on the fur side with the tails of the animal, which they do not separate from them. Their garments they tie over the shoulders, and fasten them round the middle with a belt of green skin, which is as stiff as horn. Their leggins are long, and, if they were topped with a waistband, might be called trowsers: they, as well as their shoes, are made of dressed moose, elk, or rein-deer skin. The organs of generation they leave uncovered.

The women differ little in their dress from the men, except in the addition of an apron, which is fastened round the waist, and hangs down to the knees. They are in general of a more lusty make than the other sex, and taller in proportion, but infinitely their inferiors in cleanliness. A black artificial stripe crosses the face beneath the eye, from ear to ear, which I first took for scabs, from the accumulation of dirt on it. Their hair, which is longer than that of the men, is divided from the forehead to the crown, and drawn back in long plaits behind the ears. They have also a few white beads, which they get where they procure their iron: they are from a line to an inch in length, and are worn in their ears, but are not of European manufacture. These, with bracelets made of horn and bone, compose all the ornaments which deco-

262 — SIR ALEXANDER MACKENZIE

rate their persons. Necklaces of the grisly or white bear's claws, are worn exclusively by the men.

Their arms consist of bows made of cedar, six feet in length, with a short iron spike at one end, and serve occasionally as a spear. Their arrows are well made, barbed, and pointed with iron, flint, stone, or bone; they are feathered, and from two to two feet and an half in length. They have two kinds of spears, but both are double edged, and of well polished iron; one of them is about twelve inches long, and two wide; the other about half the width, and two thirds of the length; the shafts of the first are eight feet in length, and the latter six. They have also spears made of bone. Their knives consist of pieces of iron, shaped and handled by themselves. Their axes are something like our adze, and they use them in the same manner as we employ that instrument. They were, indeed, furnished with iron in a manner that I could not have supposed, and plainly proved to me that their communication with those, who communicate with the inhabitants of the sea coast, cannot be very difficult, and from their ample provision of iron weapons, the means of procuring it must be of a more distant origin than I had at first conjectured.

They have snares made of green skin, which they cut to the size of sturgeon twine, and twist a certain number of them together; and though when completed they do not exceed the thickness of a cod-line, their strength is sufficient to hold a moose deer: they are from one and an half to two fathoms in length. Their nets and fishing lines are made of willow-bark and nettles; those made of the latter are finer and smoother than if made with hempen thread. Their hooks are small bones, fixed in pieces of wood split for that purpose, and tied round with fine watape, which has been particularly described in the former voyage. Their kettles are also made of watape, which is so closely woven that they never leak, and they heat water in them, by putting red-hot stones into it. There is one kind of them, made of spruce-bark, which they hang over the fire, but at such a distance as to receive the heat without being within reach of the blaze; a very tedious operation. They have various dishes of wood and bark; spoons of horn and wood, and buckets; bags of leather and net-work, and baskets of bark, some of which hold their fishing-tackle, while others are contrived to be carried on the back. They have a brown kind of earth in great abundance, wire which they rub their clothes, not only for ornament but utility, as it prevents the leather from becoming hard after it has been wetted. They have spruce bark in great plenty, with which they make their canoes, an operation that does not require any great portion of skill or ingenuity, and is managed in the following manner. – The bark is taken off the tree the whole length of the intended canoe, which is commonly about eighteen feet, and is sewed with watape at both ends; two laths are then laid, and fixed along the edge of the bark which forms the gunwale; in these are fixed the bars, and against them bear the ribs or timbers, that are cut to the length to which the bark can be stretched; and, to give additional strength, strips of wood are laid between them: to make the whole water-tight, gum is abundantly employed. These vessels carry from two to five people. Canoes of a similar construction were used by the Beaver Indians within these few years, but they now very generally employ those made of the bark of the birch tree, which are by far more durable. Their paddles are about six feet long, and about one foot is occupied by the blade, which is in the shape of an heart.

Previous to our departure, the natives had caught a couple of trout, of about six pounds weight, which they brought me, and I paid them with beads. They likewise gave me a net, made of nettles, the skin of a moose-deer, dressed, and a white horn in the shape of a spoon, which resembles the horn of the buffalo of the Copper-Mine River; but their description of the animal to which it belongs does not answer to that. My young men also got two quivers of excellent arrows, a collar of white bear's claws, of a great length, horn bracelets, and other articles, for which they received an ample remuneration.

Chapter 6

NORTH EAST BY NORTH

Monday; June 10 [continued]. At ten we were ready to embark. I then took leave of the Indians, but encouraged them to expect us in two moons, and expressed the hope that I should find them on the road with any of their relations whom they might meet. I also returned the beaver skins to the man who had presented them to me, desiring him to take care of them till I came back, when I would purchase them of him. Our guide expressed much less concern about the undertaking in which he had engaged, than his companions, who appeared to be affected with great solicitude for his safety.

We now pushed off the canoe from the bank, and proceeded East half a mile, when a river flowed in from the left, about half as large as that which we were navigating. We continued the same course three quarters of a mile, when we missed two of our fowling pieces, which had been forgotten, and I sent their owners back for them, who were absent on this errand upwards of an hour. We now proceeded North-East by East half a mile, North-East by North three quarters of a mile, when the current slackened: there was a verdant spot on the left, where, from the remains of some Indian timber-work, it appeared, that the natives have frequently encamped. Our next course was East one mile, and we saw a ridge of mountains covered with snow to the South-East. The land on our right was low and marshy for three or four miles, when it rose into a range of heights that extended to the mountains. We proceeded East-South-East a mile and a half, South-East by East one mile, East by South three quarters of a mile, South-East by East one mile, East by

South half a mile, North-East by East one mile, South-East half a mile, East-North-East a mile and a quarter, South-South-East half a mile, North-North-East a mile and an half: here a river flowed in from the left, which was about one-fourth part as large as that which received its tributary waters. We then continued East by South half a mile, to the foot of the mountain on the South of the above river. The course now veered short, South-West by West three quarters of a mile, East by South a quarter of a mile, South half a mile, South-East by South half a mile, South-West a quarter of a mile, East by South a quarter of a mile, veered to West-North-West a quarter of a mile, South-West one eighth of a mile, East South-East one quarter of a mile, East one sixth of a mile, South-South-West one twelfth of a mile, East South-East one eighth of a mile, North-East by East one third of a mile, East by North one twelfth of a mile, North-East by East one third of a mile, East one sixteenth of a mile, South-East one twelfth of a mile, North-East by East one twelfth of a mile, East one eighth of a mile, and East-South-East half a mile, when we landed at seven o'clock and encamped. During the greatest part of the distance we came today, the river runs close under the mountains on the left.

Tuesday, June 11. The morning was clear and cold. On my interpreter's encouraging the guide to dispel all apprehension, to maintain his fidelity to me, and not to desert in the night, "How is it possible for me," he replied, "to leave the lodge of the Great Spirit! – When he tells me that he has no further occasion for me, I will then return to my children." As we proceeded, however, he soon lost, and with good reason, his exalted notions of me.

At four we continued our voyage, steering East by South a mile and an half, East-South-East half a mile. A river appeared on the left, at the foot of a mountain which, from its conical form, my young Indian called the Beaver Lodge Mountain. Having proceeded South-South-East half a mile, another river appeared from the right. We now came in a line with the beginning of the mountains we saw yesterday: others of the same kind ran parallel with them on the left side of the river, which was reduced to the breadth of fifteen yards, and with a moderate current.

We now steered East-North-East one eighth of a mile, South-East by South one eighth of a mile, East-South-East one sixth of a mile, South-West one eighth of a mile, East-South-East one eighth of a mile, South-South-East one sixth of a mile, North-East by East one twelfth of a mile, East-South-East half a mile, South-West by West one third of a mile, South-South-East one eighth of a mile, South-South-West one quarter of a mile, North-East one sixth of a mile, South by West one fourth of a mile, East three quarters of a mile, and North-East one quarter of a mile. Here the mountain on the left appeared to be composed of a succession of round hills, covered with wood almost to their summits, which were white with snow, and crowned with withered trees. We now steered East, in a line with the high lands on the right five miles; North one twelfth of a mile, North-East by North one eighth of a mile, South by East one sixteenth of a mite, North-East by North one fourth of a mile, where another river fell in from the right; North-East by East one sixth of a mile, East two miles and an half, South one twelfth of a mile, North-East half a mile, South-East one third of a mile, East one mile and a quarter, South-South-West one sixteenth of a mile, North-East by East half a mile, East one mile and three quarters, South and South-West by West half a mile, North-East half a mile, South one third of a mile, North-East by North one sixth of a mile, East by South one fourth of a mile, South one eighth of a mile, South-East three quarters of a mile. The canoe had taken in so much water, that it was necessary for us to land here, in order to stop the leakage, which occasioned the delay of an hour and a quarter, North-East a quarter of a mile, East-North-East a quarter of a mile, South-East by South a sixteenth of a mile, East by South a twelfth of a mile, North-East one sixth of a mile, East-South-East one sixteenth of a mile, South-West half a mile, North-East a quarter of a mile, East by South half a mile, South-South-East one twelfth of a mile, East half a mile, North-East by North a quarter of a mile, South-South-East a quarter of a mile, North-East by North one twelfth of a mile, where a small river flowed in from the left, South-East by East one twelfth of a mile, South by East a quarter of a mile, South-East one eighth of a mile, East one twelfth of a mile, North-East by North a quarter of a mile, South half a mile, South-East by South one eighth of a mile, North-East one fourth of a mile, South-East by East, and South-East by South one third of a mile, East-South-East, and North-North-East one third of a mile, and South by West, East and East-North-East one eighth of a mile.

Here we quitted the main branch, which, according to the information of our guide, terminates at a short distance, where it is supplied by the snow which covers the mountains. In the same direction is a valley which appears to be of very great depth, and is full of snow, that rises nearly to the height of the land, and forms a reservoir of itself sufficient to furnish a river, whenever there is a moderate degree of heat. The branch which we left was not, at this time, more than ten yards broad, while that which we entered was still less. Here the current was very trifling, and the channel so meandering, that we sometimes found it difficult to work the canoe forward. The straight course from this to the entrance of a small lake or pond, is about East one mile. This entrance by the river into the lake was almost choked up by a quantity of drift-wood, which appeared to me to be an extraordinary circumstance; but I afterwards found that it falls down from the mountains. The water, however, was so high, that the country was entirely overflowed, and we passed with the canoe among the branches of trees. The principal wood along the banks is spruce, intermixed with a few white birch, growing on detached spots, the intervening spaces being covered with willow and alder. We advanced about a mile in the lake, and took up our station for the night at an old Indian encampment. Here we expected to meet with natives, but were disappointed; but our guide encouraged us with the hope of seeing some on the morrow. We saw beaver in the course of the afternoon, but did not discharge our pieces, from the fear of alarming the inhabitants; there were also swans in great numbers, with geese and ducks, which we did not disturb for the same reason. We observed also the tracks of moose-deer that had crossed the river; and wild parsneps grew here in abundance, which have been already mentioned as a grateful vegetable. Of birds, we saw blue jays, yellow birds, and one beautiful humming-bird: of the first and last, I had not seen any since I had been in the North-West.

Wednesday, June 12. The weather was the same as yesterday, and we proceeded between three and four in the morning. We took up the net which we had set the preceding evening, when it contained a trout, one white fish, one carp, and three jub. The lake is about two miles in length, East by South, and from three to five hundred yards wide. This I consider as the highest and Southernmost source of the Unjigah, or Peace River, latitude, 54.24 North, longitude 121 West of Greenwich, which, after a winding course through a vast extent of country, receiving many large rivers in its progress, and passing through the Slave Lake, empties itself into the Frozen Ocean, in 70 North latitude, and about 135 West longitude.

We landed and unloaded, where we found a beaten path leading over a low ridge of land of eight hundred and seventeen paces in length to another small lake. The distance between the two mountains at this place is about a quarter of a mile, rocky precipices presenting themselves on both sides. A few large spruce trees and liards were scattered over the carrying-place. There were also willows along the side of the water, with plenty of grass and weeds. The natives had left their old canoes here, with baskets hanging on the trees, which contained various articles. From the latter I took a net, some hooks, a goat's-horn, and a kind of wooden trap, in which, as our guide informed me, the ground-hog is taken. I left, however, in exchange, a knife, some fire-steels, beads, awls, &c. Here two streams tumble down the rocks from the right, and lose themselves in the lake which we had left; while two others fall from the opposite heights, and glide into the lake which we were approaching; this being the highest point of land dividing these waters, and we are now going with the stream. This lake runs in the same course as the last, but is rather narrower, and not more than half the length. We were obliged to clear away some floating drift-wood to get to the carrying-place, over which is a beaten path of only an hundred and seventy-five paces long. The lake empties itself by a small river, which, if the channel were not interrupted by large trees that had fallen across it, would have admitted of our canoe with all its lading: the impediment, indeed, might have been removed by two axe-men in a few hours. On the edge of the water, we observed a large quantity of thick, yellow, scum or froth, of an acrid taste and smell.

We embarked on this lake, which is in the same course, and about the same size as that which we had just left, and from whence we passed into a small river, that was so full of fallen wood, as to employ some time, and require some exertion, to force a passage. At the entrance, it afforded no more water than was just sufficient to bear the canoe; but it was soon increased by many small streams which came in broken rills down the rugged sides of the mountains, and were furnished, as I suppose, by the melting of the snow. These accessory streamlets had all the coldness of ice. Our course continued to be obstructed by banks of gravel, as well as trees which had fallen across the river. We were obliged to force our way through the one, and to cut through the other, at a great expence of time and trouble. In many places the current was also very rapid and meandering. At four in the afternoon, we stopped to unload and carry, and at five we entered a small round lake of about one third of a mile in diameter. From the last lake to this is, I think, in a straight line, East by South six miles, though it is twice that distance by the winding of the river. We again entered the river, which soon ran with great rapidity, and rushed impetuously over a bed of flat stones. At half past six we were stopped by two large trees that lay across the river, and it was with great difficulty that the canoe was prevented from driving against them. Here we unloaded and formed our encampment.

The weather was cloudy and raw, and as the circumstances of this day's voyage had compelled us to be frequently in the water, which was cold as ice, we were almost in a benumbed state. Some of the people who had gone ashore to lighten the canoe, experienced great difficulty in reaching us, from the rugged state of the country; it was, indeed, almost dark when they arrived. We had no sooner landed than I sent two men down the river to bring me some account of its circumstances, that I might form a judgment of the difficulties which might await us on the morrow; and they brought back a fearful detail of rapid currents, fallen trees, and large stones. At this place our guide manifested evident symptoms of discontent: he had been very much alarmed in going down some of the rapids with us, and expressed an anxiety to return. He shewed us a mountain, at no great distance, which he represented as being on the other side of a river, into which this empties itself.

Thursday, June 13. At an early hour of this morning the men began to cut a road, in order to carry the canoe and lading beyond the rapid; and by seven they were ready. That business was soon effected, and the canoe re-laden, to proceed with the current which ran with great rapidity. In order to lighten her, it was my intention to walk with some of the people; but those in the boat with great earnestness requested me to embark, declaring, at the same time, that, if they perished, I should perish with them. I did not then imagine in how short a period their apprehension would be justified. We accordingly pushed off, and had proceeded but a very short way when the canoe struck, and notwithstanding all our exertions, the violence of the current was so great as to drive her sideways down the river, and break her by the first bar, when I instantly jumped into the water, and the men followed my example; but before we could set her straight, or stop her, we came to deeper water, so that we were obliged to re-embark with the utmost precipitation. One of the men who was not sufficiently active, was left to get on shore in the best manner in his power. We had hardly regained our situations when we drove against a rock which shattered the stern of the canoe in such a manner, that it held only by the gunwales, so that the steersman could no longer keep his place. The violence of this stroke drove us to the opposite side of the river, which is but narrow, when the bow met with the same fate as the stern. At this moment the foreman seized on some branches of a small tree in the hope of bringing up the canoe, but such was their elasticity that, in a manner not easily described, he was jerked on shore in an instant, and with a degree of violence that threatened his destruction. But we had no time to turn from our own situation to inquire what had befallen him; for, in a few moments, we came across a cascade which broke several large holes in the bottom of the canoe, and started all the bars, except one behind the scooping seat. If this accident, however, had not happened, the vessel must have been irretrievably overset. The wreck becoming flat on the water, we all jumped out, while the steersman, who had been compelled to abandon his place, and had not recovered from his fright, called out to his companions to save themselves. My peremptory commands superseded the effects of his fear, and they all held fast to the wreck; to which fortunate resolution we owed our safety, as we should otherwise have been dashed against the rocks by the force of the water, or driven over the cascades. In this condition we were forced several hundred yards, and every yard on the verge of destruction; but, at length, we most fortunately arrived in shallow water and a small eddy, where we were enabled to make a stand, from the weight of the canoe resting on the stones, rather than from any exertions of our exhausted strength. For though our efforts were short, they were pushed to the utmost, as life or death depended on them. This alarming scene, with all its terrors and dangers, occupied only a few minutes; and in the present suspension of it, we called to the people on shore to come to our assistance, and they immediately obeyed the summons. The foreman, however, was the first with us; he had escaped unhurt from the extraordinary jerk with which he was thrown out of the boat, and just as we were beginning to take our effects out of the water, he appeared to give his assistance. The Indians, when they saw our deplorable situation, instead of making the least effort to help us, sat down and gave vent to their tears. I was on the outside of the canoe, where I remained till every thing was got on shore, in a state of great pain from the extreme cold of the water; so that at length, it was with difficulty I could stand, from the benumbed state of my limbs.

The loss was considerable and important, for it consisted of our whole stock of balls, and some of our furniture; but these considerations were forgotten in the impressions of our miraculous escape. Our first inquiry was after the absent man, whom in the first moment of danger, we had left to get on shore, and in a short time his appearance removed our anxiety. We had, however, sustained no personal injury of consequence, and my bruises seemed to be in the greater proportion.

All the different articles were now spread out to dry. The powder had fortunately received no damage, and all my instruments had escaped. Indeed, when my people began to recover from their alarm, and to enjoy a sense of safety, some of them, if not all, were by no means sorry for our late misfortune, from the hope that it must put a period to our voyage, particularly as we were without a canoe, and all the bullets sunk in the river. It did not, indeed, seem possible to them that we could proceed under these circumstances. I listened, however, to the observations that were made on the occasion without replying to them, till their panic was dispelled, and they had got themselves warm and comfortable, with an hearty meal, and rum enough to raise their spirits.

I then addressed them, by recommending them all to be thankful for their late very narrow escape. I also stated, that the navigation was not impracticable in itself, but from our ignorance of its course; and that our late experience would enable us to pursue our voyage with greater security. I brought to their recollection, that I did not deceive them, and that they were made acquainted with the difficulties and dangers they must expect to encounter, before they engaged to accompany me. I also urged the honour of conquering disasters, and the disgrace that would attend them on their return home, without having attained the object of the expedition. Nor did I fail to mention the courage and resolution which was the peculiar boast of the North men; and that I depended on them, at that moment, for the maintenance of their character. I quieted their apprehension as to the loss of the bullets, by bringing to their recollection that we still had shot from which they might be manufactured. I at the same time acknowledged the difficulty of restoring the wreck of the canoe, but confided in our skill and exertion to put it in such a state as would carry us on to where we might procure bark, and build a new one. In short, my harangue produced the desired effect, and a very general assent appeared to go wherever I should lead the way.

Various opinions were offered in the present posture of affairs, and it was rather a general wish that the wreck should be abandoned, and all the lading carried to the river, which our guide informed us was at no great distance, and in the vicinity of woods where he believed there was plenty of bark. This project seemed not to promise that certainty to which I looked in my present operations; besides, I had my doubts respecting the views of my guide, and consequently could not confide in the representation he made to me. I therefore dispatched two of the men at nine in the morning, with one of the young Indians, for I did not venture to trust the guide out of my sight, in search of bark, and to endeavour, if it were possible, in the course of the day, to penetrate to the great river, into which that before us discharges itself in the direction which the guide had communicated. I now joined my people in order to repair, as well as circumstances would admit, our wreck of a canoe, and I began to set them the example.

At noon I had an altitude, which gave 54.23 North latitude. At four in the afternoon I took time, with the hope that in the night I might obtain an observation of Jupiter, and his satellites, but I had not a sufficient horizon, from the propinquity of the mountains. The result of my calculation for time was 1.38.28 slow apparent time.

It now grew late, and the people who had been sent on the excursion already mentioned, were not yet returned; about ten o'clock, however, I heard a man halloo, and I very gladly returned the signal. In a short time our young Indian arrived with a small roll of indifferent bark: he was oppressed with fatigue and hunger, and his clothes torn to rags: he had parted with the other two men at sun-set, who had walked the whole day, in a dreadful country, without procuring any good bark, or being able to get to the large river. His account of the river, on whose banks we were, could not be more unfavourable or discouraging; it had appeared to him to be little more than a succession of falls and rapids, with occasional interruptions of fallen trees.

Our guide became so dissatisfied and troubled in mind, that we could not obtain from him any regular account of the country before us. All we could collect from him was, that the river into which this empties itself is but a branch of a large river, the great fork being at no great distance from the confluence of this; and that he knew of no lake, or large body of still water, in the vicinity of these rivers. To this account of the country, he added some strange, fanciful, but terrifying descriptions of the natives, similar to those which were mentioned in the former voyage.

We had an escape this day, which I must add to the many instances of good fortune which I experienced in this perilous expedition. The powder had been spread out, to the amount of eighty pounds weight, to receive the air; and, in this situation, one of" the men carelessly and composedly walked across it with a lighted pipe in his mouth, but without any ill consequence resulting from such an act of criminal negligence. I need not add that one spark might have put a period to all my anxiety and ambition.

I observed several trees and plants on the banks of this river, which I had not seen to the North of the latitude 52 such as the cedar, maple, hemlock, &c. At this time the water rose fast, and passed on with the rapidity of an arrow shot from a bow.

Friday, June 14. The weather was fine, clear, and warm, and at an early hour of the morning we resumed our repair of the canoe. At half past seven our two men returned hungry and cold, not having tasted food, or enjoyed the least repose for twenty-four hours, with their clothes torn into tatters, and their skin lacerated, in passing through the woods. Their account was the same as that brought by the Indian, with this exception, that they had reason to think they saw the river, or branch which our guide had mentioned; but they were of opinion that from the frequent obstructions in this river, we should have to carry the whole way to it, through a dreadful country, where much time and labour would be required to open a passage through it.

Discouraging as these accounts were, they did not, however, interrupt for a moment the task in which we were engaged, of repairing the canoe; and this work we contrived to complete by the conclusion of the day. The bark which was brought by the Indian, with some pieces of oil-cloth, and plenty of gum, enabled us to put our shattered vessel in a condition to answer our present purposes. The guide, who has been mentioned as manifesting continual signs of dissatisfaction, now assumed an air of contentment, which I attributed to a smoke that was visible in the direction of the river; as he naturally expected, if we should fall in with any natives, which was now very probable, from such a circumstance, that he should be released from a service which he had found so irksome and full of danger. I had an observation at noon, which made our latitude 54.23.43 North. I also took time, and found it slow apparent time 1.38.44.

Saturday, June 15. The weather continued the same as the preceding day, and according to the directions which I had previously given, my people began at a very early hour to open a road, through which we might carry a part of our lading; as I was fearful of risquing the whole of it in the canoe, in its present weak state, and in a part of the river which is full of shoals and rapids. Four men were employed to conduct her, lightened as she was of twelve packages. They passed several dangerous places, and met with various obstructions, the current of the river being frequently stopped by rafts of drift wood, and fallen trees, so that after fourteen hours hard labour we had not made more than three miles. Our course was South-East by East, and as we had not met with any accident, the men appeared to feel a renewed courage to continue their voyage. In the morning, however, one of the crew, whose name was Beauchamp, peremptorily refused to embark in the canoe. This being the first example of absolute disobedience which had yet appeared during the course of our expedition, I should not have passed it over without taking some very severe means to prevent a repetition of it; but as he had the general character of a simple fellow, among his companions, and had been frightened out of what little sense he possessed, by our late dangers, I rather preferred to consider him as unworthy of accompanying us, and to represent him as an object of ridicule and contempt for his pusillanimous behaviour; though, in fact, he was a very useful, active, and laborious man. At the close of the day we assembled round a blazing fire; and the whole party, being enlivened with the usual beverage which I supplied on these occasions, forgot their fatigues and apprehensions; nor did they fail to anticipate the pleasure they should enjoy in getting clear of their present difficulties and gliding onwards with a strong and steady stream, which our guide had described as the characteristic of the large river we soon expected to enter.

Sunday, June 16. The fine weather continued, and we began our work, as we had done the preceding day; some were occupied in opening a road, others were carrying, and the rest employed in conducting the canoe. I was of the first party, and soon discovered that we had encamped about half a mile above several falls, over which we could not attempt to run the canoe, lightened even as she was. This circumstance rendered it necessary that the road should be made sufficiently wide to admit the canoe to pass; a tedious and toilsome work. In running her down a rapid above the falls, an hole was broken in her bottom, which occasioned a considerable delay, as we were destitute of the materials necessary for her effectual reparation. On my being informed of this misfortune, I returned, and ordered Mr. Mackay, with two Indians, to quit their occupation in making the road, and endeavour to penetrate to the great river, according to the direction which the guide had communicated, without paying any attention to the course of the river before us.

When the people had repaired the canoe in the best manner they were able, we conducted her to the head of the falls; she was then unloaded and taken out of the water, when we carried her for a considerable distance through a low, swampy country. I appointed four men to this laborious office, which they executed at the peril of their lives, for the canoe was now become so heavy, from the additional quantity of bark and gum necessary to patch her up, that two men could not carry her more than an hundred yards, without being relieved; and as their way lay through deep mud, which was rendered more difficult by the roots and prostrate trunks of trees, they were every moment in danger of falling; and beneath such a weight, one false step might have attended with fatal consequences. The other two men and myself followed as fast as we could, with the lading. Thus did we toil till seven o'clock in the evening, to get to the termination of the road that had been made in the morning. Here Mr. Mackay and the Indian joined us, after having been at the river, which they represented as rather large. They had also observed, that the lower part of the river before us was so full of fallen wood, that the attempt to clear a passage through it, would be an unavailing labour. The country through which they had passed was morass, and almost impenetrable wood. In passing over one of the embarras, our dog, which was following them, fell in, and it was with very great difficulty that he was saved, as the current had carried him under the drift. They brought with them two geese, which had been shot in the course of their expedition. To add to our perplexities and embarrassments, we were persecuted by musquitoes and sand-flies, through the whole of the day.

The extent of our journey was not more than two miles South-East; and so much fatigue and pain had been suffered in the course of it, that my people, as might be expected, looked forward to a continuance of it with discouragement and dismay. I was, indeed, informed that murmurs prevailed among them, of which, however, I took no notice. When we were assembled together for the night, I gave each of them a dram, and in a short time they retired to the repose which they so much required. We could discover the termination of the mountains at a considerable distance on either side of us, which, according to my conjecture, marked the course of the great river. On the mountains to the East there were several fires, as their smokes were very visible to us. Excessive heat prevailed throughout the day.

Monday, June 17. Having sat up till twelve last night, which had been my constant practice since we had taken our present guide, I awoke Mr. Mackay to watch him in turn. I then laid down to rest, and at three I was awakened to be informed that he had deserted. Mr. Mackay, with whom I was displeased on this occasion, and the Cancre, accompanied by the dog, went in search of him, but he had made his escape; a design which he had for some time meditated, though I had done every thing in my power to induce him to remain with me.

This misfortune did not produce any relaxation in our exertions. At an early hour of the morning we were all employed in cutting a passage of three quarters of a mile, through which we carried our canoe and cargo, when we put her into the water with her lading, but in a very short time were stopped by the driftwood, and were obliged to land and carry. In short, we pursued our alternate journies, by land and water, till noon, when we could proceed no further, from the various small unnavigable channels into which the river branched in every direction; and no other mode of getting forward now remained for us, but by cutting a road across a neck of land. I accordingly dispatched two men to ascertain the exact distance, and we employed the interval of their absence in unloading and getting the canoe out of the water. It was eight in the evening when we arrived at the bank of the great river. This journey was three quarters of a mile East-North-East, through a continued swamp, where, in many places, we waded up to the middle of our thighs. Our course in the small river was about South-East by East three miles. At length we enjoyed, after all our toil and anxiety, the inexpressible satisfaction of finding ourselves on the bank of a navigable river, on the West side of the first great range of mountains.

Chapter 7

MOUNTAINS

Tuesday, June 18. It rained throughout the night and till seven in the morning; nor was I sorry that the weather gave me an excuse for indulging my people with that additional rest, which their fatigues, during the last three days, rendered so comfortable to them. Before eight, however, we were on the water, and driven on by a strong current, when we steered East-South-East half a mile, South-West by South half a mile, South-South-East half a mile, South-West half a mile, went round to North-West half a mile, backed South-South-East three quarters of a mile, South-South-West half a mile, South by East a quarter of a mile, and South-West by South three quarters of a mile. Here the water had fallen considerably, so that several mud and sand-banks were visible. There was also an hill ahead, West-South-West.

The weather was so hazy that we could not see across the river, which is here about two hundred yards wide. We now proceeded South by West one third of a mile, when we saw a considerable quantity of beaver work along the banks, North-North-West half a mile, South-West by West one mile and an half, South-South-West one third of a mile, West by South one third of a mile, South by East half a mile. Mountains rose on the left, immediately above the river, whose summits were covered with snow; South-West half a mile, South a quarter of a mile, South-East one third of a mile, South-South-West half a mile. Here are several islands, we then veered to West by South a third of a mile, South-South-East a sixth of a mile. On the right, the land is high, rocky, and covered with wood, West South-West one mile,

a small river running in from the South-East, South-West half a
mile, South three quarters of a mile, South-West half a mile,
South by West half a mile. Here a rocky point protrudes from
the left, and narrows the river to an hundred yards; South-East
half a mile, East by South one eighth of a mile. The current now
was very strong, but perfectly safe, South-East by South an
eighth of a mile, West by North one third of a mile, South by
West a twelfth of a mile, South-West one fourth of a mile. Here
the high land terminates on one side of the river, while rocks rise
to a considerable height immediately above the other, and the
channel widens to an hundred and fifty yards, West by South
one mile. The river now narrows again between rocks of a moderate height, North-North-East an eighth of a mile, veered to
South-West an eighth of a mile, South and South-West half a
mile. The country appeared to be low, as far as I could judge of
it from the canoe, as the view is confined by woods at the distance of about an hundred yards from the banks. Our course continued West by North two miles, North half a mile, North-West
a quarter of a mile, South-West two miles, North-West three
quarters of a mile; when a ridge of high land appeared in this
direction, West one mile. A small river flowed in from the
North, South a quarter of a mile, North-West half a mile, South-
South-West two miles and an half, South-East three quarters of a
mile; a rivulet lost itself in the main stream, West-North-West
half a mile. Here the current slackened, and we proceeded
South-South-West three quarters of a mile, South-West three
quarters of a mile, South by East three quarters of a mile, South-
East by East one mile, when it veered gradually to West-North-
West half a mile; the river being full of islands. We proceeded
due North, with little current, the river presenting a beautiful
sheet of water for a mile and an half, South-West by West one
mile, West-North-West one mile, when it veered round to
South-East one mile, West by North one mile, South-East one
mile, West by North three quarters of a mile, South one eighth of
a mile, when we came to an Indian cabin of late erection. Here
was the great fork, of which our guide had informed us, and it
appeared to be the largest branch from the South-East. It is about

half a mile in breadth, and assumes the form of a lake. The current was very slack, and we got into the middle of the channel, when we steered West, and sounded in sixteen feet water. A ridge of high land now stretched on, as it were, across our present direction: this course was three miles. We then proceeded West-South-West two miles, and sounded in twenty-four feet water. Here the river narrowed and the current increased. We then continued our course North-North-West three quarters of a mile, a small river falling in from the North-East. It now veered to South by West one mile and a quarter, West-South-West four miles and an half, West by North one mile and a quarter, North-West by West one mile, West a mile and a quarter: the land was high on both sides, and the river narrowed to an hundred and fifty, or two hundred yards; North-West three quarters of a mile, South-West by South two miles and an half: here its breadth again increased; South by West one mile, West-South-West half a mile, South-West by South three miles, South-South-East one mile, with a small river running in from the left, South with a strong current one mile, then East three quarters of a mile, South-West one mile, South-South-East a mile and an half; the four last distances being a continual rapid; South-West by West one mile, East-North-East a mile and an half, East-South-East one mile, where a small river flowed in on the right; South-West by South two miles and an half, when another small river appeared from the same quarter; South by East half a mile, and South-West by West one mile and a quarter: here we landed for the night. When we had passed the last river we observed smoke rising from it, as if produced by fires that had been fresh lighted; I therefore concluded that there were natives on its banks; but I was unwilling to fatigue my people, by pulling back against the current in order to go in search of them.

This river appeared, from its high water-mark, to have fallen no more than one foot, while the smaller branch, from a similar measurement, had sunk two feet and an half. On our entering it, we saw a flock of ducks which were entirely white, except the bill and part of the wings. The weather was cold and raw throughout the day, and the wind South-West. We saw smoke rising in columns from many parts of the woods, and I should have been more anxious to see the natives, if there had been any person with me who could have introduced me to them; but as that object could not be then attained without considerable loss of time, I determined to pursue the navigation while it continued to be so favourable, and to wait till my return, if no very convenient opportunity offered in the mean time, to engage in an intercourse with them.

Wednesday, June 19. The morning was foggy, and at three we were on the water. At half past that hour, our course was East by South three quarters of a mile, a small river flowing in from the right. We then proceeded South by East half a mile, and South-South-West a mile and an half. During the last distance, clouds of thick smoke rose from the woods, that darkened the atmosphere, accompanied with a strong odour of the gum of cypress and the spruce-fir. Our courses continued to be South-West a mile and a quarter, North-West by West three quarters of a mile, South-South-East a mile and a quarter, East three quarters of a mile, South-West one mile, West by South three quarters of a mile, South-East by South three quarters of a mile, South by West half a mile, West by South three quarters of a mile, South by West two miles and an half. In the last course there was an island, and it appeared to me, that the main channel of the river had formerly been on the other side of it. The banks were here composed of high white cliffs, crowned with pinnacles in very grotesque shapes. We continued to steer South-East by South a mile and an half, South by East half a mile, East one mile and a quarter, South-East by East one mile, South by East three quarters of a mile, South-East by East one mile, South-South-East half a mile, East one mile and a quarter, South by East half a mile, East a mile and an half, South-South-East three miles, and South-West three quarters of a mile. In the last course the rocks contracted in such a manner on both sides of the river, as to afford the appearance of the upper part of a fall or cataract. Under this apprehension we landed on the left shore, where we found a kind of foot-path, imperfectly traced, through which we conjectured that the natives occasionally passed with their canoes and baggage. On examining the course of the river, however, there did not appear to be any fall as we expected; but the rapids were of a considerable length and impassable for a light canoe. We had therefore no alternative but to widen the road so as to admit the passage of our canoe, which was now carried with great difficulty; as from her frequent repairs, and not always of the usual materials, her weight was such, that she cracked and broke on the shoulders of the men who bore her. The labour and fatigue of this undertaking, from eight till twelve, beggars all description, when we at length conquered this afflicting passage, of about half a mile, over a rocky and most rugged hill. Our course was South-South-West. Here I took a meridian altitude which gave me 53.42.20 North latitude. We, however, lost some time to put our canoe in a condition to carry us onwards. Our course was South a quarter of a mile to the next carrying-place; which was nothing more than a rocky point about twice the length of the canoe. From the extremity of this point to the rocky and almost perpendicular bank that rose on the opposite shore, is not more than forty or fifty yards. The great body of water, at the same time tumbling in successive cascades along the first carrying-place, rolls through this narrow passage in a very turbid current, and full of whirlpools. On the banks of the river there was great plenty of wild onions, which when mixed up with our pemmican was a great improvement of it; though they produced a physical effect on our appetites, which was rather inconvenient to the state of our provisions.

Here we embarked, and steered South-East by East three quarters of a mile. We now saw a smoke on the shore; but before we could reach land the natives had deserted their camp, which appeared to be erected for no more than two families. My two Indians were instantly dispatched in search of them, and, by following their tracks, they soon overtook them; but their language was mutually unintelligible; and all attempts to produce a friendly communication were fruitless. They no sooner perceived my young men than they prepared their bows and arrows, and made signs for them not to advance; and they thought it prudent to desist from proceeding, though not before the natives had discharged five arrows at them, which, however, they avoided, by means of the trees. When they returned with this account, I very much regretted that I had not accompanied them; and as these people could not be at any very great distance, I took Mr. Mackay, and one of the Indians with me in order to overtake them; but they had got so far that it would have been imprudent in me to have followed them. My Indians, who, I believe, were terrified at the manner in which these natives received them, informed me, that, besides their bows, arrows, and spears, they were armed with long knives, and that they accompanied their strange antics with menacing actions and loud shoutings. On my return, I found my people indulging their curiosity in examining the bags and baskets which the natives had left behind them. Some of them contained their fishing tackle, such as nets, lines, &c. others of a smaller size were filled with a red earth, with which they paint themselves. In several of the bags there were also sundry articles of which we did not know the use. I prevented my men from taking any of them; and for a few articles of mere curiosity, which I took myself, I left such things in exchange as would be much more useful to their owners.

At four we left this place, proceeding with the stream South-East three quarters of a mile, East-South-East one mile, South three quarters of a mile, South-South-West one mile, South by East three quarters of a mile, South-South-East one mile, South-South-West two miles, South-South-East three miles and a quarter, East by North one mile, South-South-East one mile and a quarter, with a rapid, South-South-West three quarters of a mile, South one mile and an half, South-East one mile and a quarter, South three quarters of a mile, and South-South-East one mile and an half. At half past seven we landed for the night, where a small river flowed in from the right. The weather was showery, accompanied with several loud claps of thunder. The banks were overshadowed by lofty firs, and wide-spreading cedars.

Thursday, June 20. The morning was foggy, and at half past four we proceeded with a South wind, South-East by East two miles, South-South-East two miles and an half, and South-

South-West two miles. The fog was so thick, that we could not see the length of our canoe, which rendered our progress dangerous, as we might have come suddenly upon a cascade or violent rapid. Our next course was West-North-West two miles and an half, which comprehended a rapid. Being close in with the left bank of the river, we perceived two red deer at the very edge of the water: we killed one of them, and wounded the other, which was very small. We now landed, and the Indians followed the wounded animal, which they soon caught, and would have shot another in the woods, if our dog, who followed them, had not disturbed it. From the number of their tracks it appeared that they abounded in this country. They are not so large as the elk of the Peace River, but are the real red deer, which I never saw in the North, though I have been told that they are to be found in great numbers in the plains along the Red, or Assiniboin River. The bark had been stripped off many of the spruce trees, and carried away, as I presumed, by the natives, for the purpose of covering their cabins. We now got the venison on board, and continued our voyage South-West one mile, South a mile and an half, and West one mile. Here the country changed its appearance; the banks were but of a moderate height, from whence the ground continued gradually rising to a considerable distance, covered with poplars and cypresses, but without any kind of underwood. There were also several low points which the river, that is here about three hundred yards in breadth, sometimes overflows, and are shaded with liard, the soft birch, the spruce, and the willow. For some distance before we came to this part of the river, our view was confined within very rugged, irregular, and lofty banks, which were varied with the poplar, different kinds of spruce fir, small birch trees, cedars, alders, and several species of the willow. Our next course was South-West by West six miles, when we landed at a deserted house, which was the only Indian habitation of this kind that I had seen on this side of Mechilimakina. It was about thirty feet long and twenty wide, with three doors, three feet high by one foot and an half in breadth. From this and other circumstances, it appears to have been constructed for three families. There were also three fireplaces, at equal distances from each other; and the beds were on either side of them. Behind the beds was a narrow space, in the form of a manger, and somewhat elevated, which was appropriated to the purpose of keeping fish. The wall of the house, which was five feet in height, was formed of very strait spruce timbers, brought close together, and laid into each other at the corners. The roof was supported by a ridge pole, resting on two upright forks of about ten feet high; that and the wall support a certain number of spars, which are covered with spruce bark; and the whole attached and secured by the fibres of the cedar. One of the gable ends is closed with split boards; the other with poles. Large rods are also fixed across the upper part of the building, where fish may hang and dry. To give the walls additional strength, upright posts are fixed in the ground, at equal distances, both within and without, of the same height as the wall, and firmly attached with bark fibres. Openings appear also between the logs in the wall, for the purpose, as I conjectured, of discharging their arrows at a besieging enemy; they would be needless for the purpose of giving light, which is sufficiently afforded by fissures between the logs of the building, so that it appeared to be constructed merely for a summer habitation. There was nothing further to attract our attention in or about the house, except a large machine, which must have rendered the taking off the roof absolutely necessary, in order to have introduced it. It was of a cylindrical form, fifteen feet long, and four feet and an half in diameter; one end was square, like the head of a cask, and a conical machine was fixed inwards to the other end, of similar dimensions: at the extremity of which was an opening of about seven inches diameter. This machine was certainly contrived to set in the river, to catch large fish; and very well adapted to that purpose; as when they are once in, it must be impossible for them to get out, unless they should have strength sufficient to break through it. It was made of long pieces of split wood, rounded to the size of a small finger, and placed at the distance of an inch asunder, on six hoops; to this was added a kind of boot of the same materials, into which it may be supposed that the fish are driven, when they are to be taken out. The house was left in such apparent order as to mark the design of its owners to return thither. It answered in every particular the description given us by our late guide, except that it was not situated on an island.

We left this place, and steered South by East one mile and a quarter when we passed where there had been another house, of which the ridgepole and supporters alone remained: the ice had probably carried away the body of it. The bank was at this time covered with water, and a small river flowed in on the left. On a point we observed an erection that had the appearance of a tomb; it was in an oblong form, covered, and very neatly walled with bark. A pole was fixed near it, to which, at the height of ten or twelve feet, a piece of bark was attached, which was probably a memorial, or symbol of distinction. Our next course was South by West two miles and an half, when we saw an house on an island, South-East by East one mile and three quarters, in which we observed another island, with an house upon it. A river also flowed from the right, and the land was high and rocky, and wooded with the epinette.

Our canoe was now become so crazy, that it was a matter of absolute necessity to construct another; and as from the appearance of the country there was reason to expect that bark was to be found, we landed at eight, with the hope of procuring it. I accordingly dispatched four men with that commission, and at twelve they returned with a sufficient quantity to make the bottom of a canoe of five fathom in length, and four feet and an half in height. At noon I had an observation, which gave me 53.17.28 North latitude.

We now continued our voyage South-East by South one mile and an half, East-South-East one mile, East-North-East half a mile, South-East two miles, South-East by South one mile, South-East six miles, and East-North-East. Here the river narrows between steep rocks, and a rapid succeeded, which was so violent that we did not venture to run it. I therefore ordered the loading to be taken out of the canoe, but she was now become so heavy that the men preferred running the rapid to the carrying her overland. Though I did not altogether approve of their proposition, I was unwilling to oppose it. Four of them undertook this hazardous expedition, and I hastened to the foot of the rapid with great anxiety, to wait the event, which turned out as I expected. The water was so strong, that although they kept clear of the rocks, the canoe filled, and in this state they drove half way down the rapid, but fortunately she did not overset; and having got her into an eddy, they emptied her, and in an half-drowned condition arrived safe on shore. The carrying-place is about half a mile over, with an Indian path across it. Mr. Mackay, and the hunters, saw some deer on an island above the rapid; and had that discovery been made before the departure of the canoe, there is little doubt that we should have added a considerable quantity of venison to our stock of provisions. Our vessel was in such a wretched condition, as I have already observed, that it occasioned a delay of three hours to put her in a condition to proceed. At length we continued our former course, East-North-East a mile and an half, when we passed an extensive Indian encampment; East-South-East one mile, where a small river appeared on the left; South-East by South one mile and three quarters, East by South half a mile, East by North one mile, and saw another house on an island; South half a mile, West three quarters of a mile, South-West half a mile, where the cliffs of white and red clay appeared like the ruins of ancient castles. Our canoe now veered gradually to East-North-East one mile and an half, when we landed in a storm of rain and thunder, where we perceived the remains of Indian houses. It was impossible to determine the wind in any part of the day, as it came a-head in all our directions.

Friday, June 21. As I was very sensible of the difficulty of procuring provisions in this Country, I thought it prudent to guard against any possibility of distress of that kind on our return; I therefore ordered ninety pounds weight of pemmican to be buried in an hole, sufficiently deep to admit of a fire over it without doing any injury to our hidden treasure, and which would, at the same time, secure it from the natives of the country, or the wild animals of the woods.

The morning was very cloudy, and at four o'clock we renewed our voyage, steering South by East one mile and a quarter, East-South-East half a mile, South by East one mile and an half, East half a mile, South-East two miles, where a large river flowed in from the left, and a smaller one from the right. We then continued South by West three quarters of a mile, East by South a mile and an half, South three quarters of a mile, South-East by East one mile, South by East half a mile, South-East three quarters of a mile, South-East by South half a mile, South-East by East half a mile, the cliffs of blue and yellow clay, displaying the same grotesque shapes as those which we passed yesterday, South-South-East a mile and an half, South by East two miles. The latitude by observation was 52.47.51 North.

Here we perceived a small new canoe, that had been drawn up to the edge of the woods, and soon after another appeared, with one man in it, which came out of a small river. He no sooner saw us than he gave the whoop, to alarm his friends, who immediately appeared on the bank, armed with bows and arrows, and spears. They were thinly habited, and displayed the most outrageous antics. Though they were certainly in a state of great apprehension, they manifested by their gestures that they were resolved to attack us, if we should venture to land. I therefore ordered the men to stop the way of the canoe, and even to check her drifting with the current, as it would have been extreme folly to have approached these savages before their fury had in some degree subsided. My interpreters, who understood their language, informed me that they threatened us with instant death if we drew nigh the shore; and they followed the menace by discharging a volley of arrows, some of which fell short of the canoe, and others passed over it, so that they fortunately did us no injury. As we had been carried by the current below the spot where the Indians were, I ordered my people to paddle to the opposite side of the river, without the least appearance of confusion, so that they brought me abreast of them. My interpreters, while we were within hearing, had done every thing in their power to pacify them, but in vain. We also observed that they had sent off a canoe with two men, down the river, as we concluded, to communicate their alarm, and procure assistance. This circumstance determined me to leave no means untried that might engage us in a friendly intercourse with them, before they acquired additional security and confidence, by the arrival of their relations and neighbours, to whom their situation would be shortly notified.

I therefore formed the following adventurous project, which was happily crowned with success. I left the canoe, and walked by myself along the beach, in order to induce some of the natives to come to me, which I imagined they might be disposed to do, when they saw me alone, without any apparent possibility of receiving assistance from my people, and would consequently imagine that a communication with me was not a service of danger. At the same time, in order to possess the utmost security of which my situation was susceptible, I directed one of the Indians to slip into the woods, with my gun and his own, and to conceal himself from their discovery; he also had orders to keep as near me as possible, without being seen; and if any of the natives should venture across, and attempt to shoot me from the water, it was his instructions to lay him low: at the same time he was particularly enjoined not to fire till I had discharged one or both of the pistols that I carried in my belt. If, however, any of them were to land, and approach my person, he was immediately to join me. In the mean time my other interpreter assured them that we entertained the most friendly disposition, which I confirmed by such signals as I conceived would be comprehended by them. I had not, indeed, been long at my station, and my Indian in ambush behind me, when two of the natives came off in a canoe, but stopped when they had got within an hundred yards of me. I made signs for them to land, and as an inducement, displayed looking glasses, beads, and other alluring trinkets. At length, but with every mark of extreme apprehension, they approached the shore, stern foremost, but would not venture to land. I now made them a present of some beads, with which they were going to push off, when I renewed my entreaties, and, after some time, prevailed on them to come ashore, and sit down by me. My hunter now thought it right to join me, and created some alarm in my new acquaintance. It was, however, soon removed, and I had the satisfaction to find that he, and these people perfectly understood each other. I instructed him to say every thing that might tend to sooth their fears and win their confidence. I expressed my wish to conduct them to our canoe, but they declined my offer; and when they observed some of my people coming towards us, they requested me to let them return; and I was so well satisfied with the progress I had made in my intercourse with them, that I did not hesitate a moment in complying with their desire. During their short stay, they observed us, and every thing about us, with a mixture of admiration and astonishment. We could plainly distinguish that their friends received them with great joy on their return, and that the articles which they carried back with them were examined with a general and eager curiosity; they also appeared to hold a consultation, which lasted about a quarter of an hour, and the result was, an invitation to come over to them, which was cheerfully accepted. Nevertheless, on our landing, they betrayed evident signs of confusion, which arose, probably from the quickness of our movements, as the prospect of a friendly communication had so cheered the spirits of my people, that they paddled across the river with the utmost expedition. The two men, however, who had been with us, appeared, very naturally, to possess the greatest share of courage on the occasion, and were ready to receive us on our landing; but our demeanor soon dispelled all their apprehensions, and the most familiar communication took place between us. When I had secured their confidence, by the distribution of trinkets among them, and treated the children with sugar, I instructed my interpreters to collect every necessary information in their power to afford me.

According to their account, this river, whose course is very extensive, runs towards the mid-day sun; and that at its mouth, as they had been informed, white people were building houses. They represented its current to be uniformly strong, and that in three places it was altogether impassable, from the falls and rapids, which poured along between perpendicular rocks that were much higher, and more rugged, than any we had yet seen, and would not admit of any passage over them. But besides the dangers and difficulties of the navigation, they added, that we should have to encounter the inhabitants of the country, who were very numerous. They also represented their immediate neighbours as a very malignant race, who lived in large subterraneous recesses: and when they were made to understand that it was our design to proceed to the sea, they dissuaded us from prosecuting our intention, as we should certainly become a sacrifice to the savage spirit of the natives. These people they described as possessing iron, arms, and utensils, which they procured from their neighbours to the Westward, and were obtained by a commercial progress from people like ourselves, who brought them in great canoes.

Such an account of our situation, exaggerated as it might be in some points, and erroneous in others, was sufficiently alarming, and awakened very painful reflections; nevertheless it did not operate on my mind so as to produce any change in my original determination. My first object, therefore, was to persuade two of these people to accompany me, that they might secure for us a favourable reception from their neighbours. To this proposition they assented, but expressed some degree of dissatisfaction at the immediate departure, for which we were making preparation; but when we were ready to enter the canoe, a small one was seen doubling the point below, with three men in it. We thought it prudent to wait for their arrival, and they proved to be some of their relations, who had received the alarm from the messengers, which I have already mentioned as having been sent down the river for that purpose, and who had passed on, as we were afterwards informed, to extend the notice of our arrival. Though these people saw us in the midst of their friends, they displayed the most menacing actions, and hostile postures. At length, however, this wild, savage spirit appeared to subside, and they were persuaded to land. One of them, who was a middle aged person, whose agitations had been less frequent than those of his companions, and who was treated with particular respect by them all, inquired who we were, whence we came, whither we were going, and what was the motive of our coming into that country.

When his friends had satisfied him as far as they were able, respecting us, he instantly advised us to delay our departure for that night, as their relations below, having been by this time alarmed by the messengers, who had been sent for that purpose, would certainly oppose our passage, notwithstanding I had two of their own people with me. He added, that they would all of them be here by sun-set, when they would be convinced, as he was, that we were good people, and meditated no ill designs against them.

Such were the reasons which this Indian urged in favour of our remaining till the next morning; and they were too well founded for me to hesitate in complying with them; besides, by prolonging my stay till the next morning, it was probable that I might obtain some important intelligence respecting the country through which I was to pass, and the people who inhabited it. I accordingly ordered the canoe to be unloaded, taken out of the water, and gummed. My tent was also pitched, and the natives were now become so familiar, that I was obliged to let them know my wish to be alone and undisturbed.

My first application to the native whom I have already particularly mentioned, was to obtain from him such a plan of the river as he should be enabled to give me; and he complied with this request with a degree of readiness and intelligence that evidently proved it was by no means a new business to him. In order to acquire the best information he could communicate, I assured him, if I found his account correct, that I should either return myself, or send others to them, with such articles as they appeared to want: particularly arms and ammunition, with which they would be able to prevent their enemies from invading them. I obtained, however, no addition to what I already knew, but that the country below us, as far as he was acquainted with it, abounded in animals, and that the river produced plenty of fish.

Our canoe was now become so weak, leaky, and unmanageable, that it became a matter of absolute necessity to construct a new one; and I had been informed, that if we delayed that important work till we got further down the river, we should not be able to procure bark. I therefore dispatched two of my people, with an Indian, in search of that necessary material. The weather was so cloudy that I could not get an observation.[27]

I passed the rest of the day in conversing with these people: they consisted of seven families, containing eighteen men; they were clad in leather, and had some beaver and rabbit-skin blankets. They had not been long arrived in this part of the country, where they proposed to pass the summer, to catch fish for their winter provision: for this purpose they were preparing machines similar to that which we found in the first Indian house we saw and described. The fish which they take in them are large, and only visit this part of the river at certain seasons. These people differ very little, if at all, either in their appearance, language, or manners, from the Rocky-Mountain Indians. The men whom I sent in search of bark, returned with a certain quantity of it, but of a very indifferent kind. We were not gratified with the arrival of any of the natives whom we expected from a lower part of the river.

---

27. The observation, already mentioned, I got on my return.

Chapter 8

POINTED CANOE

Saturday, June 22. At six in the morning we proceeded on our voyage, with two of the Indians, one of them in a small pointed canoe, made after the fashion of the Esquimaux, and the other in our own. This precaution was necessary in a two-fold point of view, as the small canoe could be sent ahead to speak to any of the natives that might be seen down the river, and, thus divided, would not be easy for them both to make their escape. Mr. Mackay also embarked with the Indian, which seemed to afford him great satisfaction, and he was thereby enabled to keep us company with diminution of labour.

Our courses were South-South-East a mile and an half, South-East half a mile, South by East four miles and an half, South-East by South half a mile, South by West half a mile, South-East by East one mile, South-South-West a mile and an half, South by East one mile and a quarter. The country, on the right, presented a very beautiful appearance: it rose at first rather abruptly to the height of twenty-five feet, when the precipice was succeeded by an inclined plain to the foot of another steep; which was followed by another extent of gently-rising ground: these objects, which were shaded with groves of fir, presenting themselves alternately to a considerable distance.

We now landed near an house, the roof of which alone appeared above ground; but it was deserted by its inhabitants who had been alarmed at our approach. We observed several men in the second steep, who displayed the same postures and menacing actions as those which we have so lately described. Our conductors went to them immediately on an embassy of friendship, and, after a very vociferous discourse, one of them was persuaded to come to us, but presented a very ferocious aspect: the rest, who were seven in number, soon followed his example. They held their bows and arrows in their hands, and appeared in their garments, which were fastened round the neck, but left the right arm free for action. A cord fastened a blanket or leather covering under the right arm-pit, so that it hung upon the left shoulder, and might be occasionally employed as a target, that would turn an arrow which was nearly spent. As soon as they had recovered from their apprehensions, ten women made their appearance, but without any children, whom, I imagine, they had sent to a greater distance, to be out of the reach of all possible danger. I distributed a few presents among them, and left my guides to explain to them the object of my journey, and the friendliness of my designs, with which they had themselves been made acquainted; their fears being at length removed, I gave them a specimen of the use to which we applied our fire-arms: at the same time, I calmed their astonishment, by the assurance, that, though we could at once destroy those who did us injury, we could equally protect those who shewed us kindness. Our stay here did not exceed half an hour, and we left these people with favourable impressions of us.

From this place we steered East by North half a mile, South by East three quarters of a mile, and South by West a mile and an half, when we landed again on seeing some of the natives on the high ground, whose appearance was more wild and ferocious than any whom we had yet seen. Indeed I was under some apprehension that our guides, who went to conciliate them to us, would have fallen a prey to their savage fury. At length, however, they were persuaded to entertain a more favourable opinion of us, and they approached us one after another, to the number of sixteen men, and several women; I shook hands with them all, and desired my interpreters to explain that salutation as a token of friendship. As this was not a place where we could remain with the necessary convenience, I proposed to proceed further, in search of a more commodious spot. They immediately invited us to pass the night at their lodges, which were at no great distance, and promised, at the same time, that they would, in the morning, send two men to introduce us to the next nation, who were very numerous, and ill-disposed towards strangers. As we were pushing from the shore, we were very much surprised at hearing a woman pronounce several words in the Knisteneaux language. She proved to be a Rocky-Mountain native, so that my interpreters perfectly understood her. She informed us that her country is at the forks of this river, and that she had been taken prisoner by the Knisteneaux, who had carried her across the mountains. After having passed the greatest part of the summer with them, she had contrived to escape, before they had reached their own country, and had re-crossed the mountains, when she expected to meet her own friends: but after suffering all the hardships incident to such a journey, she had been taken by a war-party of the people with whom she then was, who had driven her relations from the river into the mountains. She had since been detained by her present husband, of whom she had no cause to complain; nevertheless she expressed a strong desire to return to her own people. I presented her with several useful articles, and desired her to come to me at the lodges, which she readily engaged to do. We arrived thither before the Indians, and landed, as we had promised. It was now near twelve at noon, but on attempting to take an altitude I found the angle too great for my sextant.

The natives whom we had already seen, and several others, soon joined us, with a greater number of women than I had yet seen; but I did not observe the female prisoner among them. There were thirty-five of them, and my remaining store of presents was not sufficient to enable me to be very liberal to so many claimants. Among the men I found four of the adjoining nation, and a Rocky-Mountain Indian, who had been with them for some time. As he was understood by my interpreters, and was himself well acquainted with the language of the strangers, I possessed the means of obtaining every information respecting the country, which it might be in their power to afford me. For this purpose I selected an elderly man, from the four strangers, whose countenance had prepossessed me in his favour. I stated to these people, as I had already done to those from whom I had hitherto derived information, the objects of my voyage, and the very great advantages which they would receive from my successful termination of it. They expressed themselves very much satisfied at my communication, and assured me that they would not deceive me respecting the subject of my inquiry. An old man also, who appeared to possess the character of a chief, declared his wish to see me return to his land, and that his two young daughters should then be at my disposal. I now proceeded to request the native, whom I had particularly selected, to commence his information, by drawing a sketch of the country upon a large piece of bark, and he immediately entered on the work, frequently appealing to, and sometimes asking the advice of, those around him. He described the river as running to the East of South, receiving many rivers, and every six or eight leagues encumbered with falls and rapids, some of which were very dangerous, and six of them impracticable. The carrying-places he represented as of great length, and passing over hills and mountains. He depicted the lands of three other tribes, in succession, who spoke different languages. Beyond them he knew nothing either of the river or country, only that it was still a long way to the sea; and that, as he had heard, there was a lake, before they reached the water, which the natives did not drink. As far as his knowledge of the river extended, the country on either side was level, in many places without wood, and abounding in red deer, and some of a small fallow kind. Few of the natives, he said, would come to the banks for some time; but that at a certain season they would arrive there in great numbers, to fish. They now procured iron, brass, copper, and trinkets, from the Westward; but formerly these articles were obtained from the lower parts of the river, though in small quantities. A knife was produced which had been brought from that quarter. The blade was ten inches long, and an inch and an half broad, but with a very blunted edge. The handle was of horn. We understood that this instrument had been obtained from white men, long before they had heard that any came to the Westward. One very old man observed, that as long as he could remember, he was told of white people to the Southward; and that he had heard, though he did not vouch for the truth of the report, that one of them had made an attempt to come up the river, and was destroyed.

These people describe the distance across the country as very short to the Western ocean; and, according to my own idea, it cannot be above five or six degrees. If the assertion of Mr. Mears be correct, it cannot be so far, as the inland sea which he mentions within Nootka, must come as far East as 126 West longitude. They assured us that the road was not difficult, as they avoided the mountains, keeping along the low lands between them, many parts of which are entirely free from wood. According to their account, this way is so often travelled by them, that their path is visible throughout the whole journey, which lies along small lakes and rivers. It occupied them, they said, no more than six nights, to go to where they meet the people who barter iron, brass, copper, beads, &c. with them, for dressed leather, and beaver, bear, lynx, fox, and marten skins. The iron is about eighteen inches of two-inch bar. To this they give an edge at one end, and fix it to an handle at right angles, which they employ as an axe. When the iron is worn down, they fabricate it into points for their arrows and spikes. Before they procured iron they employed bone and horn for those purposes. The copper and brass they convert into collars, arm-bands, bracelets, and other ornaments. They sometimes also point their arrows with those metals. They had been informed by those whom they meet to trade with, that the white people, from whom these articles are obtained, were building houses at the distance of three days, or two nights journey from the place where they met last fall. With this route they all appeared to be well acquainted.

I now requested that they would send for the female prisoner whom I saw yesterday, but I received only vague and evasive answers: they probably apprehended, that it was our design to take her from them. I was, however, very much disappointed at being prevented from having an interview with her, as she might have given me a correct account of the country beyond the forks of the river, as well as of the pass, through the mountains, from them.

My people had listened with great attention to the relation which had been given me, and it seemed to be their opinion, that it would be absolute madness to attempt a passage through so many savage and barbarous nations. My situation may, indeed, be more easily conceived than expressed: I had no more than thirty days provision remaining, exclusive of such supplies as I might obtain from the natives, and the toil of our hunters, which, however, was so precarious as to be matter of little dependence: besides, our ammunition would soon be exhausted, particularly our ball, of which we had not more than an hundred and fifty, and about thirty pounds weight of shot, which, indeed, might be converted into bullets, though with great waste.

The more I heard of the river, the more I was convinced it could not empty itself into the ocean to the North of what is called the River of the West, so that with its windings, the distance must be very great. Such being the discouraging circumstances of my situation, which were now heightened by the discontents of my people, I could not but be alarmed at the idea of attempting to get to the discharge of such a rapid river, especially when I reflected on the tardy progress of my return up it, even if I should meet with no obstruction from the natives; a circumstance not very probable, from the numbers of them which would then be on the river; and whom I could have no opportunity of conciliating in my passage down, for the reasons which have been already mentioned. At all events, I must give up every expectation of returning this season to Athabasca. Such were my reflections at this period; but instead of continuing to indulge them, I determined to proceed with resolution, and set future events at defiance. At the same time I suffered myself to nourish the hope that I might be able to penetrate with more safety, and in a shorter period, to the ocean by the inland, western communication.

To carry this project into execution I must have returned a considerable distance up the river, which would necessarily be attended with a very serious inconvenience, if I passed over every other; as in a voyage of this kind, a retrograde motion could not fail to cool the ardour, slacken the zeal, and weaken the confidence of those, who have no greater inducement in the undertaking, than to follow the conductor of it. Such was the state of my mind at this period, and such the circumstances by which it was distressed and distracted.

To the people who had given me the foregoing information, I presented some beads, which they preferred to any other articles in my possession, and I recompensed in the same manner two of them who communicated to me the following vocabulary in the languages of the Nagailer and Amah tribes.

	The Nagailer, or Carrier-Indians.	The Atnah, or Chin-Indians.
Eye,	Nah,	Thloustin.
Hair,	Thigah,	Cahowdin.
Teeth,	Gough,	Chliough.
Nose,	Nenzeh,	Pisax.
Head,	Thie,	Scapacay.
Wood,	Dekin,	Shedzay.
Hand,	Lab,	Calietha.
Leg,	Kin,	Squacht.
Tongue,	Thoula,	Dewhasjisk.
Ear,	Zach,	Ithlinah.
Man,	Dinay,	Scuynlouch.
Woman,	Chiqoui,	Smosledgensk.
Beaver,	Zah,	Schugh.
Elk,	Yezey,	Oikoy-Beh.
Dog,	Sleing,	Scacah.
Ground-hog,	Thidnu,	Squaiquais.

Iron,	Thlisitch,	Soucoumang.
Fire,	Coun,	Teuck.
Water,	Tou,	Shaweliquoih.
Stone,	Zeh,	Ishehoineah.
Bow,	Nettuny,	Isquoinah.
Arrow,	Igah,	Squaili.
Yes,	Nesi,	Amaig.
Plains,	Thoughoud,	Spilela.
Come here,	Andezei,	Thla-elyeh.

The Amah language has no affinity to any with which I am acquainted; but the Nagailer differs very little from that spoken by the Beaver Indians, and is almost the same as that of the Chipewyans.

We had a thunder-storm with heavy rain; and in the evening when it had subsided, the Indians amused us with singing and dancing, in which they were joined by the young women. Four men now arrived whom we had not yet seen; they had left their families at some distance in the country, and expressed a desire that we should visit them there.

Sunday, June 23. After a restless night, I called the Indians together, from whom I yesterday received the intelligence which has been already mentioned, in the hope that I might obtain some additional information. From their former account they did not make the least deviation; but they informed me further, that where they left this river, a small one from the Westward falls into it, which was navigable for their canoes during four days, and from thence they slept but two nights, to get to the people with whom they trade, and who have wooden canoes much larger than ours, in which they go down a river to the sea. They continued to inform me, that if I went that way we must leave our own canoe behind us; but they thought it probable that those people would furnish us with another. From thence they stated the distance to be only one day's voyage with the current to the lake whose water is nauseous, and where they had heard that great canoes came two winters ago, and that the people belonging to them, brought great quantities of goods and built houses.

At the commencement of this conversation, I was very much surprised by the following question from one of the Indians: 'What,' demanded he, 'can be the reason that you are so particular and anxious in your inquiries of us respecting a knowledge of this country: do not you white men know every thing in the world?' This interrogatory was so very unexpected, that it occasioned some hesitation before I could answer it. At length, however, I replied, that we certainly were acquainted with the principal circumstances of every part of the world; that I knew where the sea is, and where I myself then was, but that I did not exactly understand what obstacles might interrupt me in getting to it; with which, he and his relations must be well acquainted, as they had so frequently surmounted them. Thus I fortunately preserved the impression in their minds, of the superiority of white people over themselves.

It was now, however, absolutely necessary that I should come to a final determination which route to take; and no long interval of reflection was employed, before I preferred to go over land: the comparative shortness and security of such a journey, were alone sufficient to determine me. I accordingly proposed to two of the Indians to accompany me, and one of them readily assented to my proposition.

I now called those of my people about me, who had not been present at my consultation with the natives; and after passing a warm eulogium on their fortitude, patience, and perseverance, I stated the difficulties that threatened our continuing to navigate the river, the length of time it would require, and the scanty provision we had for such a voyage: I then proceeded for the foregoing reasons to propose a shorter route, by trying the over-land road to the sea. At the same time, as I knew from experience, the difficulty of retaining guides, and as many circumstances might occur to prevent our progress in that direction, I declared my resolution not to attempt it, unless they would engage, if we could not after all proceed over land, to return with me, and continue our voyage to the discharge of the waters, whatever the distance might be. At all events, I declared, in the most solemn manner, that I would not abandon my design of reaching the sea, if I made the attempt alone, and that I did not despair of returning in safety to my friends.

This proposition met with the most zealous return, and they unanimously assured me, that they were as willing now as they had ever been, to abide by my resolutions, whatever they might be, and to follow me wherever I should go. I therefore requested them to prepare for an immediate departure, and at the same time gave notice to the man who had engaged to be our guide, to be in readiness to accompany us. When our determination to return up the river was made known, several of the natives took a very abrupt departure; but to those who remained, I gave a few useful articles, explaining to them at the same time, the advantages that would result to them, if their relations conducted me to the sea, along such a road as they had described. I had already given a moose skin to some of the women for the purpose of making shoes, which were now brought us; they were well sewed but ill shaped, and a few beads were considered as a sufficient remuneration for the skill employed on them. Mr. Mackay, by my desire, engraved my name, and the date of the year on a tree.

When we were ready to depart, our guide proposed, for the sake of expedition, to go over land to his lodge, that he might get there before us, to make some necessary preparation for his journey. I did not altogether relish his design, but was obliged to consent: I thought it prudent, however, to send Mr. Mackay, and the two Indians along with him. Our place of rendezvous, was the subterraneous house which we passed yesterday.

At ten in the morning we embarked, and went up the current much faster than I expected with such a crazy vessel as that which carried us. We met our people at the house as had been appointed; but the Indian still continued to prefer going on by land, and it would have been needless for me to oppose him. He proceeded, therefore, with his former companions, whom I desired to keep him in good humour by every reasonable gratification. They were also furnished with a few articles that might be of use if they should meet with strangers.

In a short time after we had left the house, I saw a wooden canoe coming down the river, with three natives in it, who, as soon as they perceived us, made for the shore, and hurried into the woods. On passing their vessel, we discovered it to be one of those which we had seen at the lodges. A severe gust of wind, with rain, came from the South-South-East. This we found to be a very prevalent wind in these parts. We soon passed another wooden canoe drawn stern foremost on the shore; a circumstance which we had not hitherto observed. The men worked very hard, and though I imagined we went a-head very fast, we could not reach the lodges, but landed for the night at nine, close to the encampment of two families of the natives whom we had formerly seen at the lodges. I immediately went and sat down with them, when they gave some roasted fish; two of my men who followed me were gratified also with some of their provisions. The youngest of the two natives now quitted the shed, and did not return during the time I remained there. I endeavoured to explain to the other by signs, the cause of my sudden return, which he appeared to understand. In the mean time my tent was pitched, and on my going to it, I was rather surprised that he did not follow me, as he had been constantly with me during the day and night I had passed with his party on going down. We, however, went to rest in a state of perfect security; nor had we the least apprehension for the safety of our people who were gone by land.

Monday, June 24. We were in our canoe by four this morning, and passed by the Indian hut, which appeared in a state of perfect tranquillity. We soon came in sight of the point where we first saw the natives, and at eight were much surprised and disappointed at seeing Mr. Mackay, and our two Indians coming alone from the ruins of an house that had been partly carried away by the ice and water, at a short distance below the place where we had appointed to meet. Nor was our surprise and apprehension diminished by the alarm which was painted in their countenances. When we had landed, they informed me that they had taken refuge in that place, with the determination to sell their lives, which they considered in the most imminent danger, as dear as possible. In a very short time after they had left us, they met a party of the Indians, whom we had known at this place, and were probably those whom we had seen to land from their canoe. They appeared to be in a state of extreme rage, and had their bows bent, with their arrows across them. The guide stopped to ask them some questions, which my people did not understand, and then set off with his utmost speed. Mr. Mackay, however, did not leave him till they were both exhausted with running. When the young man came up, he then said, that some treacherous design was meditated against them, as he was induced to believe from the declaration of the natives, who told him that they were going to do mischief, but refused to name the enemy. The guide then conducted them through very bad ways, as fast as they could run; and when he was desired to slacken his pace, he answered that they might follow him in any manner they pleased, but that he was impatient to get to his family, in order to prepare shoes, and other necessaries, for his journey. They did not, however, think it prudent to quit him, and he would not stop till ten at night. On passing a track that was but lately made, they began to be seriously alarmed, and on inquiring of the guide where they were, he pretended not to understand them. They then all laid down, exhausted with fatigue, and without any kind of covering: they were cold, wet, and hungry, but dared not light a fire, from the apprehension of an enemy. This comfortless spot they left at the dawn of day, and, on their arrival at the lodges, found them deserted; the property of the Indians being scattered about, as if abandoned for ever. The guide then made two or three trips into the woods, calling aloud, and bellowing like a madman. At length he set off in the same direction as they came, and had not since appeared. To heighten their misery, as they did not find us at the place appointed, they concluded that we were all destroyed, and had already formed their plan to take to the woods, and cross in as a direct a line as they could proceed, to the waters of the Peace River, a scheme which could only be suggested by despair. They intended to have waited for us till noon, and if we did not appear by that time, to have entered without further delay on their desperate expedition.

This alarm among the natives was a very unexpected as well as perilous event, and my powers of conjecture were exhausted in searching for the cause of it. A general panic seized all round me, and any further prosecution of the voyage was now considered by them as altogether hopeless and impracticable. But without paying the least attention to their opinions or surmises, I ordered them to take every thing out of the canoe, except six packages: when that was done, I left four men to take care of the lading, and returned with the others to our camp of last night, where I hoped to find the two men, with their families, whom we had seen there, and to be able to bring them to lodge with us, when I should wait the issue of this mysterious business. This project, however, was disappointed, for these people had quitted their sheds in the silence of the night, and had not taken a single article of their little property with them.

These perplexing circumstances made a deep impression on my mind, not as to our immediate safety, for I entertained not the least apprehension of the Indians I had hitherto seen, even if their whole force should have been combined to attack us, but these untoward events seemed to threaten the prosecution of my journey; and I could not reflect on the possibility of such a disappointment but with sensations little short of agony. Whatever might have been the wavering disposition of the people on former occasions, they were now decided in their opinions as to the necessity of returning without delay; and when we came back to them, their cry was – 'Let us reimbark, and be gone.' This, however, was not my design, and in a more peremptory tone than I usually employed, they were ordered to unload the canoe, and take her out of the water. On examining our property, several articles appeared to be missing, which the Indians must have purloined; and among them were an axe, two knives, and the young men's bag of medicines. We now took a position that was the best calculated for defence, got our arms in complete order, filled each man's flask of powder, and distributed an hundred bullets, which were all that remained, while some were employed in melting down shot to make more. The weather was so cloudy that I had not an opportunity of taking an observation.

While we were employed in making these preparations, we saw an Indian in a canoe come down the river, and land at the huts, which he began to examine. On perceiving us he stood still, as if in a state of suspense, when I instantly dispatched one of my Indians towards him, but no persuasions could induce him to have confidence in us; he even threatened that he would hasten to join his friends, who would come and kill us. At the conclusion of this menace he disappeared. On the return of my young man, with this account of the interview, I pretended to discredit the whole, and attributed it to his own apprehensions and alarms. This, however, he denied, and asked with a look and tone of resentment, whether he had ever told me a lie? Though he was but a young man, he said, he had been on war excursions before he came with me, and that he should no longer consider me as a wise man, which he had hitherto done.

To add to our distresses we had not an ounce of gum for the reparation of the canoe, and not one of the men had sufficient courage to venture into the woods to collect it. In this perplexing situation I entertained the hope that in the course of the night some of the natives would return, to take away a part at least of the things which they had left behind them, as they had gone away without the covering necessary to defend them from the weather and the flies. I therefore ordered the canoe to be loaded, and dropped to an old house, one side of which, with its roof, had been carried away by the water; but the three remaining angles were sufficient to shelter us from the woods. I then ordered two strong piquets to be driven into the ground, to which the canoe was fastened, so that if we were hard pressed we had only to step on board and push off. We were under the necessity of making a smoke to keep off the swarms of flies, which would have otherwise tormented us; but we did not venture to excite a blaze, as it would have been a mark for the arrows of the enemy. Mr. Mackay and myself, with three men kept alternate watch, and allowed the Indians to do as they fancied. I took the first watch, and the others, laid down in their clothes by us. I also placed a centinel at a small distance, who was relieved every hour. The weather was cloudy, with showers of rain.

Tuesday, June 25. At one I called up the other watch, and laid down to a small portion of broken rest. At five I arose, and as the situation which we left yesterday was preferable to that which we then occupied, I determined to return to it. On our arrival Mr. Mackay informed me that the men had expressed their dissatisfaction to him in a very unreserved manner, and had in very strong terms declared their resolution to follow me no further in my proposed enterprize. I did not appear, however, to have received such communications from him, and continued to employ my whole thoughts in contriving means to bring about a reconciliation with the natives, which alone would enable me to procure guides, without whose assistance it would be impossible for me to proceed, when my darling project would end in disappointment.

At twelve we saw a man coming with the stream upon a raft, and he must have discovered us before we perceived him, as he was working very hard to get on the opposite shore, where he soon landed, and instantly fled into the woods. I now had a meridional altitude, which gave 60.23 natural horizon, (the angle being more than the sextant could measure with the artificial horizon), one mile and an half distant; and the eye five feet above the level of the water, gave 52.47.51 North latitude.

While I was thus employed, the men loaded the canoe without having received any orders from me, and as this was the first time they had ventured to act in such a decided manner, I naturally concluded, that they had preconcerted a plan for their return. I thought it prudent, however, to take no notice of their transaction, and to wait the issue of future circumstances. At this moment our Indians perceived a person in the edge of the woods above us, and they were immediately dispatched to discover who it was. After a short absence they returned with a young woman whom we had seen before: her language was not clearly comprehended by us, so that we could not learn from her, at least with any degree of certainty, the cause of this unfortunate alarm that had taken place among the natives. She told us that her errand was to fetch some things which she had left behind her; and one of the dogs whom we found here, appeared to acknowledge her as his mistress. We treated her with great kindness, gave her something to eat, and added a present of such articles as we thought might please her. On her expressing a wish to leave us, we readily consented to her departure, and indulged the hope that her reception would induce the natives to return in peace, and give us an opportunity to convince them, that we had no hostile designs whatever against them. On leaving us, she went up the river without taking a single article of her own, and the dog followed. The wind was changeable throughout the day, and there were several showers in the course of it.

Though a very apparent anxiety prevailed among the people for their departure, I appeared to be wholly inattentive to it, and at eight in the evening I ordered four men to step into the canoe, which had been loaded for several hours, and drop down to our guard-house, and my command was immediately obeyed: the rest of us proceeded there by land. When I was yet at a considerable distance from the house, and thought it impossible for an arrow to reach it, having a bow and quiver in my hand, I very imprudently let fly an arrow, when, to my astonishment and infinite alarm, I heard it strike a log of the house. The men who had just landed, imagined that they were attacked by an enemy from the woods. Their confusion was in proportion to their imaginary danger, and on my arrival I found that the arrow had passed within a foot of one of the men; though it had no point, the weapon, incredible as it may appear, had entered an hard, dry log of wood upwards of an inch. But this was not all: for the men readily availed themselves of this circumstance, to remark upon the danger of remaining in the power of a people possessed of such a means of destruction. Mr. Mackay having the first watch, I laid myself down in my cloak.

Wednesday, June 26. About midnight a rustling noise was heard in the woods which created a general alarm, and I was awakened to be informed of the circumstance, but heard nothing. At one I took my turn of the watch, and our dog continued unceasingly to run backwards and forwards along the skirts of the wood in a state of restless vigilance. At two in the morning the centinel informed me, that he saw something like an human figure creeping along on all-fours about fifty paces above us. After some time had passed in our search, I at length discovered that his information was true, and it appeared to me that a bear had occasioned the alarm; but when day appeared, it proved to be an old, grey-haired, blind man, who had been compelled to leave his hiding-place by extreme hunger, being too infirm to join in the flight of the natives to whom he belonged. When I put my hand on this object of decaying nature, his alarm was so great, that I expected it would have thrown him into convulsions. I immediately led him to our fire which had been just lighted, and gave him something to eat, which he much wanted, as he had not tasted food for two days. When his hunger was satisfied, and he had got warm and composed, I requested him to acquaint me with the cause of that alarm which had taken place respecting us among his relations and friends, whose regard we appeared to have conciliated but a few days past. He replied, that very soon after we had left them, some natives arrived from above, who informed them that we were enemies; and our unexpected return, in direct contradiction to our own declarations, confirmed them in that opinion. They were now, he said, so scattered, that a considerable time would elapse, before they could meet again. We gave him the real history of our return, as well as of the desertion of our guide, and, at the same time, stated the impossibility of our proceeding, unless we procured a native to conduct us. He replied, that if he had not lost his sight, he would with the greatest readiness have accompanied us on our journey. He also confirmed the accounts which we had received of the country, and the route to the Westward. I did not neglect to employ every argument in my power, that he might be persuaded of our friendly dispositions to the inhabitants wheresoever we might meet them.

At sun-rise we perceived a canoe with one man in it on the opposite side of the river, and at our request, the blind man called to him to come to us, but he returned no answer, and continued his course as fast as he could paddle down the current. He was considered as a spy by my men, and I was confirmed in that opinion, when I saw a wooden canoe drifting with the stream close in to the other shore, where it was more than probable that some of the natives might be concealed. It might, therefore, have been an useless enterprise, or perhaps fatal to the future success of our undertaking, if we had pursued these people, as they might, through fear, have employed their arms against us, and provoked us to retaliate.

The old man informed me, that some of the natives whom I had seen here were gone up the river, and those whom I saw below had left their late station to gather a root in the plains, which, when dried, forms a considerable article in their winter stock of provisions. He had a woman, he said, with him, who used to see us walking along the small adjoining river, but when he called her he received no answer, so that she had probably fled to join her people. He informed me, also, that he expected a considerable number of his tribe to come on the upper part of the river to catch fish for their present support, and to cure them for their winter store; among whom he had a son and two brothers.

In consequence of these communications, I deemed it altogether unnecessary to lose any more time at this place, and I informed the old man that he must accompany us for the purpose of introducing us to his friends and relations, and that if we met with his son or brothers, I depended upon him to persuade them, or some of their party, to attend us as guides in our meditated expedition. He expressed his wishes to be excused from this service, and in other circumstances we should not have insisted on it, but, situated as we were, we could not yield to his request.

At seven in the morning we left this place, which I named Deserter's River or Creek. Our blind guide was, however, so averse to continuing with us, that I was under the very disagreeable necessity of ordering the men to carry him into the canoe; and this was the first act during my voyage, that had the semblance of violent dealing. He continued to speak in a very loud tone, while he remained, according to his conjecture, near enough to the camp to be heard, but in a language that our interpreters did not understand. On asking him what he said, and why he did not speak in a language known to us, he replied, that the women understood him better in that which he spoke, and he requested her, if she heard him, to come for him to the carrying-place, where he expected we should leave him.

At length our canoe was become so leaky, that it was absolutely unfit for service; and it was the unremitting employment of one person to keep her clear of water: we, therefore, inquired of the old man where we could conveniently obtain the articles necessary to build a new one; and we understood from him that, at some distance up the river, we should find plenty of bark and cedar.

At ten, being at the foot of a rapid, we saw a small canoe coming down with two men in it. We thought it would be impossible for them to escape, and therefore struck off from the shore with a design to intercept them, directing the old man at the same time to address them; but they no sooner perceived us, than they steered into the strength of the current, where I thought that they must inevitably perish; but their attention appeared to be engrossed by the situation of their canoe, and they escaped without making us the least reply.

About three in the afternoon we perceived a lodge at the entrance of a considerable river on the right, as well as the tracks of people in the mud at the mouth of a small river on the left. As they appeared to be fresh, we landed, and endeavoured to trace them, but without success. We then crossed over to the lodge, which was deserted, but all the usual furniture of such buildings remained untouched.

Throughout the whole of this day the men had been in a state of extreme ill-humor, and as they did not choose openly to vent it upon me, they disputed and quarrelled among themselves. About sun-set the canoe struck upon the stump of a tree, which broke a large hole in her bottom; a circumstance that gave them an opportunity to let loose their discontents without reserve. I left them as soon as we had landed, and ascended an elevated bank, in a state of mind which I scarce wish to recollect, and shall not attempt to describe. At this place there was a subterraneous house, where I determined to pass the night. The water had risen since we had passed down, and it was with the utmost exertion that we came up several points in the course of the day.

Thursday, June 27. We embarked at half past four, with very favourable weather, and at eight we landed, where there was an appearance of our being able to procure bark; we, however, obtained but a small quantity. At twelve we went on shore again, and collected as much as was necessary for our purpose. It now remained for us to fix on a proper place for building another canoe, as it was impossible to proceed with our old one, which was become an absolute wreck. At five in the afternoon we came to a spot well adapted to the business in which we were about to engage. It was on a small island not much encumbered with wood, though there was plenty of the spruce kind on the opposite land, which was only divided from us by a small channel. We now landed, but before the canoe was unloaded, and the tent pitched, a violent thunder-storm came on, accompanied with rain, which did not subside till the night had closed in upon us. Two of our men who had been in the woods for axe-handles, saw a deer, and one of them shot at it, but unluckily missed his aim. A net was also prepared and set in the eddy at the end of the island.

Chapter 9

CANOE BUILDING

Friday, June 28. At a very early hour of the morning every man was employed in making preparations for building another canoe, and different parties went in search of wood, watape, and gum. At two in the afternoon they all returned successful, except the collectors of gum, and of that article it was feared we should not obtain here a sufficient supply for our immediate wants. After a necessary portion of time allotted for refreshment, each began his respective work. I had an altitude at noon, which made us in 53.2.32 North latitude.

Saturday, June 29. The weather continued to be fine. At five o'clock we renewed our labour, and the canoe was got in a state of considerable forwardness. The conductor of the work, though a good man, was remarkable for the tardiness of his operations, whatever they might be, and more disposed to eat than to be active; I, therefore, took this opportunity of unfolding my sentiments to him, and thereby discovering to all around me the real state of my mind, and the resolutions I had formed for my future conduct. After reproaching him for his general inactivity, but particularly on the present occasion, when our time was so precious, I mentioned the apparent want of economy both of himself and his companions, in the article of provisions. I informed him that I was not altogether a stranger to their late conversations, from whence I drew the conclusion that they wished to put an end to the voyage. If that were so, I expressed my wish that they would be explicit, and tell me at once of their determination to follow me no longer. I concluded, however, by assuring him, that whatever plan they had meditated to pursue, it was my fixed and unalterable determination to proceed, in spite of every difficulty that might oppose, or danger that should threaten me. The man was very much mortified at my addressing this remonstrance particularly to him; and replied, that he did not deserve my displeasure more than the rest of them. My object being answered, the conversation dropped, and the work went on.

About two in the afternoon one of the men perceived a canoe with two natives in it, coming along the inside of the island, but the water being shallow, it turned back, and we imagined that on perceiving us they had taken the alarm; but we were agreeably surprised on seeing them come up the outside of the island, when we recognised our guide, and one of the natives whom we had already seen. The former began immediately to apologize for his conduct, and assured me that since he had left me, his whole time had been employed in searching after his family, who had been seized with the general panic, that had been occasioned by the false reports of the people who had first fled from us. He said it was generally apprehended by the natives that we had been unfriendly to their relations above, who were expected upon the river in great numbers at this time; and that many of the Atnah or Chin nation, had come up the river to where we had been, in the hope of seeing us, and were very much displeased with him and his friends for having neglected to give them an early notice of our arrival there. He added, that the two men whom we had seen yesterday, or the day before, were just returned from their rendezvous, with the natives of the sea coast, and had brought a message from his brother-in-law, that he had a new axe for him, and not to forget to bring a moose skin dressed in exchange, which he actually had in his canoe. He expected to meet him, he said, at the other end of the carrying-place.

This was as pleasing intelligence as we had reason to expect, and it is almost superflous to observe that we stood in great need of it. I had a meridian altitude, which gave 53.3.7 North latitude. I also took time in the fore and afternoon, that gave a mean of 1.37.42. Achrometer slow apparent time, which, with an observed immersion of Jupiter's first satellite, made our longitude 122.48 West of Greenwich.

The blind old man gave a very favourable account of us to his friends, and they all three were very merry together during the whole of the afternoon. That our guide, however, might not escape from us during the night, I determined to watch him.

Sunday, June 30. Our strangers conducted themselves with great good-humour throughout the day. According to their information we should find their friends above and below the carrying-place. They mentioned, also, that some of them were not of their tribe, but are allied to the people of the sea coast, who trade with the white men. I had a meridian altitude, that gave 53.3.17 North latitude.

Monday, July 1. Last night I had the first watch, when one of my Indians proposed to sit up with me, as he understood, from the old man's conversation, that he intended, in the course of the night, to make his escape. Accordingly at eleven I extinguished my light, and sat quietly in my tent, from whence I could observe the motions of the natives. About twelve, though the night was rather dark, I observed the old man creeping on his hands and knees towards the water-side. We accordingly followed him very quietly to the canoe, and he would have gone away with it, if he had not been interrupted in his design. On upbraiding him for his treacherous conduct, when he had been treated with so much kindness by us, he denied the intention of which we accused him, and declared that his sole object was to assuage his thirst. At length, however, he acknowledged the truth, and when we brought him to the fire, his friends, who now awoke, on being informed of what had passed, reprobated his conduct, and asked him how he could expect that the white people would return to this country, if they experienced such ungrateful treatment. The guide said, for his part, he was not a woman, and would never run away through fear. But notwithstanding this courageous declaration, at one I awakened Mr. Mackay, related to him what had passed, and requested him not to indulge himself in sleep till I should rise. It was seven before I awoke, and on quitting my tent I was surprised at not seeing the guide and his companion, and my apprehensions were increased when I observed that the canoe was removed from its late situation. To my inquiries after them, some of the men very composedly answered that they were gone up the river, and had left the old man behind them. Mr. Mackay also told me, that while he was busily employed on the canoe, they had got to the point before he had observed their departure. The interpreter now informed me that at the dawn of day the guide had expressed his design, as soon as the sun was up, to go and wait for us, where he might find his friends. I hoped this might be true; but that my people should suffer them to depart without giving me notice, was a circumstance that awakened very painful reflections in my breast. The weather was clear in the forenoon. My observation this day gave 53.3.32 North latitude.

At five in the afternoon our vessel was completed, and ready for service. She proved a stronger and better boat than the old one, though had it not been for the gum obtained from the latter, it would have been a matter of great difficulty to have procured a sufficiency of that article to have prevented her from leaking. The remainder of the day was employed by the people in cleaning and refreshing themselves, as they had enjoyed no relaxation from their labours since we landed on this spot.

The old man having manifested for various and probably very fallacious reasons, a very great aversion to accompany us any further, it did not appear that there was any necessity to force his inclination. We now put our arms in order, which was soon accomplished, as they were at all times a general object of attention.

Tuesday, July 2. It rained throughout the night, but at half past three we were ready to embark, when I offered to conduct the old man where he had supposed we should meet his friends, but he declined the proposition. I therefore directed a few pounds of pemmican to be left with him, for his immediate support, and took leave of him and the place, which I named Canoe Island. During our stay there we had been most cruelly tormented by flies, particularly the sand-fly, which I am disposed to consider as the most tormenting insect of its size in nature. I was also compelled to put the people upon short allowance, and confine them to two meals a-day, a regulation peculiarly offensive to a Canadian voyager. One of these meals was composed of the dried rows of fish, pounded, and boiled in water, thickened with a small quantity of flour, and fattened with a bit of grain. These articles, being brought to the consistency of an hasty pudding, produced a substantial and not unpleasant dish. The natives are very careful of the rows of fish, which they dry, and preserve in baskets made of bark. Those we used were found in the huts of the first people who fled from us. During our abode in Canoe Island, the water sunk three perpendicular feet. I now gave the men a dram each, which could not but be considered, at this time, as a very comfortable treat. They were, indeed, in high spirits, when they perceived the superior excellence of the new vessel, and reflected that it was the work of their own hands.

At eleven we arrived at the rapids, and the foreman, who had not forgotten the fright he suffered on coming down it, proposed that the canoe and lading should be carried over the mountain. I threatened him with taking the office of foreman on myself, and suggested the evident change there was in the appearance of the water since we passed it, which upon examination had sunk four feet and an half. As the water did not seem so strong on the West side, I determined to cross over, having first put Mr. Mackay, and our two hunters, on shore, to try the woods for game. We accordingly traversed, and got up close along the rocks, to a considerable distance, with the paddles, when we could proceed no further without assistance from the line; and to draw it across a perpendicular rock, for the distance of fifty fathoms, appeared to be an insurmountable obstacle. The general opinion was to return, and carry on the other side; I desired, however, two of the men to take the line, which was seventy fathoms in length, with a small roll of bark, and endeavour to climb up the rocks, from whence they were to descend on the other side of that which opposed our progress; they were then to fasten the end of the line to the roll of bark, which the current would bring to us; this being effected, they would be able to draw us up. This was an enterprise of difficulty and danger, but it was crowned with success; though to get to the water's edge above, the men were obliged to let themselves down with the line, run down a tree, from the summit of the rock. By a repetition of the same operation, we at length cleared the rapid, with the additional trouble of carrying the canoe, and unloading at two cascades. We were not more than two hours getting up this difficult part of the river, including the time employed in repairing an hole which had been broken in the canoe, by the negligence of the steersman.

Here we expected to meet with the natives, but there was not the least appearance of them, except that the guide, his companion, and two others, had apparently passed the carrying-place. We saw several fish leap out of the water, which appeared to be of the salmon kind. The old man, indeed, had informed us that this was the season when the large fish begin to come up the river. Our hunters returned, but had not seen the track of any animal. We now continued our journey; the current was not strong, but we met with frequent impediments from the fallen trees, which lay along the banks. We landed at eight in the evening; and suffered indescribable inconveniences from the flies.

Wednesday, July 3. It had rained hard in the night, and there was some small rain in the morning. At four we entered our canoe, and at ten we came to a small river, which answered to the description of that whose course the natives said, they follow in their journies towards the sea coast; we therefore put into it, and endeavoured to discover if our guide had landed here; but there were no traces of him or of any others. My former perplexities were now renewed. If I passed this river, it was probable that I might miss the natives; and I had reason to suspect that my men would not consent to return thither. As for attempting the woods, without a guide, to introduce us to the first inhabitants, such a determination would be little short of absolute madness. At length, after much painful reflection, I resolved to come at once to a full explanation with my people, and I experienced a considerable relief from this resolution. Accordingly, after repeating the promise they had so lately made me, on our putting back up the river, I represented to them that this appeared to me to be the spot from which the natives took their departure for the sea coast, and added, withal, that I was determined to try it; for though our guide had left us, it was possible that, while we were making the necessary preparations, he or some others might appear, to relieve us from our present difficulties. I now found, to my great satisfaction, that they had not come to any fixed determination among themselves, as some of them immediately assented to undertake the woods with me. Others, however, suggested that it might be better to proceed a few leagues further up the river, in expectation of finding our guide, or procuring another, and that after all we might return hither. This plan I very readily agreed to adopt, but before I left this place, to which I gave the name of the West-Road River, I sent some of the men into the woods, in different directions, and went some distance up the river myself, which I found to be navigable only for small canoes. Two of the men found a good beaten path, leading up an hill just behind us, which I imagined to be the great road.

At four in the afternoon we left this place, proceeding up the river; and had not been upon the water more than three quarters of an hour, when we saw two canoes coming with the stream. No sooner did the people in them perceive us than they landed, and we went on shore at the same place with them. They proved to be our guide, and six of his relations. He was covered with a painted beaver robe, so that we scarcely knew him in his fine habiliment. He instantly desired us to acknowledge that he had not disappointed us, and declared, at the same time, that it was his constant intention to keep his word. I accordingly gave him a jacket, a pair of trowsers, and an handkerchief, as a reward for his honourable conduct. The strangers examined us with the most minute attention, and two of them, as I was now informed, belonged to the people whom we first saw, and who fled with so much alarm from us. They told me, also, that they were so terrified on that occasion, as not to approach their huts for two days; and that when they ventured thither, they found the greater part of their property destroyed, by the fire running in the ground. According to their account, they were of a different tribe, though I found no difference in their language from that of the Nagailas or Carriers. They are called Nascud Denee. Their lodges were at some distance, on a small lake, where they take fish, and if our guide had not gone for them there, we should not have seen an human being on the river. They informed me that the road by their habitation is the shortest, and they proposed that we should take it.

Thursday, July 4. At an early hour this morning, and at the suggestion of our guide, we proceeded to the landing-place that leads to the strangers lodges. Our great difficulty here was to procure a temporary separation from our company, in order to hide some articles we could not carry with us, and which it would have been imprudent to leave in the power of the natives. Accordingly Mr. Mackay, and one of our Indians embarked with them, and soon run out of our sight. At our first hiding-place we left a bag of pemmican, weighing ninety pounds, two bags of wild rice, and a gallon keg of gunpowder. Previous to our putting these articles in the ground, we rolled them up in oil cloth, and dressed leather. In the second hiding-place, and guarded with the same rollers, we hid two bags of Indian corn, or maize, and a bale of different articles of merchandise. When we had completed this important object, we proceeded till half past eight, when we landed at the entrance of a small rivulet, where our friends were waiting for us.

Here it was necessary that we should leave our canoe, and whatever we could not carry on our backs. In the first place, therefore, we prepared a stage, on which the canoe was placed bottom upwards, and shaded by a covering of small trees and branches, to keep her from the sun. We then built an oblong hollow square, ten feet by five, of green logs, wherein we placed every article it was necessary for us to leave here, and covered the whole with large pieces of timber.

While we were eagerly employed in this necessary business, our guide and his companions were so impatient to be gone, that we could not persuade the former to wait till we were prepared for our departure, and we had some difficulty in persuading another of the natives to remain, who had undertook to conduct us where the guide had promised to wait for our arrival.

At noon we were in a state of preparation to enter the woods, an undertaking of which I shall not here give any preliminary opinion, but leave those who read it to judge for themselves.

We carried on our backs four bags and an half of pemmican, weighing from eighty-five to ninety pounds each; a case with my instruments, a parcel of goods for presents, weighing ninety pounds, and a parcel containing ammunition of the same weight. Each of the Canadians had a burden of about ninety pounds, with a gun, and some ammunition. The Indians had about forty-five pounds weight of pemmican to carry, besides their gun, &c. with which they were very much dissatisfied, and if they had dared would have instantly left us. They had hitherto been very much indulged, but the moment was now arrived when indulgence was no longer practicable. My own load, and that of Mr. Mackay, consisted of twenty-two pounds of pemmican, some rice, a little sugar, &c. amounting in the whole to about seventy pounds each, besides our arms and ammunition. I had also the tube of my telescope swung across my shoulder, which was a troublesome addition to my burthen. It was determined that we should content ourselves with two meals a-day, which were regulated without difficulty, as our provisions did not require the ceremony of cooking.

In this state of equipment we began our journey, as I have already mentioned, about twelve noon, the commencement of which was a steep ascent of about a mile; it lay along a well-beaten path, but the country through which it led was rugged and ridgy, and full of wood. When we were in a state of extreme heat, from the toil of our journey, the rain came on, and continued till the evening, and even when it ceased the underwood continued its drippings upon us.

About half past six we arrived at an Indian camp of three fires, where we found our guide, and on his recommendation we determined to remain there for the night. The computed distance of this day's journey was about twelve geographical miles; the course about West.

At sun-set an elderly man and three other natives joined us from the Westward. The former bore a lance that very much resembled a serjeant's halberd. He had lately received it, by way of barter, from the natives of the Sea-Coast, who procured it from the white men. We should meet, he said, with many of his countrymen who had just returned from thence. According to his report, it did not require more than six days journey, for people who are not heavily laden, to reach the country of those with whom they bartered their skins for iron, &c. and from thence it is not quite two day's march to the sea. They proposed to send two young men on before us, to notify to the different tribes that we were approaching, that they might not be surprised at our appearance, and be disposed to afford us a friendly reception. This was a measure which I could not but approve, and endeavoured by some small presents to prepossess our couriers in our favour.

These people live but poorly at this season, and I could procure no provision from them, but a few small, dried fish, as I think, of the carp kind. They had several European articles; and one of them had a strip of fur, which appeared to me to be of the sea otter. He obtained it from the natives of the coast, and exchanged it with me for some beads and a brass cross.

We retired to rest in as much security as if we had been long habituated to a confidence in our present associates: indeed, we had no alternative; for so great were the fatigues of the day in our mode of travelling, that we were in great need of rest at night.

Friday, July 5. We had no sooner laid ourselves down to rest last night, than the natives began to sing, in a manner very different from what I had been accustomed to hear among savages. It was not accompanied either with dancing, drum, or rattle; but consisted of soft, plaintive tones, and a modulation that was rather agreeable: it had somewhat the air of church music. As the natives had requested me not to quit them at a very early hour in the morning, it was five before I desired that the young men, who were to proceed with us, should depart, when they prepared to set off: but, on calling to our guide to conduct us, he said, that he did not intend to accompany us any further, as the young men would answer our purpose as well as himself. I knew it would be in vain to remonstrate with him, and therefore submitted to his caprice without a reply. However, I thought proper to inform him, that one of my people had lost his dag, or poignard, and requested his assistance in the recovery of it. He asked me what I would give him to conjure it back again; and a knife was agreed to be the price of his necromantic exertions. Accordingly, all the dags and knives in the place were gathered together, and the natives formed a circle round them; the conjurer also remaining in the middle. When this part of the ceremony was arranged, he began to sing, the rest joining in the chorus; and after some time he produced the poignard which was stuck in the ground, and returned it to me.

At seven we were ready to depart; when I was surprised to hear our late guide propose, without any solicitation on our part, to resume his office; and he actually conducted us as far as a small lake, where we found an encampment of three families. The young men who had undertaken to conduct us were not well understood by my interpreters, who continued to be so displeased with their journey, that they performed this part of their duty with great reluctance. I endeavoured to persuade an elderly man of this encampment to accompany us to the next tribe, but no inducement of mine could prevail on him to comply with my wishes. I was, therefore, obliged to content myself with the guides I had already engaged, for whom we were obliged to wait some time, till they had provided shoes for their journey. I exchanged two halfpence here, one of his present Majesty, and the other of the State of Massachuset's Bay, coined in 1787. They hung as ornaments in children's ears.

My situation here was rendered rather unpleasant by the treatment which my hunters received from these people. The former, it appeared, were considered as belonging to a tribe who inhabit the mountains, and are the natural enemies of the latter. We had also been told by one of the natives, of a very stern aspect, that he had been stabbed by a relation of theirs, and pointed to a scar as the proof of it. I was, therefore, very glad to proceed on my journey.

Our guides conducted us along the lake through thick woods, and without any path, for about a mile and an half, when we lost sight of it. This piece of water is about three miles long and one broad. We then crossed a creek and entered upon a beaten track, through an open country, sprinkled with cypress trees. At twelve the sky became black, and an heavy gust with rain shortly followed, which continued for upwards of an hour. When we perceived the approaching storm, we fixed our thin, light oil-cloth to screen us from it. On renewing our march, as the bushes were very wet, I desired our guides, they having no burdens, to walk in front, and beat them as they went: this task, they chose to decline, and accordingly I undertook it. Our road now lay along a lake, and across a creek that ran into it. The guides informed me, that this part of the country abounds in beaver: many traps were seen along the road which had been set for lynxes and martens. About a quarter of a mile from the place where we had been stopped by the rain, the ground was covered with hail, and as we advanced, the hailstones increased in size, some of them being as big as musket-balls. In this manner was the ground whitened for upwards of two miles. At five in the afternoon we arrived on the banks of another lake, when it again threatened rain; and we had already been sufficiently wetted in the course of the day, to look with complacency towards a repetition of it: we accordingly fixed our shed, the rain continuing with great violence through the remainder of the day: it was, therefore, determined, that we should stop here for the night.

In the course of the day we passed three winter huts; they consisted of low walls, with a ridge-pole, covered with the branches of the Canadian balsam-tree. One of my men had a violent pain in his knee, and I asked the guides to take a share of his burden, as they had nothing to carry but their beaver robes, and bows and arrows, but they could not be made to understand a word of my request.

Saturday, July 6. At four this morning I arose from my bed, such as it was. As we must have been in a most unfortunate predicament, if our guides should have deserted us in the night, by way of security, I proposed to the youngest of them to sleep with me, and he readily consented. These people have no covering but their beaver garments, and that of my companions was a nest of vermin. I, however, spread it under us, and having laid down upon it, we covered ourselves with my camblet cloak. My companion's hair being greased with fish-oil, and his body smeared with red earth, my sense of smelling, as well as that of feeling, threatened to interrupt my rest; but these inconveniences yielded to my fatigue, and I passed a night of sound repose.

I took the lead in our march, as I had done yesterday, in order to clear the branches of the wet which continued to hang upon them. We proceeded with all possible expedition through a level country with but little under-wood; the larger trees were of the fir kind. At half past eight we fell upon the road, shorter than that which we had travelled. The West-road river was also m sight, winding through a valley. We had not met with any water since our encampment of last night, and though we were afflicted with violent thirst, the river was at such a distance from us, and the descent to it so long and steep, that we were compelled to be satisfied with casting our longing looks towards it. There appeared to be more water in the river here, than at its discharge. The Indian account, that it is navigable for their canoes, is, I believe, perfectly correct.

Our guides now told us, that as the road was very good and well traced, they would proceed to inform the next tribe that we were coming. This information was of a very unpleasant nature; as it would have been easy for them to turn off the road at an hundred yards from us, and, when we had passed them, to return home. I proposed that one of them should remain with us, while two of my people should leave their loads behind and accompany the other to the lodges. But they would not stay to hear our persuasion, and were soon out of sight.

I now desired the Cancre to leave his burden, take a small quantity of provision, with his arms and blanket, and follow me. I also told my men to come on as fast they could, and that I would wait for them as soon as I had formed an acquaintance with the natives of the country before us. We accordingly followed our guides with all the expedition in our power, but did not overtake them till we came to a family of natives, consisting of one man, two women, and six children, with whom we found them. These people betrayed no signs of fear at our appearance, and the man willingly conversed with my interpreter, to whom he made himself more intelligible, than our guides had been able to do. They, however, had informed him of the object of our journey. He pointed out to us one of his wives, who was a native of the sea coast, which was not a very great distance from us. This woman was more inclined to corpulency than any we had yet seen, was of low stature, with an oblong face, grey eyes, and a flattish nose. She was decorated with ornaments of various kinds, such as large blue beads, either pendant from her ears, encircling her neck, or braided in her hair: she also wore bracelets of brass, copper, and horn. Her garments consisted of a kind of tunic, which was covered with a robe of matted bark, fringed round the bottom with skin of the sea otter. None of the women whom I had seen since we crossed the mountain wore this kind of tunic; their blankets being merely girt round the waist. She had learned the language of her husband's tribe, and confirmed his account, that we were at no great distance from the sea. They were on their way, she said, to the great river to fish. Age seemed to be an object of great veneration among these people, for they carried an old woman by turns on their backs who was quite blind and infirm from the very advanced period of her life.

Our people having joined us and rested themselves, I requested our guides to proceed, when the elder of them told me that he should not go any further, but that these people would send a boy to accompany his brother, and I began to think myself rather fortunate, that we were not deserted by them all.

About noon we parted, and in two hours we came up with two men and their families: when we first saw them they were sitting down, as if to rest themselves; but no sooner did they perceive us than they rose up and seized their arms. The boys who were behind us immediately ran forwards and spoke to them, when they laid by their arms and received us as friends. They had been eating green berries and dried fish. We had, indeed, scarcely joined them, when a woman and a boy came from the river with water, which they very hospitably gave us to drink. The people of this party had a very sickly appearance, which might have been the consequence of disease, or that indolence which is so natural to them, or of both. One of the women had a tattooed line along the chin, of the same length as her mouth.

The lads now informed me that they would go no further, but that these men would take their places; and they parted from their families with as little apparent concern, as if they were entire strangers to each other. One of them was very well understood by my interpreter, and had resided among the natives of the sea coast, whom he had left but a short time. According to his information, we were approaching a river, which was neither large nor long, but whose banks are inhabited; and that in the bay which the sea forms at the mouth of it, a great wooden canoe, with white people, arrives about the time when leaves begin to grow: I presume in the early part of May.

After we parted with the last people, we came to an uneven, hilly, and swampy country, through which our way was impeded by a considerable number of fallen trees. At five in the afternoon we were overtaken by a heavy shower of rain and hail, and being at the same time very much fatigued, we encamped for the night near a small creek. Our course, till we came to the river, was about South-West ten miles, and then West, twelve or fourteen miles. I thought it prudent, by way of security, to submit to the same inconveniences I have already described, and shared the beaver robe of one of my guides during the night.

Sunday, July 7. I was so busily employed in collecting intelligence from our conductors, that I last night forgot to wind up my time-piece, and it was the only instance of such an act of negligence since I left Fort Chepwyan, on the 11th of last October. At five we quitted our station, and proceeded across two mountains, covered with spruce, poplar, white birch, and other trees. We then descended into a level country, where we found a good road, through woods of cypress. We then came to two small lakes, at the distance of about fourteen miles. Course about West. Through them the river passes, and our road kept in a parallel line with it on a range of elevated ground. On observing some people before us, our guides hastened to meet them, and, on their approach, one of them stepped forward with an axe in his hand. This party consisted only of a man, two women, and the same number of children. The eldest of the women, who was probably the man's mother, was engaged, when we joined them, in clearing a circular spot, of about five feet in diameter, of the weeds that infested it; nor did our arrival interrupt her employment, which was sacred to the memory of the dead. The spot to which her pious care was devoted, contained the grave of an husband, and a son, and whenever she passed this way, she always stopped to pay this tribute of affection.

As soon as we had taken our morning allowance, we set forwards, and about three we perceived more people before us. After some alarm we came up with them. They consisted of seven men, as many women, and several children. Here I was under the necessity of procuring another guide, and we continued our route on the same side of the river, till six in the evening, when we crossed it. It was knee deep, and about an hundred yards over. I wished now to stop for the night, as we were all of us very much fatigued, but our guide recommended us to proceed onwards to a family of his friends, at a small distance from thence, where we arrived at half past seven. He had gone forward, and procured us a welcome and quiet reception. There being a net hanging to dry, I requested the man to prepare and set it in the water, which he did with great expedition, and then presented me with a few small dried fish. Our course was South-West about twelve miles, part of which was an extensive swamp, that was seldom less than knee deep. In the course of the afternoon we had several showers of rain. I had attempted to take an altitude, but it was past meridian. The water of the river before the lodge was quite still, and expanded itself into the form of a small lake. In many other places, indeed, it had assumed the same form.

Monday, July 8. It mined throughout the night, and it was seven in the morning before the weather would allow us to proceed. The guide brought me five small boiled fish, in a platter made of bark; some of them were of the carp kind, and the rest of a species for which I am not qualified to furnish a name. Having dried our clothes, we set off on our march about eight, and our guide very cheerfully continued to accompany us; but he was not altogether so intelligible as his predecessors in our service. We learned from him, however, that this lake, through which the river passes extends to the foot of the mountain, and that he expected to meet nine men, of a tribe which inhabits the North side of the river.

In this part of our journey we were surprised with the appearance of several regular basons, some of them furnished with water, and the others empty; their slope from the edge to the bottom formed an angle of about forty-five degrees, and their perpendicular depth was about twelve feet. Those that contained water, discovered gravel near their edges, while the empty ones were covered with grass and herbs, among which we discovered mustard, and mint. There were also several places from whence the water appears to have retired, which are covered with the same soil and herbage.

We now proceeded along a very uneven country, the upper parts of which were covered with poplars, a little under-wood and plenty of grass: the intervening vallies were watered with rivulets. From these circumstances, and the general appearance of vegetation, I could not account for the apparent absence of animals of every kind.

At two in the afternoon we arrived at the largest river that we had seen, since we left our canoe, and which forced its way between and over the huge stones that opposed its current. Our course was about South-South-West sixteen miles along the river, which might here justify the title of a lake. The road was good, and our next course, which was West by South, brought us onward ten miles, where we encamped, fatigued and wet, it having rained three parts of the day. This river abounds with fish, and must fall into the great river, further down than we had extended our voyage.

Tuesday, July 9. A heavy and continued rain fell through great part of the night, and as we were in some measure exposed to it, time was required to dry our clothes; so that it was half past seven in the morning before we were ready to set out. As we found the country so destitute of game, and foreseeing the difficulty of procuring provisions for our return, I thought it prudent to conceal half a bag of pemmican: having sent off the Indians, and all my people except two, we buried it under the fire-place, as we had done on a former occasion. We soon overtook our party, and continued our route along the river or lake. About twelve I had an altitude, but it was inaccurate from the cloudiness of the weather. We continued our progress till five in the afternoon, when the water began to narrow, and in about half an hour we came to a ferry, where we found a small raft. At this time it began to thunder, and torrents of rain soon followed, which terminated our journey for the day. Our course was about South, twenty-one miles from the lake already mentioned. We now discovered the tops of mountains, covered with snow, over very high intermediate land. We killed a whitehead and a grey eagle, and three grey partridges; we saw also two otters in the river, and several beaver lodges along it. When the rain ceased, we caught a few small fish, and repaired the raft for the service of the ensuing day.

Wednesday, July 10. At an early hour of this morning we prepared to cross the water. The traverse is about thirty yards, and it required five trips to get us all over. At a short distance below, a small river falls in, that comes from the direction in which we were proceeding. It is a rapid for about three hundred yards, when it expands into a lake, along which our road conducted us, and beneath a range of beautiful hills, covered with verdure, At half past eight we came to the termination of the lake, where there were two houses that occupied a most delightful situation, and as they contained their necessary furniture, it seemed probable that their owners intended shortly to return. Near them were several graves or tombs, to which the natives are particularly attentive, and never suffer any herbage to grow upon them. In about half an hour we reached a place where there were two temporary huts, that contained thirteen men, with whom we found our guide who had preceded us, in order to secure a good reception. The buildings were detached from each other, and conveniently placed for fishing in the lake. Their inhabitants called themselves Sloua-cuss-Dinais, which denomination, so far as my interpreter could explain it to me, I understood to mean Red-fish Men. They were much more cleanly, healthy, and agreeable in their appearance, than any of the natives whom we had passed; nevertheless, I have no doubt that they are the same people, from their name alone, which is of the Chepewyan language. My interpreters, however, understood very little of what they said, so that I did not expect much information from them. Some of them said it was a journey of four days to the sea, and others were of opinion that it was six; and there were among them who extended it to eight; but they all uniformly declared that they had been to the coast. They did not entertain the smallest apprehension of danger from us, and, when we discharged our pieces, expressed no sensation but that of astonishment, which as may be supposed, was proportionably encreased when one of the hunters shot an eagle, at a considerable distance. At twelve I obtained an altitude, which, made our latitude 53.4.32 North, being not far so far South as I expected.

I now went accompanied by one of my men, an interpreter, and the guide, to visit some huts at the distance of a mile. On our arrival the inhabitants presented us with a dish of boiled trout, of a small kind. The fish would have been excellent if it had not tasted of the kettle, which was made of the bark of the white spruce, and of the dried grass with which it was boiled. Besides this kind of trout, red and white carp and jub, are the only fish I saw as the produce of these waters.

These people appeared to live in a state of comparative comfort: they take a greater share in the labour of the women, than is common among the savage tribes, and are, as I was informed, content with one wife. Though this circumstance may proceed rather from the difficulty of procuring subsistence, than any habitual aversion to polygamy.

My present guide now informed me, that he could not proceed any further, and I accordingly engaged two of these people to succeed him in that office; but when they desired us to proceed on the beaten path without them, as they could not set off till the following day, I determined to stay that night, in order to accommodate myself to their convenience. I distributed some trifles among the wives and children of the men who were to be our future guides, and returned to my people. We came back by a different way, and passed by two buildings, erected between four trees, and about fifteen feet from the ground, which appeared to me to be intended as magazines for winter provisions. At four in the afternoon, we proceeded with considerable expedition, by the side of the lake, till six, when we came to the end of it: we then struck off through a much less beaten track, and at half past seven stopped for the night. Our course was about West-South-West thirteen miles, and West six miles.

Thursday, July 11. I passed a most uncomfortable night: the first part of it I was tormented with flies, and in the latter deluged with rain. In the morning the weather cleared, and as soon as our clothes were dried, we proceeded through a morass. This part of the country had been laid waste by fire, and the fallen trees added to the pain and perplexity of our way. An high, rocky ridge stretched along our left. Though the rain returned, we continued our progress till noon, when our guides took to some trees for shelter. We then spread our oil-cloth, and, with some difficulty, made a fire. About two the rain ceased, when we continued our journey through the same kind of country which we had hitherto passed. At half past three we came in sight of a lake; the land, at the same time gradually rising to a range of mountains whose tops were covered with snow. We soon after observed two fresh tracks, which seemed to surprise our guides, but they supposed them to have been made by the inhabitants of the country who were come into this part of it to fish. At five in the afternoon we were so wet and cold, (for it had at intervals continued to rain,) that we were compelled to stop for the night. We passed seven rivulets and a creek in this day's journey. As I had hitherto regulated our course by the sun, I could not form an accurate judgment of this route, as we had not been favoured with a sight of it during the day; but I imagine it to have been nearly in the same direction as that of yesterday. Our distance could not have been less than fifteen miles.

Our conductors now began to complain of our mode of travelling, and mentioned their intention of leaving us; and my interpreters, who were equally dissatisfied, added to our perplexity by their conduct. Besides, these circumstances, and the apprehension that the distance from the sea might be greater than I had imagined, it became a matter of real necessity that we should begin to diminish the consumption of our provisions, and to subsist upon two-thirds of our allowance; a proposition which was as unwelcome to my people, as it was necessary to be put into immediate practice.

Friday, July 12. At half past five this morning we proceeded on our journey, with cloudy weather, and when we came to the end of the lake several tracks were visible that led to the side of the water; from which circumstance I concluded, that some of the natives were fishing along the banks of it. This lake is not more than three miles long, and about one broad. We then passed four smaller lakes, the two first being on our right, and those which preceded on our left. A small river also flowed across our way from the right, and we passed it over a beaver-dam. A larger lake now appeared on our right, and the mountains on each side of us were covered with snow. We afterwards came to another lake on our right, and soon reached a river, which our guides informed us was the same that we had passed on a raft. They said it was navigable for canoes from the great river except two rapids, one of which we had seen. At this place it is upwards of twenty yards across, and deep water. One of the guides swam over to fetch a raft which was on the opposite side; and having encreased its dimensions, we crossed at two trips, except four of the men, who preferred swimming.

Here our conductors renewed their menace of leaving us, and I was obliged to give them several articles, and promise more, in order to induce them to continue till we could procure other natives to succeed them. At four in the afternoon we forded the same river, and being with the guides at some distance before the rest of the people, I sat down to wait for them, and no sooner did they arrive, than the former set off with so much speed, that my attempt to follow them proved unsuccessful. One of my Indians, however, who had no load, overtook them, when they excused themselves to him by declaring, that their sole motive for leaving us, was to prevent the people, whom they expected to find, from shooting their arrows at us. At seven o'clock, however, we were so fatigued, that we encamped without them: the mountains covered with snow now appeared to be directly before us. As we were collecting wood for our fire, we discovered a cross road, where it appeared that people had passed within seven or eight days. In short, our situation was such as to afford a just cause of alarm, and that of the people with me was of a nature to defy immediate alleviation. It was necessary, however, for me to attempt it; and I rested my principles of encouragement on a representation of our past perplexities and unexpected relief, and endeavoured to excite in them the hope of similar good fortune. I stated to them, that we could not be at a great distance from the sea, and that there were but few natives to pass, till we should arrive among those, who being accustomed to visit the sea coast, and, having seen white people, would be disposed to treat us with kindness. Such was the general tenor of the reasoning I employed on the occasion, and I was happy to find that it was not offered in vain.

The weather had been cloudy till three in the afternoon, when the sun appeared; but surrounded, as we were, with snow-clad mountains, the air became so cold, that the violence of our exercise, was not sufficient to produce a comfortable degree of warmth. Our course to-day was from West to South, and at least thirty-six miles. The land in general was very barren and stony, and lay in ridges, with cypress trees scattered over them. We passed several swamps, where we saw nothing to console us but a few tracks of deer.

Saturday, July 13. The weather this morning was clear but cold, and our scanty covering was not sufficient to protect us from the severity of the night. About five, after we had warmed ourselves at a large fire, we proceeded on our dubious journey. In about an hour we came to the edge of a wood, when we perceived an house, situated on a green spot, and by the side of a small river. The smoke that issued from it informed us that it was inhabited. I immediately pushed toward this mansion, while my people were in such a state of alarm, that they followed me with the utmost reluctance. On looking back I perceived that we were in an Indian defile, of fifty yards in length. I, however, was close upon the house before the inhabitants perceived us, when the women and children uttered the most horrid shrieks, and the only man who appeared to be with them, escaped out of a back door, which I reached in time to prevent the women and children from following him. The man fled with all his speed into the wood, and I called in vain on my interpreters to speak to him, but they were so agitated with fear as to have lost the power of utterance. It is impossible to describe the distress and alarm of these poor people, who believing that they were attacked by enemies, expected an immediate massacre, which, among themselves, never fails to follow such an event.

Our prisoners consisted of three women, and seven children, which apparently composed three families. At length, however, by our demeanor, and our presents, we contrived to dissipate their apprehensions. One of the women then informed us, that their people, with several others had left that place three nights before, on a trading journey to a tribe whom she called Annah, which is the name the Chepewyans give to the Knisteneaux, at the distance of three days. She added also, that from the mountains before us, which were covered with snow, the sea was visible; and accompanied her information with a present of a couple of dried fish. We now expressed our desire that the man might be induced to return, and conduct us in the road to the sea. Indeed, it was not long before he discovered himself in the wood, when he was assured, both by the women and our interpreters that we had no hostile design against him; but these assurances had no effect in quieting his apprehensions. I then attempted to go to him alone, and showed him a knife, beads, &c. to induce him to come to me, but he, in return, made an hostile display of his bow and arrows; and, having for a time exhibited a variety of strange antics, again disappeared. However, he soon presented himself in another quarter, and after a succession of parleys between us, he engaged to come and accompany us.

While these negotiations were proceeding, I proposed to visit the fishing machines, to which the women readily consented, and I found in them twenty small fish, such as trout, carp, and jub, for which I gave her a large knife; a present that appeared to be equally unexpected and gratifying to her. Another man now came towards us, from an hill, talking aloud from the time he appeared till he reached us. The purpose of his speech was, that he threw himself upon our mercy, and we might kill him, if it was our pleasure, but that from what he had heard, he looked rather for our friendship than our enmity. He was an elderly person, of a decent appearance, and I gave him some articles to conciliate him to us. The first man now followed with a lad along with him, both of whom were the sons of the old man, and, on his arrival, he gave me several half-dried fish, which I considered as a peace-offering. After some conversation with these people, respecting the country, and our future progress through it, we retired to rest, with sensations very different from those with which we had risen in the morning. The weather had been generally cloudy throughout the day, and when the sun was obscured, extremely cold for the season. At noon I obtained a meridian altitude, which gave 52.58.53 North latitude. I likewise took time in the afternoon.

Sunday, July 14. This morning we had a bright sun, with an East wind. These people examined their fishing machines, when they found in them a great number of small fish, and we dressed as many of them as we could eat. Thus was our departure retarded until seven, when we proceeded on our journey, accompanied by the man and his two sons. As I did not want the younger, and should be obliged to feed him, I requested of his father to leave him, for the purpose of fishing for the women. He replied, that they were accustomed to fish for themselves, and that I need not be apprehensive of their encroaching upon my provisions, as they were used to sustain themselves in their journies on herbs, and the inner tegument of the bark of trees, for the stripping of which he had a thin piece of bone, then hanging by his side. The latter is of a glutinous quality, of a clammy, sweet taste, and is generally considered by the more interior

Indians as a delicacy, rather than an article of common food. Our guide informed me that there is a short cut across the mountains, but as there was no trace of a road, and it would shorten our journey but one day, he should prefer the beaten way.

We accordingly proceeded along a lake, West five miles. We then crossed a small river, and passed through a swamp, about South-West, when we began gradually to ascend for some time till we gained the summit of an hill, where we had an extensive view to the South-East, from which direction a considerable river appeared to flow, at the distance of about three miles; it was represented to me as being navigable for canoes. The descent of this hill was more steep than its ascent, and was succeeded by another, whose top, though not so elevated as the last, afforded a view of the range of mountains, covered with snow, which, according to the intelligence of our guide, terminates in the ocean. We now left a small lake on our left, then crossed a creek running out of it, and at one in the afternoon came to an house, of the same construction and dimensions as have already been mentioned, but the materials were much better prepared and finished. The timber was squared on two sides, and the bark taken off the two others; the ridge pole was also shaped in the same manner, extending about eight or ten feet beyond the gable end, and supporting a shed over the door: the end of it was carved into the similitude of a snake's head. Several hieroglyphics and figures of a similar workmanship, and painted with red earth, decorated the interior of the building. The inhabitants had left the house but a short time, and there were several bags or bundles in it, which I did not suffer to be disturbed. Near it were two tombs, surrounded in a neat manner with boards, and covered with bark. Beside them several poles had been erected, one of which was squared, and all of them painted. From each of them were suspended several rolls or parcels of bark, and our guide gave the following account of them; which, as far as we could judge from our imperfect knowledge of the language, and the incidental errors of interpretation, appeared to involve two different modes of treating their dead; or it might be one and the same ceremony, which we did not distinctly comprehend: at all events, it is the practice of these people to burn the bodies of their dead, except the larger bones, which are rolled up in bark and suspended from poles, as I have already described. According to the other account, it appeared that they actually bury their dead; and when another of the family dies, the remains of the person who was last interred are taken from the grave and burned, as has been already mentioned; so that the members of a family are thus successively buried and burned, to make room for each other; and one tomb proves sufficient for a family through succeeding generations. There is no house in this country without a tomb in its vicinity. Our last course extended about ten miles.

We continued our journey along the lake before the house, and, crossing a river that flowed out of it, came to a kind of bank, or weir, formed by the natives, for the purpose of placing their fishing machines, many of which, of different sizes, were lying on the side of the river. Our guide placed one of them, with the certain expectation that on his return he should find plenty of fish in it. We proceeded nine miles further, on a good road, West-South-West, when we came to a small lake: we then crossed a river that ran out of it, and our guides were in continual expectation of meeting with some of the natives. To this place our course was a mile and an half, in the same direction as the last. At nine at night we crossed a river on rafts, our last distance being about four miles South-East, on a winding road, through a swampy country, and along a succession of small lakes. We were now quite exhausted, and it was absolutely necessary for us to stop for the night. The weather being clear throughout the day, we had no reason to complain of the cold. Our guides encouraged us with the hope that, in two days of similar exertion, we should arrive among the people of the other nation.

Monday, July 15. At five this morning we were again in motion, and passing along a river, we at length forded it. This stream was not more than knee deep, about thirty yards over, and with a stony bottom. The old man went onward by himself, in the hope of falling in with the people, whom he expected to meet in the course of the day. At eleven we came up with him, and the natives whom he expected, consisting of five men, and part of their families. They received us with great kindness, and examined us with the most minute attention. They must, however, have been told that we were white, as our faces no longer indicated that distinguishing complexion. They called themselves Neguia Dinais, and were come in a different direction from us, but were not going the same way, to the Anah-yoe Tesse or River, and appeared to be very much satisfied with our having joined them. They presented us with some fish which they had just taken in the adjoining lake.

Here I expected our guides, like their predecessors, would have quitted us, but, on the contrary, they expressed themselves to be so happy in our company, and that of their friends, that they voluntarily, and with great cheerfulness proceeded to pass another night with us. Our new acquaintance were people of a very pleasing aspect. The hair of the women was tied in large loose knots over the ears, and plaited with great neatness from the division of the head, so as to be included in the knots. Some of them had adorned their tresses with beads, with a very pretty effect. The men were clothed in leather, their hair was nicely combed, and their complexion was fairer, or perhaps it may be said, with more propriety, that they were more cleanly, than any of the natives whom we had yet seen. Their eyes, though keen and sharp, are not of that dark colour, so generally observable in the various tribes of Indians; they were, on the contrary, of a grey hue, with a tinge of red. There was one man amongst them of at least six feet four inches in height; his manners were affable, and he had a more prepossessing appearance than any Indian I had met with in my journey; he was about twenty-eight years of age, and was treated with particular respect by his party. Every man, woman, and child, carried a proportionate burden, consisting of beaver coating and parchment, as well as skins of the otter, the marten, the bear, the lynx, and dressed mooseskins. The last they procure from the Rocky-Mountain Indians. According to their account, the people of the sea coast prefer them to any other article. Several of their relations and friends, they said, were already gone, as well provided as themselves, to barter with the people of the coast; who barter them in their turn, except the dressed leather, with white people who, as they had been informed, arrive there in large canoes.

Such an escort was the most fortunate circumstance that could happen in our favour. They told us, that as the women and children could not travel fast, we should be three days in getting to the end of our journey; which must be supposed to have been very agreeable information to people in our exhausted condition.

In about half an hour after we had joined our new acquaintance, the signal for moving onwards was given by the leader of the party, who vociferated the words, Huy, Huy, when his people joined him and continued a clamorous conversation. We passed along a winding road over hills, and through swampy vallies, from South to West. We then crossed a deep, narrow river, which discharges itself into a lake, on whose side we stopped at five in the afternoon, for the night, though we had reposed several times since twelve at noon; so that our mode of travelling had undergone a very agreeable change. I compute the distance of this day's journey at about twenty miles. In the middle of the day the weather was clear and sultry.

We all sat down on a very pleasant green spot, and were no sooner seated, than our guide and one of the party prepared to engage in play. They had each a bundle of about fifty small sticks, neatly polished, of the size of a quill, and five inches long: a certain number of these sticks had red lines round them; and as many of these as one of the players might find convenient were curiously rolled up in dry grass, and according to the judgment of his antagonist respecting their number and, marks, he lost or won. Our friend was apparently the loser, as he parted with his bow and arrows, and several articles which I had given him.

Tuesday, July 16. The weather of this morning was the same as yesterday; but our fellow-travellers were in no hurry to proceed, and I was under the necessity of pressing them into greater expedition, by representing the almost exhausted state of our provisions. They, however, assured us, that after the next night's sleep we should arrive at the river where they were going, and that we should there get fish in great abundance. My young men, from an act of imprudence, deprived themselves last night of that rest which was so necessary to them. One of the strangers asking them several questions respecting us, and concerning their own country, one of them gave such answers as were not credited by the audience; whereupon he demanded, in a very angry tone, if they thought he was disposed to tell lies, like the Rocky-Mountain Indians; and one of that tribe happening to be of the party, a quarrel ensued, which might have been attended with the most serious consequences, if it had not been fortunately prevented by the interference of those who were not interested in the dispute.

Though our stock of provisions was getting so low, I determined nevertheless, to hide about twenty pounds of pemmican, by way of providing against our return. I therefore left two of the men behind, with directions to bury it, as usual, under the place where we had made our fire.

Our course was about West-South-West by the side of the lake, and in about two miles we came to the end of it. Here was a general halt, when my men overtook us. I was now informed, that some people of another tribe were sent for, who wished very much to see us, two of whom would accompany us over the mountains; that, as for themselves, they had changed their mind, and intended to follow a small river which issued out of the lake, and went in a direction very much different from the line of our journey. This was a disappointment, which, though not uncommon to us, might have been followed by considerable inconveniences. It was my wish to continue with them whatever way they went; but neither my promises or entreaties would avail: these people were not to be turned from their purpose; and when I represented the low state of our provisions, one of them answered, that if we would stay with them all night, he would boil a kettle of fish-roes for us. Accordingly, without receiving any answer, he began to make preparation to fulfil his engagement. He took the roes out of a bag, and having bruised them between two stones, put them in water to soak. His wife then took an handful of dry grass in her hand, with which she squeezed them through her fingers; in the mean time her husband was employed in gathering wood to make a fire, for the purpose of heating stones. When she had finished her operation, she filled a watape kettle nearly full of water, and poured the roes into it. When the stones were sufficiently heated, some of them were put into the kettle, and others were thrown in from time to time, till the water was in a state of boiling; the woman also continued stirring the contents of the kettle, till they were brought to a thick consistency; the stones were then taken out, and the whole was seasoned with about a pint of strong rancid oil. The smell of this curious dish was sufficient to sicken me without tasting it, but the hunger of my people surmounted the nauseous meal. When unadulterated by the stinking oil, these boiled roes are not unpalatable food.

In the mean time four of the people who had been expected, arrived, and, according to the account given of them, were of two tribes whom I had not yet known. After some conversation, they proposed, that I should continue my route by their houses; but the old guide, who was now preparing to leave us, informed me that it would lengthen my journey; and by his advice I proposed to them to conduct us along the road which had been already marked out to us. This they undertook without the least hesitation; and, at the same time, pointed out to me the pass in the mountain, bearing South by East by compass. Here I had a meridian altitude, and took time.

At four in the afternoon we parted with our late fellow-travellers in a very friendly manner, and immediately forded the river. The wild parsnep, which luxuriates on the borders of the lakes and rivers, is a favourite food of the natives: they roast the tops of this plant, in their tender state, over the fire, and taking off the outer rind, they are then a very palatable food.

We now entered the woods, and some time after arrived on the banks of another river that flowed from the mountain, which we also forded. The country soon after we left the river was swampy; and the fire having passed through it, the number of trees, which had fallen, added to the toil of our journey. In a short time we began to ascend, and continued ascending till nine at night. We walked upwards of fourteen miles, according to my computation, in the course of the day, though the straight line of distance might not be more than ten. Notwithstanding that we were surrounded, by mountains covered with snow, we were very much tormented with musquitoes.

Wednesday, July 17. Before the sun rose, our guides summoned us to proceed, when we descended into a beautiful valley, watered by a small river. At eight we came to the termination of it, where we saw a great number of moles, and began again to ascend. We now perceived many ground-hogs, and heard them whistle in every direction. The Indians went in pursuit of them, and soon joined us with a female and her litter, almost grown to their full size. They stripped off their skins, and gave the carcasses to my people. They also pulled up a root, which appeared like a bunch of white berries of the size of a pea; its shape was that of a fig, while it had the colour and taste of a potatoe.

We now gained the summit of the mountain, and found ourselves surrounded by snow. But this circumstance is caused rather by the quantity of snow drifted in the pass, than the real height of the spot, as the surrounding mountains rise to a much higher degree of elevation. The snow had become so compact that our feet hardly made a perceptible impression on it. We observed, however, the tracks of an herd of small deer which must have passed a short time before us, and the Indians and my hunters went immediately in pursuit of them. Our way was now nearly level, without the least snow, and not a tree to be seen in any part of it. The grass is very short, and the soil a reddish clay, intermixed with small stones. The face of the hills, where they are not enlivened with verdure, appears, at a distance, as if fire had passed over them. It now began to hail, snow, and rain, nor could we find any shelter but the leeward side of an huge rock. The wind also rose into a tempest, and the weather was as distressing as any I had ever experienced. After an absence of an hour and an half, our hunters brought a small doe of the reindeer species, which was all they had killed, though they fired twelve shots at a large herd of them. Their ill success they attributed to the weather. I proposed to leave half of the venison in the snow, but the men preferred carrying it, though their strength was very much exhausted. We had been so long shivering with cold in this situation that we were glad to renew our march. Here and there were scattered a few crowberry bushes and stinted willows; the former of which had not yet blossomed.

Before us appeared a stupendous mountain, whose snow-clad summit was lost in the clouds; between it and our immediate course, flowed the river to which we were going. The Indians informed us that it was at no great distance. As soon as we could gather a sufficient quantity of wood, we stopped to dress some of our venison; and it is almost superflous to add, that we made an heartier meal than we had done for many a day before. To the comfort which I have just mentioned, I added that of taking off my beard, as well as changing my linen, and my people followed the humanising example. We then set forwards, and came to a large pond, on whose bank we found a tomb, but lately made, with a pole, as usual, erected beside it, on which two figures of birds were painted, and by them the guides distinguished the tribe to which the deceased person belonged. One of them, very unceremoniously, opened the bark and shewed us the bones which it contained, while the other threw down the pole, and having possessed himself of the feathers that were tied to it, fixed them on his own head. I therefore conjectured, that these funeral memorials belonged to an individual of a tribe at enmity with them.

We continued our route with a considerable degree of expedition, and as we proceeded the mountains appeared to withdrew from us. The country between them soon opened to our view, which apparently added to their awful elevation. We continued to descend till we came to the brink of a precipice, from whence our guides discovered the river to us, and a village on its banks. This precipice, or rather succession of precipices, is covered with large timber, which consists of the pine, the spruce, the hemlock, the birch, and other trees. Our conductors informed us, that it abounded in animals, which, from their description, must be wild goats. In about two hours we arrived at the bottom, where there is a conflux of two rivers, that issue from the mountains. We crossed the one which was to the left. They are both very rapid, and continue so till they unite their currents, forming a stream of about twelve yards in breadth. Here the timber was also very large; but I could not learn from our conductors why the most considerable hemlock trees were stripped of their bark to the tops of them. I concluded, indeed, at that time that the inhabitants tanned their leather with it. Here were also the largest and loftiest elder and cedar trees that I had ever seen. We were now sensible of an entire change in the climate, and the berries were quite ripe.

The sun was about to set, when our conductors left us to follow them as well as we could. We were prevented, however, from going far astray, for we were hemmed in on both sides and behind by such a barrier as nature never before presented to my view. Our guides had the precaution to mark the road for us, by breaking the branches of trees as they passed. This small river must, at certain seasons, rise to an uncommon height and strength of current most probably on the melting of the snow; as we saw a large quantity of drift wood lying twelve feet above the immediate level of the river. This circumstance impeded our progress, and the protruding rocks frequently forced us to pass through the water. It was now dark, without the least appearance of houses, though it would be impossible to have seen them, if there had been any, at the distance of twenty yards, from the thickness of the woods. My men were anxious to stop for the night; indeed the fatigue they had suffered justified the proposal, and I left them to their choice; but as the anxiety of my mind impelled me forwards, they continued to follow me, till I found myself at the edge of the woods; and, notwithstanding the remonstrances that were made, I proceeded, feeling rather than seeing my way, till I arrived at an house, and soon discovered several fires, in small huts, with people busily employed in cooking their fish. I walked into one of them without the least ceremony, threw down my burden, and, after shaking hands with some of the people, sat down upon it. They received me without the least appearance of surprize, but soon made signs for me to go up to the large house, which was erected, on upright posts, at some distance from the ground. A broad piece of timber with steps cut in it, led to the scaffolding even with the floor, and by this curious kind of ladder I entered the house at one end; and having passed three fires, at equal distances in the middle of the building, I was received by several people, sitting upon a very wide board, at the upper end of it. I shook hands with them, and seated myself beside a man, the dignity of whose countenance induced me to give him that preference. I soon discovered one of my guides seated a little above me, with a neat mat spread before him, which I supposed to be the place of honour, and appropriated to strangers. In a short time my people arrived, and placed themselves near me, when the man by whom I sat, immediately rose, and fetched, from behind a plank of about four feet wide, a quantity of roasted salmon. He then directed a mat to be placed before me and Mr. Mackay, who was now sitting by me. When this ceremony was performed, he brought a salmon for each of us, and half an one to each of my men. The same plank served also as a screen for the beds, whither the women and children were already retired; but whether that circumstance took place on our arrival, or was the natural consequence of the late hour of the night, I did not discover. The signs of our protector seemed to denote, that we might sleep in the house, but as we did not understand him with a sufficient degree of certainty, I thought it prudent, from the fear of giving offence, to order the men to make a fire without, that we might sleep by it. When he observed our design, he placed boards for us that we might not take our repose on the bare ground, and ordered a fire to be prepared for us. We had not been long seated round it, when we received a large dish of salmon roes, pounded fine and beat up with water so as to have the appearance of a cream. Nor was it without some kind of seasoning that gave it a bitter taste. Another dish soon followed, the principal article of which was also salmon-roes, with a large proportion of gooseberries, and an herb that appeared to be sorrel. Its acidity rendered it more agreeable to my taste than the former preparation. Having been regaled with these delicacies, for such they were considered by that hospitable spirit which provided them, we laid ourselves down to rest with no other canopy than the sky; but I never enjoyed a more sound and refreshing rest, though I had a board for my bed, and a billet for my pillow.

Thursday, July 18. At five this morning I awoke, and found that the natives had lighted a fire for us, and were sitting by it. My hospitable friend immediately brought me some berries and roasted salmon, and his companions soon followed his example. The former, which consisted among many others, of gooseberries, whirtleberries and raspberries, were the finest I ever saw or tasted, of their respective kinds. They also brought the dried roes of fish to eat with the berries.

Salmon is so abundant in this river, that these people have a constant and plentiful supply of that excellent fish. To take them with more facility, they had, with great labour, formed an embankment or weir across the river for the purpose of placing their fishing machines, which they disposed both above and below it. I expressed my wish to visit this extraordinary work, but these people are so superstitious, that they would not allow me a nearer examination than I could obtain by viewing it from the bank. The river is about fifty yards in breadth, and by observing a man fish with a dipping net, I judged it to be about ten feet deep at the foot of the fall. The weir is a work of great labour, and contrived with considerable ingenuity. It was near four feet above the level of the water, at the time I saw it, and nearly the height of the bank on which I stood to examine it. The stream is stopped nearly two thirds by it. It is constructed by fixing small trees in the bed of the river in a slanting position (which could be practicable only when the water is much lower than I saw it) with the thick part downwards; over these is laid a bed of gravel on which is placed a range of lesser trees, and so on alternately till the work is brought to its proper height. Beneath it the machines are placed, into which the salmon fall when they attempt to leap over. On either side there is a large frame of timber-work six feet above the level of the upper water, in which passages are left for the salmon leading directly into the machines, which are taken up at pleasure. At the foot of the fall dipping nets are also successfully employed.

The water of this river is of the colour of asses milk, which I attributed in part to the limestone that in many places forms the bed of the river, but principally to the rivulets which fall from mountains of the same material.

These people indulge an extreme superstition respecting their fish, as it is apparently their only animal food. Flesh they never taste, and one of their dogs having picked and swallowed part of a bone which we had left, was beaten by his master till he disgorged it. One of my people also having thrown a bone of the deer into the river, a native, who had observed the circumstance, immediately dived and brought it up, and, having consigned it to the fire, instantly proceeded to wash his polluted hands.

As we were still at some distance from the sea, I made application to my friend to procure us a canoe or two, with people to conduct us thither. After he had made various excuses, I at length comprehended that his only objection was to the embarking venison in a canoe on their river, as the fish would instantly smell it and abandon them, so that he, his friends, and relations, must starve. I soon eased his apprehensions on that point, and desired to know what I must do with the venison that remained, when he told me to give it to one of the strangers whom he pointed out to me, as being of a tribe that eat flesh. I now requested him to furnish me with some fresh salmon in its raw state: but, instead of complying with my wish, he brought me a couple of them roasted, observing at the same time, that the current was very strong, and would bring us to the next village, where our wants would be abundantly supplied. In short, he requested that we would make haste to depart. This was rather unexpected after so much kindness and hospitality, but our ignorance of the language prevented us from being able to discover the cause.

At eight this morning, fifteen men armed, the friends and relations of these people, arrived by land, in consequence of notice sent them in the night, immediately after the appearance of our guides. They are more corpulent and of a better appearance than the inhabitants of the interior. Their language totally different from any I had heard; the Atnah and Chin tribe, as far as I can judge from the very little I saw of that people, bear the nearest resemblance to them. They appear to be of a quiet and peaceable character, and never make any hostile incursions into the lands of their neighbours.

Their dress consists of a single robe tied over the shoulders, falling down behind, to the heels, and before, a little below the knees, with a deep fringe round the bottom. It is generally made of the bark of the cedar tree, which they prepare as fine as hemp; though some of these garments are interwoven with strips of the sea-otter skin, which give them the appearance of a fur on one side. Others have stripes of red and yellow threads fancifully introduced toward the borders, which have a very agreeable effect. The men have no other covering than that which I have described, and they unceremoniously lay it aside when they find it convenient. In addition to this robe, the women wear a close fringe hanging down before them about two feet in length, and half as wide. When they sit down they draw this between their thighs. They wear their hair so short, that it requires little care or combing. The men have theirs in plaits, and being smeared with oil and red earth, instead of a comb they have a small stick hanging by a string from one of the locks, which they employ to alleviate any itching or irritation in the head. The colour of the eye is grey with a tinge of red. They have all high cheek-bones, but the women are more remarkable for that feature than the men. Their houses, arms, and utensils I shall describe hereafter.

I presented my friend with several articles, and also distributed some among others of the natives who had been attentive to us. One of my guides had been very serviceable in procuring canoes for us to proceed on our expedition; he appeared also to be very desirous of giving these people a favourable impression of us; and I was very much concerned that he should leave me as he did, without giving me the least notice of his departure, or receiving the presents which I had prepared for him, and he so well deserved. At noon I had an observation which gave 52.28.11 North longitude.

Chapter 10

NATIVE CANADIANS

Thursday, July 18 [continued]. At one in the afternoon we embarked, with our small baggage, in two canoes, accompanied by seven of the natives. The stream was rapid, and ran upwards of six miles an hour. We came to a weir, such as I have already described, where the natives landed us, and shot over it without taking a drop of water. They then received us on board again, and we continued our voyage, passing many canoes on the river, some with people in them, and others empty. We proceeded at a very great rate for about two hours and an half, when we were informed that we must land, as the village was only at a short distance. I had imagined that the Canadians who accompanied me were the most expert canoe-men in the world, but they are very inferior to these people, as they themselves acknowledged, in conducting those vessels.

Some of the Indians ran before us, to announce our approach, when we took our bundles and followed. We had walked along a well-beaten path, through a kind of coppice, when we were informed of the arrival of our couriers at the houses, by the loud and confused talking of the inhabitants. As we approached the edge of the wood, and were almost in sight of the houses, the Indians who were before me made signs for me to take the lead, and that they would follow. The noise and confusion of the natives now seemed to encrease, and when we came in sight of the village, we saw them running from house to house, some armed with bows and arrows, others with spears, and many with axes, as if in a state of great alarm. This very unpleasant and unexpected circumstance, I attributed to our sudden arrival, and the very short notice of it which had been given them. At all events, I had but one line of conduct to pursue, which was to walk resolutely up to them, without manifesting any signs of apprehension at their hostile appearance. This resolution produced the desired effect, for as we approached the houses, the greater part of the people laid down their weapons, and came forward to meet us. I was, however, soon obliged to stop from the number of them that surrounded me. I shook hands, as usual with such as were the nearest to me, when an elderly man broke through the crowd, and took me in his arms; another then came, who turned him away without the least ceremony, and paid me the same compliment. The latter was followed by a young man, whom I understood to be his son. These embraces, which at first rather surprised me, I soon found to be marks of regard and friendship. The crowd pressed with so much violence and contention to get a view of us, that we could not move in any direction. An opening was at length made to allow a person to approach me, whom the old man made me understand was another of his sons. I instantly stepped forward to meet him, and presented my hand, whereupon he broke the string of a very handsome robe of sea-otter skin, which he had on, and covered me with it. This was as flattering a reception as I could possibly receive, especially as I considered him to be the eldest son of the chief. Indeed it appeared to me that we had been detained here for the purpose of giving him time to bring the robe with which he had presented me.

The chief now made signs for us to follow him, and he conducted us through a narrow coppice, for several hundred yards, till we came to an house built on the ground, which was of larger dimensions, and formed of better materials than any I had hitherto seen; it was his residence. We were no sooner arrived there, than he directed mats to be spread before it, on which we were told to take our seats, when the men of the village, who came to indulge their curiosity, were ordered to keep behind us. In our front other mats were placed, where the chief and his counsellors took their seats. In the intervening space, mats, which were very clean, and of a much nearer workmanship than those on which we sat were also spread, and a small roasted salmon placed before each of us. When we had satisfied ourselves with the fish, one of the people who came with us from the last village approached, with a kind of ladle in one hand, containing oil, and in the other something that resembled the inner rind of the cocoa-nut, but of a lighter colour; this he dipped in the oil, and, having eat it, indicated by his gestures how palatable he thought it. He then presented me with a small piece of it, which I chose to taste in its dry state, though the oil was free from any unpleasant smell. A square cake of this was next produced, when a man took it to the water near the house, and having thoroughly soaked it, he returned and, after he had pulled it to pieces like oakum, put it into a well-made trough, about there feet long, nine inches wide, and five deep; he then plentifuly sprinkled it with salmon oil, and manifested by his own example that were we to eat of it. I just tasted it, and found the oil perfectly sweet, without which the other ingredient would have been very insipid. The chief partook of it with great avidity, after it had received an additional quantity of oil. This dish is considered by these people as a great delicacy; and on examination, I discovered it to consist of the inner rind of the hemlock tree, taken off early in summer, put into a frame, which shapes it into cakes of fifteen inches long, ten broad, and half an inch thick; and in this form I should suppose it may be preserved for a great length of time. This discovery satisfied me respecting the many hemlock trees which I had observed stripped of their bark.

In this situation we remained for upwards of three hours, and not one of the curious natives left us during all that time, except a party often or twelve of them, whom the chief ordered to go and catch fish, which they did in great abundance, with dipping nets, at the foot of the Weir.

At length we were relieved from the gazing crowd, and got a lodge erected, and covered in for our reception during the night. I now presented the young chief with a blanket, in return for the robe with which he had favoured me, and several other articles, that appeared to be very gratifying to him. I also presented some to his father, and amongst them was a pair of scissars, whose use

I explained to him, for clipping his beard, which was of great length; and to that purpose he immediately applied them. My distribution of similar articles was also extended to others, who had been attentive to us. The communication, however, between us was awkward and inconvenient, for it was carried on entirely by signs, as there was not a person with me who was qualified for the office of an interpreter.

We were all of us very desirous to get some fresh salmon, that we might dress them in our own way, but could not by any means obtain that gratification, though there were thousands of that fish strung on cords, which were fastened to stakes in the river. They were even averse to our approaching the spot where they clean and prepare them for their own eating. They had, indeed, taken our kettle from us, lest we should employ it in getting water from the river; and they assigned as the reason for this precaution, that the salmon dislike the smell of iron. At the same time they supplied us with wooden boxes, which were capable of holding any fluid. Two of the men that went to fish, in a canoe capable of containing ten people, returned with a full lading of salmon, that weighed from six to forty pounds, though the far greater part of them were under twenty. They immediately strung the whole of them, as I have already mentioned, in the river.

I now made the tour of the village, which consisted of four elevated houses, and seven built on the ground, besides a considerable number of other buildings or sheds, which are used only as kitchens, and places for curing their fish. The former are constructed by fixing a certain number of posts in the earth, on some of which are laid, and to others are fastened, the supporters of the floor, at about twelve feet above the surface of the ground: their length is from an hundred to an hundred and twenty feet, and they are about forty feet in breadth. Along the centre are built three, four, or five hearths, for the two-fold purpose of giving warmth, and dressing their fish. The whole length of the building on either side is divided by cedar planks, into partitions or apartments of seven feet square, in the front of which there are boards, about three feet wide, over which, though they are not immovably fixed, the inmates of these recesses generally pass, when they go to rest. The greater part of them are intended for that purpose, and such are covered with boards, at the height of the wall of the house, which is about seven or eight feet, and rest upon beams that stretch across the building. On those also are placed the chests which contain their provisions, utensils, and whatever they possess. The intermediate space is sufficient for domestic purposes. On poles that run along the beams, hang roasted fish, and the whole building is well covered with boards and bark, except within a few inches of the ridge pole; where open spaces are left on each side to let in light and emit the smoke. At the end of the house that fronts the river, is a narrow scaffolding, which is also ascended by a piece of timber, with steps cut in it; and at each corner of this erection there are openings, for the inhabitants to ease nature. As it does not appear to be a custom among them to remove these heaps of excremental filth, it may be supposed that the effluvia does not annoy them.

The houses which rest on the ground are built of the same materials, and on the same plan. A sloping stage that rises to a cross piece of timber, supported by two forks, joins also to the main building, for those purposes which need not be repeated.

When we were surrounded by the natives on our arrival, I counted sixty-five men, and several of them may be supposed to have been absent; I cannot, therefore, calculate the inhabitants of this village at less than two hundred souls.

The people who accompanied us hither, from the other village, had given the chief a very particular account of every thing they knew concerning us: I was, therefore, requested to produce my astronomical instruments; nor could I have any objection to afford them this satisfaction, as they would necessarily add to our importance in their opinion.

Near the house of the chief I observed several oblong squares, of about twenty feet by eight. They were made of thick cedar boards, which were joined with so much neatness, that I at first thought they were one piece. They were painted with hieroglyphics, and figures of different animals, and with a degree of correctness that was not to be expected from such an uncultivated people. I could not learn the use of them, but they appeared to be calculated for occasional acts of devotion or sacrifice, which all these tribes perform at least twice in the year, at the spring and fall. I was confirmed in this opinion by a large building in the middle of the village, which I at first took for the half finished frame of an house. The ground-plot of it was fifty feet by forty-five; each end is formed by four stout posts, fixed perpendicularly in the ground. The comer ones are plain, and support a beam of the whole length, having three intermediate props on each side, but of a larger size, and eight or nine feet in height. The two centre posts, at each end, are two feet and an half in diameter, and carved into human figures, supporting two ridge poles on their heads, at twelve feet from the ground. The figures at the upper part of this square represent two persons, with their hands upon their knees, as if they supported the weight with pain and difficulty: the others opposite to them stand at their ease, with their hands resting on their hips. In the area of the building there were the remains of several fires. The posts, poles and figures, were painted red and black; but the sculpture of these people is superior to their painting.

Friday, July 19. Soon after I had retired to rest last night, the chief paid me a visit to insist on my going to his bed-companion, and taking my place himself; but, notwithstanding his repeated entreaties, I resisted this offering of his hospitality.

At an early hour this morning I was again visited by the chief, in company with his son. The former complained of a pain in his breast; to relieve his suffering, I gave him a few drops of Turlington's Balsam on a piece of sugar; and I was rather surprised to see him take it without the least hesitation. When he had taken my medicine, he requested me to follow him, and conducted me to a shed, where several people were assembled round a sick man, who was another of his sons. They immediately uncovered him, and shewed me a violent ulcer in the small of his back, in the foulest state that can be imagined. One of his knees was also afflicted in the same manner. This unhappy man was reduced to a skeleton, and, from his appearance, was drawing near to an end of his pains. They requested that I would touch him, and his father was very urgent with me to administer medicine; but he was in such a dangerous state, that I thought it prudent to yield no further to the importunities than to give the sick person a few drops of Turlington's balsam in some water. I therefore left them, but was soon called back by the loud lamentations of the women, and was rather apprehensive that some inconvenience might result from my compliance with the chief's request. On my return I found the native physicians busy in practising their skill and art on the patient. They blew on him, and then whistled; at times they pressed their extended fingers, with all their strength on his stomach; they also put their fore fingers doubled into his mouth, and spouted water from their own with great violence into his face. To support these operations the wretched sufferer was held up in a sitting posture; and when they were concluded, he was laid down and covered with a new robe made of the skins of the lynx. I had observed that his belly and breast were covered with scars, and I understood that they were caused by a custom prevalent among them, of applying pieces of lighted touch wood to their flesh, in order to relieve pain or demonstrate their courage. He was now placed on a broad plank, and carried by six men into the woods, where I was invited to accompany them. I could not conjecture what would be the end of this ceremony, particularly as I saw one man carry fire, another an axe, and a third dry wood. I was, indeed, disposed to suspect that, as it was their custom to burn the dead, they intended to relieve the poor man from his pain, and perform the last sad duty of surviving affection. When they had advanced a short distance into the wood, they laid him upon a clear spot, and kindled a fire against his back, when the physican began to scarify the ulcer with a very blunt instrument, the cruel pain of which operation the patient bore with incredible resolution. The scene afflicted me and I left it.

On my return to our lodge, I observed before the door of the chief's residence, four heaps of salmon, each of which consisted of between three and four hundred fish. Sixteen women were employed in cleaning and preparing them. They first separate the head from the body, the former of which they boil; they then cut the latter down the back on each side of the bone, leaving one third of the fish adhering to it, and afterwards take out the guts. The bone is roasted for immediate use, and the other parts are dressed in the same manner, but with more attention, for future provision. While they are before the fire, troughs are placed under them to receive the oil. The toes are also carefully preserved, and form a favourite article of their food.

After I had observed these culinary preparations, I paid a visit to the chief, who presented me with a roasted salmon; he then opened one of his chests, and took out of it a garment of blue cloth, decorated with brass buttons; and another of a flowered cotton, which I supposed were Spanish; it had been trimmed with leather fringe, after the fashion of their own cloaks. Copper and brass are in great estimation among them, and of the former they have great plenty: they point their arrows and spears with it, and work it up into personal ornaments; such as collars, ear-rings, and bracelets, which they wear on their wrists, arms, and legs. I presume they find it the most advantageous article of trade with the more inland tribes. They also abound in iron. I saw some of their twisted collars of that metal which weighed upwards of twelve pounds. It is generally in bars of fourteen inches in length, and one inch three quarters wide. The brass is in thin squares; their copper is in larger pieces, and some of it appeared to be old stills cut up. They have various trinkets; but their iron is manufactured only into poniards and daggers. Some of the former have very neat handles, with a silver coin of a quarter or eighth of a dollar fixed on the end of them. The blades of the latter are from ten to twelve inches in length, and about four inches broad at the top, from which they gradually lessen into a point.

When I produced my instruments to take an altitude, I was desired not to make use of them. I could not then discover the cause of this request, but I experienced the good effect of the apprehension which they occasioned, as it was very effectual in hastening my departure. I had applied several times to the chief to prepare canoes and people to take me and my party to the sea, but very little attention had been paid to my application till noon; when I was informed that a canoe was properly equipped for my voyage, and that the young chief would accompany me. I now discovered that they had entertained no personal fear of the instruments, but were apprehensive that the operation of them might frighten the salmon from that part of the river. The observation taken in this village gave me 52.25.52 North latitude.

In compliance with the chief's request I desired my people to take their bundles, and lay them down on the bank of the river. In the mean time I went to take the dimensions of his large canoe, in which, it was signified to me, that about ten winters ago he went a considerable distance towards the midday sun, with forty of his people, when he saw two large vessels full of such men as myself, by whom he was kindly received: they were, he said, the first white people he had seen. They were probably the ships commanded by Captain Cook. This canoe was built of cedar, forty-five feet long, four feet wide, and three feet and a half in depth. It was painted black and decorated with white figures of fish of different kinds. The gunwale, fore and aft, was inlaid with the teeth of the sea-otter.[28]

When I returned to the river, the natives who were to accompany us, and my people, were already in the canoe. The latter, however, informed me, that one of our axes was missing. I immediately applied to the chief, and requested its restoration; but he would not understand me till I sat myself down on a stone, with my arms in a state of preparation, and made it appear to him that I should not depart till the stolen article was restored. The village was immediately in a state of uproar, and some danger was apprehended from the confusion that prevailed in it. The axe, however, which had been hidden under the chief's canoe, was soon returned. Though this instrument was not, in itself, of sufficient value to justify a dispute with these people, I apprehended that the suffering them to keep it, after we had declared its loss, might have occasioned the loss of every thing we carried

28. As Captain Cooke has mentioned, that the people of the sea-coast adorned their canoes with human teeth, I was more particular in my inquiries; the result of which was, the most satisfactory proof, that he was mistaken: but his mistake arose from the very great resemblance there is between human teeth and those of the sea-otter.

with us, and of our lives also. My people were dissatisfied with me at the moment; but I thought myself right then, and, I think now, that the circumstances in which we were involved, justified the measure which I adopted.

Chapter 11

Renew Voyage

Friday, July 19 [continued]. At one in the afternoon we renewed our voyage in a large canoe with four of the natives. We found the river almost one continued rapid, and in half an hour we came to an house, where, however, we did not land, though invited by the inhabitants. In about an hour we arrived at two houses, where we were, in some degree, obliged to go on shore, as we were informed that the owner of them was a person of consideration. He indeed received and regaled us in the same manner as at the last village; and to increase his consequence, he produced many European articles, and amongst them were at least forty pounds weight of old copper stills. We made our stay as short as possible, and our host embarked with us. In a very short time we were carried by the rapidity of the current to another house of very large dimensions, which was partitioned into different apartments, and whose doors were on the side. The inhabitants received us with great kindness; but instead of fish, they placed a long, clean, and well made trough before us full of berries. In addition to those which we had already seen, there were some black, that were larger than the huckle berry, and of a richer flavour; and others white, which resembled the blackberry in every thing but colour. Here we saw a woman with two pieces of copper in her under lip, as described by Captain Cook. I continued my usual practice of making these people presents in return for their friendly reception and entertainment.

The navigation of the river now became more difficult, from the numerous channels into which it was divided, without any sensible diminution in the velocity of its current. We soon reached another house of the common size, where we were well received; but whether our guides had informed them that we were not in want of any thing, or that they were deficient in inclination, or perhaps the means, of being hospitable to us, they did not offer us any refreshment. They were in a state of busy preparation. Some of the women were employed in beating and preparing the inner rind of the cedar bark, to which they gave the appearance of flax. Others were spinning with a distaff and spindle. One of them was weaving a robe of it, intermixed with stripes of the sea-otter skin, on a frame of adequate contrivance that was placed against the side of the house. The men were fishing on the river with drag-nets between two canoes. These nets are forced by poles to the bottom, the current driving them before it; by which means the salmon coming up the river are intercepted, and give notice of their being taken by the struggles they make in the bag or sleeve of the net. There are no weirs in this part of the river, as I suppose, from the numerous channels into which it is divided. The machines, therefore, are placed along the banks, and consequently these people are not so well supplied with fish as the village which has been already described, nor do they appear to possess the same industry. The inhabitants of the last house accompanied us in a large canoe. They recommended us to leave ours here, as the next village was but at a small distance from us, and the water more rapid than that which we had passed. They informed us also, that we were approaching a cascade. I directed them to shoot it, and proceeded myself to the foot thereof, where I reimbarked, and we went on with great velocity, till we came to a fall, where we left our canoe, and carried our luggage along a road through a wood for some hundred yards, when we came to a village, consisting of six very large houses, erected on pallisades, rising twenty-five feet from the ground, which differed in no one circumstance from those already described, but the height of their elevation. They contained only four men and their families. The rest of the inhabitants were with us and in the small houses which we passed higher up the river.[29] These people do not seem to enjoy the abundance of their neighbours, as the men who returned from fishing had no more than five salmon; they refused to sell one of them, but gave me one roasted of a very indifferent kind. In the houses there were several chests or boxes containing different articles that belonged to the people whom we had lately passed. If I were to judge by the heaps of filth beneath these buildings, they must have been erected at a more distant period than any which we passed. From these houses I could perceive the termination of the river, and its discharge into a narrow arm of the sea.

As it was now half past six in the evening, and the weather cloudy, I determined to remain here for the night, and for that purpose we possessed ourselves of one of the unoccupied houses. The remains of our last meal, which we brought with us, served for our supper, as we could not procure a single fish from the natives. The course of the river is about West, and the distance from the great village upwards of thirty-six miles. There we had lost our dog, a circumstance of no small regret to me.

Saturday, July 20. We rose at a very early hour this morning, when I proposed to the Indians to run down our canoe, or procure another at this place. To both these proposals they turned a deaf ear, as they imagined that I should be satisfied with having come in sight of the sea. Two of them peremptorily refused to proceed; but the other two having consented to continue with us, we obtained a larger canoe than our former one, and though it was in a leaky state we were glad to possess it.

At about eight we got out of the river, which discharges itself by various channels into an arm of the sea. The tide was out, and had left a large space covered with sea-weed. The surrounding hills were involved in fog. The wind was at West, which was a-head of us, and very strong; the bay appearing to be from one to three miles in breadth. As we advanced along the land we saw a great number of sea-otters. We fired several shots at them, but without any success from the rapidity with which they plunge under the water. We also saw many small porpoises or divers. The white-headed eagle, which is common in the inte-

---

29. Mr. Johnstone came to these houses the first day of the preceding month.

rior parts; some small gulls, a dark bird which is inferior in size to the gull, and a few small ducks, were all the birds which presented themselves to our view.

At two in the afternoon the swell was so high, and the wind, which was against us, so boisterous, that we could not proceed with our leaky vessel, we therefore landed in a small cove on the right side of the bay. Opposite to us appeared another small bay, in the mouth of which is an island, and where, according to the information of the Indians, a river discharges itself that abounds in salmon.

Our young Indians now discovered a very evident disposition to leave us; and, in the evening, one of them made his escape. Mr. Mackay, however, with the other, pursued and brought him back; but as it was by no means necessary to detain him, particularly as provisions did not abound with us, I gave him a small portion, with a pair of shoes, which were necessary for his journey, and a silk handkerchief, telling him at the same time, that he might go and inform his friends, that we should also return in three nights. He accordingly left us, and his companion, the young chief, went with him.

When we landed, the tide was going out, and at a quarter past four it was ebb, the water having fallen in that short period eleven feet and an half. Since we left the river, not a quarter of an hour had passed in which we did not see porpoises and seaotters. Soon after ten it was high water, which rendered it necessary that our baggage should be shifted several times, though not till some of the things had been wetted.

We were now reduced to the necessity of looking out for fresh water, with which we were plentifully supplied by the rills that ran down from the mountains.

When it was dark the young chief returned to us, bearing a large porcupine on his back. He first cut the animal open, and having disencumbered it of the entrails, threw them into the sea; he then singed its skin, and boiled it in separate pieces, as our kettle was not sufficiently capacious to contain the whole: nor did he go to rest, till, with the assistance of two of my people who happened to be awake, every morsel of it was devoured.

I had flattered myself with the hope of getting a distance of the moon and stars, but the cloudy weather continually disappointed me, and I began to fear that I should fail in this important object; particularly as our provisions were at a very low ebb, and we had, as yet, no reason to expect any assistance from the natives. Our stock was, at this time, reduced to twenty pounds of pemmican, fifteen pounds of rice, and six pounds of flour, among ten half-starved men, in a leaky vessel, and on a barbarous coast. Our course from the river was about West-South-West, distance ten miles.

Sunday, July 22. At forty minutes past four this morning it was low water, which made fifteen feet perpendicular height below the high-water mark of last night. Mr. Mackay collected a quantity of small muscles which we boiled. Our people did not partake of this regale, as they are wholly unacquainted with sea shell-fish. Our young chief being missing, we imagined that he had taken his flight, but, as we were preparing to depart, he fortunately made his appearance from the woods, where he had been to take his rest after his feast of last night. At six we were upon the water, when we cleared the small bay, which we named Porcupine Cove, and steered West-South-West for seven miles, we then opened a channel about two miles and an half wide at South-South-West, and had a view of ten or twelve miles into it. As I could not ascertain the distance from the open sea, and being uncertain whether we were in a bay or among inlets and channels of islands, I confined my search to a proper place for taking an observation. We steered, therefore, along the land on the left, West-North-West a mile and an half; then North-West one fourth of a mile, and North three miles to an island; the land continuing to run North-North-West, then along the island, South-South-West half a mile, West a mile and an half, and from thence directly across to the land on the left, (where I had an altitude,) South-West three miles.[30] From this position a channel, of which the island we left appeared to make a cheek, bears North by East.

---

30. The Cape or Point Menzies of Vancouver.

Under the land we met with three canoes, with fifteen men in them, and laden with their moveables, as if proceeding to a new situation, or returning to a former one. They manifested no kind of mistrust or fear of us, but entered into conversation with our young man, as I supposed, to obtain some information concerning us. It did not appear that they were the same people as those we had lately seen, as they spoke the language of our young chief, with a different accent. They then examined every thing we had in our canoe, with an air of indifference and disdain. One of them in particular made me understand, with an air of insolence, that a large canoe had lately been in this bay, with people in her like me, and that one of them, whom he called *Macubah,* had fired on him and his friends, and that *Bensins* had struck him on the back, with the flat part of his sword. He also mentioned another name, the articulation of which I could not determine. At the same time he illustrated these circumstances by the assistance of my gun and sword; and I do not doubt but he well deserved the treatment which he described. He also produced several European articles, which could not have been long in his possession. From his conduct and appearance, I wished very much to be rid of him, and flattered myself that he would prosecute his voyage, which appeared to be in an opposite direction to our course. However, when I prepared to part from them, they turned their canoes about, and persuaded my young man to leave me, which I could not prevent.

We coasted along the land[31] at about West-South-West for six miles, and met a canoe with two boys in it, who were dispatched to summon the people on that part of the coast to join them. The troublesome fellow now forced himself into my canoe, and pointed out a narrow channel on the opposite shore, that led to his village, and requested us to steer towards it, which I accordingly ordered. His importunities now became very irksome, and he wanted to see every thing we had, particularly my instruments, concerning which he must have received information from my young man. He asked for my hat, my handker-

---

31. Named by Vancouver King's Island.

chief, and, in short, every thing that he saw about me. At the same time he frequently repeated the unpleasant intelligence that he had been shot at by people of my colour. At some distance from the land a channel opened to us, at South-West by West, and pointing that way, he made me understand that *Macubah* came here with his large canoe. When we were in mid-channel, I perceived some sheds, or the remains of old buildings, on the shore; and as, from that circumstance, I thought it probable that some Europeans might have been there, I directed my steersman to make for that spot. The traverse is upwards of three miles North-West.

We landed, and found the ruins of a village, in a situation calculated for defence. The place itself was over grown with weeds, and in the centre of the houses there was a temple, of the same form and construction as that which I described at the large village. We were soon followed by ten canoes, each of which contained from three to six men. They informed us that we were expected at the village, where we should see many of them. From their general deportment I was very apprehensive that some hostile design was meditated against us, and for the first time I acknowledged my apprehensions to my people. I accordingly desired them to be very much upon their guard, and to be prepared if any violence was offered to defend themselves to the last.

We had no sooner landed, than we took possession of a rock, where there was not space for more than twice our number, and which admitted of our defending ourselves with advantage, in case we should be attacked. The people in the three first canoes, were the most troublesome, but, after doing their utmost to irritate us, they went away. They were, however, no sooner gone, than an hat, an handkerchief, and several other articles, were missing. The rest of our visitors continued their pressing invitations to accompany them to their village, but finding our resolution to decline them was not to be shaken, they, about sun-set relieved us from all further importunities, by their departure.

Another canoe, however, soon arrived, with seven stout, well-looking men. They brought a box, which contained a very fine sea-otter skin, and a goat skin, that was beautifully white. For the former they demanded my hanger, which, as may well be supposed, could not be spared in our present situation, and they actually refused to rake a yard and an half of common broad cloth, with some other articles, for the skin, which proves the unreflecting improvidence of our European traders. The goat-skin was so bulky that I did not offer to purchase it. These men also told me that *Macubah* had been there, and left his ship behind a point of land in the channel, South-West from us; from whence he had come to their village in boats, which these people represented by imitating our manner of rowing. When I offered them what they did not choose to accept for the otter-skin, they shook their heads, and very distinctly answered 'No, no.' And to mark their refusal of any thing we asked from them, they emphatically employed the same British monosyllable. In one of the canoes which had left us, there was a seal, that I wished to purchase, but could not persuade the natives to part with it. They had also a fish, which I now saw for the first time. It was about eighteen inches in length, of the shape and appearance of a trout, with strong, sharp teeth. We saw great numbers of the animals which we had taken for sea otters, but I was now disposed to think that a great part of them, at least, must have been seals.

The natives having left us, we made a fire to warm ourselves, and as for supper, there was but little of that, for our whole daily allowance did not amount to what was sufficient for a single meal. The weather was clear throughout the day, which was succeeded by a fine moon-light night. I directed the people to keep watch by two in turn, and laid myself down in my cloak.

Monday, July 22. This morning the weather was clear and pleasant; nor had any thing occurred to disturb us throughout the night. One solitary Indian, indeed, came to us with about half a pound of boiled seal's flesh, and the head of a small salmon, for which he asked an handkerchief, but afterwards accepted a few beads. As this man came alone, I concluded that no general plan had been formed among the natives to annoy us, but this opinion did not altogether calm the apprehensions of my people.

Soon after eight in the morning, I took five altitudes for time, and the mean of them was 36° 48' at six in the afternoon, 58.34 time, by the watch, which makes the achrometer slow apparent time 1h 21m 44s.

Two canoes now arrived from the same quarter as the rest, with several men, and our young Indian along with them. They brought a very few small sea-otter skins, out of season, with some pieces of raw seal's flesh. The former were of no value, but hunger compelled some of my people to take the latter, at an extravagant price. Mr. Mackay lighted a bit of touch wood with a burning-glass, in the cover of his tobacco-box, which so surprised the natives, that they exchanged the best of their otter skins for it. The young man was now very anxious to persuade our people to depart, as the natives, he said, were as numerous as musquitoes, and of very malignant character. This information produced some very earnest remonstrances to me to hasten our departure, but as I was determined not to leave this place, except I was absolutely compelled to it, till I had ascertained its situation, these solicitations were not repeated.

While I was taking a meridian, two canoes, of a larger size, and well manned, appeared from the main South-West channel. They seemed to be the fore-runners of others, who were coming to co-operate with the people of the village, in consequence of the message sent by the two boys, which has been already mentioned; and our young Indian, who understood them, renewed his entreaties for our departure, as they would soon come to shoot their arrows, and hurl their spears at us. In relating our danger, his agitation was so violent that he foamed at the mouth. Though I was not altogether free from apprehensions on the occasion, it was necessary for me to disguise them, as my people were panic struck, and some of them asked if it was my determination to remain there to be sacrificed? My reply was the same as their former importunities had received, that I would not stir till I had accomplished my object; at the same time, to humour their fears, I consented that they should put every thing into the canoe, that we might be in a state of preparation to depart. The two canoes now approached the shore, and in a short time five men, with their families, landed very quietly from them. My instruments being exposed, they examined them with much apparent admiration and astonishment. My altitude, by an artificial horizon, gave 52° 21' 33"; that by the natural horizon was 52° 20' 48" North latitude.[32]

These Indians were of a different tribe from those which I had already seen, as our guide did not understand their language. I now mixed up some vermilion in melted grease, and inscribed, in large characters, on the South-East face of the rock on which we had slept last night, this brief memorial – 'Alexander Mackenzie, from Canada, by land, the twenty-second of July, one thousand seven hundred and ninety-three.'

As I thought that we were too near the village, I consented to leave this place, and accordingly proceeded North-East three miles, when we landed on a point, in a small cove, where we should not be readily seen, and could not be attacked except in our front.

Among other articles that had been stolen from us, at our last station, was a sounding-line, which I intended to have employed in this bay, though I should not probably have found the bottom, at any distance from the shore, as the appearance both of the water and land indicated a great depth. The latter displayed a solid rock, rising, as it appeared to me, from three to seven hundred feet above high water mark. Where any soil was scattered about, there were cedars, spruce-firs, white birch, and other trees of large growth. From its precipices issued streams of fine water, as cold as ice.

The two canoes which we had left at our last station, followed us hither, and when they were preparing to depart, our young chief embarked with them. I was determined, however, to prevent his escape, and compelled him, by actual force, to come on shore, for I thought it much better to incur his displeasure, than to suffer him to expose himself to any untoward accident among strangers, or to return to his father before us. The men in the canoe made signs for him to go over the hill, and that they

---

32. This I found to be the cheek of Vancouver's Cascade Channel.

would take him on board at the other side of it. As I was necessarily engaged in other matters, I desired my people to take care that he should not run away; but they peremptorily refused to be employed in keeping him against his will. I was, therefore, reduced to the necessity of watching him myself.

I took five altitudes, and the mean of them was 29.23.48 at 3.5.53 in the afternoon, by the watch, which makes it slow apparent time

	1m 22h 38s	
In the forenoon it was	1 21 44	2 44 22
Mean of both		1 22 11
Difference nine hours going of the time-piece slow		8
		1 22 19

I observed an emersion of Jupiter's third satellite, which gave 8° 32' 21" difference of longitude. I then observed an emersion of Jupiter's first satellite, which gave 8.31.48. The mean of these observations is 8° 32' 2" which is equal to 128.2 West of Greenwich.

I had now determined my situation, which is the most fortunate circumstance of my long, painful, and perilous journey, as a few cloudy days would have prevented me from ascertaining the final longitude of it.[33]

At twelve it was high water, but the tide did not come within a foot and an half of the high water mark of last night. As soon

33. Mr. Meares was undoubtedly wrong in the idea, so earnestly insisted on by him in his voyage, that there was a North-West practicable passage to the Southward of sixty-nine degrees and an half of latitude, as I flatter myself has been proved by my former voyage. Nor can I refrain from expressing my surprise at his assertion, that there was an inland sea or archipelago of great extent between the islands of Nootka and the main, about the latitude where I was at this time. Indeed I have been informed that Captain Grey, who commanded an American vessel, and on whose authority he ventured this opinion, denies that he had given Mr. Meares any such information. Besides, the contrary is indubitably proved by Captain Vancouver's survey, from which no appeal can be made.

as I had completed my observations, we left this place: it was then ten o'clock in the afternoon. We returned the same way that we came, and though the tide was running out very strong, by keeping close in with the rocks, we proceeded at a considerable rate, as my people were very anxious to get out of the reach of the inhabitants of this coast.

Tuesday, July 23. During our course we saw several fires on the land to the Southward, and after the day dawned, their smokes were visible. At half past four this morning we arrived at our encampment of the night of the 21st, which had been named Porcupine Cove. The tide was out, and considerably lower than we found it when we were here before; the high-water mark being above the place where we had made our fire. This fluctuation must be occasioned by the action of the wind upon the water, in those narrow channels.

As we continued onwards, towards the river, we saw a canoe, well manned, which at first made from us with great expedition, but afterwards waited, as if to reconnoitre us; however, it kept out of our way, and allowed us to pass. The tide being much lower than when we were here before, we were under the necessity of landing a mile below the village. We observed that stakes were fixed in the ground along the bay, and in some places machines were fastened to them, as I afterwards learned, to intercept the seals and otters. These works are very extensive, and must have been erected with no common labour. The only bird we saw to-day was the white-headed eagle.[34]

Our guide directed us to draw the canoe out of the reach of the tide and to leave it. He would not wait, however, till this operation was performed, and I did not wish to let him go alone. I therefore followed him through a bad road encumbered with underwood. When we had quitted the wood, and were in sight of the houses, the young man being about fifteen or twenty paces before me, I was surprised to see two men running down towards me from one of the houses, with daggers in their hands and fury in their aspect. From their hostile appearance, I could

---

34. This bay was now named Mackenzie's Outlet.

not doubt of their purpose. I therefore stopped short, threw down my cloak, and put myself in a posture of defence, with my gun presented towards them. Fortunately for me, they knew the effect of fire-arms, and instantly dropped their daggers, which were fastened by a string to their wrists, and had before been held in a menacing attitude. I let my gun also fall into my left hand, and drew my hanger. Several others soon joined them, who were armed in the same manner; and among them I recognized the man whom I have already mentioned as being so troublesome to us, and who now repeated the names of Macubah and Benzins, signifying at the same time by his action, as on a former occasion, that he had been shot at by them. Until I saw him my mind was undisturbed; but the moment he appeared, conceiving that he was the cause of my present perilous situation, my resentment predominated, and, if he had come within my reach, I verily believe, that I should have terminated his insolence for ever.

The rest now approached so near, that one of them contrived to get behind me, and grasped me in his arms. I soon disengaged myself from him; and, that he did not avail himself of the opportunity which he had of plunging his dagger into me, I cannot conjecture. They certainly might have overpowered me, and though I should probably have killed one or two of them, I must have fallen at last.

One of my people now came out of the wood. On his appearance they instantly took flight, and with the utmost speed sought shelter in the houses from whence they had issued. It was, however, upwards often minutes before all my people joined me; and as they came one after the other, these people might have successively dispatched every one of us. If they had killed me, in the first instance, this consequence would certainly have followed, and not one of us would have returned home to tell the horrid fate of his companions.

After having stated the danger I had encountered, I told my people that I was determined to make these natives feel the impropriety of their conduct toward us, and compel them to return my hat and cloak which they had taken in the scuffle, as well as the articles previously purloined from us; for most of the men who were in the three canoes that we first saw, were now in the village. I therefore told my men to prime their pieces afresh, and prepare themselves for an active use of them, if the occasion should require it.

We now drew up before the house, and made signs for some one to come down to us. At length our young chief appeared, and told us that the men belonging to the canoes had not only informed his friends, that we had treated him very ill, but that we had killed four of their companions whom we had met in the bay. When I had explained to them as well as it was in my power, the falsehood of such a story, I insisted on the restoration of every thing that had been taken from us, as well as a necessary supply of fish, as the conditions of my departure; accordingly the things were restored, and a few dried fish along with them. A reconciliation now took place, but our guide or young chief was so much terrified that he would remain no longer with us, and requested us to follow with his father's canoe, or mischief would follow. I determined, however, before my departure, to take an observation, and at noon got a meridian altitude, making this place, which I named Rascal's Village, 52.23.43 North latitude.

On my informing the natives that we wanted something more to eat, they brought us two salmons; and when we signified that we had no poles to set the canoe against the current, they were furnished with equal alacrity, so anxious were they for our departure. I paid, however, for every thing which we had received, and did not forget the loan of the canoe.

Chapter 12

FRIENDLY VILLAGE

Tuesday, July 23. [continued]. The current of the river was so strong, that I should have complied with the wishes of my people, and gone by land, but one of my Indians was so weak, that it was impossible for him to perform the journey. He had been ill some time; and, indeed, we had been all of us more or less afflicted with colds on the sea coast. Four of the people therefore set off with the canoe, and it employed them an hour to get half a mile. In the mean time the native, who has been already mentioned as having treated us with so much insolence, and four of his companions, went up the river in a canoe, which they had above the rapid, with as many boxes as men in her. This circumstance was the cause of fresh alarm, as it was generally concluded that they would produce the same mischief and danger in the villages above, as they had in that below. Nor was it forgotten that the young chief had left us in a manner which would not be interpreted in our favour by his father and friends.

At length the canoe arrived, and the people declared in the most unreserved terms, that they would proceed no further in her; but when they were made acquainted with the circumstances which have just been described, their violence increased, and the greater part of the men announced their determination to attempt the mountains, and endeavour, by passing over them, to gain the road by which we came to the first village. So resolved were they to pursue this plan, that they threw every thing which they had into the river, except their blankets. I was all this time sitting patiently on a stone, and indulging the hope that, when their frantic terror had subsided, their returning reason would have disposed them to perceive the rashness of their project; but when I observed that they persisted in it, I no longer remained a silent listener to their passionate declarations, but proceeded to employ such arguments as I trusted would turn them from their senseless and impracticable purpose. After reproving my young Indian in very severe terms, for encouraging the rest to follow their mad design of passing the mountains, I addressed myself generally to them, stating the difficulty of ascending the mountains, the eternal snows with which they were covered, our small stock of provisions, which two days would exhaust, and the consequent probability that we should perish with cold and hunger. I urged the folly of being affected by the alarm of danger which might not exist, and if it did, I encouraged them with the means we possessed of surmounting it. Nor did I forget to urge the inhumanity and injustice of leaving the poor sick Indian to languish and die. I also added, that as my particular object had been accomplished, I had now no other but our common safety; that the sole wish of my heart was to employ the best means in my power, and to pursue the best method which my understanding could suggest, to secure them and myself from every danger that might impede our return.

My steersman, who had been with me for five years .in that capacity, instantly replied that he was ready to follow me wherever I should go, but that he would never again enter that canoe, as he had solemnly sworn he would not, while he was in the rapid. His example was followed by all the rest, except two, who embarked with Mr. Mackay,[35] myself, and the sick Indian. The current, however, was so strong, that we dragged up the greatest part of the way, by the branches of trees. Our progress, as may be imagined, was very tedious, and attended with uncommon labour; the party who went by land being continually obliged to wait for us. Mr. Mackay's gun was carried out of the canoe and lost, at a time when we appeared to stand in very great need of it, as two canoes, with sixteen or eighteen men, were coming down

---

35. It is but common justice to him, to mention in this place that I had every reason to be satisfied with his conduct.

the stream; and the apprehensions which they occasioned did not subside till they shot by us with great rapidity.

At length we came in sight of the house, when we saw our young Indian with six others, in a canoe coming to meet us. This was a very encouraging circumstance, as it satisfied us that the natives who had preceded, and whose malignant designs we had every reason to suspect, had not been able to prejudice the people against us. We, therefore, landed at the house, where we were received in a friendly manner, and having procured some fish, we proceeded on our journey.

It was almost dark when we arrived at the next house, and the first persons who presented themselves to our observation were the turbulent Indian and his four companions. They were not very agreeable objects; but we were nevertheless well received by the inhabitants, who presented us with fish and berries. The Indians who had caused us so much alarm, we now discovered to be inhabitants of the islands, and traders in various articles, such as cedar-bark, prepared to be wove into mats, fish-spawn, copper, iron, and beads, the latter of which they get on their own coast. For these they receive in exchange roasted salmon, hemlock-bark cakes, and the other kind made of salmon roes, sorrel, and bitter berries. Having procured as much fish as would serve us for our supper, and the meals of the next day, all my people went to rest except one, with whom I kept the first watch.

Wednesday, July 24. After twelve last night, I called up Mr. Mackay, and one of the men, to relieve us, but as a general tranquillity appeared to prevail in the place, I recommended them to return to their rest. I was the first awake the morning, and sent Mr. Mackay to see if our canoe remained where we left it; but he returned to inform me that the Islanders had loaded it with their articles of traffic, and were ready to depart. On this intelligence I hurried to the water side, and seizing the canoe by the stem, I should certainly have overset it, and turned the three men that were in it, with all their merchandise, into the river, had not one of the people of the house, who had been very kind to us, informed me that this was their own canoe, and that my guide had gone off with ours. At the same moment the other two Indians who belonged to the party, jumped nimbly into it, and pushed off with all the haste and hurry that their fears may be supposed to dictate.

We now found ourselves once more without a guide or a canoe. We were, however, so fortunate as to engage, without much difficulty, two of these people to accompany us; as, from the strength of the current, it would not have been possible for us to have proceeded by water without their assistance. As the house was upon an island, we ferried over the pedestrian party to the main bank of the river, and continued our course till our conductors came to their fishing ground, when they proposed to land us, and our small portion of baggage; but as our companions were on the opposite shore, we could not acquiesce, and after some time persuaded them to proceed further with us. Soon after we met the chief, who had regaled us in our voyage down the river. He was seining between two canoes, and had taken a considerable quantity of salmon. He took us on board with him, and proceed upwards with great expedition. These people are surprisingly skilful and active in setting against a strong current. In the roughest part they almost filled the canoe with water, by way of a sportive alarm to us.

We landed at the house of the chief, and he immediately placed a fish before me. Our people now appeared on the opposite bank, when a canoe was sent for them. As soon as they had made their meal of fish, they proceeded on their route, and we followed them, the chief and one of the natives having undertaken to conduct us.

At five in the afternoon we came to two houses, which we had not seen in going down. They were upon an island, and I was obliged to send for the walking party, as our conductors, from the lateness of the hour, refused to proceed any further with us till the next day. One of our men, being at a small distance before the others, had been attacked by a female bear, with two cubs, but another of them arrived to his rescue, and shot her. Their fears probably prevented them from killing the two young ones. They brought a part of the meat, but it was very indifferent. We were informed that our former guide, or young chief, had passed this place, at a very early hour of the morning, on foot.

These people take plenty of another fish, besides salmon, which weigh from fifteen to forty pounds, This fish is broader than the salmon, of a greyish colour, and with an hunch on its back; the flesh is white, but neither rich nor well flavoured. Its jaw and teeth are like those of a dog, and the latter are larger and stronger than any I had ever seen in a fish of equal size: those in front bend inwards, like the claws of a bird of prey. It delights in shallow water, and its native name is Dilly.

We received as many fish and berries from these people as completely satisfied our appetites. The latter excelled any of the kind that we had seen. I saw, also, three kinds of gooseberries, which, as we passed through the woods, we found in great abundance.

Thursday, July 25. I arose before the sun, and the weather was very fine. The men who were to accompany us went to visit their machines, and brought back plenty of fish, which they strung on a rope, and left them in the river. We now embarked thirteen in a canoe, and landed my men on the South bank, as it would have been impracticable to have stemmed the tide with such a load. The under-wood was so thick that it was with great difficulty they could pass through it. At nine we were under the necessity of waiting to ferry them over a river from the South, which is not fordable. After some time we came to two deserted houses, at the foot of a rapid, beyond which our boatmen absolutely refused to conduct us by water. Here was a road which led opposite to the village. We had, however, the curiosity to visit the houses, which were erected upon posts; and we suffered very severely for the indulgence of it; for the floors were covered with fleas, and we were immediately in the same condition, for which we had no remedy but to take to the water. There was not a spot round the houses, free from grass, that was not alive, as it were, with this vermin.

Our guides proposed to conduct us on our way, and we followed them on a well-beaten track. They, however, went so fast, that we could not all of us keep up with them, particularly our sick Indian, whose situation was very embarrassing to us, and at length they contrived to escape. I very much wished for these men to have accompanied us to the village, in order to do away any ill impressions which might have arisen from the young chief's report to his father, which we were naturally led to expect would not be in our favour.

This road conducted us through the finest wood of cedar trees that I had ever seen. I measured several of them that were twenty-four feet in girth, and of a proportionate height. The alder trees are also of an uncommon size; several of them were seven feet and an half in circumference, and rose to forty feet without a branch; but my men declared that they had, in their progress, seen much larger of both kinds. The other wood was hemlock, white birch, two species of spruce-firs, willows, &c. Many of the large cedars appeared to have been examined, as I suppose by the natives, for the purpose of making canoes, but finding them hollow at heart, they were suffered to stand. There was but little underwood, and the soil was a black rich mould, which would well reward the trouble of cultivation. From the remains of bones on certain spots, it is probable that the natives may have occasionally burned their dead in this wood.

As it was uncertain what our reception might be at the village, I examined every man's arms and ammunition, and gave Mr. Mackay, who had unfortunately lost his gun, one of my pistols. Our late conductors had informed us that the man whom we left in a dying state, and to whom I had administered some Turlington's balsam, was dead; and it was by no means improbable that I might be suspected of hastening his end.

At one in the afternoon we came to the bank of the river, which was opposite to the village, which appeared to be in a state of perfect tranquillity. Several of the natives were fishing above and below the weir, and they very readily took us over in their canoes. The people now hurried down to the water side, but I perceived none of the chief's family among them. They made signs to me to go to his house; I signified to them not to crowd about us, and indeed drew a line, beyond which I made them understand they must not pass. I now directed Mr. Mackay, and the men to remain there, with their arms in readiness, and to keep the natives at a distance, as I was determined to go alone to the chief's house; and if they should hear the report of my pistols, they were ordered to make the best of their way from these people, as it would then be equally fruitless and dangerous to attempt the giving me any assistance, as it would be only in the last extremity, and when I was certain of their intention to destroy me, that I should discharge my pistols. My gun I gave to Mr. Mackay, when, with my loaded pistols in my belt, and a poniard in my hand, I proceeded to the abode of the chief. I had a wood to pass in my way thither, which was intersected by various paths, and I took one that led to the back instead of the front of the house; and as the whole had been very much altered since I was here before, I concluded that I had lost my way. But I continued to proceed, and soon met with the chief's wife, who informed me, that he was at the next house. On my going round it, I perceived that they had thrown open the gable ends, and added two wings, nearly as long as the body, both of which were hung round with salmon as close as they could be placed. As I could discover none of the men, I sat down upon a large stone near some women who were supping on salmon toes and berries. They invited me to partake of their fare, and I was about to accept their invitation, when Mr. Mackay joined me, as both himself and all my party were alarmed at my being alone. Nor was his alarm lessened by an old man whom he met in the wood, and who made use of signs to persuade him to return. As he came without his gun, I gave him one of my pistols. When I saw the women continue their employment without paying the least attention to us, I could not imagine that any hostile design was preparing against us. Though the non-appearance of the men awakened some degree of suspicion that I should not be received with the same welcome as on my former visit. At length the chief appeared, and his son, who had been our guide, following him: displeasure was painted in the old man's countenance, and he held in his hand a bead tobacco pouch which belonged to Mr. Mackay, and the young chief had purloined from him. When he had approached within three or four yards of me, he threw it at me with great indignation, and walked away. I followed him, however, until he had passed his son, whom I took by the hand, but he did not make any very cordial return to my salutation; at the same time he made signs for me to discharge my pistol, and give him my hanger which Mr. Mackay had brought me, but I did not pay the least attention to either of his demands.

We now joined the chief, who explained to me that he was in a state of deep distress for the loss of his son, and made me understand that he had cut off his hair and blackened his face on the melancholy occasion. He also represented the alarm which he had suffered respecting his son who had accompanied us; as he apprehended we had killed him, or had all of us perished together. When he had finished his narrative, I took him and his son by their hands, and requested them to come with me to the place where I had left my people, who were rejoiced to see us return, having been in a state of great anxiety from our long absence. I immediately remunerated the young chief for his company and assistance in our voyage to the sea, as well as his father, for his former attentions. I gave them cloth and knives, and, indeed, a portion of every thing which now remained to us. The presents had the desired effect of restoring us to their favour; but these people are of so changeable a nature, that there is no security with them. I procured three robes and two otter-skins, and if I could have given such articles in exchange as they preferred, I should probably have obtained more. I now repre-sented the length of the way which I had to go, and requested some fish to support us on our journey, when he desired us to follow him to the house, where mats were immediately arranged and a fish placed before each of us.

We were now informed, that our dog, whom we had lost, had been howling about the village ever since we left it, and that they had reason to believe he left the woods at night to eat the fish he could find about the houses. I immediately dispatched Mr. Mackay, and a man, in search of the animal, but they returned without him.

When I manifested my intention to proceed on my journey, the chief voluntarily sent for ten roasted salmon, and having attended us with his son, and a great number of his people, to the last house in the village, we took our leave. It was then half past three in the afternoon.

I directed Mr. Mackay to take the lead, and the others to follow him in Indian files, at a long and steady pace, as I determined to bring up the rear. I adopted this measure from a confusion that was observable among the natives which I did not comprehend. I was not without my suspicions that some mischief was in agitation, and they were increased from the confused noise we heard in the village. At the same time a considerable number came running after us; some of them making signs for us to stop, and others rushing by me. I perceived also, that those who followed us were the strangers who live among these people, and are kept by them in a state of awe and subjection; and one of them made signs to me that we were taking the wrong road. I immediately called out to Mr. Mackay to stop. This was naturally enough taken for an alarm, and threw my people into great disorder. When, however, I was understood, and we had mustered again, our Indian informed us, that the noise we heard was occasioned by a debate among the natives, whether they should stop us or not. When, therefore, we had got into the right road, I made such arrangements as might be necessary for our defence, if we should have an experimental proof that our late and fickle friends were converted into enemies.

Our way was through a forest of stately cedars, beneath a range of lofty hills, covered with rocks, and without any view of the river. The path was well beaten, but rendered incommodious by the large stones which lay along it.

As we were continuing our route, we all felt the sensation of having found a lost friend at the sight of our dog; but he appeared, in a great degree, to have lost his former sagacity. He ran in a wild way backwards and forwards; and though he kept our road, I could not induce him to acknowledge his master. Sometimes he seemed disposed to approach as if he knew us;

and then, on a sudden, he would turn away, as if alarmed at our appearance. The poor animal was reduced almost to a skeleton, and we occasionally dropped something to support him, and by degrees he recovered his former sagacity.

When the night came on we stopped at a small distance from the river, but did not venture to make a fire. Every man took his tree, and laid down in his clothes, and with his arms, beneath the shade of its branches. We had removed to a short distance from the path; no centinel was now appointed, and every one was left to watch for his own safety.

Friday, July 26. After a very restless, though undisturbed night, we set forward as soon as day appeared, and walked on with all possible expedition, till we got to the upper, which we now called Friendly Village, and was the first we visited on our outward journey.

It was eight in the morning of a very fine day when we arrived, and found a very material alteration in the place since we left it. Five additional houses had been erected and were filled with salmon: the increase of inhabitants was in the same proportion. We were received with great kindness, and a messenger was dispatched to inform the chief, whose name was Soocomlick, and who was then at his fishing-weir, of our arrival. He immediately returned to the village to confirm the cordial reception of his people; and having conducted us to his house, entertained us with the most respectful hospitality. In short, he behaved to us with so much attention and kindness, that I did not withhold any thing in my power to give, which might afford him satisfaction. I presented him with two yards of blue cloth, an axe, knives, and various other articles. He gave me in return a large shell which resembled the under shell of a Guernsey oyster, but somewhat larger. Where they procure them I could not discover, but they cut and polish them for bracelets, ear-rings, and other personal ornaments. He regretted that he had no sea-otter skins to give me, but engaged to provide abundance of them whenever either my friends or myself should return by sea; an expectation which I thought it right to encourage among these people. He also earnestly requested me to bring him a gun and ammunition. I might have procured many curious articles at this place, but was prevented by the consideration that we must have carried them on our backs upwards of three hundred miles through a mountainous country. The young chief, to his other acts of kindness, added as large a supply offish as we chose to take.

Our visit did not occasion any particular interruption of the ordinary occupation of the people; especially of the women, who were employed in boiling sorrel, and different kinds of berries, with salmon-roes, in large square kettles of cedar wood. This pottage, when it attained a certain consistency, they took out with ladles, and poured it into frames of about twelve inches square and one deep, the bottom being covered with a large leaf, which were then exposed to the sun till their contents became so many dried cakes. The roes that are mixed up with the bitter berries, are prepared in the same way. From the quantity of this kind of provision, it must be a principal article of food, and probably of traffic. These people have also portable chests of cedar, in which they pack them, as well as their salmon, both dried and roasted. It appeared to me, that they eat no flesh, except such as the sea may afford them, as that of the sea-otter and the seal. The only instance we observed to the contrary, was in the young Indian who accompanied us among the islands, and has been already mentioned as feasting on the flesh of a porcupine; whether this be their custom throughout the year, or only during the season of the salmon fishery; or, whether there were any casts of them, as in India, I cannot pretend to determine. It is certain, however, that they are not hunters, and I have already mentioned the abhorrence they expressed at some venison which we brought to their village. During our former visit to these people, they requested us not to discharge our fire-arms, lest the report should frighten away the salmon, but now they expressed a wish that I should explain the use and management of them. Though their demeanour to us was of the most friendly nature, and they appeared without any arms, except a few who accidentally had their daggers, I did not think it altogether prudent to discharge our pieces; I therefore fired one of my pistols at a tree marked for the purpose, when I put four out of five buck-shot, with which it was loaded, into the circle, to their extreme astonishment and admiration.

These people were in general of the midde stature, well-set, and better clothed with flesh than any of the natives of the interior country. Their faces are round, with high cheek bones, and their complexion between the olive and the copper. They have small grey eyes with a tinge of red; they have wedge heads, and their hair is of a dark brown colour, inclining to black. Some wear it long, keep it well combed, and let it hang loose over their shoulders, while they divide and tie it in knots over the temples. Others arrange its plaits, and bedawb it with brown earth, so as to render it impervious to the comb; they, therefore, carry a bodkin about them to ease the frequent irritation, which may be supposed to proceed from such a state of the head. The women are inclined to be fat, wear their hair short, and appear to be very subject to swelled legs, a malady that, probably, proceeds from the posture in which they are always sitting: as they are chiefly employed in the domestic engagements of spinning, weaving, preparing the fish, and nursing their children, which did not appear to be numerous. Their cradle differed from any that I had seen; it consisted of a frame fixed round a board of sufficient length, in which the child, after it has been swathed, is placed on a bed of moss, and a conductor contrived to carry off the urinary discharge. They are flung over one shoulder by means of a cord fastened under the other, so that the infant is always in a position to be readily applied to the breast, when it requires nourishment. I saw several whose heads were inclosed in boards covered with leather, till they attain the form of a wedge. The women wear no clothing but the robe, either loose or tied round the middle with a girdle, as the occasion may require, with the addition of a fringed apron, already mentioned, and a cape, in the form of an inverted bowl or dish. To the robe and cap, the men add, when it rains, a circular mat with an opening in the middle sufficient to admit the head, which extending over the shoulders, throws off the wet. They also occasionally wear shoes of dressed mooseskin, for which they are indebted to their neighbours. Those

parts, which among all civilized nations are covered from familiar view, are here openly exposed.

They are altogether dependent on the sea and rivers for their
sustenance, so that they may be considered as a stationary people; hence it is that the men engage in those toilsome employ-
ments, which the tribes who support themselves by the chase,
leave entirely to the women. Polygamy is permitted among
them, though, according to my observation, most of the men
were satisfied with one wife, with whom, however, chastity is
not considered as a necessary virtue. I saw but one woman
whose under lip was split and disfigured with an appendant
ornament. The men frequently bathe, and the boys are continually in the water. They have nets and lines of various kinds and
sizes, which are made of cedar bark, and would not be known
from those made of hemp. Their hooks consist of two pieces of
wood or bone, forming when fixed together, an obtuse angle.

Their spears or darts are from four to sixteen feet in length;
the barb or point being fixed in a socket, which, when the animal
is struck, slips from it: thus the barb being fastened by a string to
the handle, remains as a buoy; or enables the aquatic hunter to
tire and take his prey. They are employed against sea-otters,
seals, and large fish.

Their hatchets are made principally of about fourteen inches
of bar-iron, fixed into a wooden handle, as I have already
described them; though they have some of bone or horn: with
these, a mallet and wooden wedge, they hew their timbers and
form their planks. They must also have other tools with which
they complete and polish their work, but my stay was so short,
my anxiety so great, and my situation so critical, that many circumstances may be supposed to have escaped me.

Their canoes are made out of the cedar tree, and will carry
from eight to fifty persons.

Their warlike weapons, which, as far as I could judge, they
very seldom have occasion to employ, are bows and arrows,
spears, and daggers. The arrows are such as have been already
described, but rather of a slighter make. The bows are not more
than two feet and an half in length; they are formed of a slip of

red cedar; the grain being on one side untouched with any tool, while the other is secured with sinews attached to it by a kind of glue. Though this weapon has a very slender appearance, it throws an arrow with great force, and to a considerable distance. Their spears are about ten feet long, and pointed with iron. Their daggers are of various kinds, being of British, Spanish, and American manufacture.

Their household furniture consists of boxes, troughs, and dishes formed of wood, with different vessels made of watape. These are employed, according to their several applications, to contain their valuables and provisions, as well as for culinary purposes, and to carry water. The women make use of muscle-shells to split and clean their fish, and which are very well adapted to that purpose.

Their ornaments are necklaces, collars, bracelets for the arms, wrists, and legs, with ear-rings, &c.

They burn their dead, and display their mourning, by cutting their hair short, and blackening their faces. Though I saw several places where bodies had been burned, I was surprised at not seeing any tomb or memorial of the dead, particularly when their neighbours are so superstitiously attentive to the erection and preservation of them.

From the number of their canoes, as well as the quantity of their chests and boxes, to contain their moveables, as well as the insufficiency of their houses, to guard against the rigours of a severe winter, and the appearance of the ground around their habitations, it is evident that these people reside here only during the summer or salmon season, which does not probably last more than three months. It may be reasonably inferred, therefore, that they have villages on the sea-coast, which they inhabit during the rest of the year. There it may be supposed they leave the sick, the infirm, and the aged; and thither they may bear the ashes of those who die at the place of their summer residence.

Of their religion I can say but little, as my means of observation were very contracted. I could discover, however, that they believed in a good and an evil spirit: and that they have some forms of worship to conciliate the protection of one, and perhaps to avert the enmity of the other, is apparent from the temples which I have described; and where, at stated periods, it may be presumed they hold the feasts, and perform the sacrifices, which their religion, whatever it may be, has instituted as the ceremonials of their public worship.

From the very little I could discover of their government, it is altogether different from any political regulation which had been remarked by me among the savage tribes. It is on this river alone that one man appears to have an exclusive and hereditary right to what was necessary to the existence of those who are associated with him. I allude to the salmon weir, or fishing place, the sole right to which confers on the chief an arbitrary power. Those embankments could not have been formed without a very great and associated labour; and, as might be supposed, on the condition that those who assisted in constructing it should enjoy a participating right in the advantages to be derived from it. Nevertheless, it evidently appeared to me, that the chief's power over it, and the people, was unlimited, and without control. No one could fish without his permission, or carry home a larger portion of what he had caught, than was set apart for him. No one could build an house without his consent; and all his commands appeared to be followed with implicit obedience. The people at large seemed to be on a perfect equality, while the strangers among them were obliged to obey the commands of the natives in general, or quit the village. They appear to be of a friendly disposition, but they are subject to sudden gusts of passion, which are as quickly composed; and the transition is instantaneous, from violent irritation to the most tranquil demeanor. Of the many tribes of savage people whom I have seen, these appear to be the most susceptible of civilization. They might soon be brought to cultivate the little ground about them which is capable of it. There is a narrow border of a rich black soil, on either side of the river, over a bed of gravel, which would yield any grain or fruit, that are common to similar latitudes in Europe.

The very few words which I collected in their language are as follows:

Zimilk,	Salmon.
Dilly,	A fish of the size of a salmon, with canine teeth.
Sepnas,	Hair of the head.
Kietis,	An axe.
Clougus,	Eyes.
Itzas,	Teeth.
Ma-acza,	Nose.
Ich-yeh,	Leg.
Shous-shey,	Hand.
Watts,	Dog.
Zla-achle,	House.
Zimnez,	Bark mat robe.
Couloun,	Beaver or otter ditto.
Dichts,	Stone.
Neach,	Fire.
Ulkan,	Water.
Gits com,	A mat.
Shiggimia,	Thread.
Till-kewan,	Chest or box.
Thlogatt,	Cedar bark.
Achmioul,	Beads got upon their coast.
II-caiette,	A bonnet.
Couny,	A clam shell.

Nochasky,	A dish composed of berries and salmon roes.
Caiffre,	What?

Chapter 13

BEAVER ROBES

Friday, July 26 [continued]. At eleven in the morning we left this place, which I called Friendly Village, accompanied by every man belonging to it, who attended us about a mile, when we took a cordial leave of them; and if we might judge from appearances, they parted from us with regret.

In a short time we halted, to make a division of our fish, and each man had about twenty pounds weight of it, except Mr. Mackay and myself, who were content with shorter allowance, that we might have less weight to carry. We had also a little flour, and some pemmican. Having completed this arrangement with all possible expedition, we proceeded onwards, the ground rising gradually, as we continued our route. When we were clear of the wood, we saw the mountain towering above, and apparently of impracticable ascent. We soon came to the fork of the river, which was at the foot of the precipice, where the ford was three feet deep, and very rapid. Our young Indian, though much recovered, was still too weak to cross the water, and with some difficulty I carried him over on my back.

It was now one in the afternoon, and we had to ascend the summit of the first mountain before night came on, in order to look for water. I left the sick Indian, with his companion and one of my men, to follow us, as his strength would permit him. The fatigue of ascending these precipices I shall not attempt to describe, and it was past five when we arrived at a spot where we could get water, and in such an extremity of weariness, that it was with great pain any of us could crawl about to gather wood for the necessary purpose of making a fire. To relieve our anxiety, which began to increase every moment for the situation of the Indian, about seven he and his companions arrived; when we consoled ourselves by sitting round a blazing fire, talking of past dangers, and indulging the delightful reflection that we were thus far advanced on our homeward journey. Nor was it possible to be in this situation without contemplating the wonders of it. Such was the depth of the precipices below, and the height of the mountains above, with the rude and wild magnificence of the scenery around, that I shall not attempt to describe such an astonishing and awful combination of objects; of which, indeed, no description can convey an adequate idea. Even at this place, which is only, as it were, the first step towards gaining the summit of the mountains, the climate was very sensibly changed. The air that fanned the village which we left at noon, was mild and cheering; the grass was verdant, and the wild fruits ripe around it. But here the snow was not yet dissolved, the ground was still bound by the frost, the herbage had scarce begun to spring, and the crowberry bushes were just beginning to blossom.

Saturday, July 27. So great was our fatigue of yesterday, that it was late before we proceeded to return over the mountains, by the same route which we had followed in our outward journey. There was little or no change in the appearance of the mountains since we passed them, though the weather was very fine.

Sunday, July 28. At nine this morning we arrived at the spot, where we slept with the natives on the 16th instant, and found our pemmican in good condition where we had buried it.

The latitude of this place, by observation, when I passed, I found to be 52.46.32. I now took time, and the distance between sun and moon. I had also an azimuth, to ascertain the variation.

We continued our route with fine weather, and without meeting a single person on our way, the natives being all gone, as we supposed, to the Great River. We recovered all our hidden stores of provisions, and arrived about two in the afternoon of Sunday, August the 4th, at the place which we had left a month before.

A considerable number of Indians were encamped on the opposite side of the small river, and in consequence of the weather, confined to their lodges: as they must have heard of, if not seen, us, and our arms being out of order from the rain, I was not satisfied with our situation; but did not wish to create an alarm. We, therefore, kept in the edge of the wood, and called to them, when they turned out like so many furies, with their arms in their hands, and threatening destruction if we dared to approach their habitations. We remained in our station till their passion and apprehensions had subsided, when our interpreter gave them the necessary information respecting us. They proved to be strangers to us, but were the relations of those whom we had already seen here, and who, as they told us, were upon an island at some distance up the river. A messenger was accordingly sent to inform them of our arrival.

On examining the canoe, and our property, which we had left behind, we found it in perfect safety; nor was there the print of a foot near the spot. We now pitched our tent, and made a blazing fire, and I treated myself, as well as the people, with a dram; but we had been so long without tasting any spirituous liquor, that we had lost all relish for it. The Indians now arrived from above, and were rewarded for the care they had taken of our property with such articles as were acceptable to them.

Monday, August 5. At nine this morning I sent five men in the canoe, for the various articles we had left below, and they soon returned with them, and except some bale goods, which had got wet, they were in good order, particularly the provisions, of which we were now in great need.

Many of the natives arrived both from the upper and lower parts of the river, each of whom was dressed in a beaver robe. I purchased fifteen of them; and they preferred large knives in exchange. It is an extraordinary circumstance, that these people, who might have taken all the property we left behind us, without the least fear of detection, should leave that untouched, and purloin any of our utensils, which our confidence in their honesty gave them a ready opportunity of taking. In fact, several articles were missing, and as I was very anxious to avoid a quarrel with the natives, in this stage of our journey, I told those who remained near us, without any appearance of anger, that their relations who were gone, had no idea of the mischief that would result to them from taking our property. I gravely added, that the salmon, which was not only their favourite food, but absolutely necessary to their existence, came from the sea which belonged to us white men; and that as, at the entrance of the river, we could prevent those fish from coming up it, we possessed the power to starve them and their children. To avert our anger, therefore, they must return all the articles that had been stolen from us. This finesse succeeded. Messengers were dispatched to order the restoration of every thing that had been taken. We purchased several large salmon of them and enjoyed the delicious meal which they afforded.

At noon this day, which I allotted for repose, I got a meridian altitude, which gave 53.24.10. I also took time. The weather had been cloudy at intervals.

Tuesday, August 6. Every necessary preparation had been made yesterday for us to continue our route to day; but before our departure, some of the natives arrived with part of the stolen articles; the rest, they said, had been taken by the people down the river, who would be here in the course of the morning, and recommended their children to our commiseration, and themselves to our forgiveness.

The morning was cloudy, with small rain, nevertheless I ordered the men to load the canoe, and we proceeded in high spirits on finding ourselves once more so comfortably together in it. We landed at an house on the first island, where we procured a few salmon, and four fine beaver skins. There had been much more rain in these parts than in the country above, as the water was pouring down the hills in torrents. The river consequently rose with great rapidity, and very much impeded our progress.

The people on this river are generally of the middle size, though I saw many tall men among them. In the cleanliness of their persons they resemble rather the Beaver Indians than the Chepewyans. They are ignorant of the use of fire arms, and their only weapons are bows and arrows, and spears. They catch the larger animals in snares, but though their country abounds in them, and the rivers and lakes produce plenty of fish, they find a difficulty in supporting themselves, and are never to be seen but in small bands of two or three families. There is no regular government among them; nor do they appear to have a sufficient communication or understanding with each other, to defend themselves against an invading enemy, to whom they fall an easy prey. They have all the animals common on the West side of the mountains, except the buffalo and the wolf; at least we saw none of the latter, and there being none of the former, it is evident that their progress is from the South-East. The same language is spoken, with very little exception from the extent of my travels down this river, and in a direct line from the North-East head of it in latitude 53° or 74° to Hudson's Bay; so that a Chepewyan, from which tribe they have all sprung, might leave Churchill River, and proceeding in every direction to the North-West of this line without knowing any language except his own, would understand them all: I except the natives of the sea coast, who are altogether a different people. As to the people to the Eastward of this river, I am not qualified to speak of them.

At twelve we ran our canoe upon a rock, so that we were obliged to land in order to repair the injury she had received; and as the rain came on with great violence, we remained here for the night. The salmon were now driving up the current in such large shoals, that the water seemed, as it were, to be covered with the fins of them.

Wednesday, August 7. About nine this morning the weather cleared, and we embarked. The shoals of salmon continued as yesterday. There were frequent showers throughout the day, and every brook was deluged into a river. The water had risen at least one foot and an half perpendicular in the last twenty-four hours. In the dusk of the evening we landed for the night.

Thursday, August 8. The water continued rising during the night; so that we were disturbed twice in the course of it, to remove our baggage. At six in the morning we were on our way, and proceeded with continual and laborious exertion, from the increased rapidity of the current. After having passed the two carrying places of Rocky Point, and the Long Portage, we encamped for the night.

Friday, August 9. We set off at five, after a rainy night, and in a foggy morning. The water still retained its height. The sun, however, soon beamed upon us; and our clothes and baggage were in such a state that we landed to dry them. After some time we re-embarked, and arrived at our first encampment on this river about seven in the evening. The water fell considerably in the course of the day.

Saturday, August 10. The weather was cloudy with slight showers, and at five this morning we embarked, the water falling as fast as it had risen. This circumstance arises from the mountainous state of the country on either side of the river, from whence the water rushes down almost as fast as it falls from the heavens, with the addition of the snow it melts in its way. At eight in the evening we stopped for the night.

Sunday, August 11. At five this morning we proceeded with clear weather. At ten we came to the foot of the long rapid, which we ascended with poles much easier than we expected. The rapids that were so strong, and violent in our passage downwards, were now so reduced, that we could hardly believe them to be the same. At sun-set we landed and encamped.

Monday, August 12. The weather was the same as yesterday, and we were on the water at a very early hour. At nine we came to a part of the river where there was little or no current. At noon we landed to gum the canoe, when I took a meridian altitude, which gave 54.11.36 North latitude. We continued our route nearly East, and at three in the afternoon approached the fork, when I took time, and the distance between the sun and moon. At four in the afternoon we left the main branch. The current was quite slack, as the water had fallen six feet, which must have been in the course of three days. At sunset we landed and took our station for the night.

Tuesday, August 13. There was a very heavy rain in the night, and the morning was cloudy; we renewed our voyage, however, at a very early hour, and came to the narrow gut between the mountains of rock, which was a passage of some risk; but fortunately the state of the water was such, that we got up without any difficulty, and had more time to examine these extraordinary rocks than in our outward passage. They are as perpendicular as a wall, and give the idea of a succession of enormous Gothic churches. We were now closely hemmed in by the mountains, which have lost much of their snow since our former passage by them. We encamped at a late hour, cold, wet, and hungry: for such was the state of our provisions, that our necessary allowance did not answer to the active cravings of our appetites.

Wednesday, August 14. The weather was cold and raw, with small rain, but our necessities would not suffer us to wait for a favourable change of it, and at half past five we arrived at the swampy carrying-place, between this branch and the small river. At three in the afternoon the cold was extreme, and the men could not keep themselves warm even by their violent exertions, which our situation required; and now I gave them the remainder of our rum to fortify and support them. The canoe was so heavy that the lives of two of them were endangered in this horrible carrying place. At the same time it must be observed, that from the fatiguing circumstances of our journey, and the inadequate state of our provisions, the natural strength of the men had been greatly diminished. We encamped on the banks of the bad river.

Thursday, August 15. The weather was now clear, and the sun shone upon us. The water was much lower than in the downward passage, but as cold as ice, and, unfortunately, the men were obliged to be continually in it to drag on the canoe. There were many embarras, through which a passage might have been made, but we were under the necessity of carrying both the canoe and baggage.

About sun-set we arrived at our encampment of the 13th of June, where some of us had nearly taken our eternal voyage. The legs and feet of the men were so benumbed, that I was very apprehensive of the consequences. The water being low, we made a search for our bag of ball, but without success. The river was full of salmon, and another fish like the black bass.

Friday, August 16. The weather continued to be the same as yesterday, and at two in the afternoon we came to the carrying-place which leads to the first small lake; but it was so filled with drift wood, that a considerable portion of time was employed in making our way through it. We now reached the high land which separates the source of the Tacoutche Tesse or Columbia River, and Unjigah, or Peace River: the latter of which, after receiving many tributary streams, passes through the great Slave Lake, and disembogues itself in the Frozen Ocean, in latitude 69½ North, longitude 135 West from Greenwich; while the former, confined by the immense mountains that run nearly parallel with the Pacific Ocean, and keep it in a Southern course, empties itself in 46.20 North latitude and longitude 124 West from Greenwich.

If I could have spared the time, and had been able to exert myself, for I was now afflicted with a swelling in my ancles, so that I could not even walk, but with great pain and difficulty, it was my intention to have taken some salmon alive, and colonised them in the Peace River, though it is very doubtful whether that fish would live in waters that have not a communication with the sea.

Some of the inhabitants had been here since we passed; and I apprehend, that on seeing our road through their country, they mistook us for enemies, and had therefore deserted the place, which is a most convenient station; as on one side, there is great plenty of white fish, and trout, jub, carp, &c. and on the other, abundance of salmon, and probably other fish. Several things that I had left here in exchange for articles of which I had possessed myself, as objects of curiosity, were taken away. The whirtle berries were now ripe, and very fine of their kind.

Saturday, August 17. The morning was cloudy, and at five we renewed our progress. We were compelled to carry from the lake to the Peace River, the passage, from the falling of the water, being wholly obstructed by driftwood. The meadow through which we passed was entirely inundated; and from the state of my foot and ancle, I was obliged, though with great reluctance, to submit to be carried over it.

At half past seven we began to glide along with the current of the Peace River; and almost at every canoe's length we perceived Beaver roads to and from the river. At two in the afternoon, an object attracted our notice at the entrance of a small river, which proved to be the four beaver skins, already mentioned to have been presented to me by a native, and left in his possession to receive them on my return. I imagine, therefore, that being under the necessity of leaving the river, or, perhaps, fearing to meet us again, he had taken this method to restore them to me; and to reward his honesty, I left three times the value of the skins in their place. The snow appeared in patches on the mountains. At four in the afternoon we passed the place where we found the first natives, and landed for the night at a late hour. In the course of the day we caught nine outards, or Canada geese, but they were as yet without their feathers.

Sunday, August 18. As soon as it was light we proceeded on our voyage, and drove on before the current, which was very much diminished in its strength, since we came up it. The water indeed was so low, that in many parts it exposed a gravelly beach. At eleven we landed at our encampment of the seventh of June, to gum the canoe and dry our clothes: we then re-embarked, and at half past five arrived at the place, where I lost my book of memorandums, on the fourth of June, in which were certain courses and distances between that day and the twenty sixth of May, which I had now an opportunity to supply. They were as follow:

North-North-West half a mile, East by North half a mile, North by East a quarter of a mile, North-West by West a quarter of a mile, West-South-West half a mile, North-West a mile and a quarter, North-North-West three quarters of a mile, North by East half a mile, North-West three quarters of a mile, West half a mile, North-West three quarters of a mile, West-North-West one mile and a quarter, North three quarters of a mile, West by North one quarter of a mile, North-West one mile and an half, West-North-West half a mile, North-North-West three quarters of a mile, West one quarter of a mile, North-North-East half a mile, North-North-West two miles, and North-West four miles.

We were seven days in going up that part of the river which we came down to-day; and it now swarmed, as it were, with beavers and wild fowl. There was rain in the afternoon, and about sun-set we took our station for the night.

Monday, August to. We had some small rain throughout the night. Our course to-day was South-South-West three quarters of a mile, West-North-West half a mile, North half a mile, North-West by West three quarters of a mile, North by West half a mile; a small river to the left, South-West by West three quarters of a mile, West-North-West a mile and an half, North-West by North four miles, a rivulet on the right, West-North-West three quarters of a mile; a considerable river from the left, North-North-West two miles, North half a mile, West-North-West one mile and an half; a rivulet on the right, North-West by West one mile and a quarter, West-North-West one mile, West-South-West a quarter of a mile, North-North-West half a mile, North-West half a mile, West-South-West three quarters of a mile, North-West by West three miles, West-South-West three quarters of a mile, North-West by West one mile; a small river on the right, South-West a quarter of a mile, West-North-West, islands, four miles and an half, a river on the left, North half a mile, West a quarter of a mile, North a quarter of a mile North-West by West three quarters of a mile, North-North-East three quarters of a mile, North-West by North half a mile, West-North-West a mile and an half, and North-West by North half a mile. The mountains were covered with fresh snow, whose showers had dissolved in rain before they reached us. North-West three quarters of a mile, South-West a quarter of a mile, North a mile and three quarters, West-North-West a mile and a quarter, North-West a mile and an half, North-North-West half a mile, West-North-West a quarter of a mile, North half a mile; here the current was slack: North-West by North half a mile, North-West by West a quarter of a mile, North-North-West a quarter of a mile, North-West by West one mile and a quarter, North half a mile, North-East by North one mile and three quarters, South-West one mile and a quarter, with an island, North by East one mile, North-West. Here the other branch opened to us, at the distance of three quarters of a mile.

I expected from the slackness of the current in this branch, that the Western one would be high, but I found it equally low. I had every reason to believe that from the upper part of this branch, the distance would not be great to the country through which I passed when I left the Great River; but it has since been determined otherwise by Mr. J. Finlay, who was sent to explore it, and found its navigation soon terminated by falls and rapids.

The branches are about two hundred yards in breadth, and the water was six feet lower than on our upward passage. Our course, after the junction, was North-North-West one mile, the rapid North-East down it three quarters of a mile, North by West one mile and a quarter, North by East one mile and an half, East by South one mile, North-East two miles and an half, East-North-East a quarter of a mile; a rivulet; East by South one mile and an half, North-East two miles, East-North-East one mile, North-North-East a quarter of a mile, North-East by East half a mile, East-South-East a quarter of a mile, East-North-East half a mile, North-East two miles, North-East by East two miles and a quarter, South-East by East a quarter of a mile; a rivulet from the left; East by North a mile and an half, East by South one mile, East-North-East one mile and three quarters; a river on the right; North-North-East three quarters of a mile, North-East a mile and an half, North-East by East a mile and a quarter, East-North-East half a mile, and North-East by North half a mile. Here we landed at our encampment of the 27th of June, from whence I dispatched a letter in an empty keg, as was mentioned in that period of my journal, which set forth our existing state, progress, and expectation.

Tuesday, August 20. Though the weather was clear, we could not embark this morning before five, as there was a rapid very near us, which required day-light to run it, that we might not break our canoe on the rocks. The baggage we were obliged to carry. Our course was North by East a mile and an half, North-North-East a mile and an half down another rapid on the West side; it requires great care to keep directly between the eddy current, and that which was driving down with so much impetuosity. We then proceeded North-North-West, a river from the right a mile and a quarter, North-North-East a mile and an half, a river from the left; North one mile and three quarters, North-East two miles, North-East by East two miles and a quarter, East by North one mile, North-East by East four miles, a river from the left, and East by South a mile and an half. Here was our encampment on the 26th of May, beyond which it would be altogether superfluous for me to take the courses, as they are inserted in their proper places.

As we continued our voyage, our attention was attracted by the appearance of an Indian encampment. We accordingly landed, and found there had been five fires, and within that number of days, so that there must have been some inhabitants in the neighbourhood, though we were not so fortunate as to see them. It appeared that they had killed a number of animals, and fled in a state of alarm, as three of their canoes were left carelessly on the beach, and their paddles laying about in disorder. We soon after came to the carrying-place called the Portage de la Montagne de Roche. Here I had a meridian altitude, which made the latitude 56.3.51 North.

The water, as I have already observed, was much lower than when we came up it, though at the same time, the current appeared to be stronger from this place to the forks; the navigation, however, would now be attended with greater facility, as there is a stony beech all the way, so that poles, or the towing line, may be employed with the best effect, where the current overpowers the use of paddles.

We were now reduced to a very short allowance; the disappointment, therefore, at not seeing any animals was proportioned to our exigences, as we did not possess at this time more than was sufficient to serve us for two meals. I now dispatched Mr. Mackay and the Indians to proceed to the foot of the rapids, and endeavour in their way to procure some provisions, while I prepared to employ the utmost expedition in getting there; having determined, notwithstanding the disinclination of my people, from the recollection of what they had suffered in coming that way, to return by the same route. I had observed, indeed that the water which had fallen fifteen feet perpendicular, at the narrow pass below us, had lost much of its former turbulence.

As dispatch was essential in procuring a supply of provisions, we did not delay a moment in making preparation to renew our progress. Five of the men began to carry the baggage, while the sixth and myself took the canoe asunder, to cleanse her of the dirt, and expose her lining and timbers to the air, which would render her much lighter. About sun-set Mr. Mackay and our hunters returned with heavy burdens of the flesh of a buffalo: though not very tender, it was very acceptable, and was the only animal that they had seen, though the country was covered with tracks of them, as well as of the moose-deer and the elk. The former had done rutting, and the latter were beginning to run. Our people returned, having left their loads mid-way on the carrying place. My companion and myself completed our undertaking, and the canoe was ready to be carried in the morning. An hearty meal concluded the day, and every fear of future want was removed.

Wednesday, August 21. When the morning dawned we set forwards, but as a fire had passed through the portage, it was with difficulty we could trace our road in many parts; and with all the exertion of which we were capable, we did not arrive at the river till four in the afternoon. We found almost as much difficulty in carrying our canoe down the mountain as we had in getting it up; the men being not so strong as on the former occasion, though they were in better spirits; and I was now enabled to assist them, my ancle being almost well. We could not, however, proceed any further till the following day, as we had the canoe to gum, with several great and small poles to prepare; those we had left here having been carried away by the water, though we had left them in a position from fifteen to twenty feet above the water-mark, at that time. These occupations employed us till a very late hour.

Thursday, August 22. The night was cold, and though the morning was fine and clear, it was seven before we were in a state of preparation to leave this place, sometimes driving with the current, and at other times shooting the rapids. The latter had lost much of their former strength; but we, nevertheless, thought it necessary to land very frequently, in order to examine the rapids before we could venture to run them. However, the canoe being light, we very fortunately passed them all, and at noon arrived at the place where I appointed to meet Mr. Mackay and the hunters; there we found them, with plenty of excellent fat meat, ready roasted, as they had killed two elks within a few hundred yards of the spot where we then were. When the men had satisfied their appetites, I sent them for as much of the meat as they could carry. In coming hither, Mr. Mackay informed me, that he and the hunters kept along the high land, and did not see or cross the Indian path. At the same time, there can be no doubt but the road from this place to the upper part of the rapids is to be preferred to that which we came, both for expedition and safety.

After staying here about an hour and an half, we proceeded with the stream, and landed where I had forgotten my pipe-tomahawk and seal, on the eighteenth of May. The former of them I now recovered.

On leaving the mountains we saw animals grazing in every direction. In passing along an island, we fired at an elk, and broke its leg; and, as it was now time to encamp, we landed; when the hunters pursued the wounded animal, which had crossed over to the main land, but could not get up the bank. We went after it, therefore, in the canoe, and killed it. To give some notion of our appetites, I shall state the elk, or at least the carcase of it, which we brought away, to have weighed two hundred and fifty pounds; and as we had taken a very hearty meal at one o'clock, it might naturally be supposed that we should not be very voracious at supper; nevertheless, a kettle full of the elk flesh was boiled and eaten, and that vessel replenished and put on the fire. All that remained, with the bones, &c. was placed, after the Indian fashion round the fire to roast, and at ten next morning the whole was consumed by ten persons and a large dog, who was allowed his share of the banquet. This is no exaggeration; nor did any inconvenience result from what may be considered as an inordinate indulgence.

Friday, August 23. We were on the water before day-light; and when the sun rose a beautiful country appeared around us, enriched and animated by large herds of wild cattle. The weather was now so warm, that to us, who had not of late been accustomed to heat, it was overwhelming and oppressive. In the course of this day we killed a buffalo and a bear; but we were now in the midst of abundance, and they were not sufficiently fat to satisfy our fastidious appetites, so we left them where they fell. We landed for the night, and prepared ourselves for arriving at the Fort on the following day.

Saturday, August 24. The weather was the same as yesterday, and the country increasing in beauty; though as we approached the Fort, the cattle appeared proportionably to diminish. We now landed at two lodges of Indians, who were as astonished to see us, as if we had been the first white men whom they had ever beheld. When we had passed these people not an animal was to be seen on the borders of the river.

At length, as we rounded a point, and came in view of the Fort, we threw out our flag, and accompanied it with a general discharge of our fire-arms; while the men were in such spirits, and made such an active use of their paddles, that we arrived before the two men whom we left here in the spring, could recover their senses to answer us. Thus we landed at four in the afternoon, at the place we left on the ninth of May. Here my voyages of discovery terminate. Their toils and their dangers, their solicitudes and sufferings, have not been exaggerated in my description. On the contrary, in many instances, language has failed me in the attempt to describe them. I received, however, the reward of my labours, for they were crowned with success.

As I have now resumed the character of a trader, I shall not trouble my readers with any subsequent concern, but content myself with the closing information, that after an absence of eleven months, I arrived at Fort Chepewyan, where I remained, for the purposes of trade, during the succeeding winter.

The following general, but short, geographical view of the country may not be improper to close this work, as well as some remarks on the probable advantages that may be derived from advancing the trade of it, under proper regulations, and by the spirit of commercial enterprize.

By supposing a line from the Atlantic, East, to the Pacific, West, in the parallel of forty-five degrees of North latitude, it will, I think, nearly describe the British territories in North America. For I am of the opinion, that the extent of the country to the South of this line, which we have a right to claim, is equal to that to the North of it, which may be claimed by other powers.

The outline of what I shall call the first division, is along that track of country which runs from the head of James-Bay, in about latitude 51 North, along the Eastern coast, as far North as to, and through, Hudson's Straits, round by Labrador; continuing on the Atlantic coast, on the outside of the great islands, in the gulf of St. Laurence, to the river St. Croix, by which it takes its course, to the height of land that divides the waters emptying themselves into the Atlantic, from those discharged into the river St. Laurence. Then following these heights, as the boundary between the British possessions, and those of the American States, it makes an angle Westerly until it strikes the discharge of Lake Champlain, in latitude 45 North, when it keeps a direct West line till it strikes the river St. Laurence, above Lake St. Francis, where it divides the Indian village St. Rigest; from whence it follows the centre of the waters of the great river St. Laurence: it then proceeds through Lake Ontario, the connection between it and Lake Erie; through the latter. and its chain of connection, by the river Detroit, as far South as latitude 42 North, and then through the lake and river St. Clair, as also Lake Huron, through it continues to the Strait of St. Mary, latitude 46 ½ North; from which we will suppose the line to strike to the East of North, to the head of James-Bay, in the latitude already mentioned.

Of this great tract, more than half is represented as barren and broken, displaying a surface of rock and fresh water lakes, with a very scattered and scanty proportion of soil. Such is the whole coast of Labrador, and the land, called East Main to the West of the heights, which divide the waters running into the river and gulf of St. Laurence, from those flowing into Hudson's Bay. It is consequently inhabited only by a few savages, whose numbers are proportioned to the scantiness of the soil; nor is it probable, from the same cause, that they will encrease. The fresh and salt waters, with a small quantity of game, which the few, stinted woods afford, supply the wants of nature: from whence, to that of the line of the American boundary, and the Atlantic ocean, the soil, wherever cultivation has been attempted, has yielded abundance; particulary on the river St. Laurence, from Quebec upwards, to the line of boundary already mentioned; but a very inconsiderable proportion of it has been broken by the ploughshare.

The line of the second division may be traced from that of the first at St. Mary's, from which also the line of American boundary runs, and is said to continue through Lake Superior, (and through a lake called the Long Lake which has no existence), to the Lake of the Woods, in latitude 49.37 North, from whence it is also said to run West to the Mississipi, which it may do, by giving it a good deal of Southing, but not otherwise; as the source of that river does not extend further North than latitude 47.38 North, where it is no more than a small brook; consequently, if Great-Britain retains the right of entering it along the line of division, it must be in a lower latitude, and wherever that may be, the line must be continued West, till it terminates in the Pacific Ocean, to the South of the Columbia. This division is then bounded by the Pacific Ocean on the West, the Frozen Sea and Hudson's Bay on the North and East. The Russians, indeed, may claim with justice, the islands and coast from Behring's Straits to Cook's Entry.

The whole of this country will long continue in the possession of its present inhabitants, as they will remain contented with the produce of the woods and waters for their support, leaving the earth, from various causes, in its virgin state. The proportion of it that is fit for cultivation is very small, and is still less in the interior parts: it is also very difficult of access; and whilst any land remains uncultivated to the South of it, there will be no temptation to settle it. Besides, its climate is not in general sufficiently genial to bring the fruits of the earth to maturity. It will also be an asylum for the descendants of the original inhabitants of the country to the South, who prefer the modes of life of their forefathers, to the improvements of civilisation. Of this disposition there is a recent instance. A small colony of Iroquois emigrated to the banks of the Saskatchiwine, in 1799, who had been brought up from their infancy under the Romish missionaries, and instructed by them at a village within nine miles of Montreal.

A further division of this country is marked by a ridge of high land, rising, as it were, from the coast of Labrador, and running nearly South-West to the source of the Utawas River, dividing the waters going either way to the river and gulf of St. Laurence and Hudson's Bay, as before observed. From thence it stretches to the North of West, to the Northward of Lake Superior, to latitude 50 North, and longitude 89 West, when it forks from the last course at about South-West, and continues the same division of waters until it passes North of the source of the Mississipi. The former course runs, as has been observed, in a North-West direction, until it strikes the river Nelson, separating the waters that discharge themselves into Lake Winipic, which forms part of the said river, and those that also empty themselves into Hudson's Bay, by the Albany, Severn, and Hay's or Hill's Rivers. From thence it keeps a course of about West-North-West, till it forms the banks of the Missinipi or Churchill River, at Portage de Traite, latitude 55.25 North. It now continues in a Western direction, between the Saskatchiwine and the source of the Missinipi, or Beaver River, which it leaves behind, and divides the Saskatchiwine from the Elk River; when, leaving those also behind, and pursuing the same direction it leads to the high land that lies between the Unjigah and Tacoutche rivers, from whence it may be supposed to be the same ridge. From the head of the Beaver River, on the West, the same kind of high ground runs to the East of North, between the waters of the Elk River and the Missinipi forming the Portage la Loche, and continuing on to the latitude 57¼ North, dividing the waters that run to Hudson's Bay from those going to the North Sea: from thence its course is nearly North, when an angle runs from it to the North of the Slave Lake, till it strikes Mackenzie's River.

The last, but by no means the least, is the immense ridge, or succession of ridges of stony mountains, whose Northern extremity dips in the North Sea, in latitude 70 North, and longitude 135 West, running nearly South-East, and begins to be parallel with the coast of the Pacific Ocean, from Cook's entry, and so onwards to the Columbia. From thence it appears to quit the coast, but still continuing, with less elevation, to divide the waters of the Atlantic from those which run into the Pacific. In those snow-clad mountains rises the Mississippi, if we admit the Missisouri to be its source, which flows into the Gulph of Mexico; the River Nelson, which is lost in Hudson's Bay; Mackenzie's River, that discharges itself into the North Sea; and the Columbia emptying itself into the Pacific Ocean. The great River St. Laurence and Churchill River, with many lesser ones, derive their sources far short of these mountains. It is, indeed, the extension of these mountains so far South on the sea-coast, that prevents the Columbia from finding a more direct course to the sea, as it runs obliquely with the coast upwards of eight degrees of latitude before it mingles with the ocean.

It is further to be observed, that these mountains, from Cook's entry to the Columbia, extend from six to eight degrees in breadth Easterly; and that along their Eastern skirts is a narrow strip of very marshy, boggy, and uneven ground, the outer edge of which produces coal and bitumen: these I saw on the banks of Mackenzie's River, as far North as latitude 66. I also discovered them in my second journey, at the commencement of the rocky mountains in 56 North latitude, and 120 West longitude; and the same was observed by Mr. Fidler, one of the servants of the Hudson's Bay Company, at the source of the South branch of the Saskachiwine, in about latitude 52 North, and longitude 112½ West[36] Next to this narrow belt are immense plains, or meadows, commencing in a point at about the junction of the River of the Mountain with Mackenzie's River, widening as they continue East and South, till they reach the Red River at its confluence with the Assiniboin River, from whence they take a more Southern direction, along the Mississippi towards Mexico. Adjoining to these plains is a broken country composed of lakes, rocks, and soil.

From the banks of the rivers running through the plains, there appeared to ooze a saline fluid, concreting into a thin, scurf on the grass. Near that part of the Slave River where it first loses the name of Peace River, and along the extreme edge of these plains, are very strong salt springs, which in the summer concrete and crystallize in great quantities. About the Lake Dauphin, on the South-West side of Lake Winipic, are also many salt ponds, but it requires a regular process to form salt from them. Along the West banks of the former is to be seen, at intervals, and traced in the line of the direction of the plains, a soft rock of lime-stone, in thin and nearly horizontal stratas, particularly on the Beaver, Cedar, Winipic and Superior lakes, as also in the beds of the rivers crossing that line. It is also remarkable that, at the narrowest part of Lake Winipic, where it is not more than two miles in breadth, the West side is faced with rocks of this stone thirty feet perpendicular; while, on the East side, the rocks are more elevated, and of a dark-grey granite.

The latter is to be found throughout the whole extent North of this country, to the coast of Hudson's Bay, and as I have been informed, along that coast, onwards to the coast of Labrador; and it may be further observed, that between these extensive ranges of granite and lime-stone are found all the great lakes of this country.

There is another very large district which must not be forgotten; and behind all the others in situation as well as in soil, produce, and climate. This comprehends the tract called the Barren Grounds, which is to the North of a line drawn from Churchill, along the North border of the Rein-Deer Lake, to the North of the Lake of the Hills and Slave Lake, and along the North side of the latter to the rocky mountains, which terminate in the North

36. Bitumen is also found on the coast of Slave Lake, in latitude 60 North, near its discharge by Mackenzie's River; and also near the forks of the Elk [Athabasca] River.

Sea, latitude 70 North, and longitude 135 West; in the whole extent of which no trees are visible, except a few stinted ones, scattered along its rivers, and with scarce any thing of surface that can be called earth; yet, this inhospitable region is inhabited by a people who are accustomed to the life it requires. Nor has bountiful Nature withheld the means of subsistence; the rein deer, which supply both food and clothing, are satisfied with the produce of the hills, though they bear nothing but a short curling moss, on a species of which, that grows on the rocks, the people themselves subsist when famine invades them. Their small lakes are not furnished with a great variety offish, but such as they produce are excellent, which, with hares and partridges, form a proportion of their food.

The climate must necessarily be severe in such a country as we have described, and which displays so large a surface of fresh water. Its severity is extreme on the coast of Hudson's Bay, and proceeds from its immediate exposure to the North-West winds that blow off the Frozen Ocean.

These winds, in crossing directly from the bay over Canada and the British dominions on the Atlantic, as well as over the Eastern States of North America to that ocean, (where they give to those countries a length of winter astonishing to the inhabitants of the same latitudes in Europe), continue to retain a great deal of force and cold in their passage, even over the Atlantic, particularly at the time when the sun is in its Southern declination. The same winds which come from the Frozen Ocean, over the barren grounds, and across frozen lakes and snowy plains, bounded by the rocky mountains, lose their frigid influence, as they travel in a Southern direction, till they get to the Atlantic Ocean, where they close their progress. Is not this a sufficient cause for the difference between the climate in America, and that of the same latitude in Europe?

It has been frequently advanced, that the difference of clearing away the wood has had an astonishing influence in meliorating the climate in the former: but I am not disposed to assent to that opinion in the extent which it proposes to establish, when I consider the very trifling proportion of the country cleared, com-

---

pared with the whole. The employment of the axe may have had some inconsiderable effect; but I look to other causes. I myself observed in a country, which was in an absolute state of nature, that the climate is improving; and this circumstance was confirmed to me by the native inhabitants of it. Such a change, therefore, must proceed from some predominating operation in the system of the globe which is beyond my conjecture, and, indeed, above my comprehension, and may, probably, in the course of time, give to America the climate of Europe. It is well known, indeed, that the waters are decreasing there, and that many lakes are draining and filling up by the earth which is carried into them from the higher lands by the rivers: and this may have some partial effect.

The climate on the West coast of America assimilates much more to that of Europe in the same latitudes: I think very little difference will be found, except such as proceeds from the vicinity of high mountains covered with snow. This is an additional proof that the difference in the temperature of the air proceeds from the cause already mentioned.

Much has been said, and much more still remains to be said on the peopling of America. On this subject I shall confine myself to one or two observations, and leave my readers to draw their inferences from them.

The progress of the inhabitants of the country immediately under our observation, which is comprised within the line of latitude 45 North, is as follows: that of the Esquimaux, who possess the sea coast from the Atlantic through Hudson's Straits and Bay, round to Mackenzie's River, (and I believe further) is known to be westward: they never quit the coast, and agree in appearance, manners, language, and habits with the inhabitants of Greenland. The different tribes whom I describe under the name of Algonquins and Knisteneaux, but originally the same people, were the inhabitants of the Atlantic coast, and the banks of the river St. Laurence and adjacent countries: their progress is Westerly, and they are even found West and North as far as Athabasca. On the contrary, the Chepewyans, and the numerous tribes who speak their language, occupy the whole space between the Knisteneaux country and that of the Esquimaux, stretching behind the natives of the coast of the Pacific, to latitude 52 North, on the river Columbia. Their progress is Easterly; and, according to their own traditions, they came from Siberia; agreeing in dress and manner with the people now found upon the coast of Asia.

Of the inhabitants of the coast of the Pacific Ocean we know little more than that they are stationary there. The Nadowasis or Assiniboins, as well as the different tribes not particularly described, inhabiting the plains on and about the source and banks of the Saskatchiwine and Assiniboin rivers, are from the Southward, and their progress is North-West.

The discovery of a passage by sea, North-East or North-West from the Atlantic to the Pacific Ocean, has for many years excited the attention of governments, and encouraged the enterprising spirit of individuals. The nonexistence, however, of any such practical passage being at length determined, the practicabilty of a passage through the continents of Asia and America becomes an object of consideration. The Russians, who first discovered that, along the coasts of Asia no useful or regular navigation existed, opened an interior communication by rivers, & through that long and wide-extended continent, to the strait that separates Asia from America, over which they passed to the adjacent islands and continent of the latter. Our situation, at length, is in some degree similar to theirs; the non-existence of a practicable passage by sea, and the existence of one through the continent, are clearly proved; and it requires only the countenance and support of the British Government, to increase in a very ample proportion this national advantage, and secure the trade of that country to its subjects.

Experience, however, has proved, that this trade, from its very nature cannot be carried on by individuals. A very large capital, or credit, or indeed both, is necessary, and consequently an association of men of wealth to direct, with men of enterprise to act, in one common interest, must be formed on such principles, as that in due time the latter may succeed the former, in continual and progressive succession. Such was the equitable and successful mode adopted by the merchants from Canada, which has been already described.

The junction of such a commercial association with the Hudson's Bay Company, is the important measure which I would propose, and the trade might then be carried on with a very superior degree of advantage, both private and public, under the privilege of their charter, and would prove, in fact, the complete fulfilment of the conditions, on which it was first granted.

It would be an equal injustice to either party to be excluded from the option of such an undertaking; for if the one has a right by charter, has not the other a right by prior possession, as being successors to the subjects of France, who were exclusively possessed of all the then known parts of this country, before Canada was ceded to Great-Britain, except the coast of Hudson's Bay, and having themselves been the discoverers of a vast extent of country since added to his Majesty's territories, even to the Hyperborean and the Pacific Oceans?

If, therefore, that company should decline, or be averse to engage in, such an extensive, and perhaps hazardous, undertaking, it would not, surely, be an unreasonable proposal to them, from government, to give up a right which they refuse to exercise, on allowing them a just and reasonable indemnification for their stock, regulated by the average dividends of a certain number of years, or the actual price at which they transfer their stock.

By enjoying the privilege of the company's charter, though but for a limited period, there are adventurers who would be willing, as they are able, to engage in, and carry on the proposed commercial undertaking, as well as to give the most ample and satisfactory security to government for the fulfilment of its contract with the company. It would, at the same time, be equally necessary to add a similar privilege of trade on the Columbia River, and its tributary waters.

If however, it should appear that the Hudson's Bay Company have an exclusive right to carry on their trade as they think proper, and continue it on the narrow scale, and with so little benefit to the public as they now do; if they should refuse to enter into a co-operative junction with others, what reasonable cause can they assign to government for denying the navigation of the bay to Nelson's River; and, by its waters, a passage to and from the interior country, for the use of the adventurers, and for the sole purpose of transport, under the most severe and binding restrictions not to interfere with their trade on the coast, and the country between it and the actual establishments of the Canadian traders.[37]

By these waters that discharge themselves into Hudson's Bay at Port Nelson, it is proposed to carry on the trade to their source, at the head of the Saskatchiwine River, which rises in the Rocky Mountains, not eight degrees of longitude from the Pacific Ocean. The Tacoutche or Columbia river flows also from the same mountains, and discharges itself likewise in the Pacific, in latitude 46.20. Both of them are capable of receiving ships at their mouths, and are navigable throughout for boats.

The distance between these waters in only known from the report of the Indians. If, however, this communication should prove inaccessible, the route I pursued, though longer, in consequence of the great angle it makes to the North, will answer every necessary purpose. But whatever course may be taken from the Atlantic, the Columbia is the line of communication from the Pacific Ocean, pointed out by nature, as it is the only navigable river in the whole extent of Vancouver's minute survey of that coast: its banks also form the first level country in all the Southern extent of continental coast from Cook's entry, and, consequently, the most Northern situation fit for colonization, and suitable to the residence of a civilized people. By opening

37. Independent of the prosecution of this great object, I conceive that the merchants from Canada are entitled to such an indulgence, (even if they should be considered as not possessing a rightful claim,) in order that they might be enabled to extend their trade beyond their present limits, and have it in their power to supply the natives with a larger quantity of useful articles; the enhanced value of which, and the present difficulty of transporting them, will be fully comprehended when I relate, that the tract of transport occupies an extent of from three to four thousand miles, through upwards of sixty large fresh water lakes, and numerous rivers; and that the means of transport are slight, bark canoes. It must be observed, that those waters are intercepted by more than two hundred rapids, along which the articles of merchandise are chiefly carried on men's backs, and over an hundred and thirty carrying-places, from twenty-five paces to thirteen miles in length, where the canoes and cargoes proceed by the same toilsome and perilous operations.

this intercourse between the Atlantic and Pacific Oceans, and forming regular establishments through the interior, and at both extremes, as well as along the coasts and islands, the entire command of the fur trade of North America might be obtained, from latitude 48 North to the pole, except that portion of it which the Russians have in the Pacific. To this may be added the fishing in both seas, and the markets of the four quarters of the globe. Such would be the field for commercial enterprise, and incalculable would be the produce of it, when supported by the operations of that credit and capital which Great Britain so pre-eminently possesses. Then would this country begin to be remunerated for the expences it has sustained in discovering and surveying the coast of the Pacific Ocean, which is at present left to American adventurers, who without regularity or capital, or the desire of conciliating future confidence, look altogether to the interest of the moment. They, therefore, collect all the skins they can procure, and in any manner that suits them, and having exchanged them at Canton for the produce of China, return to their own country. Such adventurers, and many of them, as I have been informed, have been very successful, would instantly disappear from before a well-regulated trade.

It would be very unbecoming in me to suppose for a moment, that the East India Company would hesitate to allow those privileges to their fellow-subjects which are permitted to foreigners, in a trade that is so much out of the line of their own commerce, and therefore cannot be injurious to it.

Many political reasons, which it is not necessary here to enumerate, must present themselves to the mind of every man acquainted with the enlarged system and capacities of British commerce, in support of the measure which I have very briefly suggested, as promising the most important advantages to the trade of the united kingdoms.

The End

Printed in the United States
1441700002B/130